King of Beaver Island

KING OF
BEAVER ISLAND

*The Life and Assassination
of James Jesse Strang*

છે.

Roger Van Noord

University of Illinois Press
Urbana and Chicago

Manufactured in the United States of America

C 5 4 3 2 1

This book is printed on acid-free paper.

Library of Congress Cataloging-in-Publication Data

Van Noord, Roger, 1941–
  King of Beaver Island.

  Bibliography: p.
  Includes Index.
    1. Strang, James Jesse, 1813–1856.   2. Mormons—
Michigan—Biography.   3. Church of Jesus Christ of Latter Day Saints
(Strangites)—History.   4. Mormon Church—History.
I. Title.
BX8680.S88S87   1988   289.3'3 [B]   87–11261
ISBN 0–252–01472–3 (alk. paper)

Contents

Acknowledgments

THE SEED FOR THIS BOOK was planted during a hunting trip to Beaver Island in the fall of 1971. During a break in our pursuit of grouse, Larry Gustin, Don Eve, and I talked with a leader of the Beaver Island Historical Society about reports that he had the robe and crown from the 1850 coronation of King Strang. The man said he indeed had them, at his home, but when we expressed interest in seeing them, he demurred, saying he hadn't made a practice of showing them in public. He asked where we were staying and said he might get back with us. We doubted he would.

That evening there was a knock at our motel door. It was the man, with a cardboard box. Inside the box was a red robe, a gold metal crown, and a wooden scepter. We took turns trying on the robe and crown, posing for pictures, then journalistic skepticism took over. Gustin and I were newspaper reporters, and we questioned the man about how he had obtained the objects and why he thought they were authentic. There were no convincing answers. There were labels in the robe, and we took down the information on them. Days later, some checking revealed that the companies listed on the labels had not existed at the time of the coronation. It was my first brush with what would be innumerable examples of the inaccuracy of handed-down history involving James Jesse Strang.

In the next several years, Gustin and I discussed writing a book about Strang. Gustin, however, first was busy writing a biography of Billy Durant, the creator of General Motors, then he became involved in editing a picture history of Flint, Michigan. In the summer of 1978, I went to the National Archives in Washington, D.C., to search for new material on Strang in contemporary sources. The hunt was a success, and my appetite for research was whetted. Gustin, meanwhile, had decided to co-author a history of the Buick

Motor Division and dropped out of the Strang project. He continued to offer valuable advice, and to him goes substantial credit for the idea to take a fresh look at Strang.

That first research trip was followed by many others to libraries and archives across the country, from Yale University's Beinecke Rare Book and Manuscript Library in New Haven, Connecticut, to the Mormon Church Archives in Salt Lake City. The staffs at these and the other libraries were almost without exception helpful. Ann Fahnestock, of the Barker Memorial Library in Fredonia, N.Y., gave assistance well beyond the routine, as did John Cumming, when he was director of Clarke Historical Library at Central Michigan University. I was aided immeasurably by Flint Public Library staff members, who obtained books and microfilm, then printed reams of paper copies from the microfilm, saving me time and eyesight.

Special thanks are due historian Helen Collar for a personal tour of Beaver Island one summer day, my brother Carl Van Noord for some research in New York City and at Yale, Jane Van Oss for helping me locate reference material, Alice Lethbridge and Mike and Juli Riha for saving me additional trips to Salt Lake City, and the Arbons, a Mormon couple who spent hours answering my questions about their religion. For other assistance and advice, I owe a debt to Alan N. MacLeese, Cumming, Harriet Arnold, and my wife, Sharon. My wife and our son, Ryan, also endured several "vacations" with an ulterior motive—to do a little research on the side. On one of these, we made a side trip to Beaver Island, to be there for what Strang's followers called King's Day, the anniversary of his coronation. I was curious whether present-day islanders would acknowledge the anniversary. The day passed without public notice of one of the most unusual events in American history.

Roger Van Noord
April 1987

Preface

AS A FARM BOY, on the New York frontier, he didn't travel much. Except in his mind. Even in his early childhood, he spent days sitting on the floor, thinking, his mind wandering "over fields that old men shrink from."

As a young man, his wandering thoughts became more focused. One day, a few months after his nineteenth birthday, James Jesse Strang tried to concoct a plan to marry Victoria, the thirteen-year-old heir to the British crown—a rather unrealistic goal, especially for an American in 1832.

"I shall try if there is the least chance," Strang wrote of the marriage bid. "My mind has allways been filled with dreams of royalty and power."

Victoria became queen five years later. And although she would marry another in 1840, the dream that had taken root in Strang's youth—the grand dream of a kingdom and power—endured.

In 1844, when Strang was thirty-one and a lawyer in the Wisconsin Territory, a volley of shots fired by a mob would give him the opportunity to take his first steps on the road to royalty. In the years ahead he would assume imperial titles, undergo a formal coronation, and establish a kingdom. In 1856 another volley of shots would end it all.

A skeptical follower of Strang wrote: "No man can serve two masters. You cannot serve a temporal king and a Republican government at the same time. The thing is preposterous." And yet, under Strang, such a system survived for six years on Beaver Island, the largest island in Lake Michigan.

What kind of man was this imperial dreamer, whose dreams came true?

On September 11, 1846, Strang visited a New York City phrenologist. S. R. Wells found Strang to have a "comprehensive" mind;

a "versatility" of talent; a faculty to win confidence and adapt to circumstances; a fondness for debate, with tongue and pen; and both energy and perseverence, as long as he was engaged in a cause.

This appears a reasonable assessment of a man who would persuade his followers to help him form an island kingdom, a man who would write and carry out an extensive code of conduct for that kingdom, and a man who would conduct a variety of debates in his newspaper and on the floor of a state legislature.

Wells also said Strang did not have "a very brilliant imagination." Strang was, however, a man of vision who foresaw the Civil War more than twenty-five years before it began and predicted that a bridge would join the two Michigan peninsulas a century before the Mackinac Bridge was built.

The phrenologist made one gross blunder. "Should you undertake to play the hypocrite," Wells wrote, ". . . you would very soon expose yourself in some way, for you have not tact and cunning enough to enable you to carry it out into any great speculation or enterprise." Strang, throughout his career, had a reputation for cunning. He also was a lightning rod for accusations involving the sincerity of his religious claims. And he did carry out a great speculation and enterprise, the creation of a kingdom in an antimonarchical atmosphere.

At nineteen, Strang was a self-proclaimed atheist, which fell in line with Wells's statement that Strang lacked spirituality of mind and devotional feeling. Yet Strang later would maintain that two years before his phrenological examination an angel had ordained him as the ruler of God's people and that he was the successor to the Mormon prophet, Joseph Smith.

Strang was a man of contrasts and contradictions: a one-time strident opponent of polygamy who would have five wives, a prophet and a shrewd political tactician, a bookish editor and an incendiary propagandist, a legislator and a lawbreaker. He balanced the powers of his Beaver Island kingdom and the state, and took advantage of each. He deferred to civil law when it was overpowering or when it suited his purpose. He skillfully walked a tightrope, seemingly always a step from extinction, and through the force of his personality made himself and his followers a power to be feared.

His timing in establishing the island kingdom was fortuitous. He caught the era of the sidewheel steamer at the flood and used it to build the island's economy into preeminence at the Straits of Mackinac. At his death the railroad lines from the East had reached Chicago; therefore many goods and passengers no longer had to go over the hump of Michigan's Lower Peninsula and past Beaver Island.

Bias and misinformation about Strang have made it difficult for biographers to present a balanced portrait of this complex, controversial leader. Milo M. Quaife's *The Kingdom of Saint James*, published in 1930, has stood for more than fifty years as the most competent look at Strang's career. Quaife amassed key documents relating to Strang and interviewed contemporaries of Strang, but his benchmark biography is flawed and now outdated. Quaife appears too unwilling to question Strang's activities or veracity. Although Quaife obtained the letter of appointment, he sidestepped the issue of forgery. Quaife's work is marred by his confusing the sequence of events relating to Strang's covenant, placing Strang's public acknowledgment that he was practicing polygamy five years too early, overstating the population of the Mormon kingdom on Beaver Island by accepting Strang's figures at face value, and erroneously having the warship *Michigan* returning to Beaver Island ten days after the shooting of Strang. The more recent studies of Strang have mainly replowed the ground covered by Quaife.

Using a lode of previously untapped information, including contemporary journals, documents, letters, and newspaper accounts, this biography provides a fresh perspective on the events surrounding the coronation of Strang, his trial on federal charges in Detroit, his remarkable career in the state legislature, the accusations of Mormon thievery, his perennial conflicts with non-Mormons in his region, his assassination, and the exodus, at gunpoint, of his followers from Beaver Island.

This narrative is based, where possible, on original sources, keeping in mind the possible biases for or against the Mormon leader. Strang himself, through his autobiography, diary, letters, and publications, is a major source. But although Strang was an editor who professed a high regard for fairness, he headed a partisan, propagandist press, and any history that relies solely on Strang's version of events is not accurate. Letters, journals, and newspaper accounts often offer the necessary balance.

The story of James Jesse Strang is fascinating, and I have attempted to let the story tell itself. In the narrative, the terms "Saints" and "Mormons" are used interchangeably for members of the churches headed by Joseph Smith, Brigham Young, and Strang, while the term "Gentiles" is used the Mormon way, meaning everyone who was not a Mormon. In differentiating between the followers of Strang and Brigham Young, the terms "Strangites" and "Brighamites" are used, which is the way Strang's supporters and the Utah Mormons referred to each other.

King of Beaver Island

Chapter 1

Opportunity

ON THAT FEVERED DAY in Carthage, Billy Hamilton was stationed with a friend in the cupola of the courthouse. Their assignment: be on the lookout for a body of men approaching the town. Using a field glass, the two boys had been keeping watch for five hours when, at about 4 P.M., they spotted a swarm of men just beyond a stand of trees about two miles to the northwest. Billy's friend delivered this information to the captain of the local militia, the Carthage Greys.[1]

About forty-five minutes later the boys saw at least 100 armed men emerge from those trees. In single file the men began walking toward town, using an old rail fence for a screen. The men were trailing their muskets and rifles alongside their legs, to hide the long barrels. Billy and his friend scrambled down from the cupola and ran for the militia captain, but he was nowhere to be found. The captain had stressed that they were to report only to him, and by the time the boys located him, the men had reached the Carthage jail.[2]

Inside the jail was the Mormon prophet, Joseph Smith. Outside, guarding the jail, were seven of the Carthage Greys, their guns loaded with powder but no balls. Earlier that day the officer in charge of the guard detail had predicted that Joseph Smith would die before sundown.[3]

The jail, a two-story stone building, had its cells on the second floor. Adjacent to the cells was a larger room, with a double bed and chairs. That room had three windows without bars and a door without a lock. Joseph Smith was sitting in that room with Hyrum Smith, his brother and fellow prisoner, and with two Mormon visitors, John Taylor and Willard Richards. The windows were wide open for some relief on the hot, muggy day, and in an attempt to revive their spirits, the men had just drunk some wine.[4]

Three days earlier Joseph Smith had given himself up amid the

I

anti-Mormon unrest that followed his destruction of an opposition newspaper. The *Nauvoo Expositor* had the temerity to challenge Smith in his own fiefdom—the City of Nauvoo, which was about fifteen miles from Carthage in western Illinois. In its only edition, on June 7, 1844, the paper accused Smith of various iniquities and abuses. The *Expositor* referred to polygamy and secret societies at Nauvoo and implied that Smith was a "self-constituted monarch." Smith called the charges libelous and, with the backing of the Nauvoo City Council, had the *Expositor's* press and type demolished and burned as a public nuisance.[5]

The action against the *Expositor* provided new grist for the anti-Mormon hate mill, which called for the extermination of the Mormon leaders. And on June 17 Joseph and Hyrum Smith and fifteen other Mormons were arrested on charges of riot in destroying the *Expositor's* press. A court in Nauvoo, however, released them, stirring anti-Mormon passions into a frenzy. Citizens from throughout the area joined militia units and drilled, preparing for a war with Nauvoo. Joseph Smith countered by mustering the Nauvoo Legion, the Mormon militia.[6]

Illinois Governor Thomas Ford, fearing a civil war in the area, warned Smith that if he did not turn himself in for a trial in Carthage, the county seat, he would call out the state militia and Nauvoo could be destroyed. Smith eventually decided to go to Carthage to face the charges. Ford promised protection and a fair trial.[7]

Joseph and Hyrum Smith rode into Carthage just before midnight on June 24. After a hearing in the afternoon of the 25th, they were released on bond. But earlier that same day, a new charge had been made against the Smiths—treason against the state for calling out the Legion. That evening, without a hearing, the Smiths were sent to jail on the treason charge, on an order signed by a justice of the peace who was an active anti-Mormon and who also was the captain of the Carthage Greys, which included some of the Mormons' bitterest enemies. The Smiths protested the lack of a hearing, to no avail: they were escorted to jail.[8]

The men Billy Hamilton saw approaching the jail two days later had faces blackened with gunpowder. Their clothes were turned inside out. Most were members of the state militia's Warsaw

2

regiment, which had been dismissed earlier by Governor Ford. Although part of the regiment had gone home to nearby Warsaw, these men had not. They had business at the jail.[9]

As the men closed in, the guards on the steps of the jail fired a volley from point-blank range. No one was hit. The mob seized the guards and threw them aside. One guard, not in on the charade, resisted.[10]

When he heard the volley of several shots, Willard Richards peered out a window. A black-faced horde was at the jailhouse door! Joseph Smith pulled out a six-shooter and Hyrum a single-shot pistol; both weapons had been smuggled in. Taylor grabbed a hickory cane and Richards a knotty walking stick.[11]

A shower of shots echoed up the stairway to the second floor. Some balls, fired through the open windows, slammed into the ceiling. With no lock to protect them, the Mormons braced themselves against the door to the room. The attackers pounded up the stairs and tried to shove their way in. One shot blasted through the door and hit Hyrum Smith near his nose. He fell backward, moaning. More shots struck his body.[12]

Joseph Smith began emptying his revolver into the stairway landing. The gun reported three times, but misfired three others. Taylor flailed with his club at gun barrels sticking through the doorway, spoiling the aim of the gunmen.[13]

The Mormons' situation was hopeless. More men with muskets and rifles crowded into the doorway. The Mormons' guns were empty. Taylor ran toward a window, deciding to jump and take his chances with the mob below. A shot from the doorway hit him in the thigh, and he fell on the windowsill. Then a shot from outside hit him in the chest and knocked him back into the room. Taylor was wounded twice more before he could roll for cover under the bed, where he was hit again.[14]

Joseph Smith dropped his gun and sprang for the window opposite the door. He was shot twice from the doorway and once from outside. Smith pitched forward out the window and fell heavily to the ground on his left side—dead.[15]

Then came the cry: "He's leaped the window!" The shooting stopped inside, and the men on the stairs ran down to the yard, leaving Hyrum Smith dead on the floor, Richards with a flesh wound of the ear, and Taylor bleeding under the bed. Richards dragged Taylor into a cell and covered him with a mattress to hide him. The watch in Taylor's vest pocket had been smashed by a shot, stopping it at 5:16 and perhaps saving his life. The assassination had taken two minutes.[16]

When Billy Hamilton heard the first shots, he realized that if he waited for the Carthage militia to get organized, he would miss the action. Billy took off for the jail and arrived just as Smith fell to the ground. One member of the mob went up to Smith's body and said: "He is dead, boys!" Its object accomplished, the mob quickly headed back toward the woods.[17]

Billy Hamilton climbed the stairway to the jail's second floor, where the only body he could find was Hyrum Smith's. His curiosity satisfied, Billy decided to go home. About a block from the jail, he met the company of the Carthage Greys, marching in formation toward the jail, as if on dress parade, with guns at the shoulder and flag flying: a purposeful march, and much too late.[18]

Like the mob, the Carthage Greys feared the coming of the Mormons to exact revenge. And within hours, almost all of the residents and citizen-soldiers of Carthage had fled in a panic—in wagons, on horseback, and on foot. Many left doors and windows open. Carthage was a temporary ghost town.[19]

≥ ≥ ≥

James Jesse Strang would claim that at 5:30 P.M. on June 27, shortly after Joseph Smith had been killed in Carthage, an angel came to him at Burlington, Wisconsin. The angel, Strang said, anointed his head with oil, to ordain him as ruler of God's people, and told him: "Thou shalt save his people from their enemies. . . . While the day of the wicked abideth, shalt thou prepare a refuge for the oppressed and for the poor and needy."[20]

This new ruler of God's people was short, with an almost insignificant appearance on first impression. He was thirty-one years old and a lawyer in the Wisconsin Territory; he had been a Mormon for less than five months. For Strang, the fateful events of 1844 had begun with a February visit to Nauvoo, the Mecca of Mormonism. He went to see both the city and its Number 1 citizen—Joseph Smith.[21]

Nauvoo boasted a population of 11,000 Mormons, with perhaps 4,000 more living nearby. Five years earlier, much of Nauvoo had been an unsettled lowland peninsula, jutting into the Mississippi River. Joseph Smith and his followers had transformed that soggy site into a bustling city that was running neck and neck with Chicago for the title of largest city in Illinois.[22]

For many visitors, the first sign of Nauvoo was the half-finished Mormon temple, a commanding stone presence on the bluff overlooking the city. Below the temple was a proliferation of stores and homes built of wood, stone, brick, and logs. A Masonic Hall had just been completed, and many other public buildings and homes were in the works.[23]

Strang was impressed—with the city and with Joseph Smith, a tall, fine-looking man with light hair and an easy manner. Smith had many visitors, and Strang, traveling with a friend who was a high priest in the church, had a definite entrée.[24]

Smith generally received visitors in his office. One of his clerks told what these visits were like. "Persons of almost all professions—Doctors, Lawyers, Priests . . . seemed anxious to get a good look at what was then considered very wonderful: a man who should dare to call himself a prophet, announce himself as a seer and ambassador of the Lord. Not only were they anxious to see, but also to ask hard questions, to ascertain his depth."[25]

One of the visitors was Charles Francis Adams, John Quincy Adams's son, who met with Smith a few months after Strang did. Adams found Smith to be a "mixture of shrewdness and extravagant self-conceit, of knowledge and ignorance, of wisdom and folly."[26]

Here was Joseph Smith, a man of humble beginnings who, despite his educational shortcomings, had founded a religion and had become mayor of perhaps the largest city of Illinois and lieutenant-general of the Nauvoo Legion, a Mormon militia of 4,000 men. And just before Strang had arrived, the thirty-eight-year-old Smith had decided to run for president of the United States. If Joseph Smith could do all this, then the possibilities for

James Jesse Strang—with his cunning and far superior education—were even more exciting.[27]

Before the month was out, Strang was a Mormon convert. On
February 25, a Sunday, Joseph Smith baptized Strang in the unfinished temple. A week later, on March 3, Strang was ordained an
elder of the church by Hyrum Smith, Joseph's older brother.[28] Ambitious for power and fame, Strang had hitched his wagon to the
Mormon star.

Despite all of the appearances of vitality, all was not well with
Joseph Smith and Nauvoo early in 1844. Dissension was brewing
within the city, and on the outside non-Mormons were outraged by
reports of secret practices in Nauvoo and were fearful of the power
represented by the Nauvoo Legion. They also resented the Mormons' political clout. Some of the more rabid Mormon-haters told
Smith that his days were numbered.[29]

The Mormons had been uprooted before, and once again
Joseph Smith began to consider locations for a new sanctuary.
Learning of Strang's extensive knowledge of geography, Smith questioned him closely about the advantages and disadvantages of several
areas in the far West.[30]

Strang had an idea for a Mormon refuge closer to Nauvoo. He
proposed that a Mormon settlement be formed immediately, about
225 miles to the northeast, in the area in which he lived in the
Wisconsin Territory. Strang touted the benefits of the area—at the
edge of a fertile prairie on the White River near Burlington, about
fifteen miles north of Illinois in southeastern Wisconsin. Joseph
Smith urged Strang to submit a written report on the settlement
possibilities there.[31]

After returning home, Strang worked on the report, completing it on May 24. A few days later the friend who had accompanied
Strang to Nauvoo added a concurring note. The friend was Aaron
Smith, an elder and high priest in the Mormon church but no relation to Joseph and Hyrum. The report was mailed at the end
of May.[32]

Strang probably was unaware that his report arrived in Nauvoo
at a time when Joseph Smith was preoccupied with the cataclysmic
events that led to his assassination. Nor could Strang have been

aware that while he was in the Burlington area on June 27, his royal destiny was being promoted at Carthage.

          ❧   ❧   ❧

The news of the assassination of Joseph Smith traveled slowly—by letter, by mailed newspaper, and by word of mouth, not by telegraph. Just one month earlier, Morse had sent his historic message: "What hath God wrought!"

A week after the assassination, the news had reached Milwaukee, about thirty miles from Burlington. On July 5 the *Milwaukee Commercial Herald* printed the story, and three days later, it said editorially, "Whether another leader will be found capable of supplying the place of Smith . . . remains to be seen."[33]

According to Strang, the news from Carthage had not yet reached the Burlington area when a letter from Nauvoo arrived at the Burlington post office on July 9. The letter, bearing the postmark "Nauvoo June 19," was picked up by Strang's law partner, C. P. Barnes. Barnes delivered it to Strang, who was with Aaron Smith at the time.[34]

The letter was to become one of the most important—and controversial—documents in the history of the Mormon religion. Strang used it, buttressed later by his word about being anointed by the angel, as his authority to be Joseph Smith's successor.

The "letter of appointment," as Strang called it, was signed by Joseph Smith and dated June 18, nine days before Smith's assassination and less than four months after Strang had been baptized into the Mormon church. In the letter Smith acknowledged Strang's report proposing a Mormon settlement near Burlington. Smith said he had planned to reject Strang's proposal "for the present," but that God had "ruled it otherwise."[35]

Smith predicted his martyrdom and seemingly reported God's assistance in naming a successor. He related a vision in which God told him that to James J. Strang "shall the gathering of the people be for he shall plant a stake of Zion in Wisconsin. . . . there shall my people have peace & rest & shall not be mooved . . . and the name of the city shall be called voree which is being interpreted garden of peace." The letter closed with this "appointment" of Strang: "if evil befall me thou shalt lead the flock to pleasant pastures." [36]

Strang—armed with the letter—began making plans to stake his claim to the church that Smith built. Elsewhere in the country, many of the church leaders, still stumping for Smith for president, were just learning about the assassination. Nauvoo was practically rudderless through this period, mainly because it had been stripped of its leadership for the presidential campaign. At the time of Smith's death, Sidney Rigdon—the vice-presidential candidate—and ten of the twelve apostles were out campaigning, leaving apostles John Taylor and Willard Richards as the chief officials in Nauvoo. [37]

With Joseph Smith dead, Rigdon was the lone surviving member of the church's highest ranking body, the First Presidency. But Rigdon's standing with the Smiths, and with the people, had been on the decline. Would Rigdon automatically assume the leadership of the church? Or would that role be filled by the Quorum of Twelve, the apostles? Or would it be passed on through Joseph to his son, then twelve, with Joseph's brother, William, acting as regent? These were among the possibilities being discussed in Nauvoo when James Jesse Strang began to project himself into the picture with the letter of appointment. [38]

Brigham Young, the president of the Twelve and the leading apostle in prestige and ability, had been in Boston when the Smiths were shot on June 27. It was not until July 9 that he heard rumors of the assassinations. When those reports were confirmed, he headed for Nauvoo. [39]

While Nauvoo awaited Young's arrival, Strang was already off showing his flag—the letter of appointment. On July 26 Strang left the Burlington area on foot to attend a conference in Michigan. Circling the southern end of Lake Michigan, he was joined in Indiana by Aaron Smith, whom the letter of appointment named as Strang's counselor. They walked north to Florence, in southwestern Michigan, where on August 5 they joined a group of Mormon elders holding the conference. Strang presented the letter and stated the case for the gathering at Voree. [40]

Among the dozen elders present was Moses Smith, Aaron's brother, who was married to a sister of Strang's wife. One of the first settlers in the Burlington area, Moses Smith had since moved to Nauvoo.[41]

According to Strang, the conference agreed that Moses Smith, who had been preaching in Michigan, and another elder, Norton Jacob, would take a copy of the letter of appointment to Nauvoo. Smith was a supporter of Strang; Jacob definitely was not. In Florence, Jacob preached vehemently against the letter.[42] In his private journal, Jacob wrote that the letter "carried on its face the marks of a base forgery, being written throughout in printed characters. . . . The thing no doubt was framed by Aaron Smith and James J. Strang."[43]

Two other elders, Crandell Dunn and Harvey Green, joined Jacob in a tirade against Strang. Dunn and Green, the presiding high priests in Michigan, advised Strang and Aaron Smith to end their mission and return home. Strang said he quietly told them they could not command someone "whom God had placed at their head."[44]

Dunn, in a letter written two years after the confrontation with Strang in Florence, said he had detected flaws in the letter of appointment and subjected Strang to questioning that put him on the defensive. Dunn's letter also had flaws, such as maintaining the postmark on the letter was black when it should have been red. The postmark was red. Dunn also claimed that Strang admitted he had not been ordained as prophet.[45] Indeed, there is no contemporary evidence that Strang had mentioned the angel's visit to anyone before the conference.

Ten years later, Strang would maintain that on the day of Smith's death he had told his household of the angel's visit and that on the next day the story became known in the neighborhood. He said he also had mentioned the angel to Mormon families with whom he stayed en route to Florence. To believe that after telling people about the angel's visit he then had confessed that he had not been ordained, Strang said, "It is necessary to believe not only that I am a liar and an imposter, but more than an idiot."[46]

A story of another vision also had become linked with the

letter of appointment. Strang reported that he received this vision on June 18, the date of the letter of appointment. In this vision, Strang said, he was carried in spirit to the top of a hill that overlooked the future site of Voree. Before him was a city of stone, with gardens and streets and shops and people—a thriving, happy community. In a vast hall, Strang—surrounded by counselors, priests, and orators—addressed the people with "the spirit of prophesy." [47]

After Florence, Strang and Aaron Smith carried the letter of appointment from town to town, as far east as Sandusky, Ohio. For four weeks, the letter was on display before they returned home to Wisconsin by boat via the Great Lakes. [48]

In Nauvoo, Rigdon had arrived on August 3, ready to gain control of the church by being named the church "guardian." Rigdon reported that on the day of Smith's assassination he also had had a vision. The revelation, he said, made it clear that he should be named guardian and that there could be no successor to Joseph Smith as Prophet, Seer, and Revelator. [49]

Rigdon had wanted a meeting on August 6 to gain approval of his plan, but he postponed the meeting until August 8. [50] This gave Brigham Young a chance to play his stronger hand.

With the arrival of Young and four other apostles late on August 6, Rigdon's hopes of grabbing the reins of the church slipped away. The Twelve received the endorsement that Rigdon alone had sought. Under Young's leadership the Twelve took over the job of running the church, leaving the office of Prophet, Seer, and Revelator vacant. [51]

Young also took action against his rivals. On August 24 Moses Smith and Norton Jacob returned to Nauvoo, bearing a copy of the letter of appointment. Smith's reception was harsh: several apostles told him the revelation included in the letter to Strang was false and threatened him with excommunication if he persisted in preaching about it. A shy, unassuming man, Smith left the scene of confrontation by joining a group of Mormons who were heading off to explore the West. [52]

On August 26 direct action was taken against Strang. The Twelve, declaring that Strang and Aaron Smith were leading Saints astray by means of a false revelation, excommunicated them. The action was published as a warning to Mormons in the Nauvoo *Times and Seasons* on September 2.

On September 8 Rigdon was excommunicated. By the end of the year, the church hierarchy was so firmly in Young's hands that he was signing letters not as the president of the Twelve but as president of the church. Rigdon left Nauvoo and began organizing his own church.[53] He never again was a serious rival of Young: that role would be filled by James Jesse Strang.

Strang was no shy, unassuming rival. Despite his excommunication, he stated his case forcefully. "I am delivered over to the buffetings of Satan," he wrote late in 1844, "yet when I pray God answers. I lay hands on the sick and they recover. I can speak in new tongues. . . . Is it not rather strange if God gave such gifts to men who believe not in him and blaspheme his name continually. . . . If I am not what I profess to be, I am of all men most wicked."[54]

Chapter 2

Dreams of Royalty

WHO WAS JAMES JESSE STRANG, the man who bragged of gifts from God? A descendant of a Huguenot wine merchant who fled religious persecution in France. A sixth-generation New Yorker.[1] A dreamer whose dreams were coming true.

His parents, Clement Strang and Abigail James, had been born on opposite banks of the Hudson River near the Revolutionary War battleground of Saratoga. They married in Saratoga County in the summer of 1810. By 1813 the couple—with their young son, David—had moved west to the state's Finger Lakes region and settled in the rolling countryside south of Scipio in Cayuga County. There, on March 21, 1813, their second child, also a son, was born. He was named Jesse James after Abigail's father (Jesse would later reverse his first two names). Five years later, there would be a third child in the family, a daughter, Myraette.[2]

As a baby, Jesse had poor health. Forty-two years later, in the beginnings of an autobiography, Strang would write that infancy to him meant sickness and suffering. His early recollections, he wrote, "produced a kind of creeping sensation akin to horror." He once was so near death that plans were made for his burial.[3]

By his third birthday, his family had moved twice. In August 1814 the Strangs left Scipio for Manlius, about forty miles to the northeast. After seventeen months the family headed west again, this time to Chautauqua County in the southwestern corner of the state.[4] The Strangs settled two miles northeast of Forestville in the township or town of Hanover, one of the more sparsely populated areas of the state. It was there that Jesse grew up. And for him, the early years were not pleasant.[5]

Besides the burden of bad health, he bore the label of an imbecile: "all who knew me, except my parents, thought me scarcely more than idiotic."[6] Perhaps it was his appearance, his oversize forehead, or his personality, withdrawn and brooding. "Long weary days I sat on the floor, thinking, thinking, thinking! occasionally asking a strange, uninfantile question and never getting an answer. My mind wandered over fields that old men shrink from, seeking rest and finding none till darkness gathered thick around and I burst into tears and cried aloud, and with a voice scarcely able to articulate told my mother that my head ached."[7]

Strang said he had little inclination to play and was seldom cheerful. He attended the district school until he was twelve, but the terms usually were short and the teachers ill-qualified. The instructors gave him little or no attention, as if he were too stupid to learn. His classmates ridiculed or ignored him. His continued poor health curtailed his attendance. Not counting the time he was sick, Strang estimated that he had received the equivalent of about six months of schoolhouse education before his twelfth birthday.[8] Books were his substitute for school, and he read voraciously, often by candle and firelight at night.

Although Strang never said a great deal about his early days, he did report that he was tenderly and carefully guided as a youth and that his mother played the major role. Wherever he went, he had to ask permission from his mother and give a complete account of his doings on his return. "I always told mother the truth. I couldn't even talk to nor kiss one of the girls but I had to tell mother all about it, what she said and what I said."[9] Strang recalled being "very slightly whipped" by his father twice and by his mother once.[10] And one time his father exercised discipline by sending him away to school.[11]

That occasion was when Jesse, at fifteen, was learning about love, although a more physical than romantic kind, from an unwed mother of one child. Nancy Crawford was about twenty years old, though she looked younger. Three years later, a few months after he had begun a diary, Jesse wrote about Nancy in a private code.[12]

According to Jesse, Nancy was "a young lady of neither property or character, and by association the attachment became so strong that I allmost thought her a part of myself." She was "of an easy disposition though not contented, fascinating in her manner, though not allways agreeable, violent and vehement in the mild and agreeable passions, yet fickle and changeable."[13] They began seeing each other in August, and the opposition of his parents and friends increased the attraction. That fall, Jesse's father made the financial sacrifice necessary to separate the couple by sending him to Fredonia Academy.[14]

The academy, about ten miles away in Fredonia, was the first in the county and had been open only two years. Tuition was $3 per quarter for most students, and out-of-town students boarded with local families for about $1 per week. Jesse rang the bell to halve his tuition costs in the winter quarter.[15] He was one of ninety-eight students, thirty-three of them girls, and he took courses in arithmetic and grammar. The academy, with its library of 140 books, opened avenues of thought for him.[16] It would leave a mark on Jesse James Strang far beyond arithmetic and grammar.

Although Jesse studied so hard he became sick, his months at Fredonia did not succeed in making him forget Nancy. They corresponded throughout the fall and winter. In the spring, when Jesse returned home, they picked up where they had left off. Perhaps for this reason, Jesse was back in school in June for the latter half of the spring quarter, taking algebra. The quarter ended in July, and Jesse went home again. He found Nancy anxious to get married.[17]

Although Nancy had one child, she did not want another until she was married. She wanted to marry Jesse immediately; he kept putting her off. Whether she had become pregnant again is not clear, but marriage seemed paramount in her mind. If Jesse would not marry her, maybe someone else would. She became engaged to another man. Then the engagement fell through, and she began to see Jesse again. This time they talked seriously of marriage, apparently with the emphasis on "talked." For once again another marriage opportunity came up, and this time Nancy married the other man.[18]

Two years later, approaching his nineteenth birthday, Jesse was on the verge of getting involved with another sexually experienced woman. He was teaching school at the time in Randolph, about twenty-five miles southeast of Forestville.[19] Eight weeks after his arrival, it was common gossip that he was courting a woman named Mary Torrance in the presence of her husband. Jesse admitted that she had kissed him playfully a number of times and that he would have returned the kisses had it not been for the consequences. He remembered his experience with Nancy Crawford and showed some restraint. "I really wanted to do the other thing," Strang wrote, "and believe I might have done it too by careful management if I had tried . . . but I am somewhat inclined to a certain evil which is easier avoided than corrected," he confessed in code. "I am fond of female company."[20] This from a young man who eventually would have five wives.

ૉ ૉ ૉ

One of the books Jesse had carried with him to Randolph was about Napoleon—a significant choice, for he had begun to dream more and more about power and empire. And as the school year closed, with Strang facing the prospect of going back to being "no more than a common farmer," he wrote that he was sorry that he had not made more progress in preparing for his "great designs" for "revolutionizeing government and countrie." He lamented that he had never done "one great thing." He felt he ought to have been "a member of an Assembly or a Brigadier General before this time if I am ever to rival Caesar or Napoleon, which I have sworn to."[21]

Strang, who was too young to have been in the state assembly, realized he had a long way to go before he could reach his imperial dream. At times he became discouraged and was tempted to settle down and marry, but he needed a vocation, or at least some means of support. "I am at a loss what to do: sometimes I think of going into the service of the fur company; sometimes I think of studying the law; and sometimes of speculating either in this or some foreign country; I have even thought of an intrigue for power with foreign princes." In the back of his mind, the dreams of empire were so deeply imprinted that they could not easily be erased.[22] His internal debate between dreams and practicality continued.

Outwardly, Strang was showing a great facility for debating ideas with other men. His only real rival here had been his best friend, Benjamin Perce, but Perce had moved away. Debates were held almost every week, and Strang, with his loud and rapid way of speaking, was on the winning side of nearly all of these contests. A decision in his internal debate was not clear-cut, but he was keeping score.[23]

Strang recorded his dreams and ambitions in his diary, which he began at the age of eighteen and continued until he was twenty-three. His diary not only gives a fascinating peek at his life during this period, but also reveals, through the deciphering of the private code he used for the most personal sections, many thoughts and actions he obviously wished to remain secret. Thus the credibility of these coded sections, many of which testify to an unbalanced desire for distinction, is all the more enhanced. The diary discloses a driven young man who recorded his achievements and his inadequacies and failures; a man of authority, yet bookish; a purposeful man torn between humble service ("I intend to make serving the people my business through life"[24]) and arrogant ambition.

On May 27, a few months after his nineteenth birthday and after his teaching job had ended, Strang occupied himself with a mind game: trying to concoct a plan for him to marry Victoria, the heir to the British crown. She had turned thirteen three days earlier. Strang wrote: "I shall try if there is the least chance. My mind has allways been filled with dreams of royalty and power."[25] Taking note of a war in Europe, he exclaimed: "O! If I was King of England I would try my fortune in the bloody field."[26]

It was during this year that Strang began reversing the order of his first two names when he signed his diary. Perhaps he wanted to avoid comparisons with a celebrated murderer, Jesse Strang, who had been executed four years earlier for killing an Albany woman's husband, at her request.[27] Or perhaps he realized that King James sounded more regal than King Jesse.

That summer, however, James Jesse Strang, the man who would be king, was resolved to be a priest, a lawyer, a conqueror, and a legislator—"unless I find better business."[28] Although this resolution may have sounded a bit brash, even to him, time proved it remarkably successful.

In December, his eye on one of those four goals, Strang began to study law with borrowed books. He studied up to fifteen hours a day, with half of that time devoted to law, half to politics and a variety of other books. "I know not what my prospects are but this much I know—I will never be a member of the bar when I am afraid of any of equal experience in the state. I should rather be the best hunter in an Indian tribe than a common place member of the New York bar."[29]

And yet he remained ambivalent about law as a career. "I will study faithfully day and night for seven years if by so doing I can make a respectable Lawyer, and if I can not I think I will try the mercantile business. Nevertheless if called upon in a good cause, I should prefer the profession of arms if I could accomodate my mind to it."[30]

As 1832 drew to a close, Strang was preoccupied with national affairs, in particular the nullification controversy, in which South Carolina declared federal tariff increases null and void. In the midst of this controversy, pitting North against South, Strang predicted a civil war, twenty-eight years before the fact. "Disunion with all the horrors of anarchy and civil war are stareing us in the face," he wrote.[31] A week earlier, unknown to Strang, Joseph Smith had made a similar prediction, which later was cited as proof of his prophetic power.[32]

Strang saw opportunity in potential revolution. "Amidst all the evils of the disturbances of our national affairs there is one consolation: that is if our government is overthrown, some master spirit may form another. May I be the one. I tremble when I write but it is true."[33] He wrote this in code.

Meanwhile, Strang was accepting a master spirit, the "Spirit of Nature," as the ruler of the universe, while he was rejecting the religion of his youth. Until his late teens, Strang had belonged to the largest church in the county, a Baptist church in Forestville. The Second Baptist Church of Hanover had been organized in 1817, with Strang's parents as two of twenty-nine charter members. Strang had been baptized at the age of twelve and had been an active member, even serving as church clerk for a time. But during his late teens Strang "seemed to lose his spirituality and become somewhat skeptical," according to his sister, Myraette. This may have been connected with a "difficulty" in the church, a difficulty that apparently led to a church split in about 1831.[34]

Religion in that hellfire and damnation region, which came to be described as the "burned-over district" because it would be burned-over by many evangelical expeditions, had become a touchy subject for Strang. He found himself trying to keep peace between his burgeoning independence of thought and his parents' unquestioning beliefs. In his diary, Strang noted that a revival had been held nearby, but that nearly half of the converts had returned to their "wallowing." At that time, many revivalists scorned any reading other than the Bible and biblical tracts, and to Strang, a lover of books and a seeker of knowledge, this anti-intellectualism was heresy.[35] In the end, the church lost Strang: he was expelled for holding opinions contrary to church doctrine.[36]

The depth of Strang's anti-church views are revealed in his diary entries. He saw "one people propagating its religion by fire and sword; another revileing the first for its cruelty and yet using the more deadly weapons of calumny and slander in its own cause, persecuting by word and act in common life all who dare to believe a little more or a little less than its own standard." And he remarked pointedly: "Parents teaching their own children to believe certain principles without evidence of their truth, and even that it is blasphemy to ask or wish for it."[37]

In Randolph, Strang had been called on to pray and discuss religious subjects. "Sometimes I consent just to please the people," he wrote in his first use of his diary code, which substituted symbols for the alphabet. "It is all a mere mock of sounds with me, for I can no longer believe the nice speculative contradictions of our divine theologians of our age. Indeed it is a long time since I have really believed these dogmas but every examination leaves less evidence and I have about given it up."[38]

He was being coached in his examination by Thomas Paine's *Age of Reason*, in which Paine set forth his view of theology and his reasons for not believing the Bible.[39] The word of God is the creation, Paine said, and through the creation, man reads the handwriting of God; all other Bibles are forgeries.

Under the intellectual prodding of Paine's book, Strang examined his Baptist religion and found it to be a collection of absurdities. And yet, in desperation, when his mind was in a muddle, he still considered being a priest, even though he confessed, in code, that he was the "perfect atheist." He said he did not admit this publicly "lest I bring my father grey hair with sorrow to the grave."[40]

A reading of Shelley's "Queen Mab" also helped lead Strang toward a view of the "Spirit of Nature" as the ruler of the universe.[41] Strang had rejected much of the intuitive faith of his parents' religion, and now he was substituting a mystical communion with nature.

> What have posterity to do with me? Well time shall answer. I have no trouble on that point. It is writen. Not in the Alcoran. Not in the Bible. Not in the will of the priesthood. Not in the good pleasure of him who claims the keys of heaven and earth and hell. No. Not in secret decrees, the inscrutiable designs, the preordained determinations of a forever changing merciful and cruel creature of superstitious imagination seated high in heaven on a dazzleing and resplendent throne and gazed on by successive millions of human beings. But it is writen, writen in the constitution of nature and in the native bent and vigor of the mind.[42]

Strang believed that man could rely on his own wits and creativity, without any intermediary, Bible, mysterious decree, or superstitiously imagined God. Strang called himself a "cool Philosopher" compared with the "restless Christians" he saw about him.[43] Faced with a conflict between emotionalism and rationalism, he had come down on the side of the latter: he was thinking his way into a theology of the mind. And yet, more than a decade later, after the assassination of Joseph Smith, this anti-emotionalist would claim to have talked with a messenger from God.

For a philosopher, debate is a natural outlet. But when free thinkers dare to challenge all assumptions in their debates, even religions are not sacred. And the debating societies that Strang joined were under almost constant attack by religious "bigots" of the community. Strang felt pressure to abandon the debating societies, but he resisted these "conscience keepers."[44]

In debate, the keeper of Strang's conscience envied a trait one of his colleagues had. This friend could appear sincere and reasonable in uttering the greatest absurdities and was so skillful that he did not care which side he took in a debate.[45] Strang stored that trait for future reference. Later in life, he would learn to use fabrication for a cause: his cause.

Strang continued his slow progress in the study of law. A summer of farming, a winter of teaching, and another season of farming divided his attention and left him depressed. It was an opportune time for something to lift his spirits, and that something came in July.[46]

Strang had been chosen to give a temperance address, and since it was his first attempt at public speaking, he nervously approached the assignment, even though he had years of debating experience. He wrote the speech out. "I believe I could speak as well without writing but I shall not try it first." The speech boosted his morale and his confidence. "It is done. After this experiment, with my experience in debating I may safely ever consider myself perfectly at home in publick speaking."[47]

After his temperance speech, Strang felt more cheerful about working as a farmer for his father and others to earn money. He carried a book in his pocket to study when he could, and off and on that year he also studied law with a tutor in Silver Creek, a village a few miles north of Forestville, on Lake Erie. He began to prepare to take court cases to earn money to pay for part of his expenses.[48]

In November, in Silver Creek, he still was waiting for his first case: "Mud and rain but no law. I have had no business yet and begin to think I shall get very little here. I only want a beginning." Later that day Strang was retained on two lawsuits. "Well no down heartedness, no horrors now," he wrote. "The course is commenced. The first step is taken and the road to honour or obloquy is allready tried. The result a few years will determine."[49]

His failure to become an overnight success at anything but debating and public speaking had forced Strang to view his situation more realistically. His dreams of power and empire were being tempered, and his most ambitious thoughts were now preoccupied with fame. He had read part of Sir Walter Scott's *Waverly* and he was not impressed. "If Scott gained his popularity by writing such a work or a series of such works who could not be immortal? . . . I have better writing."[50] When he learned that Westminster Palace, the eleventh-century building that housed the British Parliament, was gutted by fire, he observed: "All the works of man are destined to decay. Monuments of greatness . . . fall before the tooth of time. . . . And fame, fame alone of all the productions of man's folly may survive."[51]

On New Year's Day, 1835, Strang noted the passing of another year, "gone in the way of the world, and passed as others have passed their days who have died in obscurity. Curse me eternally if that be my fate. I know it is in my power to make it otherwise."[52] He was feeling guilty about attending and helping to organize a New Year's ball, even though it turned out to be a "glorious frolic." The ball had met with opposition, but he did not care. "I must let this suffice for a long time. Frolicking is not the business for me to become rich or great by: thank fortune: or fate."[53]

Two months later, on the same day, two efforts that could have earned Strang money ended in setback. Some land speculation fell apart, and he lost a race for the office of Hanover town constable by five votes. The day's events left Strang thinking of becoming a farmer.[54]

But the prospect of farming was not pleasant. "I have not seen enough of the world; played enough wild pranks, nor acted my part in its contentions. I have not yet learned to desire that station which I consider most happy. . . . If my present aspirations are too high, I may as well abandon my future hopes, mark out a different course, and content myself to live that life which I now believe the least unhappy."[55]

What he enjoyed most was politics, even when he lost: "busy from monday morning till tuesday evening without sleeping or scarcely eating in 20 sprees, half a dozen frays, and a dozen quarrels, without injuring or being injured by any one, and for politics. . . . During that forty hours all was stratagem: every man I met was laying a plan to surprise some other one, and a lot of willy fellows spent a night in watching my movements all to no purpose."[56]

He tried to take his losses philosophically: "Ill fortune is frequently the best fortune; and probably it may be so now . . . it is a matter of remark and complaint with my friends that I keep up the same eternal smile and apparent satisfaction whether successful or unsuccessful. Yet that fact is probably for my happiness. I find much satisfaction in looking on the world the smooth side out, though I might prefer acting my part rather roughly."[57]

At the end of March, after eight months in Silver Creek, the would-be lawyer—lacking business and feeling a bit sorry for himself—left for Forestville and entered a period of trial in his life. "I have neither friends, vassals, or money," he wrote. "I was not born to fortune, name [or] influence. I was never the favourite of accident or chance. No man ever gave me a dollar. . . ."[58]

Then, early in June, he came down with a severe case of smallpox. There were more than 300 pocks on his face and all burned like fire. One salve for his affliction was that he was nursed by Wealthy Smith, which was only appropriate, since he had caught the disease while attending her.[59]

Strang had been seeing Wealthy for more than a year, during which time they had become known as a couple. The previous summer they were to stand up together at a friend's wedding, and Strang felt ticklish about it. "After paying my respects to her since last winter," he wrote in his diary, "it will be taken for more than it is worth. But, Go ahead. I may take her at last," indicating that even then his feeling for her had advanced beyond casual friendship.[60]

Late in June, still suffering from the effects of smallpox, Strang was sued for helping his brother, David, gain clear title to a mill. The answers to many obvious questions about the case are shrouded by time, but it is known that in January Strang had embarked on a major land speculation, an activity he would continue throughout his life. For most Americans during that period, land was the principal opportunity for investment. Strang's plan was to make several hundred dollars in a year so he would not have to neglect his studies to work. But those hopes had been dashed.[61]

The focus of Strang's speculation was land on which there was a mill worth $400. He expected the title to the mill to fail, and then, because he owned the land on which it sat, he would own the mill. But David bought the mill, and James ended up selling his brother the land at cost, thus giving David firm control of the mill.[62]

The mill was valuable enough for competing interests to fight over it, and Strang became the target of three lawsuits for helping his brother gain ownership.[63] Strang ended up crossing swords with some of the most influential men in Forestville: these men, he said, not only thwarted his every attempt at doing business but also "knowingly engaged in circulating the most corrupt falsehood against me." He noted that two persons even went to an attorney's office and offered to perjure themselves in the attempt to ruin him.[64]

His free-thinking ways also had others awaiting his comeuppance. "Clergymen and their pious followers prayed the overwhelming vengeance of the allmighty on the heaven daring Infidel who Providence had thrown in their power," Strang wrote. "Men who have said in their hearts and spoken with their lips 'There is no God' thanked fate and fortune that I should soon fall."[65]

The suits eventually were dropped, but not without Strang himself being accused of perjury. Again, the details are not known. A nineteen-man grand jury heard his case. No indictment was returned, as eighteen of the jurors decided Strang was not guilty. "Forestvill spit its venom in vain," Strang wrote. And he added: "I shall never forget the friends who were faithful at that moment. For my intention to my enemies, let the light of future judgment reveal it."[66]

One casualty of the mill affair was Strang's relationship with Wealthy Smith. Wealthy apparently gave some credence to what was being said about Strang, and their correspondence was broken off. Wealthy did not even want to speak to him again—but her mind would change within a year. Later, in a letter to Wealthy, Strang wrote: "Once, you had a mind which I believed not time nor fortune could change. And had anyone told me you would sacrifice your brightest prospects; violate the strongest affection; and discard the most faithful friendship at the beck of those whom you knew to be worthless, because, forsooth, they were your relatives, I would have treated him as a base slanderer."[67]

Four months later, in October, Strang remembered his friends and enemies again, in an accident at David's mill. On the day of the accident the water level in the millpond was higher than ever before, with the flow sheeting swiftly over the dam. Seeking to dislodge some driftwood, Strang was walking along a board from the head of the flume when the board broke, dumping him into the pond. The current quickly pushed Strang against the dam, about six feet from the flume. David reached out a board. But when Strang pulled himself toward his brother with the aid of the board, the force of the current loosened his body's grip on the dam. He was going over! He landed on the rocks below, and the roiling current carried him downstream underwater, yet he seldom touched bottom. He grabbed at anything and everything. He grabbed a limb, but it broke. He was carried under a jumble of driftwood and wedged at the bottom. For half a minute he fought his way out from under the wood. The current carried him further downstream. Bringing himself above water, he saw what he hoped was land. He hit a rock and was sucked under again. This time when he came up, he made contact with a log, which swung him around, and he latched onto it. The log turned out to be a tree lodged in the middle of the creek, about 150 yards downstream from the dam.[68]

"What a multitude of thoughts were crowded together in that short spase of time," Strang wrote that night. ". . . how did imagination picture the obsequies of my end; Friends sobing around; my poor heartbroken mother sinking by my pale remains; those who in life had injured me deep as hatred could conceive or malice could invent standing in clusters round talking perhaps that the hand of God had done it, and then offering their consoling (ah! vile) assistance."[69]

Strang climbed above water on the tree and rested his quivering limbs. David came on the run. After learning that his brother was all right, the next question was how to get him ashore from the middle of the creek, with water flowing swiftly on either side. Strang directed David to go around to the opposite bank, where there were some trees, and fell one of them toward him. David chopped one down, and Strang used this bridge to reach shore.[70]

Six weeks later, Strang again thought about death as the year approached its end. "O! time, time how quickly thou fliest away. What has become of the past? I have lived allmost twenty-three years. Behind is allmost blank, while ahead is only thick darkness. Should I die now, I have lived in vain. O! the curse: to have done nothing for posterity."[71]

⊱ ⊱ ⊱

Many families in western New York state were selling out and heading west to a new frontier. Prompted partly by the situation in Forestville, Strang was thinking about moving, too.[72] Of his prospects in Forestville, Strang wrote: "I know it was a common opinion among my most intimate friends that hatred and falsehood had done their work too well, and that I must either abandon the scenes of my childhood and the associations of my youth and exile myself to distant and unknown lands or ultimately sink beneath the accumulated weight of misfortunes which had fallen upon me."[73]

There was a strong lure for Strang to go west, to the Wisconsin Territory. His best friend, Benjamin Perce, had moved there in 1835, with Moses Smith, Perce's brother-in-law. Together the men explored the western end of what is now Racine County. Smith carved a jackknife claim on a tree at the present site of Burlington, and Perce settled two miles farther west on the future site of Voree.[74]

Early in 1836 many friends and relatives of the pair also had settled in the area. And because of Smith, who had been an ardent Mormon since 1832, and his brother, Aaron, the area became a center of Mormonism. The Smiths would be named the highest officials for the church's Wisconsin region.[75]

Strang decided to stay in New York state—but not in Forestville. Both he and his parents moved elsewhere in the same county in 1836. His decision not to head west was made with some reluctance, though he also had thought about going to the Florida Territory, which was in the middle of a war with the Seminole Indians, and to Texas, which a few weeks earlier had won its independence after a war with Mexico. Strang was still dreaming of glory on the field of battle. "I wish to go there [to Texas] but if I should Mother would cry herself to death. They need help and well deserve it," he wrote.[76]

Strang was glad he did not have a family, and yet he thought of settling down: "man was formed for society. Without it he is hardly human. Every man at middle age should have about him a wife and family."[77] Strang had been courting Benjamin Perce's sister, Mary, since winter, and they had become engaged. But in May the engagement was broken, and Strang was upset. "It was a total, radical and unmitigated failure," he wrote, "without one redeeming circumstance. She could have done but one act more. Only informed me that when we meet again it must be as total strangers. . . . By heavens she is mine. I will steal her heart in an hour she thinks not. I know she can and must and will love me."[78]

Once again Strang felt so close and yet so far, and he was frustrated. He was a sensual man, and in one diary entry he wrote: "but how do I curse man's weaker passions—no, finer but stronger passions on reading of 'the lass that made the bed for him.' "[79] The reference was to Robert Burns's poem about a short but sweet one-night affair with a woman "that made the bed."

> I kiss'd her o'er and o'er again,
> And ay she wist na what to say.
> I laid her 'tween me an' the wa'—
> The lassie thocht na long till day.

Three weeks later their engagement was renewed with the help of Mary's aunt, who had first introduced them.

Meanwhile, Strang was again reading law in Silver Creek, where he had accumulated a 120-volume library. By the end of June he had moved to Clear Creek, where he was busy handling lawsuits and seeking the assistance of a former law tutor in getting admitted to the bar.[80] In October 1836 Strang would be admitted to the practice of law in the Court of Common Pleas in Chautauqua County, thus becoming one of about three-dozen lawyers in the county.[81] (That same year another largely self-educated man, Abraham Lincoln, became a lawyer in Illinois. Both had grown up on a farm. Both read every book they could get their hands on and were experts in quoting the Bible. Both showed early talent as speakers and debaters, and both had a sharp wit, though with Lincoln the emphasis was on the wit and with Strang it was on the sharp. Both would serve as postmasters and both would be legislators. Both would be assassinated.)

Relatively little is known about Strang's life from the end of 1836 through 1843. One reason is that after five years he had stopped writing his diary, lacking the money to buy another blank book.

In September, nearly four months after the diary ended, Strang began taking steps to marry Mary Perce. First, there was the problem of Wealthy Smith, who had attempted to renew their correspondence and wanted to talk to him. Strang agreed to talk but left no hope of rekindling an old flame: "there can be no reason for a correspondence of the kind you propose unless I am to offer you my hand," Strang wrote. "It is impossible. I have taken much time to consider upon the subject; have called to mind the tender ties that once bound us together; have presented to mind in the most favorable light the possible consequences of such an act and the only possible conclusion is that it must be fraught with disappointment to you and misery to both of us." Then Strang turned blunt and almost brutally frank, leaving Wealthy no maneuvering room.

To be connected through life with the indecision of character which according to your declaration has been so fatal to your happiness during the past year would be to me the greatest possible misfortune. I will not say that in this you are different from what you ever have been, but I will say you are different from what I once supposed you were . . .

I loved you once, beautiful and kind,
We plighted an eternal vow.
A change came—you have broken that vow.
So altered are your face and mind
'Twere perjury to love you now.

Nor can I see wherein I have any better assurance of your continued affection, than I had heretofore when it was so easily broken. . . . If you were to search your own heart, I believe you would find no more reason to bestow your affection on me than on any of those you have endeavored to love since our correspondence was broken off.

Strang said the mill affair had afforded him "useful information" by showing him his real friends. "I regard that time as a thorough test of friendship," he wrote Wealthy, and ". . . had you remained faithful at that time you would have afforded me at once the most convincing proof that you loved me not for what I possess but for what I was." In one of three poems in the letter, Strang concluded: "The plant of love once touched with frost, can never spring again." He closed: "Our correspondence is ended; and had you not particularly requested an interview, I should add we must see each other no more. James J. Strang."[82]

Less than two weeks after Strang firmly cut any ties to Wealthy Smith, he wrote Mary Perce's father in Virginia, asking permission to marry her. In a self-confidently respectful letter that contained expressions of diffidence, Strang said he would not insult Perce's understanding "by pretending myself a subject of those violent passions which so often die in their sweetness. On the contrary, my partiality to Miss Perce is the result of a perfect conviction of her moral and intellectual worth, and I think I may say is of a kind and degree which may endure unimpaired as long as life lasts."[83]

By return mail, William L. Perce, who was in the candling business, gave his wholehearted consent. He told Strang that he was "certainly as well pleased to trust [my daughter] to you as any gentleman in the circle of my acquaintance. . . . I fervently hope you may neither of you have cause for sorrow & that you may not be disappointed. You must not expect too much." He told Mary that she had been a dutiful daughter. "Do not let me hear that you are a stubborn wife but remember to make home pleasant to your husband." He urged them to get married as soon as convenient.[84]

James Jesse Strang and Mary Abigail Perce were married on November 20, 1836, in Silver Creek. He was twenty-three and she eighteen, two weeks older than Strang's sister, Myraette.[85] By marrying Mary, Strang became a brother-in-law to his best friend, and in a letter to Benjamin Perce, Strang said that had he wanted other sufficient inducements for the marriage, that would have been one. "I ever regretted that fate had not made us members of the same family."[86]

Since the wedding had already taken place, Strang wrote Benjamin that it would not be well for him to ask if he had made a wise choice. "But I have chosen the companion of my life for those qualities which are enduring and agreeable in every stage of life and every possible circumstance of fortune. If it is not well done I have only to say I have acted with the utmost care and deliberation—and that every appearance is yet more than satisfactory." A rather dispassionate appraisal by a man who mentioned in the same letter that he was "subject to as warm passions as most men."[87] One can speculate that Strang chose Mary more with his mind than with his heart, in a reaction to the unhappy breakup of his relationship with Wealthy Smith. In any event, several weeks after the marriage,

Strang recommended the wedded state to Benjamin, a confirmed bachelor. "If you are ever to exchange your free, unhassled state for the society of women, it is now time. . . . Nothing else can be of equal importance to the happiness of social life. And you will agree with me that happiness is the only proper inducement to such a connection."[88]

The accuracy of these assessments of married life could be questioned, however, for they were made by one who wasn't living with his wife. James and Mary began their marriage apart, he living, working, and supposedly pinching pennies in the Ellington area, about twenty miles south of Forestville, and she living first with her mother and then with a family friend in the middle of the next county. They corresponded frequently, and throughout that winter he visited her when he got the chance, which was not often.[89]

In one of his first letters, Strang started out in an overly formal way, then, shifting to an "aw, shucks" manner, kidded her about how "this getting married ain't the thing what it's cracked up to be if a poor fellow must sit here with four holes in his coat and not half a fire and no body to do his wanting . . . afore I was married any of the girls would do my patching for love of me and not take a cent for 't, but now they act skeered at me and daren't do any thing at all at all for me. . . . What the D——l shall I do. As for keeping you here, that's out of the question—it would not take at all, and I do not know of any other remedy. So by hokey I believe I'll wear my clothes without mendin.'"[90]

At other times he did not feel like teasing, as he sat in his room after midnight, tired and alone, with half a dozen papers unopened on the table and a dozen on the floor that he had just read. "My clothes on every chair in the room . . . not three sticks of wood in the world and too much business to get any." He was lonely and he told Mary so. "Before this very short absence I did not know that I loved you as much as I really do though I thought I loved you as much as possible."[91]

During the winter, he worried about the effect of the cold weather on his health, and on hers, too. He thought a move to the warmer climate of Florida might be beneficial. She apparently was ill as often as he thought he was, and he urged her to follow her doctor's orders.

I fear you will not be careful enough. For even that spirit and animation which renders you so lovely must be sometimes curbed or your loveliness will cease and your health and happiness too.

> There be none of Beauty's daughters
> With a magick like thee;
> And like musick on the waters
> Is thy sweet voice to me . . .
> So my spirit bows before thee
> To listen and adore thee;
> With a full but soft emotion
> Like the swell of summer's ocean.[92]

In contrast to Strang's poetry and sharp-eyed description, Mary's letters to him were usually mundane, and she felt inadequate about her writing. "I cannot write. I do not know what or how to write. I never did."[93] She offered to play chess with him by mail, but there is no indication that they did. Her letters often were filled with a list of requests—to visit her, to write often, to obtain her some cloth or school supplies, such as quills or books. Mary was attending school off and on, when her health permitted, studying French and Latin, in particular.[94]

Occasionally she would respond to the teasing and not do a bad job of it. After James mentioned that she was able to do her own kissing without too much trouble but may need some help in talking, she responded by playing on the fact that they were living apart. "Dd you want to know what my business is here?" she asked. "If you do not wish to know burn the letter now. If you do, my business is to engage men to go to Virginia and work for Papa. I have engaged one man. Am I not doing good business?" And she closed that letter by writing: "I remain yours until the first of next week when if I do not see you, beware."[95]

To a friend of Mary's, Strang complained that Mary was "jealous-minded."[96] She accused him of being neglectful, and he admitted that up to a point she was right. But he had not neglected his letter writing. And he asked that she never again address him as Mr. James J. Strang, as she once did. "It is too distant, too cold—too formal. You are my dear Mary and if I am your dear

Jamie, I ask no more. But I do wrong to mention it. You have as much right to your way as I have to mine."[97]

In the spring Mary joined him for a time in Ellington, and then they traveled south, apparently through Pennsylvania and Maryland to visit her father in Virginia and also to see if the more southern climate would improve her health. They were back in New York, however, with her pregnant by the start of the new year.[98]

Strang spent the first part of 1838 practicing law and working on his father's new farm west of Mayville. In May he bought a lot in the Ellington area, where he used his political contacts among the Democrats to be appointed Ellington postmaster in November.[99]

Along with the postmaster's job, Strang soon had another responsibility: a daughter, Mary, was born in July, and she was followed two years later by another daughter, Myraette.[100] Mary was the light of her parents' life. Strang's mother called her the most playful child she had ever seen, and a family friend said she was the prettiest child in the world. When the younger Mary was staying with Strang's parents while his wife was ill, his sister said: "She gives away so many kisses that there will be none left for you." Myraette said Mary was "as happy as a little queen, she says she is happier than Victoria."[101]

Strang had settled down and deferred his great dreams for day-to-day responsibility. He continued to serve as Ellington postmaster for nearly five years, and he also managed the political affairs of the Democratic party in that area, which was predominantly Whig.[102]

Early in 1843, Strang became editor and publisher of the weekly *Randolph Herald* in the neighboring county. By that time Strang had swallowed his religious skepticism, publicly at least, and he and his wife joined the Baptist church in Randolph. But after nearly seven years of marriage, Strang got the itch to head west.[103]

In the summer of 1843 Strang began winding up his business affairs. He sold the *Randolph Herald* in June, then placed advertisements in that paper and others offering to act as a land buyer and collection agent in the west. On August 18 Strang, his wife, and two children loaded their trunks aboard his carriage and headed for Illinois and eventually the Wisconsin Territory.[104]

In Wisconsin the Strangs moved in with Benjamin Perce, who had built one of the first frame homes in the Burlington area. The clapboard home was located in a beautiful farming area west of town. Perce also had built a store in Burlington and was a justice of the peace—and a land speculator.[105]

In Burlington Strang established a law practice with Caleb P. Barnes, whom Strang had known in New York.[106] Even in law, Strang aimed to set himself apart. A justice of the Wisconsin Supreme Court told of a suit brought by Strang when the judge was a justice of the peace in the Burlington area. Strang sued to recover the value of honey that he claimed had been stolen from his client's apiary by the bees of a neighbor. "Whoever heard of a lawsuit based on such grounds?" the judge asked. "And yet Strang conducted the case with great shrewdness and made a most plausible argument. He was continually bringing up unexpected points in law cases, and using arguments that would have been thought of by no one else. I think he liked the notoriety that resulted from that sort of thing."[107]

Notoriety was a magnet for Strang and his dreams of immortal fame. He was on his way for a date with Joseph Smith. And within five months of his introduction to Smith, Strang would leap from the level of fresh convert to a man proclaiming himself to be the new head of the church.

In the fall of 1843, shortly before this crucial period, an event occurred that may have inclined Strang toward his bold bid for power. Strang and his family became severely ill and his older child died. The death of the bubbly Mary "seemed to wear very heavily on him," Strang's sister wrote.[108] Psychologically, Strang may have taken his daughter's death as an indication that time could play against his great dreams, and that the time to act was now.

After he became an advocate of Mormonism, Strang soon abandoned his law practice for the pulpit.[109] From that time on, he brought his legal discipline to bear on his orderly—yet flamboyant—approaches to pressing his claim to the mantle that had been worn by Joseph Smith.

Chapter 3

The Rajah Manchou Plates

FOR SIX MONTHS AFTER the assassination of Joseph Smith, the people in the Burlington area were not told about the letter of appointment or about the impending gathering at Voree, "lest they should be induced to ask unreasonable prices for their lands." Spreading God's word had taken a back seat to price consciousness—or speculative motives. But on January 5, 1845, Strang and his followers held a church meeting in the home of Aaron Smith, where elders were assigned to preach in that area about the letter and Voree.[1] Before the end of the year, almost everyone in that vicinity would notice happenings at Voree.

Two weeks after that January meeting, Strang revealed a vision in which God promised to reward the faithful and required tithing of the Latter Day Saints' time and labor to establish the holy city of Voree. "Serve and obey me," God said in the vision, "and I will give unto [Strang] the plates of the ancient records . . . and he shall translate them."[2] Strang's story was about to take a few pages from that of Joseph Smith's.

Two decades earlier in upstate New York, Joseph Smith, then seventeen, also had received a vision. In it, the angel Moroni told Joseph of a book written on gold plates, buried in a nearby hill. Although the plates were in a strange language, Moroni said they could be translated by using two stones, Urim and Thummim, deposited with the plates. (In the Old Testament the Urim and Thummim were set into the breastplate of judgment worn by the high priest; they were the medium for revelation of the will of God to his people.) With the help of Moroni, Joseph found the plates in a stone box under a large rock near Manchester, but the angel prevented him from taking them until exactly four years later.

After he had begun translating the plates, Smith took three witnesses into a woods, where an angel appeared with the plates and turned them over, one by one, so the witnesses could see them. The three then signed a statement saying they had seen the engravings.

33

Smith translated the plates into the Book of Mormon, which he published in 1830, the same year he founded the Church of Jesus Christ of Latter-day Saints.

The Book of Mormon tells the history of the Nephites and other ancient inhabitants of North America who had migrated to this continent from ancient Palestine long before the birth of Christ. The book includes the story of a visit to the Nephites by Christ after his resurrection. The Nephites eventually were destroyed almost to a man in a battle fought near Manchester in 385 A.D. One of the survivors of that battle was Moroni, the last of the Nephite historians, who deposited the plates that Smith had dug up. Most of those plates had been written by Moroni's father, Mormon, and were completed by Moroni.

Strang's angel, who did not have a name, appeared before him on September 1, 1845, and gave him the Urim and Thummim, two translucent stones that were used like a crystal ball. In spirit, the angel took Strang to a hill near the White River in Voree and showed him plates buried under an oak tree in an earthen case. Strang said he saw this by the Urim and Thummim.[3] On September 13 Strang took Aaron Smith and three other witnesses to the hill. The witnesses, in signed statements, said that Strang led them to an oak tree about a foot in diameter and that Strang asked them to look for any sign the sod had been disturbed. The witnesses reported none. The four men dug up the tree, while Strang kept his distance. After digging through the topsoil and subsoil, the men worked with a pickax and shovel to dig through the clay. Suddenly the shovel clunked against something—a stone about a foot square and three inches thick. Below the stone was a case of slightly baked clay embedded in the hard clay soil. Inside were three plates of brass, small enough to fit in a hand.[4]

On one of the six sides of the three plates was a landscape view, apparently of the prairie and the range of hills where the men had dug. On another was a drawing of a man wearing a cap (or a crown?) with a scepter in his hand; he was surrounded by symbols that had direct parallels to the Mormon church hierarchy. The witnesses said the other four sides "are very closely covered with what appears to be alphabetic characters but in a language of which we have no knowledge."[5]

Unlike Smith, Strang showed the plates to his followers. Then, using the Urim and Thummim, he began translating the strange marks, which he later said were related to lost Levantine languages of the eastern Mediterranean. Five days later, on September 18, he completed the translation.[6] The plates, Strang said, were the record of Rajah Manchou of Vorito, a surviving member of a people slain in battle. Some parts of the translation clearly pertained to Strang and his claim to be the head of the Mormon church. Manchou said God told him: "The forerunner men shall kill, but a mighty prophet there shall dwell. I will be his strength and he shall bring forth thy record. Record my words and bury them in the hill of promise."[7]

The parallels were obvious. The forerunner was the assassinated Joseph Smith, and the prophet, Strang. And what of Rajah Manchou, whose name was a blend of Asian mystery? That Manchou was related in any way to Moroni is not clear. What is apparent is that the esoteric characters on Manchou's brass plates bear little resemblance to those said to have been copied from Moroni's plates of gold.[8] And unlike Moroni's several appearances to Joseph Smith, Rajah Manchou of Vorito, or his works, did not appear in subsequent acts of Strang's drama. He was not heard from again.

On September 21, in a barn in Voree, Strang and the four witnesses told "an immense concourse of people" about the plates and the translation.[9] According to Strang, the story of the plates "waked up the whole country to a high state of excitement."[10] Several area newspapers noted the discovery, and many people came to examine the ground and the plates.

Among the newspapermen who came was C. Latham Sholes, editor of the nearby *Southport* (later *Kenosha*) *Telegraph*. Sholes, who would hold several offices in Wisconsin state government and help develop the first practical typewriter, filed this report:

> we visited the gentleman alluded to as seer or prophet. . . .
> [He] appears to us a very intelligent man, devoid of anything like
> enthusiasm; and, so far as we could judge, honest and earnest in all
> he said. The men who subscribe the statement [of the finding of the
> plates] are said to be among the most honest and intelligent in the
> neighborhood; and, taking it altogether, it is something to stagger

ordinary credulity. The popular opinion will doubtless call it a humbug. So should we from the natural impulse of our mind. But when
testimony appears in opposition to such impulse, we are content—to
have no opinion about it.[11]

The *Southport American* chided Sholes for his neutral stance and
labeled him the "brass plates" editor. "We begin to believe that
those 'brass plates' he pretends to have seen were only reflections of
his own face in some mud puddle on the road. If so, the difficulty
we imagined in translating their meaning is at once dispelled."[12]

The *Racine Advocate* noted the "certified" digging up of the
plates and said it had "heard it talked about that a pretended
prophet . . . has been endeavoring to find a pretext for gaining a
foothold in Wisconsin for his fanatical followers." The *Advocate* expressed the hope that no citizen of Wisconsin would give "the least
encouragement . . . to the abominable delusion and blasphemous
humbug of Mormonism."[13]

In rebuttal, Sholes said: "When we become satisfied of our own
infallibility, we will not spare the use of the term [humbug] but at
present, we know there are more things in Heaven and Earth than
we ever dreamed in our philosophy, therefore we shall let humbugs
develop themselves without denouncing them in advance."[14]

Visitors attracted by the story discovered that Strang was
living with his family in a decidedly unpretentious manner in
Benjamin Perce's home. As for the thirty-two-year-old prophet himself, visitors found him to possess characteristics that normally
would not attract attention in a crowd: he was short and slender; he
was mild-mannered; he was plainly, almost shabbily, dressed.
Behind his exceptionally high forehead, however, was no ordinary
mind.[15] And his challenge to Brigham Young was no ordinary
challenge.

Strang knew he needed all the weapons that he could muster
to battle Young, who would be defending an entrenched position in
the church. An authoritative presence, Young was a dozen years
older than Strang, and he cut the more imposing figure: he was tall
and heavy-set, with an "eagle" nose and a firm mouth. Both had
reddish-brown hair, but Young was clean-shaven during this period,
while Strang is believed to have had a full beard.[16]

The discovery of the brass plates gave Strang another "cannon" to complement his letter of appointment. Strang had one other, more basic, advantage over Young. The Mormon church had been founded by a prophet, seer, and revelator who his followers believed had communicated with angels and God himself. Like Smith, Strang had revelations and had discovered ancient plates, which he also translated with seer stones. Strang capitalized on his prophetic gift and on Young's acknowledgment that he lacked it.

In assuming control of the church, Young told the Saints that they were without a prophet. Strang later pounced on that statement, pointing to the words of a familiar Mormon hymn: "A church without a prophet, / is not the church for me; / It has no head to lead it, / in it I would not be." Many who subscribed to the sentiments of that hymn would subscribe to the claims of Prophet Strang. And in Nauvoo, where Young was still refusing to issue revelations, that hymn would be "dropped like a hot potato."[17]

That fall, while Strang was advancing plans to develop Voree as a city of refuge, the Mormons under Young were planning to leave Nauvoo to seek a new refuge, for the tide of violence was again rising in that area. On the evening of September 9 a group of anti-Mormons were meeting in a schoolhouse south of Warsaw when shots were fired into the building. No one was injured, but retaliation against the Mormons was planned. On the next night a few nearby Mormon homes were torched, as were a great number of others in the days and nights to follow. On the morning of September 16 the officer in charge of the guards at the Carthage jail during the assassination of Joseph and Hyrum Smith was himself shot and killed, by a Mormon.[18]

By the end of the month more than 100 Mormon homes had been destroyed by fire. No one knew how to stop the violence—unless the Mormons were to leave. The Mormons began putting their homes and farms up for sale, and preparations were made to move the entire church to the West.[19]

Meanwhile, Strang was launching an offensive against Young. On October 12 the Saints at Voree agreed to start a publication to tell Mormons about the letter of appointment, the plates, and Voree. Two months later it was decided that 1,000 copies would be printed and circulated immediately.[20]

Thus was born the *Voree Herald*, the trumpet with which Strang rallied his church. With the publication of the first issue at the end of December 1845, Strang gained stature as a rival to Young.[21] The first issue included the text of the letter of appointment, the story of the revelation about the plates, the statement of the four Saints who dug them up, Strang's translation of the plates, and an epistle from Strang to all the elders in the church. Under the slogan, "Truth shall prevail," a bit of one-upmanship on the "Truth will prevail" slogan of the Nauvoo *Times and Seasons*, the issue was a call to all Mormons to reject Young and gather at Voree.

In his epistle Strang urged the Saints to "follow the true Shepherd," and he stated that the letter of appointment made him that shepherd. Strang said church doctrine clearly indicated that it was the duty of Joseph Smith before his martyrdom to appoint a successor. "If he has not done so then we have no evidence that he was a Prophet." (Ironically, the same argument would apply to Strang years later.)

With such logic, Strang attempted to persuade the Saints. He also warned them: "Many of you are about to . . . go into an unexplored wilderness among savages. . . . The voice of God has not called you to this. . . . When the herd comes, the savages shall pursue . . . and the men in whom you trusted when you rejected the promises of God shall leave you early and not be found of you in your greatest need." This statement was calculated to give pause to the "herd" of Nauvoo Saints who were getting ready to trek west.

In the next paragraph, Strang offered an alternative: "Let the oppressed flee for safety unto Voree and let the gathering of people be there."

The *Voree Herald*, the first paper in the Burlington area, had less than a dozen subscribers for that first issue.[22] Undoubtedly its impact was greater. One thousand copies were printed, and many of the remaining 988 were distributed by elders on missions, thus helping spread the word and the influence of Strang's church. Even the little notation, "Published monthly by the Church of Jesus Christ of Latter Day Saints," certainly rankled the headquarters of the Church of Jesus Christ of Latter-day Saints in Nauvoo.

Soon after the first issue of the *Voree Herald* was off the press, Strang joined several elders in a thrust into Mormon territory in northern Illinois. On January 7, 1846, at St. Charles, Strang encountered Reuben Miller, who had been appointed by the Brighamite apostles to organize a company of 100 families at Ottawa. Miller's company was to join twenty-four others for the western journey, and he had received almost unanimous support for the trip.[23]

Strang and Miller agreed to a debate about church authority. Before an audience of about sixty Saints, Strang talked first, advancing his claims for four hours "in his rapid manner." Miller then said Strang's points were indeed supported by church doctrine and confessed he was unable to rebut them. As a result, almost all of those at the debate who had supported the Brighamite apostles began to question the Twelve's authority to run the church and became receptive to Strang's claims.[24] In a month-long campaign in northern Illinois, Strang gained the private support of Miller and was able to convert 300 who had been loyal to the Twelve.[25] In that region the fortunes had tilted toward James Jesse Strang.

Miller returned to Nauvoo bearing firsthand information about Strang.[26] The apostles were concerned about the reports of conversions. On January 24, 1846, in the midst of last-minute preparations to leave Nauvoo, the Twelve wrote a lengthy warning to the Saints near Ottawa. The letter, signed by Brigham Young, described Strang as an excommunicated member of the church and a "wicked liar." Strang's revelations, Young said, were "pretended," and his letter from Joseph Smith a "base and wicked forgery."[27] The apostles knew they were vulnerable to Strang, especially if their western expedition failed. The salvos from Brigham Young were designed to protect the Brighamite flanks and keep in line those who stayed behind.

"Is it not surprisingly strange," Young asked, "that Joseph Smith should appoint a man to succeed him in the presidency of the church some seven or ten days before his death, and yet not tell it to the High Council, nor to any of the authorities of the church . . . ? If Mr. Strang had received his appointment from Joseph, why did he not come here upon the death of Joseph and take charge of the church, and lead them to Voree? Because his own guilty heart would not let him come near the Furnace of trial. . . . Now Brethren, if you shall think propper to listen to the falsehoods of Mr.

Strang after this letter is laid before you, Bro. Miller is instructed to cut you off from the church." But Brother Miller was himself flirting with Strang's cause. Within a few days, he would come out in favor of the new prophet.[28]

It should be noted that Strang's unwillingness to go near the "Furnace of trial" in Nauvoo was probably based on fear for his safety. An example of how unsafe it was for Strang's followers in Nauvoo came one day after Young's letter was written. Strang had sent a mission of four elders, including Moses Smith, to Nauvoo to advocate the gathering at Voree and to oppose the planned exodus to the West.[29] On January 25, the first Sunday the four were in Nauvoo, Smith and the other elders sought permission to speak at a meeting in the temple. They received no definite reply. Inside the temple a number of Young's supporters spoke against Smith and Strang. The Brighamite speeches increased the curiosity of many in the crowd. After the meeting broke up and the crowd left the temple, Smith was surrounded by hundreds of people who wanted to hear from him and about Strang. Smith and the other Strangite elders took turns mounting a large stone to speak. They had talked to the crowd for about two hours when a Nauvoo police officer ordered the crowd to disperse. When the crowd did not, another police officer showed up with a number of knife- and pistol-toting Mormons, who threatened the Strangites and sought to capture them. The four elders escaped and found refuge in the home of a Strangite.[30]

By the next Sunday the curiosity about Strang had increased to such a pitch that the Brighamites decided to give Moses Smith a chance to speak in the temple, hoping they could browbeat him. But the shy Smith made a bold defense of Strang, despite the clamor and ridicule of the crowd. A number of speakers blasted Smith and Strang, and a voice vote was taken by the congregation to cut Smith off from the church. The vote also forbade Saints either to listen to any advocate of Strang's cause or to read the *Voree Herald*.[31]

Other Strangites later gave graphic testimony that the Brighamites used threats and violence to drive those who would not support them from the church and from Nauvoo. They told of "Aunt Peggy"—a whipping. One Strangite said Young and others often warned: "They had better look out. I'll send Aunt Peggy after them." They told of whittling societies, which were used to clear the streets of apostates and other undesirables through harassment and scare tactics. The whittlers would surround a victim and slice shavings off wooden sticks until the victim got the point. A Strangite reported one case in which twenty men with bowie knives hounded a man and kicked and rolled him in the mud for three-quarters of a mile. They told of threats of "greasing and swallowing"—the tying of one end of a rope to a victim, and the other to a large stone, which would be dumped into the Mississippi River.[32]

Strang himself suggested that John P. Greene, the city marshal of Nauvoo, was put out of the way after he stated publicly that Joseph Smith had appointed Strang to succeed him. According to testimony, when the Saints were questioning Sidney Rigdon's right to lead the church after the death of Smith, Greene said: "They need not trouble themselves about it, for Joseph had appointed [James J. Strang] to stand in his stead." Strang added that Greene "died very mysteriously a few days after" making that statement.[33]

On February 4 the trek west began, with the first of the Mormons boarding flatboats with their wagons, teams, and other belongings to cross the Mississippi. Four and a half months later, wagons had reached Council Bluffs, 300 miles away on the Missouri River at the western border of the Iowa Territory. Behind those lead wagons, several thousand Mormons were stretched across the territory.[34]

Meanwhile, Strang was sniping at the caravan through the *Voree Herald*. Those who left Nauvoo "have been very unfortunate," the *Herald* said. "Nearly all their provisions are spoiled, and clothing mildewed, so that it is falling to pieces. They are now dependent on roots, bark, and an insufficient supply of game, to save them from starvation."[35] That was very nearly true. But Strang published other reports that were not. Under the heading RUMOR, the *Herald* printed: "That P. P. Pratt [one of the Brighamite apostles] has been assassinated.—That Brigham Young has been shot, and his recovery is doubtful. It is ascertained that the mortality in the camp is without a parallel in this country. Many entire families are dead."[36] By labeling the reports as rumor, Strang gave himself an out if they were wrong; by publishing the reports, he produced as much negative publicity as if they had been true. In printing another rumor about Brighamite doom and gloom, Strang provided a backhanded disclaimer: "The thing is probable enough, but the information is not such as to give the least appearance of authenticity to it. It may be true. If no such thing has happened, it probably will." [37]

The Brighamite apostles needed to combat Strang's attempts to lure away those Saints who were wavering in their resolve to make the trip west. Apostle Orson Hyde disseminated a message from the Lord in which the spirit of the Lord said that at no time had he appointed Strang to lead his people and that he supported the move of the Saints to the West. Hyde accused the Strangites of telling the "most horrid lies. . . . When they are here, in [Nauvoo], they will say that many hundreds have joined them in some other parts, and when they go to some other parts, they will say that many thousands have fallen in with Mr. Strang in Nauvoo, when the plain fact is, that I do not know of ten persons in Nauvoo that have joined Mr. Strang. There are none who join him except a few Rigdonites, and some few others who are restless and unruly spirits that would disgrace almost any society." [38]

If Strangism had had little impact in the Nauvoo area, as Hyde asserted, why the bluster? Indeed, Moses Smith and his fellow elders were credited by Strang with converting "hundreds from the delusions of Brighamism" before they returned to Voree in the spring from their mission in Nauvoo and the surrounding region. [39] And all of them were not malcontents and Rigdonites; a few were ranking leaders in the church.

One who joined Strang was Apostle John E. Page, and another was Reuben Miller. On February 15, the day Young crossed the Mississippi, Miller wrote to Strang from Nauvoo, disclosing that Strang already had an active following there. "There are many that will be at Voree in the course of six weeks. Many that would go if they had the means." [40]

Joseph Smith's family had refused to join the western trek. In fact, Emma Smith, Joseph's widow, had denounced the "tyrants" who had "seized" the government of the church. [41] After reading this, Strang wrote to her in Nauvoo on February 22, 1846. "I have never forgotten the kindness shown me by yourself and your husband (now gone home to God) on my visit to Nauvoo two years since, and hope the time may be when I shall be able to return all your kindnesses with interest." Strang closed by tactfully asking for her support in his efforts for "the salvation" of Nauvoo.[42]

Although Emma Smith's support would have been a coup, Strang needed more than symbolism. He needed counselors of the first rank. It was then that a fateful correspondence began with John Cook Bennett, who for a year and half had served as Joseph Smith's closest adviser. Bennett, one of the most controversial figures in the history of Mormonism, sensed the potential of the gathering at Voree and offered his assistance.[43] Bennett put Strang in an awkward position. Here was a man of considerable talent and energy, but with a highly questionable reputation. Illinois Governor Thomas Ford called him "probably the greatest scamp in the western country."[44] Nevertheless, Strang had to act to fill his leadership posts if he wanted to launch a full-scale recruiting drive while the Brighamites were most vulnerable. And Bennett had one overriding qualification: experience as a Mormon leader.

At the time of his correspondence with Strang, Bennett presented himself as a professor of medicine at the "Literary and Botanico-Medical College" in Cincinnati. In 1840, when he had offered his services to Joseph Smith, Bennett was the quartermaster general of the Illinois state militia. That fall he helped draft a series of unique charters for the City of Nauvoo and lobbied for their approval by the state. By the end of 1840 the charters were signed into law. The charters incorporated Nauvoo into a virtual city-state, provided for a university in the city, and allowed the city to control its own militia, the Nauvoo Legion.[45]

Smith showed the extent of his gratitude to Bennett early in 1841. In February Bennett was made the first mayor of Nauvoo, chancellor of the proposed Nauvoo university, and major general of the Legion. In April Bennett was chosen to temporarily fill Sidney Rigdon's position in the First Presidency, the church's highest ranking body, until Rigdon's health improved.[46]

Smith prized Bennett's sophistication, but it was Bennett's worldliness, especially his womanizing, that got him into trouble in Nauvoo. A dapper man—he was 5' 9", with black hair streaked

with gray, dark eyes and a complexion to match on a thin face—
Bennett presented himself to Nauvoo society as a very eligible
bachelor. But in July 1841 Smith received a letter confirming an
earlier report that the thirty-six-year-old Bennett had a wife and
children in Ohio. Smith confronted him with the letter. Shortly
thereafter, Bennett took poison. Fortuitously, the act was discovered
in time to administer an antidote. The suicide attempt apparently
helped make a Bennett repentance convincing, and Smith took no
public action against him then.[47]

But in the spring of 1842, after rumors were published about
promiscuous intercourse and polygamy in Nauvoo, after reports that
Bennett's womanizing had been sanctioned by the prophet and after
Smith smelled a plot against his life during a sham battle of the
Legion, Smith did act. He persuaded Bennett to resign as mayor
and steps were taken to expel him from the church.[48]

In June the prophet made the excommunication public and
explained: "[Bennett] went to some of the females of the city who
knew nothing of him but as an honorable man," Smith said, "and
began to teach them that promiscuous intercourse between the sexes
was a doctrine believed in by the Latter-day Saints, and that there
was no harm in it . . . that myself and others of the authorities of
the Church, not only sanctioned but practiced the same wicked
acts." Through such lies, Smith said, Bennett seduced innocent
females.[49] There is evidence, however, that by this time polygamy
was being practiced by a tightly closed circle of the highest church
officials, even though publicly the practice was denied.[50]

Soon after leaving the church, Bennett authored sensational
exposés of life among the Mormons at Nauvoo. His disclosures included accounts of seductions and attempted seductions by Smith
and other Mormon leaders, of polygamy, of swindles, and of plots
against the U.S. government and enemies of the church.[51] The Mormons countered with their own exposé. In an extra edition the
Nauvoo Wasp declared Bennett a "spoiler of character and virtue, and
a living pestilence," and accused him of adultery, fornication, and
buggery.[52] The "graceless vagabond" also was accused of promising
abortions to women if he made them pregnant.[53]

Throughout the history of the Mormon church, it is remarkable that often the church's most determined enemies were former

associates of its leaders. Some of the most vitriolic language against church leaders came in exchanges between the leaders and former insiders who had been "delivered over to the buffetings of Satan." The Bennett case is a graphic example. Joseph Smith and John Cook Bennett traded charges of licentiousness and other acts that would be unspeakable in most families—except that they talked about them publicly, at length and in lurid detail.

In view of Bennett's controversial background, Strang had reason to be suspicious of Bennett's willingness to travel to Voree. Bennett had been blamed with introducing the "spiritual wife" doctrine (polygamy) among the Mormons,[54] and he might have been seeking another opportunity to develop that religious principle—and, thereby, his amours.

Bennett quickly ingratiated himself with Strang. He inundated the prophet with ideas, he recommended actions, and he acted as a press agent for Strang and Voree. In a barrage of letters to Strang, he proclaimed his virtues with his usual extravagance, underscoring phrases with single and double lines for emphasis. He gave promise to be a man who could open doors for Voree.

In an early letter Bennett asked Strang if he could get his old job as counselor and member of the First Presidency: "but whatever place I am to occupy, I wish it to be by revelation and commandment." On March 29 Bennett wrote Strang that he had resigned his position to join him. "Can I depend upon my old place?"[55] Two days later, Bennett wrote: "For about four years past 'I have not been myself,' for my spirits have been depressed and gloomy; but I have felt like a young lion let loose ever since I heard of your glorious movement. While you will be the Moses of the last days, I hope to be your Joshua, my old position, while you stand as the crowned Imperial Primate, I will be . . . your General-in-Chief."[56] To Strang, the mention of a crown must have been royally sweet music.

Bennett advised Strang to invite Joseph Smith's only surviving brother, William, to come to Voree as church patriarch and to "take with him his mother, with the mummies and papyrus—the bodies of Joseph and Hyrum—etc., etc. as all these things would have an astonishing effect in congregating the people at Voree. Make a desperate effort now for it is highly important."[57] The collection of four Egyptian mummies and several scrolls of papyri had been part of a traveling exhibition that the Saints purchased in Ohio. Joseph Smith said one of the scrolls had been written by Abraham while in Egypt and contained an account of the creation. Modern scholars say the papyri appear to be ordinary Egyptian funeral documents.[58] Strang would not get the mummies or the bodies, but he would get evidences of support from the Smith family.[59]

Strang did not indicate any doubt about Bennett's more eccentric suggestions. And he did show confidence in Bennett's recommendations about choosing counselors: "Sidney Rigdon will not, in my opinion, go for you: but, if he will, make him one of your Councillors instead of me; but, by all means, make George J. Adams the other Councillor. . . . Adams will accept."[60] Bennett was correct: Rigdon did not answer the call to Voree, but Adams did.

Adams's reputation in the church was almost as black as Bennett's. Before his excommunication, Adams had been in great demand as a Mormon lecturer and was described as a perfect terror in using Bible quotations in debate. In 1843 Adams faced an adultery charge after returning from a two-year mission to England with a wife and child, even though he already had a wife and family in Nauvoo. In 1844 Adams was accused of embezzling church funds and teaching and practicing polygamy.[61]

Adams successfully sidestepped these charges for a time.[62] At one point, Adams was advised to "act a little more reserved relative to female society."[63] Then, after it became apparent that the spiritual wife system was following him throughout the East, the church excommunicated him in April 1845.[64] "Under the sacred garb of religion," Brigham Young said, "he had been practising the most disgraceful and diabolical conduct."[65]

Adams then hooked up with William Smith in opposition to the Brighamites. Smith, who had been named church patriarch by the Brighamites after Joseph Smith's death, was cut off from the church for apostasy in October 1845. By February 1846 Adams had forsaken William Smith—or Smith him. Adams was then reported to be the manager of a theater in St. Louis.[66]

Before joining the Mormon church in 1840, Adams had been an evangelist who doubled as an actor. After becoming a Mormon, he helped put on shows in Nauvoo. His forte was the role of Shakespeare's hump-backed tyrant, Richard III. Despite his smallish stature, he made a distinctive stage presence with his deep-set eyes, prominent hooked nose, and long black hair. His acting, however, apparently left something to be desired—especially with the nasal twang he affected.[67]

Like the charlatan king in *Huckleberry Finn*, Adams would prove to be a drunkard and a consummate con man. (In fact, the case has been made that Mark Twain used Adams as his model for the king.)[68] This was the rogue Strang chose, on the advice of Bennett, a pretty fair scamp himself, to be one of his chief aides.

Adams predicted that Strang would hear that he was a drinker of liquor but added: "It is a base phalshood, put afloat to destroy me and my influence." Adams said the Brighamites were jealous of him—"but they have faild [to destroy me] for I draw crowds whereaver and wheneaver I lift up my voice." He called a report that he was fond of women "a base lie." His proof: phrenological evidence that his amativeness was low. "I don't mention these things because I care about them partikularly—but only to let you know that I know all about them."[69]

In a letter to Adams on May 5, Strang commented on the complaints that had been made against him. "I have only to say now that if you are guilty you must do so no more." Strang said he hoped there would be no "raking up of old scores."[70] With this pardon, Adams joined Strang's organization.

The pardon followed the lines of an earlier plea made by Bennett in a letter to Strang. "Let us all be brethren good and true, forever, and let the errors of the past be buried in oblivion—forget and forgive should ever be prominent in our Christian vocabulary"[71]—especially if men like Bennett and Adams were helping to direct the show.

Chapter 4

Stirrings of a Royal Order

WITH THE ARRIVAL of John Cook Bennett in Voree came stirrings of a royal order, of a kingdom, and of power for James Jesse Strang. "I have many things to tell you when I come that I cannot commit to paper—some very important indeed," Bennett had written Strang on June 2, 1846.[1] One "thing" Bennett apparently had in mind took shape a month later.

The Voree into which Bennett was introduced that summer was a town betwixt and between. It was not a city of 10,000 inhabitants, as many newspapers said. Nor was it nonexistent, as others claimed. With its many new arrivals, Voree looked more like an encampment than a town.[2]

The *Voree Herald* reported that it certainly was not a rich community. "Its population dwell in plain houses; in board shanties, in tents, and sometimes many of them in the open air, and if any of those good truth telling Christians who say Voree is NON EST will call here of a sunday we will show them a congregation of from one to two thousand people, besides those who stay at home."[3] Dissident insiders, however, estimated that the Mormon population did not exceed 500 in Voree and the adjacent country, and the smaller figure appears closer to the truth.[4]

The Saints who gathered at Voree could buy lots for about $50 an acre. Shortly after the *Voree Herald* announced that price, Strang replied to accusations that he was the owner of a large tract of land at Voree and was trying to get rich by selling it acre by acre.[5] Strang said he owned only a couple acres, on the outskirts of Voree, the only land he possessed "on the face of the broad earth."[6]

But Strang had been a speculator for a decade, and if he did not have an interest in the "several hundred lots" being offered for sale, how could he state with certainty that the price was fixed? Land records show that much of the land at Voree was then owned by Benjamin Perce, Strang's closest friend, brother-in-law, and fellow speculator. At the end of 1846 Perce would sell 650 acres of his

Voree holdings to his brother. The listed price, $30 per acre, was about five times the per-acre price that Perce paid for 200 of the acres four months earlier. This raises the suspicion that the brothers were attempting to inflate the value of the land artificially to promote speculation.[7]

The land "scandal" prompted Strang to detail how he had devoted himself untiringly to the ministry. In less than two years, he claimed, he had traveled more than 4,000 miles, 3,000 on foot, on church business. Writing of himself in the third person, he added: "He has supported a wife and two children, and though he has received assistance with liberality from a few poor brethren, he has never asked a man for one cent. . . . he has traveled with his feet bare and blistered, gone days without food, ate raw potatoes and raw corn, slept out in storms, waded and swam rivers in cold weather."[8] Because of these sacrifices, church members would do something for him.

Shortly after July 1, on the heels of Bennett's arrival, Strang reported a revelation giving instructions to the Saints on building him a home. The revelation also commanded the Saints to build a temple and Strang was told to "take a great covenant" of all who were taught the "mysteries of the Kingdom."[9]

In Strang's papers is a note penned by Bennett, stating that Constantine the Great received a command from heaven to institute an "Order of the Illuminati" for the defense of the Christian religion.[10] Centuries later, Bennett would help create an order under that name in Voree. The Order of Illuminati formed in July 1846 was both a secret society and a paramonarchical organization with an imperial primate, a grand council, and noblemen. It bound Strang's followers to him absolutely and provided the pattern for sovereign authority in his later kingdom.

On July 6 Strang was proclaimed imperial primate, and Bennett was named his general-in-chief. There followed on that and succeeding nights a procession of chevaliers, marshals, sirs, earls, cardinals, and other Illuminati. In Bennett's room in Burlington—with Bennett officiating—these men took the covenant, with their right hands touching a cross lying on a Bible. They promised to "ever conceal, and never reveal, any of the ceremonies, secrets and misteries of the order."[11]

The oath began religiously enough: "I believe in God the Father, Almighty Sovereign of Heaven and Earth; and in the Lord Jesus Christ, his son and right Lord of the earth; and in the Holy Spirit, which inspires men to righteousness; and in the Holy Catholic and Apostolic Church of the Saints; and in James J. Strang, the Prophet of God, Apostle of the Lord Jesus, and Chief Pastor of the Flock." Then the initiates gave Strang absolute secular power as they promised to "uphold, sustain and obey the said James J. Strang . . . as the Imperial primate and actual Sovereign Lord and King on Earth . . . and will yield obedience to the revelations he shall give; the Laws made by the Grand Council of Nobles of God's Kingdom with his concurrence; and the decrees he shall make." To stress their fealty to Strang, those joining the order summarily renounced "all allegiance to any and every other Potentate, State and Nation." They also pledged to maintain the Kingdom of God's "dominion, integrity, and inviolability in defiance of any and every power, state and nation as long as life lasts." Then they learned a series of passwords, a common grip (three fingers within three), and a common sign (three fingers of the right hand to the mouth). [12]

After taking the oath, the initiates' heads were anointed from the "chalice of sacred oil," creating each an Illuminatus "in the name of the Father, and of the Son, and of the Holy Ghost, and by the authority of the Holy Priesthood and the special edict" of Strang, the "absolute sovereign." [13] With these subjects, Imperial Primate Strang had finally reached the status of king on earth. His coronation as king—and the founding of his kingdom—were years away, however.

A month later Bennett reported that 117 persons had taken the covenant, as the oath became known, "and all are highly delighted." Bennett, with his usual flourish of excess, drew up diplomas for the initiates and urged Strang to have them printed "in a splendid manner." [14]

Bennett also was delighted with Voree. His medical practice was prosperous, and he reported "there was never better feeling in any community on earth than there is here at this time." [15] But Bennett and the secret order were sowing seeds of discord that would be harvested in the fall.

In creating the secret order, Strang had taken another page from the book of Joseph Smith. On March 11, 1844, just eight days after Strang had been ordained an elder in Nauvoo, Smith had secretly formed a special council, commonly called the Council of Fifty because that was about how many members it had. The members, organized as princes in the Kingdom of God, swore their allegiance to Smith, who was ordained as king.[16]

≈ ≈ ≈

In August, with his sovereign authority attested to, Strang headed east to recruit more subjects. The first stop in this invasion of Brighamite strongholds was Kirtland, Ohio, the first major center of Mormonism in the 1830s.

With Brigham Young and most of his chief lieutenants straggling across the Plains, Strang seized the moment. He had the support of Joseph Smith's mother, Lucy, and his sole surviving brother, William. And a few months earlier, in a letter printed in the *Voree Herald*, William Smith claimed that "the whole Smith family," except for Hyrum Smith's widow, had given its backing to Strang and had said the "wilderness move is not of God."[17] Strang, with the endorsement of relatives of the martyred prophet, pressed his claim to leadership of the church with startling success.

Accompanied by William Smith, who had been ordained as patriarch and an apostle in Strang's church, Strang arrived in Kirtland on August 7 for a four-day conference. Several hundred persons heard Strang preach four times, once for eight hours. The conference upheld Strang as prophet, and Strangites took over legal possession of the Mormon temple at Kirtland.[18]

Strang then headed toward Pittsburgh, Philadelphia, New York, and Boston. This invasion, according to Strang's press, would turn into a triumphal procession. The Brighamites did not totally leave the field of battle, but they did avoid hand-to-hand combat with Strang and his leaders.[19]

In Philadelphia Orson Hyde and John Taylor, two Brighamite apostles, blasted Strang at long range. They derided Strang's letter of appointment, and Taylor called Strang "an impostor, a false and wicked man."[20] Under attack, Strang challenged Taylor and Hyde to debate who had the authority to lead the church. Perhaps wisely, Hyde and Taylor declined a war of words with Strang. Pointing out that the Brighamites had cut Strang off from the church, Hyde and Taylor said: "After Lucifer was cut off and thrust down to hell, we have no knowledge that God ever condescended to investigate the subject or right of authority with him."[21]

Hidden behind this adroit riposte was a reluctance to debate that was almost certainly prompted by the knowledge that in any public discussion, Strang would likely prick that festering sore of the Brighamites—polygamy. In the April issue of the *Voree Herald*, Strang noted that Hyde, in his March revelation, "says (and pretends that God said it), 'Behold James J. Strang hath cursed my people.' " Strang said the curse was on Hyde and other ministers of the gospel who taught that "fornication and adultery are ordinances in God's house." Copies of the curse, Strang said, were distributed in Nauvoo and produced "much excitement." In that descriptive curse, Strang trundled out his high-powered verbal artillery: "may their bones rot in the living tomb of their flesh. . . . May peace and home be names forgotten to them, and the beauty they have betrayed to infamy; may it be to their eyes a crawling mass of putridity and battening corruption; its delicate hues a sickly light that glares from universal corruption; its auburn tresses the posthumous growth of temples of crawling worms; its fragrant breath the blast of perdition. With desires insatiate may each gratification turn to burning bitterness and glowing shame."[22]

In an issue of the *Herald* that was published after his bid for a debate was turned down, Strang again attacked Hyde, this time for shunning a confrontation with George J. Adams. "Why did he tell one of the Saints in Cincinnati, that he was extremely anxious to see him, and a few minutes after as he saw Elder Adams stepping on the steamboat, sneak away and lock himself up in a state-room?"[23]

Through articles in the *Herald*, Strang belittled his opposition. Another Brighamite apostle, Parley P. Pratt, gave Strang another opportunity. Pratt, whom a fellow apostle had dubbed the "Archer of Paradise," evidently had gotten himself into a scrape in Boston and was being pursued by the police. "The Archer shot himself— out of Boston," the *Herald* reported, and added that he was being chased by "notes for borrowed money, writs for seducing wives, and warrants for adultery." [24]

The *Herald* also heralded successes in the eastern mission. In Pittsburgh, the paper said, the Saints "have nearly all returned to the true order"—the church led by Strang; in Philadelphia the Strangites were "flourishing"; in New York the church was "restored to order and the scattered sheep are gathering up"; and in Boston Strang and Adams received a "most cordial greeting." [25] Strang also claimed the backing of most of the Mormon churches in Ohio, Michigan, Indiana, Illinois, New Jersey, and the New England states.

In meetings on the eastern mission the focus generally was on Strang, whom one newspaper found to be a diminutive, ill-favored, insignificant-looking man with an earnest, energetic manner. "When preaching, he appears like a man trying with all of his might to convince others that he had something very important to tell them and that it was absolutely necessary that they should believe it." [26]

Besides preaching, prayers, and singing, the meetings could include selling Bibles and tracts, and even dancing. [27] Strang often exhibited the brass plates and the letter of appointment, which Brigham Young had branded a "wicked forgery," even though he had never examined it.

The controversial letter consisted of two sheets of paper, with the text on three sides. The fourth side served as the envelope and contained Strang's name and address, the 18¾ cent postage rate, and the "Nauvoo June 19" postmark, hand-stamped in red ink. Envelopes were not yet widely used in America, and postage stamps would not be issued for another three years. Some Brighamites insisted that the postmark was too large and that it was in black ink, not red, as it should have been. Strang easily proved the postmark was the right color and size. The Brighamites also found a small dot at the left of the top of the J in June in the postmark. Obviously, they said, the dot should not have been there, and this proved the letter was a forgery. But Strang located other letters mailed from Nauvoo on June 19. On each was the same dot. [28] Strang was jubilant. "How could the forger know that on that particular day . . . a little splinter would get into the mailing stamp, and mark every

letter with one dot which ought not to be there? . . . this dot, once
the sole ground of impeachment of this letter of appointment, has
thus established its genuineness." But doubts about the letter persisted. In an attempt to remove them, Strang presented evidence
that the letter was indeed prophetic. The letter predicted "great
calamities are comeing on the church," and the events in Hancock
County bore this out. Strang also said that the letter, in which
Joseph Smith foresaw his martyrdom, was received at Burlington
before any notice of his death or arrest.[29]

Although news of Smith's assassination may not have become
common knowledge in the Burlington area until after Strang received the letter, some newspapers in larger cities nearby reported
it as many as five days before the letter was received on July 9. The
Chicago Daily Journal carried the assassination in an extra on July 4.
The *Southport Telegraph* received the reports the same day but did
not print them until July 16 because they were vague and contra-
dictory. The *Milwaukee Commercial Herald* had the story on July 5,
via a "gentleman from Chicago." Strang, an ex-newspaperman who
traveled widely, could have picked up the news on his travels and
used it to his advantage. One indication this may have been the case
was that the Smith letter predicted his "visage" would be "marred."
Initial reports of the assassination erroneously had Smith receiving
the "contents of 27 rifles" rather than three shots.

The style of the letter also came under attack as being unlike
Smith. Brigham Young himself concluded: "Mr. Strang has high
strains of poetry here, but not a word of truth."[30] Indeed, parts of
the letter are reminiscent of Strang's writing; one passage in Strang's
diary discusses a spiritual experience similar to this one in the letter:
"The Almighty came from his throne of rest. He clothed himself
with light as with a garment. He appeared & moon & stars went
out. the earth dissolved in space. I trod on air & was borne on wings
of cherabims, the sweetest strains of heavenly musick thrilled in my
ear but the notes were low & sad as though they sounded the re-
quiem of martyred prophets."[31]

The Brighamites appear to have missed a chance to scuttle the
legitimacy of the letter from the beginning. Instead of concentrat-
ing on the postmark and the style of the letter, they should have

offered comparisons of Joseph Smith's signature as evidence, for the letter's signature does not resemble Smith's throughout his later years.[32]

The authenticity of the letter also is suspect because it is printed rather than in script. One historian says that in all Mormon history, this is the only document known in this style.[33] Another expert says that the body of the letter was printed by the same person who signed the letter. Smith usually dictated his letters to a clerk, and it is highly unlikely that he would have printed a letter himself rather than writing it in script.[34]

A close examination of the letter reveals that it was written on two kinds of paper.[35] It is possible that the covering sheet, which bears the address and postmark, was sent to Strang from someone in Nauvoo on June 19, but that the inside sheet was not.

After receiving the letter, Strang could have discarded the inside sheet that contained the original message. A forger could have begun a letter on both sides of a new sheet of paper and concluded it on the back of the envelope sheet that had been sent from Nauvoo. Since the "envelope" was addressed in printed characters, he could have tried to duplicate those characters throughout the body of the letter. One variance stands out: the lower case G's of the address are more distinctive than those in the letter.

Another anomaly is that the letter has a postscript that Strang did not include in published versions or other copies.[36] The postscript—"P S Write me soon & keep me advised of your progress from time to time"—seems a bit too casual for a document of such import and seems to ignore the prophet's vision of impending martyrdom. Strang may have decided that the postscript weakened his case for being named Smith's successor.

Based on the time it took other mail from Nauvoo to reach the Burlington area, a letter sent from Nauvoo on June 19 should have arrived in Burlington by July 3. Such a letter could have been a reply—and an unfavorable one at that—to Strang's report on the possibilities for creating a Mormon settlement near Burlington. And if a negative or lukewarm reponse had been received at about the same time Strang heard reports of Smith's assassination, Strang could have been prompted to forge a letter in a bold bid for power.

But if the Nauvoo letter did come from Smith, a forger would have had a Smith signature to copy, and the signature on the letter should have more closely resembled Smith's.

The letter was not the only Strangite relic targeted for abuse during Strang's eastern mission. The brass plates also came under attack, and Strang defended his translation of the inscriptions. Strang wrote, "The world and the Saints know just what I have told them, and what God has revealed to them." Then, drawing a parallel with Joseph Smith that helped shield him from further questions, Strang said: "That is all they know of the plates which Joseph translated. God made him a witness of the work, and the world must take the translation on his testimony. So he made me a witness after Joseph's death, and has vouchsafed me proper evidence of this calling, and the world will have to take this translation on my testimony." [37]

His translation, Strang wrote a Brighamite, had been tested "by a body of learned men, acquainted with the modern discoveries shedding light on the lost Levantine languages. And the result satisfied them that this record was written in a language bearing a common relation to all the languages spoken in the earliest ages in the Levant, and that the translation was genuine." Craftily, Strang added that it "would be too tedious to relate the process by which these tests were made, and they might not be well understood, except by men of profound learning; but they were made by those who wished to make a case against me, and the result was clearly in my favor." [38] Strang never said who this body of learned men included.

Over the next ten years former Strangites would charge that Strang had fashioned the plates out of pieces cut from a brass kettle. Forty years later Isaac Scott, a one-time leader in the church, wrote that C. P. Barnes had told him that both the letter of appointment and the plates were hoaxes, concocted by Strang, Benjamin Perce, and himself to help sell lands they owned at Voree. "Mr. Barnes said their aim, in the first place, was to have Joseph Smith appoint a gathering place, or Stake, on their lands, but as Smith was killed about this time, they changed their plans and concluded to make Strang Smith's successor and that would make a sure thing of building up Voree." According to Scott, Barnes said Strang "dictated every word" of the letter of appointment. "He said they made the 'plates' out of Ben [Perce]'s old kettle and engraved them with an old saw file and . . . that when completed they put acid on them to corrode them and give them an ancient appearance; and that to deposit them under the tree, where they were found, they took a large auger . . . which Ben [Perce] owned, put a fork handle on the auger and with it bored a long slanting hole under a tree on 'The Hill of Promise,' as they called it, laying the earth in a trail on a cloth as taken out, then put the 'plates' in, tamping in all the earth again, leaving no trace of their work visible."

About the covenant, Scott wrote that Barnes said Strang rejected advice to go slow: "We tried to persuade him not to introduce it into the church until the people were better prepared for its introduction."[39]

                 ❧   ❧   ❧

On leaving the East, Strang had to feel good about the mission. He had reason to believe that the size of his church and his influence were drawing ever closer to Young's, especially with Young occupied in dragging his flock slowly across the Plains. Thus, it likely was a confident James J. Strang who stopped in western New York state to see relatives and friends on his way back to Voree. It was three years since he had left New York.

Strang found his parents and his brother and sister worried about his welfare, both spiritual and physical. His family harbored the hope that he would rejoin the Baptist church, and, a year before, his sister had passed along a letter certifying that both he and his wife were members in good standing of the Baptist church at Randolph. Myraette hoped they would use these papers to join a Baptist church out west.[40] But they did not, and even Mary joined the Mormon church, to her father's displeasure. W. L. Perce called Mormonism a "cursed doctrine."[41]

Strang's parents knew he was deeply involved in the prophet business because he had been sending home the *Voree Herald*, in which were printed the letter from Smith, the story of the discovery of the plates, and articles about his battle for control of the Mormon church. On reading the *Herald*, his sister spoke for the whole family when she wrote: "When I think of my beloved brother, in a far off land, the propagator of strange doctrines; my heart sinks within me; & I know not how to address you. I have nothing to say in regard to the motives which may have actuated you; but I entreat, I beg you, in that name of all that is near and dear to you, all that is sacred; pause, and think of the solemn and fearful responsibility you have taken upon you."[42]

Wealthy Smith was less sparing of his feelings. In a letter written after he had visited her that fall, she declared that she was dissatisfied because they had not had a chance for a long talk. (As a side note, it is interesting to speculate on what would have happened if Strang had married Wealthy Smith, an intelligent, perceptive woman. Would Wealthy have been able to channel Strang's ambitions toward less exotic pursuits? And, in that event, would Strang simply have been less happy?) To Wealthy, it was a great mystery why Strang had become a Mormon. She said she thought Mormonism a delusion and Joseph Smith an imposter "because his prophesies and his revelations have never proved true. I have more confidence in God than to believe that he would reveal to a person that they could go to such a place and . . . they would live there in peace, and never be molested. I believe that was the revelation he had . . . when he went to Nauvoo. . . . I have no confidence in such revelations, (have you?) for either God or Joe Smith must have told a falsehood, and certainly I would believe God." Then Wealthy became more personal. "What your object could have been in joining them, I am at a loss to know, unless it was for the sake of gain, or (as I have often heard you say) to immortalize your name, for it does not seem possible that you can be a sincere believer in mormonism, but after all I have a better opinion of you than to think that you would try to deceive people." Wealthy closed, her love for Strang still apparent. "My pen is getting worn, my candle is burning low and I am getting very sleepy, so I will bid you good evening and go to bed and think of former times."[43]

During his return to Chautauqua County, Strang checked out his feeling that as a prophet he was without honor in his own county. Earlier that year, the *Mayville Sentinel* had accused him of selling a farm he did not own and suggested he had absconded from the county after being arrested on charges related to the farm deal.[44]

John C. Bennett, who had sent Strang a copy of the article, tried his best to hush it up, but Strang printed portions of it in the *Voree Herald*.[45] This would be typical of Strang throughout his career. Rather than allow critical rumors or press comments to fester, he would reprint the reports in his newspapers, even those that contained strong anti-Strang sentiments. Sometimes he would reprint negative stories without comment, as if to show his disdain, but more often he would begin an immediate counteroffensive.

In the case of the *Mayville Sentinel* article, Strang used the better part of two pages of the *Herald* in an attempt to demolish the charges, point by point, and he sent 200 copies of that issue into Chautauqua County. Regarding the charges made by the *Sentinel*, there is evidence only that Strang did have financial problems before leaving the county in 1843. He even tried to settle some debts later by offering creditors lots in Voree for speculation.[46]

As editor of the church newspaper, Strang also served notice that he would give space to opposing views. "We stand ready and willing and anxious to meet the religious world, and the champions of each and every sect, in fair open discussion," said the man who was both a skillful debater and writer. Indeed, Strang would open his columns to some of his most rabid opponents, even the Brighamites. But he hoped for similar treatment: "We call upon our opponents, also, to open the columns of their papers for the investigation of truth, and if they decline doing so we can only attribute it to a fear that they shall be unable to satisfy their own followers of the soundness of their positions."[47]

One of the truths Strang debated in his newspaper was the origin of Jesus. Contrary to the Apostles' Creed, which states "I believe in Jesus Christ, God's only son, our Lord, who was conceived by the Holy Ghost, born of the Virgin Mary," Strang believed that Christ was the literal human descendant of David.[48] This tenet is one of the major differences between Strang's church and that of the Utah Mormons, who believe in the Virgin Birth.

According to Strang, Jesus Christ "came in the flesh as the Messiah," in fulfillment of the word of God from the prophets. He said the Catholic church, however, was unwilling that its founder be the son of a poor carpenter and resorted to the heathen fable of children begotten of gods on beautiful women, and filled all their books and creeds with a story, fit only for heathen mythology, of a liaison of the God of heaven with a Hebrew peasant girl." Strang observed that if the "Catholic" account is true, Christ was not of the lineage of David. "Jewish genealogies are always reckoned in the male line; never in the female. . . . Two of the evangelists, Matthew and Luke, have given the genealogy from Abraham to Joseph, the husband of Mary, for the especial purpose of showing that in the male line, Jesus Christ was literal descendant of Abraham, Judah and David. If the husband of Mary was not the father of Christ, what have we to do with his genealogy?"[49]

🊔 🊔 🊔

On August 2, the day before he left on the eastern mission, Strang had addressed the Saints at Voree for three hours. He admonished them against every appearance of disagreement and every subject of controversy.[50] But to no avail. By the time Strang returned home in October, a number of insurrections had taken place in Voree, and several of Strang's leaders had come out against him or the covenant.[51] Chief among the dissidents were Aaron Smith, his counselor, and Reuben Miller, president of the Voree stake.

Miller challenged Strang's claims to head the church and accused him of altering his description of the way the angel had designated him as Joseph Smith's successor. Miller maintained that Strang had first said the angel did not touch him, but stood before him with uplifted hands. Strang replied that he had always said the angel anointed his head with oil.[52] There is no evidence other than a church record, however, that Strang had said anything about an anointing until after the January mission to Illinois. And Miller claimed the references to an anointing in that church record were not written until after that mission, a year and a half after Smith's death.[53]

In September 1846 Miller published a pamphlet entitled, *James J. Strang, Weighed in the Balance of Truth, and Found Wanting.* Strang dismissed the pamphlet with the comment that it was "small potatoes, and few in a hill."[54] Late that year, Miller would be excommunicated after a trial on charges of apostasy, schism, lying, and publishing a libel against Strang and the church. After his break with Strang, Miller rejoined the church of Brigham Young.[55]

Aaron Smith had been kept in the dark about the Order of the Illuminati. And in September, after he learned about the covenant, he came out against it, declaring that he knew by revelation that it was not of God.[56] In October, with Strang still absent, Aaron Smith and other dissidents targeted the man believed responsible for the covenant, the man who had become Strang's chief adviser. They put John C. Bennett on trial. The charges—teaching such false doctrines as polygamy and concubinage, threatening life, and ridiculing sacred things—were similar to those Bennett had faced in Nauvoo. According to testimony in the Voree trial on October 4, Bennett had told one Saint that there was no harm in illicit intercourse. And a high priest said Bennett had told him that when women came to confess sins, he would have a good chance to have "connection" with them. After deciding that the charges were sustained by the evidence, the council of what Strang called "Pseudo Mormons" or "Pseudoes" voted to expel Bennett from the church.[57] The action, however, had little immediate effect on Bennett's position in the church.

Strang's newspaper dismissed that dissident council as a "mere packed concern, got up without even the semblence of order or authority, to destroy a man of distinguished talent and faithfulness, by means of prejudice, falsehood, and third- and fourth-handed tell-tale rumour." For once, the Strangite news organ did not list the charges and referred to them only in vague terms. The paper said Bennett was not excommunicated nor was he found guilty of any particular offense.[58]

Not all of the opposition to Bennett was in Voree. One member of the church in Ottawa, Illinois, wrote letters to Strang that were critical of his appointment of Bennett. "I cannot understand how a prophet of the Lord can take such a man as [Bennett] for a bosom friend and councillor when you so well know what his character has been . . . and if testimony can be relied on he is no better now. How can you condemn others for what you approve in him?" The woman still gave some backhanded support for Strang. "I am not disposed to give up our prophet yet. We do not find one every day and they are not so plenty that we can afford to throw one away without good reason."[59]

One of the "Pseudoes" who testified against Bennett was Collins Pemberton, whom Strang had ordained an elder just three months before. A few days after the trial, in a church conference on October 8, Pemberton attempted to discuss the secret covenant. But Bennett objected, and the focus of that session was shifted to preaching, denying Pemberton a forum.[60]

After Strang returned from the East, he called an October 25 meeting of the high council and Pemberton was summarily excommunicated for, among other reasons, disorderly conduct in meetings of the church. And as for Aaron Smith, whom God had named a counselor in the letter of appointment, Strang reported a revelation on November 6 in which God said Aaron should no longer hold that position.[61]

Seeing that Strang was not about to take action against Bennett or the covenant, Aaron Smith called a meeting of his group of dissidents for December 7. Those who attended attacked the covenant as dangerous and voted to withdraw fellowship from those who adhered to it. The same night, Strang and his supporters met and purged a half-dozen more dissidents from positions of authority in the church. Those purged included four members of the twelve-member high council at Voree.[62]

On the evening of December 8, the dissident group made public a series of resolutions, one of which declared that the covenant would lead to "abject slavery, binding us by horrid oaths to obey all the edicts, mandates and commands of the absolute sovereign and pontiff, leaving us no alternative but to become dupes and accomplices of wicked men and oppression." The "Pseudoes" had obtained a purported copy of the covenant, and the resolution was a reaction to that understated version.[63]

According to the dissidents, Strang had declared on his return from the East that, although the covenant was a revelation from God, it was not a part of the Gospel, and that any man dissatisfied with the covenant could withdraw from it and still be a member of the church. But now, the "Pseudoes" said, Strang was expelling the best members in the church for covenant-breaking.[64]

Also on December 8 Aaron Smith was charged with covenant-breaking, lying, heresy, and schism. The Strangites reported that Smith had pleaded guilty to the first two charges and that the latter two were "fully sustained." Smith was excommunicated.[65]

The attacks of Miller and the "Pseudoes" had drawn blood, and Strang had fifty-five of his supporters, most of them members of the secret Order of the Illuminati, sign a statement that there was no secret organization in Voree that was repugnant to, or inconsistent with, the book of Doctrine and Covenants of the church. But the Strangites did not deny the existence of a secret order and even made references to Masonic orders. If the Masons could have secret orders and kings, what was all the fuss about in Voree?[66] In a bit of sophistry, Strang reportedly argued that there were no secret societies in the church because there were no societies whose existence was not known. If known to exist, he said, the societies could not be considered secret.[67] The statement signed by the fifty-five men was published in *Zion's Reveille*, the successor to the *Voree Herald*. (Strang had changed the name in a bid to wake up the brethren "from their lethargy" and get them to "spend at least as much time in examining their own hearts as seeking for the faults of their neighbours.")[68]

It was Strang who spent much time—and space in the *Zion's Reveille*—finding fault with the detailed charges against himself and Bennett, especially regarding the secret order, in "Pseudo" broadsides and newspapers. The *Reveille* articles also found fault with the anti-Strang neighbors involved—"some who are guilty of lasciviousness and abominable iniquities, such as teaching the spiritual wife doctrine."[69] In the worst Mormon tradition, each side drenched their former friends in calumny, as the Strangites and the "Pseudoes" traded accusations of thievery, polygamy, and moral leprosy.

The damage to Strang's church from the schisms, the purges, and the bad publicity was extensive, and there was a considerable loss of members—and branches of the church in major cities. Although the secret order advanced Strang's moves toward a political kingdom, those followers who were seeking a church centered around spiritual values were disillusioned, and many left the fold.[70]

In the midst of all the problems of their church, 130 Strangites held a "most sumptuous feast" on New Year's Day, 1847. It was called "one of the most pleasant festivals the church has ever witnessed . . . truly a feast of love." During the event, Strang's new house was dedicated.[71]

The house was a small log dwelling, 10 by 14 feet. Though the Saints had been given instructions in a revelation on building a house for Strang and though many Saints pledged money or time, Strang said he paid more than half of the expense and the house still needed some work.[72] In return for the work on his house, Strang apparently had promised something special, an "extraordinary endowment" or "heavenly illumination," rendering the recipient impregnable to "all the shafts of Satan." And the next night twenty-four Saints met at Strang's house, most likely for some ceremonies in connection with the Order of the Illuminati. According to the *Ottawa* (Illinois) *Free Trader*, Strang concluded the ceremonies by anointing heads with a holy oil that had a "queer" smell, and in a darkened room "the heads of all shone as if lit up by the brightness of the sun and great was the rejoicing of the Saints."[73]

The rejoicing at this miracle became muted within three days, however, when a group of forty Strangite defectors in and around Voree mounted a barrage of accusations, charging that "all was not gold that glittered" and that the Saints had been tricked. Voree buzzed about the illumination for weeks. Several defectors eventually charged that the ointment used in the anointing was a mixture of olive oil and phosphorus, which would have illuminated any ceremony held in the dark. They also said that when the ointment was rubbed a bit too vigorously on the head of one initiate who had thinner locks, the friction and the phosphorus caused not only a glow but an actual fire to surround his head.[74]

Strang subsequently admitted that ordinances of some kind had been administered at his house that day and that they usually were referred to as the "Illumination." He said that as the meeting was not public, "much curiosity has always been felt to know what they were." To the phosphorus and oil charge, Strang weakly responded that the combination "only produces a dim light in a warm dark room. It barely makes itself visible, and could not possibly for a single moment be mistaken for the glory of God,"[75] attributing more cynicism and objectivity to the Saints than religious people of that revivalist period generally possessed.

William Smith, the prophet's brother, said he had examined the "holy oil" and found it to contain phosphorus. He called Strang a base imposter, an infidel, and a liar. But Smith did not make these comments until after he had been excommunicated from Strang's church for adultery and apostasy. After his expulsion, in October 1847, Smith went on a lecture tour, in which he exposed alleged frauds of Mormonism, much in the manner of Bennett in 1842. Smith also accused Strang of making the brass plates from an old kettle and of writing the letter of appointment.[76]

Strang said Smith was not within 150 miles of the illumination and did not know any more about it than the emperor of Japan. He added that it had become fashionable for every man, when he was cut off from the church, to cry "Iniquity! Iniquity!! for the purpose of covering up his wickedness in the fierceness of his outcry against others. . . . Though you have been a mean man all your life; though you was a liar and a backbiter before you joined the church; a heretic and a swindler while in it, and are an apostate and a hypocrite now—just get up the biggest lie you can possibly invent upon the prophet and the church. Spice it strongly with criminal accusations; enrich it with incongruities and impossibilities, and you will suddenly find yourself a respectable man and a gentleman."[77]

Also in October 1847 John C. Bennett was quietly excommunicated. In June Strang had announced that Bennett had been removed from all official standing for suppressing letters addressed to Strang and teaching unsound doctrine. Bennett was expelled for "apostacy, conspiracy to establish a stake by falsehood, deception, & c. and various immoralities."[78] Unlike at Nauvoo, Bennett accepted his fate without any indication that he intended to exact retribution. He quietly went home to Plymouth, Massachusetts, and devoted himself to the raising and breeding of chickens.[79]

Bennett and Smith were not the only ranking church leaders who faced serious accusations. So did George J. Adams.

The Boston branch of the church wrote Strang that it wanted nothing to do with Adams. His actions on a mission there had caused the branch to suspend public meetings. The branch accused

Adams of teaching that it was not wrong to commit adultery under certain circumstances, of being drunk, and of renting halls for which he paid nothing, even though collections were taken for that purpose.[80] It was obvious that Adams was up to his old tricks. He apparently was associating with drunken rowdies and cementing his reputation for playing with women and at spiritual wifery. In Boston there was evidence that he was returning to his old habit of preaching on the Sabbath, and going on stage during the rest of the week, to the detriment of his religious mission.[81]

In the summer of 1847, in the midst of his problems in Boston, Adams tried to shift some of the blame to Bennett. It had become clear that Bennett was on the way out, and Adams turned on his former sponsor. In a letter to Strang, Adams called Bennett a corrupt man: "he is all self—he has injured you very much. . . . His name attached to the cause has paralyzed all my efforts." Adams then made a bid for Bennett's spot as Strang's chief aide. Adams said he knew he was a sinner, but added that he also was an "honest man, a true man, a faithful friend."[82]

Despite the complaints, Strang took no action against Adams and even gave him tacit approval to play the stage. Strang said he was no advocate of "theatricals," but wanted to know if Adams "made a more lewd or unchristian appearance on stage than King David dancing naked before the maids of Israel."[83]

Chapter 5

Beaver Island

VOREE, THE "GARDEN OF PEACE," had hardly been peaceful. And like many a garden, its space was limited—too limited for a kingdom. A kingdom, Strang had determined, needed an abundance of inexpensive land to attract and hold settlers. Strang had one other apparent requirement: isolation from competing influences.

Strang was preparing to relocate his flock, although he was not being prodded by mobs or threats, as the Mormons in Nauvoo had been. The first public hint that Strang was thinking beyond the bounds of Voree came in the *Voree Herald* of March 1846, shortly after Young began leading the Nauvoo Saints west. In an article attacking the western migration, Strang said Joseph Smith had not planned that move. Smith, he said, had only planned to establish a stake among the Indians. "What he did devise would have been accomplished before now but for apostate usurpation, and shall be soon in spite of it."

Seven months later, after he returned from the East, Strang said the place for such an Indian mission "has already been pointed out by the finger of God, and measures for its occupation are now far advanced." He gave no further details except to say that "the situation is a most delightful one, in immediate proximity to vast numbers of Indians, and secure from molestation of any kind." [1]

Shortly after this statement appeared, the word was leaked by the "Pseudoes" that Voree was to be abandoned for an Indian mission on Big Beaver Island in northern Lake Michigan, despite the letter of appointment's declaration that the people in the stake of Voree "shall not be mooved." [2] At about the same time Reuben Miller reported that he had heard the "kingdom was about to have a dominion." [3]

Strang's newspaper denied that Voree was to be abandoned. The paper said Voree would indeed be built as "one of the stakes of

Zion," to fulfill the revelation given to Joseph Smith, but admitted that the Indian mission, on Big Beaver Island, would be the "great corner stake of Zion" in accordance with another revelation.[4]

In the January 14, 1847, issue of the *Zion's Reveille*, Strang reported a vision he had had on August 25 at Elizabeth on the Monongahela River, as he was beginning his eastern mission. "I beheld a land amidst wide waters, and covered with large timber, with a deep broad bay on one side of it"—a description that fit Big Beaver Island. God told him that "here shall God establish his people . . . and from hence shall the gospel of the kingdom go unto the tribes," Strang said. He was told he would see the land with his own eyes before he returned home to Voree. The steamer he took from Buffalo to Voree did pass by the Beaver Islands. According to one report, Strang's boat was forced to take shelter there during a storm and he liked what he saw. Big Beaver, or Beaver Island, was not the only island Strang had his eye on, however. He also had made inquiries about others in the vicinity of Michigan, including Belle Isle near Detroit.[5]

Beaver Island is the largest in Lake Michigan. The fifty-eight-square-mile island was then unpopulated by white men except at a couple of fishing and trading settlements. The federal government was surveying the island and was about to sell land there for $1.25 per acre, much cheaper than the $50-per-acre price in Voree. And for a church people who were mainly poor, this was a key consideration. Beaver Island was also remote: it is about twenty miles from the northwestern shoulder of Michigan's Lower Peninsula, the northern half of which was still wilderness.

The first documented presence of a white man on the island came in the spring of 1832, when a visit was made by Father Frederic Baraga, a Roman Catholic missionary. Baraga found a village of Indians in "eight pitiable huts of tree bark." He baptized twenty-two on that trip but later ran into opposition from other Indians, and the Christian Indians decided to move to a mainland mission.[6]

The earliest white settlements on the island appear to date from the late 1830s, shortly after Michigan became a state in 1837. Among the earliest settlers were Alva Cable and his nephew, James, who established a trading house there for fishermen and Indians.[7] Other early arrivals were men connected with the North West

Co., of Rochester, New York, which also opened a trading post. Both groups located on a natural harbor on the northeast side of the island.

During the winter of 1846–47 Strang corresponded with John Fisk, an agent of the North West Co., about his plans to settle on the island. Fisk, who lived in Rochester, said he would cooperate with the Mormons in developing the place—even offering a boat to transport them there. Fisk described the island as "one of the most lovely places in the great west" and as "an earthly paradise" destined to become a refuge for the Mormons.[8]

In March 1847 the Beaver Islands became part of an organized township, named after an Indian chief who lived there. On May 1 the first Peaine Township meeting was held at the Cables' store. The township offices were filled by representatives of the trading and fishing posts, as they would be for the next few years.[9] Then the political balance of power would shift.

A harbinger of that shift came ten days after the first township meeting, when Strang and four of his followers landed in a hooker, or small fishing boat. The arrival was not one befitting an imperial primate. The Mormons had no money and less than two days' provisions, and they had been forced to sell their blankets to complete their passage. Once ashore, they made a camp of hemlock boughs and lived mainly on leeks and beechnuts during their first day of roaming the island.[10] Strang said they were not well-received, even though Fisk had said he directed those in charge of the North West trading house to help the Mormons explore the island.

Despite Strang's statement, the Mormons appear to have received some cooperation, in the form of jobs and the use of a boat. The jobs allowed them to acquire more provisions, and they used the boat to explore the Beaver shoreline and a few of the Beaver group's eleven other islands. The largest of these islands, Garden Island just to the north, is one-eighth the size of Beaver, which is thirteen miles long and half as wide.[11]

The Mormons learned that most of the white settlers on Beaver were connected with the trading houses. The year-round residents included three white families, a handful of white men with Indian wives, and twenty or thirty other men who had families elsewhere. Most of the men were fishermen and the fishing business helped increase the number of men—and boys—on the island to about 100 in the summer. And on the northern side of the island, there were forty to fifty Indian families, predominantly Chippewas, who also subsisted mainly through fishing.[12]

A key feature of the island for the fishermen was the harbor, which the sailors called Paradise Bay. Strang described it as the best in the Great Lakes. A land-locked cove with an entrance a quarter-mile wide, the harbor was large enough—about a mile across—to hold hundreds of vessels.[13]

The harbor and the rest of the island was bordered by sandy and stony beaches, with some stands of pine. The interior was level or gently rolling, and the island forest was dominated by beech and maple trees. In the swampier areas the Mormons found cedar—suitable for fence posts, rails, and shingles. The soil, although sandier than at Voree, was deemed good enough for farming and grazing once the trees were cleared. The island contained at least seven lakes, ranging up to two miles long, but no beaver.[14]

The Mormons were pleased with what they had found. There was a seemingly inexhaustible supply of pine and hardwoods for building and for selling as cordwood to passing steamers. There was the proximity of the lake's best fishing grounds for lake trout and whitefish. And there was good land in almost unlimited acreage. Although the land had not been offered for sale by the federal government, federal officials had told the Saints that until it was, they could preempt the right to buy the land by settling it, then buy it when it was put on the market.[15]

Strang and his four followers built a cabin on the island. Four weeks after their arrival, Strang and two of them returned to Voree, leaving Gurdon Brown and R. Frederick Mills on the island, the first Mormon settlers. In Voree the Saints adopted the ambitious policy to purchase the entire Beaver Islands group and divide it among the Mormons who wished to settle there.[16] But first there was the matter of money. Cheap land was almost a necessity if Strang were to develop an empire. Strang hoped his richer followers would provide the money to buy land, but if they did not, the majority of his scrawny flock would be hard-pressed to scratch up the cash even at the federal government's minimum price of $1.25 an acre.

As evidenced by the circumstances of his arrival on Beaver Island, Strang was poor, too. He sent his letters unsealed because he could not afford sealing wafers. His best coat and pants were worn and did not match.[17] Writing of himself in the third person, Strang gave this recommendation to Saints he visited: "Give him nothing but water to drink. It is so long since he has drank anything else, he might not know what it was. Give him neither cake, pies, or sweet meats. He will remember in bitterness that his children at home can have none."[18] And yet Strang was not averse to accepting contributions of provisions and money from the Saints, even using payments for subscriptions to the church newspaper for travel expenses.[19]

One church leader, John E. Page, wondered why Strang should be doing menial work, such as carrying stone for a mason fixing his fireplace chimney, when he could be spending his time editing the newspaper. "If he had the means [to hire a hodcarrier] at 50 to 75 cents a day, he could work with pen for church and world," Page wrote, adding a plea for money: "Ye rich! . . . send him some of your V's, X's and C's."[20]

Besides the business of maintaining a home and editing a weekly paper, Strang as the leader of a church in turmoil was carrying on formal debates in his newspaper and an extensive private correspondence in an attempt to strengthen his church. Often he would write into the early morning hours.[21]

The work and the controversy took a toll on Strang, physically and mentally. In the midst of the expulsions of Bennett and Smith, plus Smith's charges against him and the church, the prophet asked his readers: "Did you ever write when your mind was dark, and your head seemed spinning round like a great wheel; or when all your ideas seemed lost in the bottom of a deep, dark well, from whence you could scarcely draw them up; and when, having got them marshaled in order, you would forget them or loose them in the darkness before you could write them down? Then you don't know what toil is."[22] This was the low state of a most brilliant Mormon in 1847.

Meanwhile, in the summer of 1847, several Mormon families had moved to Beaver Island. Some became dissatisfied and left permanently; a few others left for the winter only, intending to return.

As winter approached, the Mormon population on the island was eighteen, including five men and their families.[23]

In January 1848, with the survey of Beaver Island complete, the federal government gave notice that the land there would be put up for sale the following summer.[24] Under the Pre-emption Act of 1841, those living on the island had first claim and could buy up to 160 acres at the minimum price ($1.25 an acre), without competitive bidding. Such buyers only needed to prove their occupancy and improvements and pay for the land before the public auction.[25]

On July 17 the lands were formally opened to sale. Strang, who had been on Beaver Island a few weeks earlier, apparently did not have the money to buy all the land—that would have cost at least $40,000, and the initial settlers and trading post operators had the first chance to buy some of it. About $3,000 would have given Strang control of the key portions of the island, but he did not buy any land from the federal government until 1849.[26]

One of the two Mormons who did buy land from the United States in 1848 was Marvin M. Aldrich, the president of the Mormon stake on the island. Aldrich bought 42.80 acres on the south side of the harbor entrance for $53.50. The other Mormon bought forty acres a half-mile south of Aldrich's land.[27]

Alva Cable bought thirty-nine acres at his dock and store on Whiskey Point, on the north side of the entrance to the harbor. And James Cable bought ninety-six acres on the bay on the island's southeast side, where he had established an operation similar to his uncle's.[28] The other big non-Mormon influences on the island also acquired land at the harbor. Eri James Moore and Randolph Dinsmore, the resident agents of the North West Co., bought 150 acres, which included the trading post and the other buildings of the company on the west side of the harbor.[29] Moore and Dinsmore had been living on the island since the spring of 1846.

Later in 1848 Moore sold three choice one-acre lots to Mormons for $65. By selling the lots, Moore regained most of the $77.56 he had paid for his sixty-two acres.[30] For him, it had become worthwhile to deal with the Mormons, whose population was increasing on the island.

There were sixty-two Mormons on the island in the winter of 1848–49, the second one there for the Mormons.[31] Amid the privations and loneliness of that winter, two of the Saints, Samuel Shaw and Levi Parmeter, "broke out in revelations." In Parmeter's revelation, God appointed Gurdon Brown, one of the original Mormon settlers, as prophet, while Parmeter was "the lion to come out of the thicket" and destroy the Gentiles, as the Mormons on the island called the non-Mormons. Shaw prophesied that the Indians were about to "go from house to house in the dead of night and butcher the people." Only by entering into the covenant that Shaw and Parmeter presented could the settlers avert actions by the Indians.[32] The local stake brought the new prophets to trial and cut them off from the church: "There are many spirits here, and some very strange ones too," Aldrich wrote Strang.[33]

During the summer of 1849 a church conference was held at the City of James (the Mormons had named the harbor settlement after Strang). Most of the leaders attended. The conference improved the impression many had of the island and its prospects.[34]

During 1849 the Mormon settlement on the island was reported to have grown from twelve families and sixty-two persons to nearly fifty families, which would put the Mormon population at about 250, if the family-population ratio held true.[35] Strang maintained that steamboat captains were dissuading some would-be settlers from landing at Beaver Island. When persuasion failed, he said, the boats frequently refused to stop there. These captains, Strang said, were undoubtedly opposing the Mormon settlement at the instigation of the traders and fishermen on the island.[36]

For the settlers, the first object was to build a home. The Mormon houses were typically two stories high and built of squared logs, whitewashed outside and in. After their houses were up, the settlers began to clear their land and plant crops. A hoe and a good ax were all that a man needed to start a new life on the island. If he ran short of provisions, he could walk to the harbor to chop cordwood, for choppers were paid at least fifty cents a cord. At the end of a week of chopping, he could tote home sixty pounds of flour and a chunk of pork to feed his family.[37]

The wharf owners sold the wood to the steamboats for up to $1.50 a cord, and prices rose with demand. There were about eighty-five steamers on the Great Lakes at that time, and during that season, steamboats would stop at the island about sixty times, providing an ample market for the cordwood. The steamers needed about 150 cords for a round trip from Buffalo to Chicago, and they usually took on wood when they could. When they faced long runs across the lake, they filled their wood bins and stacked the overflow on deck.[38]

Since the island roads often were simply paths through cedar swamps, there was yet little market for trees felled on inland farms that were not near the harbor: it was too difficult to haul the logs to the harbor. So the logs not needed for building were burned for firewood—or simply burned.[39] The thud of the ax and the smell of smoke were two constants in the daily lives of the settlers.

That summer the Mormons began two major projects: building a tabernacle near the harbor and building a road through a swamp into the island's interior, where there was some good farmland. Although several families settled in the interior that year, there is no indication that they bought the land, and they probably were squatters. The Mormons were more active in buying land on the island that year, but the land they bought was in the harbor area.[40]

In his only purchase of land from the federal government, Strang paid $88.81 for seventy-one acres of beachfront land on the northeast side of the harbor.[41] Strang was offered some of the prime harborfront land formerly held by the North West Co. for $1,200, but $600 was his best counteroffer. Money apparently was no longer in short supply for him.[42]

While Strang was beginning to move his headquarters to Beaver Island, Brigham Young had succeeded in moving his to an "island" in the West. And while Strang counted his followers at his new location in the hundreds, Young counted his in the thousands. Young's new stronghold was a budding island of civilization in the valley of the Great Salt Lake, a thousand miles from the western frontier. After traveling 300 miles west from Nauvoo in 1846, Young had wintered in a settlement that became known as Winter Quarters, on the western bank of the Missouri River near Council Bluffs. With a population of about 3,500, Winter Quarters was the largest of a half-dozen major Mormon stopping points that winter. Sickness decimated the population of Winter Quarters: 600 died in one year.[43] And Strang, back in Voree, was not reluctant to print reports about Young's troubles. "Many are suffering severely for want of food and raiment," the *Zion's Reveille* said. "An almost entire destitution prevails."[44] One man wrote the *Reveille* that his father and three other members of his family had died on the trek west. "And my mother, now 66 years of age, has been compelled to sleep on the open prairie, in the snow, without tent or bed. This is but the common tale of woe in all the camp."[45]

Young and his aides were not shy about belittling Strang either. Young commented that "contending with Strangism is like sitting up barley corns to see them fall over."[46] And while he was in Winter Quarters, Young received a report on the church branches in the East that said "Strangism has about run its course."[47]

At Winter Quarters and the other settlements on the route west, some of the Mormons decided the hardships were too much to deal with and headed back east. Most, however, continued west in the spring.[48] In April 1847 Young led a vanguard of 144 men, three women, and two children north and west from Winter Quarters in seventy-three wagons.[49] In late July Young's party entered "a broad open valley, about 20 miles wide and 30 long . . . at the north end of which the broad waters of the Great Salt Lake glistened in the sunbeams."[50] A week after reaching the valley, the pioneers laid out Great Salt Lake City. Other caravans, with a total of 1,750 people, arrived that year.[51]

Young returned to Winter Quarters for the winter, and there he decided to revive the church hierarchy created by Joseph Smith. With the backing of the Twelve and a church conference, Young became prophet, seer, and revelator. In 1848 Young and two parties totaling about 1,900 Saints traveled from Winter Quarters to Great Salt Lake City. By the end of the year nearly 4,000 Mormons were living in the valley.[52] In 1849, the *New York Tribune* reported that the Mormons in Salt Lake City had cultivated every inch of available land and were growing yellow wheat, Indian corn, oats, potatoes, flax, and garden vegetables. The shops in the center of town were busy, and the community seemed to be thriving.[53]

೩ ೩ ೩

Great Salt Lake City may have been thriving, but Voree definitely was not. Like Nauvoo, Voree was a city in transition, except that Voree, unlike Nauvoo, was a city that never was, and now, because of the plans for Beaver Island, never would be.

In the summer of 1848, four years after the letter of appointment ordered the gathering at Voree, a visiting member of the church estimated that there were only 300 to 400 followers of Strang living there, surrounded by a "good number" of apostates. These apostates, he said, "beset every newcomer with all sorts of the vilest and most wicked accusations against the Saints, especially the Prophet, in which they not infrequently succeed in destroying their faith."[54]

Cognizant of the troubles at Voree, particularly after the departures of Bennett and William Smith, Brigham Young wrote that "Strangism is strangled beyond hope."[55] Yet Young knew that Strang, with his ability, was still a major competitor for converts. And early in 1848 one of Young's brothers, Phineas, stopped in Voree to talk with Strang, and perhaps to scout the competition.[56] But if Brigham Young tried to seek a rapprochement with Strang, the overture was rejected.

What Phineas Young saw at Voree barely looked like a village. It was almost entirely devoid of public buildings, and work on the temple, ordered built by revelation on July 1, 1846, had hardly begun. More progress was being made on a Tower of Zion, which was to be the storehouse of food and supplies for the church's Order of Enoch. At the end of 1849 the tower had risen to a story and a half.[57] For the most part, the houses at Voree were scattered, standing alone in the midst of fields, far from roads.[58] Strang said the building of Voree was delayed in part by the poverty of the people there: "The rich would not and the poor could not buy those lands and accomplish the work required."[59]

The rich may have been reluctant to buy land because it would belong to the church under the communistic Order of Enoch. Just before the Mormon exploration of the Beaver Islands a conference had named Strang as trustee for the church, with all land acquired by the church to be held in his name. And on January 12, 1848, Strang and eleven followers established the Order of Enoch, combining their belongings and organizing the twelve families as one household, with Strang as the patriarch.[60] On that date, Strang bought 560 acres of Voree land from his brother-in-law, W. L. Perce, Jr., for the Order. A month later Strang said the order had sixty poor members who were sharing each others' joys and sorrows, toils and possessions.[61]

The members of the order were also bearing burdens that other church members were not. They were supporting ninety percent of the church operations, including the newspaper, which by 1849 had only eighty paid subscribers—even though Strang continually begged for more. To cut expenses and keep God's law, the order had a number of proscribed activities: using tea, coffee, or tobacco and eating sugar, spices, and dried fruit. The members also were to abstain from luxuries of every kind and dress plainly in a uniform style.[62]

Perhaps understandably, there was no rush to join the order. At the end of 1848 it included about 150 persons, about half of the Saints in Voree.[63] In a revelation on January 7, 1849, the Saints were denounced as a "stiff-necked and rebellious people." Rewards were promised those who would pay their tithes, build the temple and the Tower of Zion, and live in the order. Those who did not were warned of being cast out and persecuted.[64] Still there was no great response.

In August a new tack was tried: baptism for the dead. Under this doctrine, established by Joseph Smith, Saints could secure the spiritual advantages of baptism for dead relatives and others designated by God. These baptisms, along with other church "mysteries," had to take place in the temple, away from the gaze of the ungodly. But there was no temple in Voree. This problem was solved when, as Strang reported, Jesus Christ sent the prophet Elijah to inform Strang that he was giving those in the Order of Enoch the dispensation to receive baptisms for the dead until the temple was built.[65] After all this had been set in order, Strang and his followers repaired to the White River, which had been sanctified for the baptisms. There, Strang and a "large number" of other Saints proceeded to undergo baptism for their deceased relatives.[66]

These efforts to push the communistic association quietly

petered out—along with the Order of Enoch—as the building of the kingdom began in earnest on Beaver Island. So many families left Voree for the island that early in 1850 one church leader estimated that only fifteen men remained who were "good in the faith."[67] There would be no communistic associations in the kingdom, but Beaver Island would have some unusual associations, in a family way.

Chapter 6

Elvira and Charlie

S OMETHING HAPPENED to persuade Strang to do an about-face
on polygamy. Perhaps he suffered a recurrence of the sexual
frustrations that plagued him as a young man, and he em-
braced polygamy as a vehicle to gratify his desires. Perhaps his advisers, John Cook Bennett and George J. Adams, who had been
teaching a form of plural marriage for some time (if the preponder-
ance of testimony can be believed), recommended polygamy because
it had been a doctrine of Joseph Smith's. Perhaps he met an intelligent, wholesome girl he wanted to marry and decided polygamy
was the only way. Perhaps all of the above are true. Or, perhaps, as
Strang said, God revealed that polygamy was allowed.

Polygamy, under several guises, was being practiced covertly
by leading Mormons when Strang met Joseph Smith in 1844, although it would not be openly admitted until 1852.[1] Strang may
have known about the Mormon practice when he first met Smith—
there were strong rumors about it well before then. At that time
polygamy among Mormons often was referred to as the spiritual
wife doctrine or spiritual wifery.

No matter what the name, Strang railed against polygamy in
his early years as a prophet. At one point Strang—whom a revelation from God once called "meeker than Moses and more patient
than Job"[2]—even cursed those who taught it. That curse was published in the April 1846 issue of the *Voree Herald* and was pro-
nounced by Strang not only on those who taught polygamy but also
on those who taught that deceit, plundering unbelievers, and adultery were required by God in the building of his kingdom. Later
the curse would apply to James Jesse Strang.

It is interesting to note that in a surviving copy of that issue
of the *Herald*, the word polygamy has been blacked out from the
above list of evils. Some Saint may have seen a conflict between the
curse, which Strang said came from God, and the later revelation
that polygamy could be a part of the kingdom. Such a startling

change of heart on God's part could be interpreted as evidence that Strang was not a prophet.

With the arrival of Bennett and Adams in the church, reports began surfacing of various "immoralities," including the teaching of polygamy, in Voree and in other church branches. At about the time Bennett was facing charges of teaching polygamy in October 1846, Strang was reported to be set "as Flint" against iniquity, especially the spiritual wife system.[3] A few months later a church official said that spiritual wifery could have no place in the church and that it was trampled to dust as soon as it made an appearance at Voree.[4] It was not to be trampled long. But maybe, as at Nauvoo, the church leaders at Voree were being cautious in practicing polygamy, fearing a public backlash.

While on a mission early in 1847, Ebenezer Page, soon to be an apostle, referred to such caution in a letter to Strang. Under the heading of "Confidentialy," Page wrote: "I think I shall not giv my hand to any while I am in this contry for sum are inform of my wife west & my enimis hav ben heard to say that if I did so & so the law should hav affect. I will omit for the present."[5]

In July 1847 Strang wrote an editorial titled "Polygamy not possible in a free government," in which he stated that polygamy could only be sustained in an "arbitrary or despotic government."[6] (He would lend support to that statement on Beaver Island.) Two weeks later Strang commented that his opinions on the subject were unchanged and unchangeable. His view, he said, was based on a full consideration of all the scriptures, both ancient and modern.[7]

Strang professed astonishment that it should be necessary for him to state his views on polygamy. Throughout his travels, he said, he had "uniformly and most distinctly discarded and declared heretical the so called 'spiritual wife system' and everything connected therewith. . . . I now say distinctly, and I defy contradiction, that the man or woman does not exist on earth or under the earth who ever heard me say one word, or saw me do one act, savoring in the least of spiritual wifery or any of the attending abominations."[8]

That was about as categorical as a denial could be, but Strang still found himself being driven to distraction by suspicion and accusations. In August 1848 Strang wrote that both Saints and apostates were dogging his footsteps and that they seemed perfectly willing to believe the worst about him and his sexual habits. "I cannot step into a house but in a half hour it is known by half the neighborhood." Strang bitterly presented the type of dialogue he sensed took place when Saints and apostates discussed where he had gone:

> SAINT: What do you suppose Brother Strang has gone there for?
>
> APOSTATE: Anybody might know what a man goes where there is a woman for. (As if there wasn't usually a woman in every house, Strang added as an aside.)
>
> SAINT: Oh, I don't know. I don't think Brother Strang is quite so bad as that; do you really think so?—But I wish he would be more prudent.[9]

Strang said that a year earlier he had preached in Jefferson County, New York, over six days. There he again set his face as flint against "certain doctrines of devils," alluding to polygamy and other illicit intercourse, and he said that never did his actions vary from his testimony. "Yet I have now letters laying before me, written in that region, in which I am accused of criminal intercourse with more than 40 different Saints there, including every sister in the church in that region, of whom I have the slightest recollection, and several of whom I do not so much as know they exist."[10] Strang may have been set like flint against polygamy, but his activities in Jefferson County were not limited to the purely religious. In Strang's papers are four locks of feminine hair presented to him while he was there.[11]

In September 1848 the official policy of the church was still strongly against polygamy. In the September 7 issue of the *Gospel Herald*, John E. Page, the president of the apostles, reminded the various branches of the church to suspend advocates of the spiritual wife doctrine. Within a year of that order, Strang himself would secretly take a second wife.

It may have all started with Elvira Field, an intelligent, attractive girl. Elvira was nearly eighteen when she first met Strang, at a time when Strang said he was particularly vulnerable.[12] Strang told Elvira that after his first child died in 1843, his wife refused to have sex with him.[13] But this was a half-truth or may just have been part of Strang's line to persuade Elvira to become his second wife, because Mary did give birth to two children after the death of their firstborn. One of Strang's intimates wrote a letter that appears to back up Strang's comment about Mary. "I know all about the wife business. . . . If your wife would do by you as she did by him (long before he thought of [Elvira] or any other wife) you would come [to Elvira] or some other fair deal." [14]

Strang believed that a man projected his personality and achieved a degree of immortality through his children: the more children, the more descendants, the more immortality. [15] If, indeed, his wife had turned a cold shoulder and divorce was out of the question, especially for a prophet, one solution would have been polygamy. If Joseph Smith practiced polygamy, why shouldn't he? And Elvira Field presented a full-bodied opportunity.

Elvira Eliza Field was born in Ohio. When she was fourteen, her family moved to Michigan and settled in Eaton County, while Elvira moved in with an uncle in nearby Washtenaw County to continue her education. In 1846, at sixteen, she began work as a schoolteacher. [16]

Elvira's parents had joined the church of Joseph Smith, and after he was assassinated, they became followers of Strang. Elvira did, too. [17] In 1848 she made plans to attend an April conference in Voree and declared her intention to join the Order of Enoch. Strang was informed that if he were seeking a good schoolteacher, she was one. [18] But Elvira was not to become the schoolmistress of Voree; she became, instead, the prophet's first polygamous wife and an intellectual mate throughout the rest of his life.

Strang sent George J. Adams to make the proposal. Adams likely had done a similar service for others in advocating the spiritual wife doctrine. This time there was a twist. Elvira would be no ordinary plural wife. Adams told Elvira that a kingdom soon would be established on earth with Strang as king and that she would be a queen. [19] Laws for this kingdom, including an authorization for polygamy, were being revealed to Strang by God. [20]

Adams persuaded Elvira to become the secret wife of Strang. They were married on Beaver Island on July 13, 1849, with Adams conducting the ceremony before two other apostles. [21] The marriage would be kept secret until after the kingdom was established. Strang and Elvira honeymooned at Sault Ste. Marie. Publicly, he said that he went there to meet with the Indians and that he even made a voyage into Lake Superior in a bark canoe. He also visited the land office at the Soo to make his purchase of harborfront land on Beaver Island.[22] After that trip, there was a report that Strang and Adams had gone to the Soo, or somewhere else, with two women and had a "regular drinking and 'frigging' spree."[23]

The Soo trip behind him, Strang traveled to southern Michigan, apparently to return Elvira to the home of her parents, before returning to Voree to institute the procedure for the baptism for the dead and to prepare for late summer conferences at Voree and Beaver Island. Preparations also were being made for another trip to the East that winter, to attract settlers for Beaver Island.[24]

Strang wanted his new wife to accompany him on his trip east. To do this in secrecy required intricate logistics and a stunning ruse. Elvira's dark hair was cut to a masculine length, and she dressed in men's clothing, to fit her undercover role as Strang's sixteen-year-old private secretary, Charles J. Douglass.[25] "Charlie" probably left first and met Strang at Buffalo.

In September Strang traveled with his legal wife and family by boat and buggy to New York's Chautauqua County, where Mary and their three children remained with relatives. Strang then took steamboats, probably accompanied by Charlie, from Buffalo to Albany on the Erie Canal and down the Hudson River to New York City and a conference there.[26]

The four-day conference in New York began on October 5 without Strang and Charlie, who had not yet arrived. On the first day Adams glowingly described the spirit of the Saints, the features of Beaver Island, and the qualities of Strang. This song of praise was echoed by a new apostle, Lorenzo Dow Hickey,[27] who soon would voice an entirely different tune about Strang and pose awkward moments for Charlie.

Hickey, named after the revivalist Lorenzo Dow, joined the church of Joseph Smith in 1842 and soon became an elder. After Smith's death, Hickey supported Brigham Young until the spring of 1846, when he converted to Strang's church. While seeking converts for Strang in Michigan, Hickey was once suspended for false teachings but was reinstated early in 1847.[28]

A year and a half later, at Lapeer, Michigan, he was too poor to travel or even subscribe to the church newspaper. "God's work is as dear to me as ever," he wrote Strang, "and I mean before long to be more active in the work. . . . I have been taught some things by vision of night, and dreams, which has been a great satisfaction to me."[29]

In April 1849 Hickey returned to Voree for a conference. On the first day of that conference, he delivered a benediction in his biblical style, King James version; on the second day he preached; on the third day he was named an apostle. By fall he had moved his wife and family to Beaver Island. At a conference on the island, he and other apostles were given missions for fall and winter.[30] One of Hickey's first stops was New York City.

After Strang arrived at the New York conference on October 7, things proceeded fairly smoothly, at first. At one point Strang resolved a dispute over whether a "colored" man could hold the priesthood. The conference, in line with a revelation by Strang, ordained a black man as an elder.[31] By contrast, the church of Brigham Young would have a longstanding policy of denying the priesthood to blacks, a prohibition affirmed earlier that year by Young.[32]

Later that same evening the conference approved sending Hickey on a mission to Philadelphia and New Jersey. At Strang's suggestion, a decision was delayed for a day on a proposal that Hickey be accompanied by Increase Van Deusen, who had just returned to Strang's fold.[33] Van Deusen had joined Strang at Voree for a time in 1846. After being ordained an elder, Van Deusen had been assigned a mission to New York.[34] But he also found time to publish and hawk an exposé he had written about Mormonism at Nauvoo. Strang regarded Van Deusen as a potential troublemaker because his publication had revealed a Nauvoo endowment he apparently had sworn not to reveal.[35] And secrets were precious to Strang. On October 8, the last day of the conference, it was decided after considerable discussion that Van Deusen could accompany Hickey on the mission. During the debate, in an implied criticism of Van Deusen, Strang brought up the inviolability of oaths.[36]

Hickey headed for Philadelphia, but without Van Deusen, for on October 14 Van Deusen was still in New York, trying to get a church meeting to listen to a revelation he had had. Strang would not let him speak. Van Deusen insisted so strenuously that Strang threatened to call the police. The ruckus continued after the meeting adjourned.[37] The substance of Van Deusen's revelation was that Hickey had died before he had reached Philadelphia and that Strang soon would be dead also. The next day, after going to Connecticut, Van Deusen had another revelation, which he mailed to Strang. This revelation said that whoever followed the "pernicious ways" of Adams and Strang would be damned.[38]

A few days later Hickey returned to New York, alive but perhaps not so well. On October 18 he was suspended by Strang for neglecting his mission to "follow after the diabolical revelations" of Van Deusen and for "most gross lying and slander" about Adams and Samuel Graham, another of Strang's top advisers and the new president of the apostles.[39]

Another act in the melodrama involving Hickey and Van Deusen took place the following Sunday, October 21, and was reported in the *Gospel Herald*, over the name of C. J. Douglass.[40] As Hickey and Van Deusen met Strang and Charlie on the way to a morning meeting that Sunday, they greeted the couple cordially. Charlie reported that "the cloud that had rested on Hickey's brow for several days was gone, but a kind of nervous twitching which sometimes marks incipient insanity, and not infrequently follows great mental excitement, remained." He was a time bomb, about to explode. Strang preached from the text: "I will not know a wicked person." At the beginning of his sermon, Charlie reported, Hickey and Van Deusen "seemed to be in ecstacies," evidently thinking that Strang's scathing rebuke was designed for Adams and Graham. But when Strang "declared the end of those who backbite and take up a reproach against their neighbor . . . the smiling demon in them was roused to fury: sitting on their seats in the congregation, they writhed, changed color, and gesticulated." Strang concluded that God would give him the victory over all the enemies of righteousness. As another Saint started to lead the congregation in a hymn, Hickey rose, trembling with rage, and started to speak, but Strang forbade him. When Hickey persisted, Strang said he could speak at the meeting scheduled for that night. Hickey sat down, saying he was satisfied.

As soon as the meeting was over, however, Hickey grabbed the attention of the congregation and told the members he had something important to communicate. Hickey said he had just received letters from his wife on Beaver Island that proved Strang was guilty of adultery, fornication, spiritual wifery, and all the abominations that were ever practiced at Nauvoo. Hickey denounced Strang as a liar, an imposter, a false prophet, and a dangerously wicked man.

Strang tried to respond, with his "clerk" at his side, but the confusion was so great that he could not be heard. Van Deusen thrust his hands in Strang's face and chest and screamed in a high-pitched voice: "You are guilty, you are guilty, you are guilty!" With Van Deusen repeatedly clutching at him and with both Van Deusen and Hickey screaming at him, Strang withdrew from the meeting place.

That afternoon, in a church meeting attended by Hickey, Strang denied the charges and alluded to the disturbance apologetically. Strang said that Hickey had based his charges solely on three letters and that Hickey had read the letters to him. The letters, Strang said, did not contain one word concerning him, his conduct, or his policies. Strang said the letters were merely those of a homesick woman, complaining of the hardships she suffered and feared during the absence of her husband. Strang called on Hickey to produce the letters and read them before the congregation. Hickey refused.

Strang said he had no fear of all the lies that evil men and apostates could invent against him, if he could only have the opportunity of confronting them in any well-ordered assembly. Charlie's report of the uproar stated that Strang convinced the Saints that Hickey's accusations were false. "He speaks of the matter as of no moment, and seems to feel no concern about it."

The next day, the conduct of Van Deusen and Hickey was investigated: Van Deusen was excommunicated, and Hickey was suspended after he again refused to produce the letters. Fanned by Van Deusen's suspicions and those in the letters, Hickey's faith in the prophet had been shattered and he suffered a breakdown. Hickey spent some time in the Tombs (the New York City jail) and was sent to a "lunatic asylum."[41]

Later Hickey came to Adams, begging forgiveness, confessing

86

his sins, and asking Adams to cast the devils out of him. Adams said he did. Adams also reported that when he had a chance at a meeting, he bound up the devils so tightly in Van Deusen that Van Deusen could not speak—no mean feat—and "trembled like a reed shaken in the wind. After the meeting he raged a little. Bro. Hickey told him to his face that he was a liar, a knave, a puppy and a scoundrel." [42]

Adams accepted Hickey back into the fold and sent him on a mission to Philadelphia and New Jersey. Adams also wrote Strang, urging Hickey's reinstatement. "I am afraid he will die if we do not let him preach." [43] Hickey also wrote Strang, begging forgiveness and saying he felt like Nebuchadnezzar after he had been driven out and, as a madman, ate grass like an ox. "All I have to say is I love you as I have never loved before. . . . I ask your counsel & advise that I may do the thing that will please God. I heard your voice; it seemed sweet to me." [44]

Strang forgave him, and Hickey reverted to a loyal follower, although one still not enjoying full mental health. Some information, perhaps Adams had told him of the revelation on polygamy, had been given him that altered everything. "There is a dreadful storm ahead," Hickey wrote, apparently referring to the coming announcement on polygamy, "& unless we can calm it I am afraid the boat will take a rock. I am willing to do all I can do to calm the waters." [45]

For several weeks Hickey had had no word from his wife. He begged Strang for any information about Beaver Island. In mid-December Hickey learned that his wife had left the island in mid-November and that she, with their three children, had returned to Lapeer. [46] Hickey was anxious to leave the East and rejoin his family. He suggested a mission among the Indians near Lapeer, and he was back in that city by February. Within a few months he would return to the island and eventually take three polygamous wives, more than any other Saint except Strang. The first child of his polygamous marriages would be named Elvira, after Elvira Field. [47]

At Strang's next stops on his tour, in Philadelphia and Baltimore, the gossip quickened. There were references to the private secretary and his suspicious curves. Saints began to discuss Charlie's physiological peculiarities in detail. Strang assumed an air of wounded dignity and challenged his accusers to prove Charlie was a girl. Apparently no one demanded a physical examination.[48]

One woman reported that she had a dream in which Charlie was a woman. "A pretty way that is to pretend to have the gift of revelation," Strang responded. "I wonder if she has a daughter that she would be willing to give to him for a bedfellow. . . . I shall be there some of these times to stay overnight, and if she thinks I have a girl with me she will of course send him with the girls to bed. That will tell what she thinks."[49] One man said he asked Strang if Charlie had ever been on the island and that Strang answered no. The man persisted, saying he must have seen Charlie's sister on the island. Strang tried to change the subject. Later, the man said, he recognized Charlie as a girl he had seen on the island by a certain mark on her face and by the shape of her head.[50]

Earthier evidence was reported by a woman at whose house Charlie and Strang stayed. She said bloody cloths, "which women sometimes use," had been found wrapped in a flap torn from a shirt Charlie had. "Oh Gemini, thought I! The cat's out of the bag, sure enough! Oh dear! This pseudo Charlie turns out to be a filthy and abominable menstruous hussy! But when I examined the bed—Oh dear! . . . O Strang, Whang-Strambang, hocus pocus-pocus!!!"[51]

And the ruse went on. In Baltimore Charlie was named secretary of the two-day conference and wrote an article for the *Gospel Herald* denouncing slandering among the Saints. Echoing a comment Strang had made a few years earlier, Charlie said the Saints "are all too ready and willing to hear and cherish an evil report of a brother and sister."[52]

Others did not want to be surprised if Strang chose to reveal polygamy. Graham wrote Strang in his phonetic code about the "woman fikzion" and asked Strang to reply. "There is no one here to See my letters, you can write as plain as you pleas. I want to act in unizon with your feeling."[53]

Meanwhile, Strang's long-suffering wife was living with Strang's parents, trying to remain patient while she nursed their children through lengthy bouts with whooping cough and bilious fever.[54] It is unlikely she knew the truth about Charlie or she would not have been as calm about Strang's delays in visiting her or in making arrangements for her to join him. Plaintively, Mary wrote to him: "You told me before I left home that you would help me take care of the children so that they should not be a burden on me if I would only come. It is hard work to take care of children away from home. I have had two of them at the same time so sick that I feared they would die."[55]

Mary asked James to write about his plans. "I have held my self in constant reddines for traveling the last three months and shall continue so to do until further directions." She reminded him that she had said she would much rather stay home than go east. "If I had money I would take the children and go home." Why didn't he write more often? "Mother and all here have been quite anxious about you on account of your not writing for so long a time." And she asked him how she was supposed to know where to write since he had given her no directions about addressing her mail.[56]

Strang's long absence even raised his mother's suspicions. She wondered what had occupied him that he had to be apart from his family so long. "I hope you will endeavor to be with them more . . . do not let your whole soul be taken up in trying to make yourself appear great in the eyes of man that must soon die and turn to dust."[57]

In a letter couched in half-truths and larded with bids for sympathy, Strang wrote to Mary on January 25. Hickey, he said, "raised a muss which it took much time to put down; and after repenting and coming back he was not half a man." Strang said he had been subjected "to so many disappointments that I am not able to do what I know I ought to, and am at a loss which way to turn. . . . I have felt sorrow enough that you could not be with me here, but, Mary, I feel a little down now and am glad you are not here. . . . I have not been well one hour in (two months) and my spirits begin to flag. I have only kept up by the exercise of an iron will and if that gives way I shall sink. Charlie is sinking rapidly and today can scarsely help me at all. I have been bed rid some but have not quit my labours." His weight, he reported, had dropped from 162 pounds to about 145 in about two months. He soon would be head-

ing Mary's way. "I don't know how long I may be on the way, but
it is quite likely I shall be obliged to stop a Sunday in each of the
large cities to raise the money to travel with. . . . I think we have
accomplished a good work in coming down here. But I am very sure
I shall never undertake such a journey again with such indifferent
means. It is well enough for me but don't do so well for a family."
He closed affectionately: "Kiss the children for me. Tell them their
father is coming to see them. I dream about them every night and
you are scarsely absent from my thoughts, waking or sleeping.
Truly & sincerely, Jas. J. Strang."[58]

Polygamy was just one of the secrets Strang was not ready to
reveal to the world—or to his wife. And in the *Gospel Herald* he
published an admonition under the heading, "Keep a secret." "Anything revealed in confidence should be kept a secret. There is no
greater breach of good manners and Christian faith, than to reveal
that which has been placed in the secrecy of your own bosom. . . .
A confiding friend may tell you a hundred things, which whispered
abroad, would bring him into contempt and ridicule, and injure his
character through life."[59]

In a frank letter to John C. Bennett written on the same day
he wrote his wife, Strang expanded on that theme. "You are aware
Gen., that every man has his own particular frailties: faults of character sometimes peculiarly his; sometimes very prominent amid
many virtues." Strang wrote that "some mischief" might result
from public revelations of such. Strang noted that he was a preacher
of the gospel. "You are doubtless aware that preachers see more of
real life, more exciting scenes, more of the incidents of man's life as
it is, and womans too, than any other class of men. They are quite
as likely to have a hand in them too."[60]

A week later, Elvira as C. J. Douglass wrote Strang from Baltimore, where he had left her while he went to Washington. Charlie
still was sick, suffering from a hard cold and "still growing thin."
The letter was understated and formal because of her undercover
role. The only personal allusion in the letter was a reference to the
"rather lonesome evenings" she was spending since Strang had left.[61]

Meanwhile, no one in Elvira's family knew where she had gone
that fall. Her brother, Albert, who was two years older, had gone

90

to look for her. Six months after her secret marriage, he was still traveling around Michigan, seeking a clue to her whereabouts. When he found out she was married to Strang, he was angry—but he continued to be a follower of Strang. Like Elvira, he had taken the covenant the previous summer.[62]

Strang trumpeted the success of his eastern mission. He said that although the elders encountered the most violent opposition in the history of the church, they silenced it and produced a "rich harvest."[63]

In Washington Strang's business had been more political than spiritual, with less certain results. Strang was seeking a lighthouse for Beaver Island, to increase its attractiveness as a refueling stop for steamships. More important, Strang wanted the federal government to set aside the Beaver Islands for the Saints and the Saints alone, a retracing of the Mormon idea for an independent Mormon nation-state. After his visit, Strang reported that he had enlisted some support for a "just and free distribution of vacant lands among the landless, for a perpetual inheritance according to the principles of the law of God."[64] The key word was free. Adams had defiantly described the lands as being exempt from taxation and said the law of the kingdom of God would be kept there. Another leader said the Saints were not under the law of the Gentiles. A year earlier, on January 7, 1849, Strang had reported a revelation in which God said Beaver Island, along with the other islands of the Great Lakes, had been given to the Saints for a possession.[65]

On his way home from the East, Strang met his family in Buffalo.[66] While there, on April 6, 1850, he composed a "Memorial" formally asking President Zachary Taylor and Congress for the right to settle and forever occupy the uninhabited land in the islands in Lake Michigan. Strang also asked the federal government to stop selling the island land to non-Mormons. In cataloging the crimes against the Mormons and their exiles, Strang said: "We have not been suffered to live with other men. Shall we not be permitted to live alone?"[67]

Several copies of the request for the land were printed at Voree and mailed to Washington. One copy went before the U.S. Senate, which referred it to the Committee on Public Lands on June 15.

Asked for a recommendation on the request, the commissioner on public lands wrote the committee on August 30 that the only way Strang and the Mormons could obtain the land, consistent with current laws, would be to buy it. Any other plan, the commissioner said, would be claimed as a precedent to such an extent that it would completely subvert the federal land system. Based on his comments, the committee dropped the request from further consideration.[68] By that time, though, Beaver Island had become a kingdom.

Portion of a page from Strang's diary (1831 to 1836) showing a key coded section (July 27, 1832, when Strang was nineteen):

". . . vice, misery, and wretchedness; gold, monarchy and murder; kings priests and parisites, are man's perpetual associates. My heart sickens at the thought, and my whole soul shrinks with horror at the idea, and I wish that I had not been born.

"I am a perfect atheist, but do not profess it lest I bring my father grey hair with sorrow to the grave"

"Aug 5th Some time since took a resolution which I now solemnly confirm: to be a Priest, a Lawyer, a Conquerer, and a Legislator unless I find better business."

Yale University Library

Nauvoo, Illinois, in the mid-1840s. Strang was baptized in the temple in February 1844. *Church Archives, Church of Jesus Christ of Latter-day Saints.*

Nauvoo June 18th 1844

My dear son Your epistle of may 24th proposing the planting a stake of zion in wisconsin and the gathering the saints there was duly received & I with most of the breathren whose advise I called in were of opinion that you was deceived by a spirit not of this world great but not good, brother Hyrum however thought otherwise and favored the project not doubting it was of God I however determined to return you an unfavourable answer for the present but oh the littleness of man in his best earthly state not so the will of the Almighty, God hath ruled it otherwise and a message from the throne of grace directed me as it hath inspired you and the faith which thou hast in the shepherd the stone of Israel hath been repaid to thee a thousand fold and thou shalt be like unto him but the flock shall find rest with thee and God shall reveal to thee his will concerning them I have long felt that my present work

— So spake the Almighty God of heaven thy duty is made plain and if thou lackest wisdom ask of God in whose hands I trust thee & he will give thee unsparingly for if evil befall me thou shalt lead the flock to pleasant pastures God sustain thee

Joseph Smith.

James J. Strang

PS Write me soon y keep me advised of you progress from time to time

Portions of two pages of "letter of appointment" that Strang claimed he received from Joseph Smith in July 1844. *Yale University Library.*

One follower called this picture the most natural he had seen of James J. Strang. Photo believed taken about a year before Strang's assassination. *State Archives of Michigan.*

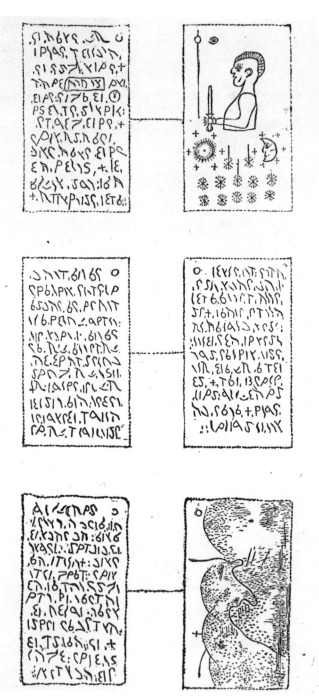

A reproduction of the six sides of the three Rajah Manchou plates. *State Historical Society of Wisconsin.*

This photograph (taken after the turn of the century) shows the Hill of Promise, where the Rajah Manchou plates were uncovered in Voree. *State Historical Society of Wisconsin.*

A peaceful view of the site of Voree, the Garden of Peace, today.

The house where Strang's parents lived while they were in Voree. A mortally wounded Strang was taken here shortly before he died in Voree, and Strang's Voree newspaper is believed to have been printed here for a time. The house still exists. *1905 photograph from State Historical Society of Wisconsin.*

James Jesse Strang.

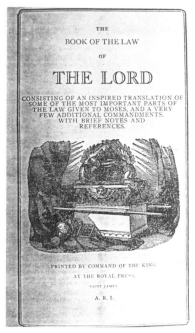

Cover of the Book of the Law of the Lord, which authorized polygamy in the kingdom.

Strang's first polygamous wife, El-vira Field, posing in 1849–50 as Charles J. Douglass, Strang's private secretary. *Clarke Historical Library.*

Map of Beaver Island, drawn in 1852 by a Mormon, James M. Greig. The harbor, with St. James just to the west, is at the upper right. *State Archives of Michigan.*

Chapter 7

The Coronation

THE GROWTH OF THE MORMON settlement on Beaver Island was shifting the balance of power away from the island's original traders and fishermen. Perhaps out of frustration with their changing fortunes, the non-Mormons on the island exhibited a desire to confront the Mormons; Strang said a "decided animosity" developed between the Mormons and their neighbors while he was in the East. [1]

There were several incidents during the winter of 1849–50. In one, several Mormons hewing timber for the tabernacle were chased off by a large group of men from Whiskey Point, on the opposite side of the harbor. One Mormon was severely beaten when he refused to stop working. In another, two "damned Mormons" were assaulted at a New Year's party. Mormons also were harassed by drunken fishermen when they called for mail at the Whiskey Point post office. "Some [Mormons] were struck, and some had letters taken from them before they left the office," Strang said. He reported that fishermen, "pretending to be drunk, went to the houses of Mormons when the men were absent, and exposed their persons in a beastly manner, accompanied with vile language and threats of violence." [2]

At the start of the winter Mormons had disagreed about whether they should associate with non-Mormons on the island. [3] The incidents gave Mormons a reason to avoid them. By the end of winter Strang said, "The distinction of Mormon and Gentile [or non-Mormon] came into use, and a line of distinction in society became visible and broad. However, the Mormons never resisted nor retaliated" [4]—until the spring of 1850.

That spring the Mormons flexed their collective muscle, electing a majority of the officers for Peaine Township, which encompassed the Beaver Islands. That spring also brought a large influx of Mormons as the various missionaries returned with a number of settlers. [5] The *Gospel Herald* said it had reason to believe "the emigration will increase rapidly for some time to come. Different persons, well informed, vary in their estimates for this season from 800 to 2,000."[6] These estimates were vastly overblown, but one can imagine the effects the predictions had on the island's original occupants.

Strang arrived from the East on April 12, making a steerage passage from Buffalo with his family and a small company of Saints from Washington, D.C. He stayed at the island for a few weeks, helping emigrants find places to settle, before continuing to Voree. Strang and the other leading men of the church were moving with their families from Voree to St. James, as the city on the harbor was now called, intending to make it the permanent headquarters of the church.[7]

For the Mormon settler, the move to the island often was not without harassment. Most settlers landed at the Whiskey Point wharf, where Strang said they were greeted with threats. "A dozen men would generally surround a family of emigrants and order them back on the boat, telling them that they were preparing to drive off and kill all the Mormons, and had combined to prevent any more from landing."[8] Most boats, Strang said, refused to land at the dock on the harbor's western side, close to the Mormon settlements.[9] That dock was operated by Eri James Moore, a resident agent of the North West Co. Moore and his wife had joined the Mormon church. The other resident agent, Randolph Dinsmore, had not joined but did have business dealings with the Mormons.

The harassment precipitated a marked change in the behavior of the Mormons, Strang said. "They publicly announced that they should submit to injury and aggression no longer—that they would return blow for blow and stroke for stroke, and would punish every man who insulted or intruded upon them."[10] Fishermen and sailors who went to Mormon meetings for mischievous purposes were eyed by Mormon guards who walked up and down the aisles with heavy canes. The first sign of a disturbance by a non-Mormon was the signal for dragging the offender out. Anyone who objected to such treatment was also summarily ejected. Strang said this put an end to disruptions of the meetings—at least from the inside. On the outside, Gentile teamsters generally made sure they worked their oxen on the Mormon Sabbath (Saturday) and hauled their loads past the Mormon meeting place.[11] About this the Mormons could do little.

Another run-in with the Gentiles involved a cow that Strang had loaned to a poor woman afflicted with palsy. During the winter, a fisherman stole the cow and sold it to a fisherman named Patrick Sullivan, who threatened to "kill any damned Mormon who came for her." In the spring, Strang went for his cow, and while he was prodding it home, the Irish fishermen in Sullivan's neighborhood gathered with shillelaghs to stop him. The Irishmen were met by an equal number of Mormons, forcing a standoff. Strang continued to drive the cow home. Sullivan eventually went to Mackinac, the Michilimackinac County seat and an island about fifty miles to the east, to file a complaint against Strang.[12]

Sullivan lodged his complaint with Justice of the Peace Charles M. O'Malley. Although O'Malley had an Irish background, he also was a candidate for county delegate to the state constitutional convention, and he knew he had little hope of election without the full support of the Mormons on Beaver Island. O'Malley wrote Strang that he would "prevent any trouble from the cow matter," and he talked Sullivan into dropping the complaint, much to Sullivan's chagrin.[13]

Seeking to buttress his position with Strang, O'Malley wrote that his opponent, William N. MacLeod, had said "the Mormons can not tell what course to take, until the petty-fogger they call the prophet gets a vission from above." And reacting to Strang's desire to break off the Beaver Islands from the rest of the state and create a new territory, O'Malley said that if he were elected in May, he would try to do this with the entire northern portion of the state.[14]

While O'Malley told the Mormons what they wanted to hear, MacLeod took the opposite approach. MacLeod, who like O'Malley was a former state representative,[15] had strong doubts about the separation idea. He wrote Strang that Congress, with the consent of the legislature, could create a new state out of Michigan's boundaries, but that it could never impinge on the state's sovereignty by legislating part of the state back to a territory. O'Malley's "ruse,"

MacLeod said, was a "disgraceful imposture, displaying either a pitiful ignorance that should disqualify him for the office, or else the fraud of a mountebank deserving the lash."[16]

In a letter Strang pointed out that on the key question of separation, "Mr. MacLeod was immoderately opposed to us. We could not support him and did not oppose him."[17] Instead, many Mormons sat on their hands.

Although Peaine Township cast thirty-nine of its forty-three votes for O'Malley, that number was not enough, for O'Malley lost countywide, 123 to 99. The vote total in Peaine indicated the Mormons were not sold on O'Malley. In an election the year before, Peaine had cast sixty-one votes, and the township's population had increased since then. In that election, Peaine had shown its political clout by providing the margin of victory for the winners of county offices.[18] In the O'Malley-MacLeod race, Strang himself pointed out that a number of voters over which he exercised "some small degree of influence" did not vote.[19]

Even though the Mormons had not supported MacLeod, two months later he did Strang an unsolicited political favor as a delegate to the constitutional convention. MacLeod, a former Presbyterian minister who had taken up the study of law, was described by a fellow delegate as the most brilliant of the 100 men at the convention.[20] In a letter to Strang, MacLeod said he had the confidence of the delegates at the convention and noted: "Your sect is not a popular one amongst politicians, and it would not be a difficult matter to affect your interest injuriously." But he said he would "return good for evil—and hope that by so doing I may convince you of my sincerity in wishing your friendship."[21] As good as his word, MacLeod was instrumental in increasing the political clout of Strang and others who lived in areas with sizable Indian populations. MacLeod's proposal, which was supported by the convention, would give the voting franchise to "civilized persons of Indian descent, not members of any tribe." MacLeod said the convention delegates apparently did not grasp the implications of the clause. "Their object was to gratify me in permitting half-breeds only to vote. But you will see that a pure Indian when he leaves his tribe and conforms to the habits of the whites, may also claim that right."[22] Strang used that clause later in his career. The proposed constitution, after its adoption by the people, took effect January 1, 1851.[23]

❧ ❧ ❧

Shortly after his victory in the cow case, Strang began making final plans toward fulfilling his youthful dreams of royalty. He scheduled his coronation for the close of the July 1850 conference on Beaver Island.

Strang's authority for becoming king and establishing a kingdom on Beaver Island was a series of revelations and a translation of what he called the Plates of Laban, all of which would become The Book of the Law of the Lord, the code of conduct for the Saints in the island kingdom. The Book of the Law consisted of an "inspired translation of some of the most important parts of the law given to Moses, and a very few additional commandments." The translation, Strang said, was made from a copy of the ancient Book of the Law, which was kept in the Ark of the Covenant in ancient Israel. That book was withheld from previous translators and later lost, he said. The Book of the Law would be the fourth book the Strangites considered sacred; the other three were the Bible, the Book of Mormon, and the book of Doctrine and Covenants of the church.[24]

As early as February 1849, Strang had mentioned the existence of some "remaining plates."[25] A year later Strang was working on a translation while in the East.[26] The metallic plates, Strang said later, dated from long before the Babylonian captivity. Their discovery remains a mystery. Seven Saints, all apostles, testified that they had examined the plates, eighteen in number, each about 7⅜ by 9 inches. These Plates of Laban were thus larger in size and greater in quantity than the plates of Rajah Manchou. The Plates of Laban, the witnesses said, were engraved with "beautiful antique workmanship, bearing a striking resemblance to the ancient oriental languages" and were "occasionally embellished with beautiful pictures."[27]

One key portion of Strang's Book of the Law was not translated from those plates, however. That portion, written by Strang "by inspiration of God," involved the calling of a king. It states that God "hath chosen his servant James to be king." [28]

Some followers of Strang—and even some modern-day writers—have argued that for Mormons the terms "king" and "kingdom" were mere religious symbols without temporal or political overtones. Mark Strang, the king's grandson, wrote that the title "King in Zion" simply "designated the head man in the Church comparable to 'Pope' in the Roman Catholic hierarchy, or 'Potentate' in a fraternal order, or 'Moderator' in the Presbyterian church. It was a religious office deriving its power from the consent of the church members. No secular authority nor any authority whatsoever over non-members was imputed to the office." [29]

In Strang's kingdom, however, the king would not only have ecclesiastical powers but also control over secular and civil affairs. And when his various authorities were combined with the fealty required of those who had taken the oath of the Order of the Illuminati, his power was absolute.

What kind of kingdom Strang had in mind is indicated by an article written by "Charles J. Douglass" in the November 15, 1849, issue of the *Gospel Herald*. A "kingdom of God must shortly be established to fulfill the scripture. You know what constitutes a kingdom. In a kingdom, there must be a king, laws, officers to execute those laws, dominion, or a certain extent of country to rule, and subjects, people under the law, ruled by the king, punished by the officers, if they commit crimes. This constitutes a kingdom. . . . This kingdom, when established, will keep increasing until it becomes a great nation, and fills the whole earth." Indeed, Strang's kingdom would be so traditional that his enemies would call its establishment treason. Samuel Graham, one of Strang's advisers, also knew what kind of kingdom Strang wanted. After it was established on the island, he wrote: "Oh King live Forever. . . . May your Brethren ever attend by you until the dominion of all the earth Shall be given US! US!! Our Selves!" [30]

Strang's enemies in the Beaver Island area did not know that he had such regal plans. They did know that they did not want the Mormons on the island. And in May 1850, according to Strang, the traders and fishermen there issued an invitation to their counterparts throughout that region to come to Whiskey Point for a "glorious and patriotic celebration of Independence" on the Fourth of July. This celebration was to be climaxed by driving off the Mormons.[31]

At the same time, Strang issued an invitation for the Saints to attend a general assembly on the island during the same period, from July 1 through July 6.[32] Strang also had let it be known to a select few that he intended to hold an "organization of the kingdom" on July 8.

One notable figure who sent his regrets was John C. Bennett, a poultry farmer in Plymouth, Massachusetts.[33] In a letter, Bennett wished Strang "every success" and added these intriguing comments: "Should it be necessary to organize the 'Imperial Guard' so soon, please notify me immediately, and name such men as it is your pleasure for me to appoint to offices in that organization. . . . I hope you will organize on a grand scale—let the 'Imperial Guard' be magnificent. . . ."[34] Despite his appearance of involvement with that typical flourish of advice, Bennett would not be a part of Strang's island history.

Some of those who made plans to attend the assembly had no inkling of what regal matters were to transpire. One of the elders on his way to Beaver Island was Stephen Post, who lived in the East and had two younger brothers living on the island. Post had never met Strang and was eager to do so. Post arrived at Beaver Island four days before the assembly was to begin.[35]

Post found the harbor as beautiful as he could imagine, with a sand beach and a sprinkling of houses. The major structures in the harbor panorama included the round-log buildings and a dock on Whiskey Point to the northeast and the dock owned by Eri J. Moore on the west. To the southwest, on a gentle bluff, stood the tabernacle, a large squared-log building that was partly completed. On the southern point of the harbor was a large squared-log house, a group of smaller ones, and the frame for a steam saw mill under construction. Post's brothers, Leonard and Warren, were working on the saw mill. He learned that Strang was not on the island but was expected any day.[36]

Strang arrived with a boatload of lumber on Friday, June 28. (Two weeks later, Strang would buy the boat, a schooner, for $1,000, evidence the eastern mission had borne some monetary fruit.)[37] On Saturday, the Mormon Sabbath, a meeting was held in a grove on the west side of the harbor. There, Post met Strang, who read a chapter in Genesis and addressed the congregation. Post was rather unimpressed and wrote in his journal that he would have picked out Strang to be a libertine.[38]

On Sunday morning Post met a young woman who lived with Strang. She was dressed in pantalets—long loose trousers gathered closely about the ankles—covered by a skirt that came down to her knees. Post commented on the oddity of her costume, comments to which she took spirited exception. The young woman's name, he learned, was Elvira Field. Her style of dress, he found out, was typical of many Mormon women on the island.[39] They were ahead of the times: a year later feminist Amelia Bloomer would become famous for wearing a similar costume, dubbed bloomers. Only then would the style begin to make its appearance in the nation's large cities.[40]

After Elvira Field left, Post was asked if he knew her. When he answered no, he was told that Field was Charles J. Douglass. He recollected seeing the name in the church newspaper and Douglass's being with Strang on the eastern mission. He recalled thinking that Strang had authored an article signed by Douglass. Post was shocked: he thought Elvira a lewd woman and Strang guilty of a gross corruption.[41]

The revelation about Douglass weighed heavily on Post's mind, but he disguised his feelings as much as he could and went to work on the tabernacle, which was being built of hewn timber, as opposed to the stone plan for the temple at Voree.[42] The outside dimensions of the tabernacle were 60 by 100 feet, and it had a partition through it, making two rooms. The smaller of the two, 60 by 30 feet, was the closer to being finished. This room had joists overhead, made of peeled fir, and the first story was almost completed. The front of the tabernacle was to be 42 feet high, with a tower for a clock, bell, and lighthouse.[43]

Some workers were hauling lumber from the boat for use as roofing and flooring for the tabernacle. Just as Post was leaving for the day, Strang and Elvira walked by, arm in arm. Strang had been handling lumber at the boat and was dressed only in a shirt and pants, as opposed to his usual black suit and top hat. Elvira was wearing an ordinary dress and a sun bonnet. Strang glanced toward

Post, then he and Elvira continued on. Post went to his boarding house reflecting on the depravity of man.[44] Two months later, Post still was dwelling on the situation of Strang and Elvira, and he posed this "hypothetical" case in a letter to his brother Warren. The case was of Jo. Sill, who had a chaste, discreet wife and met by appointment a young lady whom he dressed in male apparel. Sill preaches purity and opposes polygamy, spiritual wifery, and any kind of lasciviousness and debauchery. After a mission, during which he is accompanied by the young lady in disguise, Sill returns with so much renown that even his wife does not seem to mind his having an "incognito." The young man is transformed into a young lady, and the question arises over what to call her. Mr. Sill says to call her Miss Sill. This is hard for the brethren to mouth, so they simply call her Sally.[45]

ﻮ ﻮ ﻮ

The Saints had high expectations for the July assembly. They felt it could be one of the grandest events of the church's history. On July 1 Post and a few others prepared seats in the tabernacle, and the conference began. On July 2 Post and his brother Leonard went early to the tabernacle to take the covenant, under the supervision of George J. Adams.[46] They were among twelve to take the oath at that time. About 110 more would swear allegiance to Strang in the next week.[47]

As at Voree, the covenant usually was administered while the initiate's right hand touched or grasped a wooden cross resting on a Bible, aptly, the King James version. Sometimes several persons touched the cross at the same time. The covenant was read sentence by sentence, and the initiate nodded his or her assent at the end of each sentence. After the oath was completed, the initiates signed their names in the covenant book.[48]

At Voree Strang and Bennett generally administered the covenant, with Adams doing most of the ceremonies on Beaver Island. Adams said he had repeated the covenant so often he could recite its varied provisions by heart. He had even administered it to children as young as nine.[49] How much understanding the children had is open to doubt. One thirteen-year-old admitted: "I took the covenant. Don't know what a covenant is." [50] Those taking the covenant were told there was nothing objectionable in it, nothing in it they could not live up to, and nothing rendering them liable to any law. [51]

Post was taken aback that the covenant resembled the oath that was reported to have existed three years earlier, the one that raised the ire of dissidents in Voree and was the focus of qualified denials from church leaders. Post wrote that although he would advise all who lived on the island to take the covenant, he hoped that it would not be perverted to the worst of purposes. [52]

On the morning of July 3 Post went to Strang's house to see the brass plates found at Voree. The house was a rude log dwelling on the bluff, about a quarter mile south of the tabernacle. A square, story-and-a-half structure, the house was constructed of hewn logs fastened by wooden pegs. It had two rooms on the ground floor and two sleeping rooms above. There was only one door. [53] The plates were in Strang's pocket, and he readily handed them over for Post to see. Post found the quality of the brass like that of the French brass in kettles. "With all the faith & confidence that I could exercise, all that I could realize was that Strang made the plates himself, or at least that it was possible that he made them." [54]

An artist was at work at Strang's house, making a flag for the king-to-be. On the flag was a sun and the figure of a man with a crown on his head and a scepter in his hand. The coronation was approaching. Another man arrived at this moment, carrying some large frogs for Strang; Strang said they made excellent eating. [55]

That morning, in a meeting of the assembly, Adams said Mormons had been told that a mob was to be formed on the Fourth to break up the assemblies of the Mormons and drive them from the island. This was the first indication during the assembly that the fishermen planned to carry out their "Independence" threat. Adams, whom the Mormons called the "Big Gun," warned that every person who was with the Gentile mob would die. [56]

That evening Strang was also talking tough. "I will execute with my own hands the sentence of death against all mobs who may attempt to disturb or injure us. I wish all men to understand that we do not pretend to hold these lands by any right of the government," Strang said, admitting that he did buy a few parcels of land to satisfy fellow Mormons. Strang's adrenaline was flowing. He was talking so fast that no one could take thorough notes. He said he doubted the "cowardly devils will have the courage to attempt [to drive them off the island] either by day or night." [57]

Strang's loud talk was backed up with a big stick. Unbeknownst to the fishermen and the traders, Strang had acquired a two-pound cannon, some powder, and lead. (Later he was accused of saying that his followers had stolen and buried the cannon at Voree until they came to Beaver Island.) [58] Besides the cannon, a number of Mormons had armed themselves with rifles and pistols. A guard was set up to patrol the beach and harbor area. Other men were drilling. [59]

Strang said he doubted there would be any danger, but he wanted the Mormons to be ready. He recommended that everyone have a weapon. Those who had none, he said, could swing a smooth stone tied in the corner of their handkerchief. Strang had what he called a blue hen's egg in his pocket. It was a piece of lead the shape of an egg with a hole through it and a cord attached, for swinging. [60]

One of the small rooms at the tabernacle was used for an armory, and the guards reported for duty and were relieved there. Strang was there part of the time that night. At midnight he and another Mormon took some guns and went around to Whiskey Point, where any Gentile action against the Mormons was expected to begin. All was quiet. Four Indian canoes had landed near Moore's dock, and the Indians were settled down near Dinsmore's store for the night. A vessel came into the harbor to get wood for a trip to Chicago, but it had only a few hands on board. A peaceful night. [61]

Peaceful is not the impression that Strang left of that night in the history he wrote four years later. He has several fishing boats, filled with armed men, arriving at Whiskey Point. And in his history Strang played a more heroic role. That night, while the enemy was carousing on the Point, Strang wrote, he and some others went on a reconnaissance mission. They poured some of the enemy powder in the lake and put tobacco in one of their barrels of whiskey, causing those who drank it to become exceedingly tipsy. [62]

Strang may have been playing for the gallery's sympathy in his history, and he may have been trying to whip up some hysteria in his speeches to the Mormons at the time. Warning of a coming mob would be one of the best ways to unite the Mormons against a common foe and convince them that a strong ruler—or king—was needed. If that was Strang's purpose, he seems to have succeeded. The Mormons were ready. The mob? It had yet to make an appearance, according to Stephen Post, the lone known witness who kept a journal of those days.

The Fourth of July dawned as a beautiful day on the island. After breakfast, Strang's cannon boomed from a position a few rods south of the tabernacle.[63] This "national salute," Strang said, was the first intimation to the Gentiles that the Mormons had such a formidable weapon. "They were not a little alarmed when they discovered that at every boom of the cannon the balls skipped along the water, past Whiskey point, scarcely two rods from them."[64]

Strang said that before the booming surprise had time to abate, a delegation of Mormons called on Peter McKinley, the owner of the store and dock at the Point.[65] (Alva Cable, who had built the dock and store there, had sold out to McKinley in the face of the Mormon tide and consolidated his operations with those of his nephew, James Cable, on the southeastern side of the island. Other Gentile families were also moving from the harbor to Cable's Bay, which had become a Gentile fishing settlement.)[66] The Mormons told McKinley that since his place was considered the headquarters of the Gentiles, he would be held responsible for any attack, and the first gun fired would be the signal to destroy his store and everyone in it. "Notice was also given to all the Gentiles having property on the island, that if they joined in, furnished, or even associated with the mob, they would be taken as enemies, and their homes made as bare as a sand bank."[67]

The cannon was hauled in front of the tabernacle and a guard stationed by it. Four armed guards were assigned to duty on top of the unfinished walls of the tabernacle during the services that day. Patrols were constantly on the lookout for the enemy.[68]

The meetings that day were understandably tense. In the afternoon a few men came over from the Point, as did the sailors from the Chicago-bound boat. One man was quite intoxicated and talked in the services. Stephen Post said that once or twice he thought he heard "the clink of steel as though a hundred hands were feeling to see if their weapons were ready." The drunk was eventually escorted out. There was no real disturbance, and several other Gentiles left at about the same time. After the service was over, a call was made for a few men to work on the tabernacle, when what was really wanted was some guards for the evening. Strang and Elvira Field showed up for a while; the "mob" did not.[69]

After the Fourth, there was less talk of mobs and more and more excitement about the prospect of setting up a kingdom.[70] Strang gave several reasons to explain later why the mob had not shown up. He said the Gentiles organizing the mob had been disappointed that a number of fishermen did not show up, some of the resident traders were anxious to postpone the attack because they feared it would fail and the Mormons would take revenge, and some were fearful that the Mormons were too well prepared. "Indecision and disorder prevailed, and they were unable to agree upon a leader. . . . It soon became evident that the spirit of the undertaking had oozed out, and that the difficulty would pass away without blood letting. The mob dispersed, and the Mormons went on with their Conference."[71]

One order of business was filling the Quorum of the Twelve. Four new apostles were ordained—Samuel P. Bacon, Warren Post, Edward Preston, and Hiram P. Brown. They joined eight holdovers: Samuel Graham, Jehiel Savage, Ebenezer Page, Samuel Bennett, James Blakeslee, Phineas Wright, Lorenzo Dow Hickey, and A. N. Hosmer.[72]

‽ ‽ ‽

On July 8 (Elvira Field's twentieth birthday), James Jesse Strang was crowned king. And it was that sometimes actor, sometimes evangelist George J. Adams who managed the production, borrowing ideas from England and Israel. Adams designed the costumes and much of the scenery and acted as the master of ceremonies.[73]

As the day dawned, several Mormons were still working on the arrangements. Some had been painting all night on screens made of cloth, stretched over wooden frames. The cloth was sized white with lime paint and glue and then painted with various scenes for placement in the tabernacle. Before the ceremony, the covenant had been taken by more Saints, and, in general, all of those who attended the coronation were members of the Order of the Illuminati.[74]

By 10 A.M. an audience of 235 people had filed into the tabernacle and had taken seats. They faced what had been turned into a stage, an elaborate one for the frontier. On either side were cloth panels, one a duplication of the king's flag with a life-size figure of a man wearing a crown and holding a scepter, and on the other a man holding a cross and a trumpet. Directly behind were panels painted to look like drapery. A piece of painted drapery was stretched overhead from one side to the other to hide the fir joists from view. And a large curtain obscured everything behind it.[75]

The curtain went up at about 10, revealing the stage, which was about a foot and a half higher than the rest of the tabernacle. The stage was covered with carpet and surrounded by canvas and cloth panels on which pillars were painted to represent the interior of a palace. In the center of the platform was a large chair made of boards and covered with painted cloth. This throne included another of the compromises the frontier had forced on the coronation: the seat and arms were stuffed with moss from Norway pine. In the chair was James Jesse Strang.[76]

Dressed in a flowing, floor-length robe of red flannel, trimmed with white flannel with black specks, Strang held a wooden scepter. On his breast was a large metal star. On his head was a miter ornamented with metal stars. Strang's costume, made by the women of the church under Adams's instructions, resemble those worn by Jewish high priests. The ornaments on Strang's costume were Masonic regalia that Adams had purchased in the East.[77]

Seated in the background behind Strang were the twelve apostles and a few other church officials. After an opening prayer, Strang told the audience that he was a Jew, a descendant of the House of David, and that he had inherited the throne of Israel through the lineage of David.[78] Strang claimed his appointment as king by a revelation from God. The revelation, later printed in the Book of the Law of the Lord, states that God "hath chosen his servant James to be King. . . . He hath established him a prophet above the kings of the earth; and appointed him king in Zion: by his own voice did he call him, and he sent his angels unto him to ordain him."[79]

Strang had conveniently forgotten that his first name was Jesse and not James. And there is no indication, other than his statements, that he had Jewish blood. His revelation that he was chosen of God to be king followed a pattern set by Joseph Smith. In his translation of the Book of Mormon, Smith prophesied the coming of a "choice seer" whose name would be Joseph, meaning himself.

Adams then took over the coronation program. Dealing with royalty was nothing new to him. As an actor, he often had played the title role in Shakespeare's play about Richard III, who successfully plotted to have himself crowned king of England. Now Adams was about to crown another plotter.

The crown, designed by Strang and Elvira, had been made of paper, with gilt stars and trimmings, in the style of those worn by English kings. Adams called for the royal diadem. Samuel Graham brought it. Adams placed the circlet on Strang's head.[80] Strang, who had once dreamed of being king of England and of marrying Victoria before she became queen of England, had become one with royalty: he was King James the First.

The coronation accomplished, Adams knelt before the feet of his king. Strang placed the "scepter of Judah," a turned stick about twenty inches long, on Adams's head to ordain him as prime minister. In like manner the king called eight men to be nobles in the kingdom and serve on a privy council.[81]

Adams then led the crowd in a cheer for the new king: "Long live James, King in Zion!" The king stood and asked the congregation to stand, too. Then he gave orders that his flag be raised and guns be fired in a royal salute.[82] The coronation was over.

The next morning the king called his first official meeting at the tabernacle, with his privy council and the twelve apostles. The subject: laws of the kingdom. Even though Strang had publicly linked up with Elvira, to the point of strolling arm in arm with her about the island, he still was not ready to make public his doctrine of polygamy. And to quiet rumblings in different quarters that polygamy would be sanctioned by the church, he proclaimed a law "for the peace of families and the purity of the Kingdom of God." With the concurrence of the council and the apostles, Strang said: "From this time forth, one man shall have but one wife, and let no person make any contract or bargain in anticipation of any other law."[83] But Strang had already made such a bargain: nine months after making that statement, his first polygamous child would be born to his first polygamous wife. The child, a son, would be named Charles J. Strang after Charles J. Douglass.[84]

The doctrine of polygamy would be published, in couched language, in the Book of the Law at about the same time as that first polygamous birth. Perhaps the timing of a public announcement was even discussed on July 9, when the king and his advisers conducted business behind closed doors after the council meeting. Even after the law on polygamy was published, Saints with full knowledge of polygamy would neither confirm or deny it, waiting for the right moment to make the doctrine public.[85]

In the Book of the Law, Strang gave permission for polygamy in a chapter called "Household Relations." Instead of definitely approving it, Strang would cleverly back into an authorization of polygamy—ordering the Saints not to take more than one wife if several conditions were not met. "Thou shalt not take unto thee a multitude of wives disproportionate to thy inheritance, and thy substance: nor shalt thou take wives to vex those thou hast; neither shalt thou put away one to take another." The Saints would be commanded to "be fruitful and multiply," with the proviso that all of the children be born to wives, thus prohibiting concubines. There also would be sanctions against adultery and marrying certain blood relatives. Men would be obligated to marry widows of brothers.[86]

The explosive nature of polygamy would be proven in the next year when a number of Saints left the church shortly after learning that more than one wife was allowed.[87] One of those who separated from Strang during that period was his wife, Mary, but her departure did not coincide with her discovery that her husband was practicing polygamy. Although exactly when and how she found out is not known, she did have ample evidence. Mary was on the island in the fall for the 1850 federal census, in which Elvira Field was listed both as a member of Strang's household and that of her parents, who were living on the island with her brother. Even though he now was king, Strang listed his occupation as lawyer. Mary was on the island after the doctrine on Household Relations was published early in 1851, and she was there after Elvira's first child was born in April. Mary moved away with her children at the end of that spring. Although she left in the midst of a crisis for the kingdom, Mary also left with a loathing for island living; she had always been opposed to making her home there.[88]

For some time Mary had known that Strang lacked consideration for her feelings, a trait that had been magnified since he married Elvira, and he often left Mary to deal with their children while he traveled. Strang showed he was aware of some of his faults in a letter to a married woman who had propositioned him by letter. "I am not very selfish," Strang wrote in politely rebuffing her advances, "but I bear no contradiction; my remarks on the most commonplace subjects, are sharp and cutting. I am cold, stern, uncommunicative, petulent, and exceedingly difficult to please." Although Strang said he was not disposed to meddling in most matters, he said that in those in which he took an interest, he did "exact the most rigid and implicit obedience. I never give a reason why I should be obeyed. I bear no importunity. No excuse can be satisfactory. I can not be trifled with a single moment, and not infrequently am most seriously vexed because my unspoken wants are not anticipated." Such a man, Strang wrote to the woman, could hardly be anyone's ideal beau.[89] And yet this man was to have five wives—and keep four happy.

Strang continued his busy week on Wednesday, July 10, with a discussion of inheritances, a Mormon term referring to land assigned individuals by the church. In a meeting in the tabernacle Strang answered questions about his revelation of July 8, in which God had given the Saints the islands of the Great Lakes as an inheritance, delegating to the king the power of apportioning the land. This revelation was a confirmation of what had been the apparent policy for some time. The practice of assigning inheritances was remarkable because neither the church nor the king had title to the land on Beaver Island. Strang gave Saints "title" and the right to settle on certain parcels of federal land that ranged from 40 to 160 acres.[90]

The Saints did not buy any land from the federal government that year because God had granted them the land. And perhaps because of the presence of the Saints on the island, the non-Mormons did not buy any either. The Mormons were barred from selling or giving away their inheritances, which ensured that the land remained under control of the king. The inheritances were not free. Under the Book of the Law, those who joined the kingdom could not receive an inheritance until they gave the king a tenth of all they possessed.[91]

After the meeting on inheritances, Strang and other Saints attended a dance at the home of James M. Greig, the church bishop. Young and old mixed and danced. Strang went with Elvira, but although she danced, he did not: he sat and read newspapers he had just received. At a pause in the party, Greig stated that he wanted to dedicate himself and his belongings to God. He took some water and sprinkled it through the room while pronouncing a dedication. Strang followed suit and asked a blessing.[92]

The previous few days had been momentous on the island. They had also been eventful in the nation's capital. On July 9, the day after Strang's coronation, President Zachary Taylor died. He was succeeded by Vice-President Millard Fillmore, who had been born in the same New York county as Strang. Like Strang, he was the son of a frontier farmer and had little formal schooling. Like Strang, he had been admitted to the New York bar at twenty-three. In 1851 Fillmore, as the head of the nation, would have an arresting influence on Strang, the head of an island kingdom within the nation's borders.

Chapter 8

"Hunting Mormons like Wild Beasts"

A FTER THE CORONATION, there were indications that George J. Adams was wearing out his welcome on the island. On August 1, 1850, Adams left on a mission to Ohio in a huff, complaining of ill treatment by one of the island's leading Mormons, Hezekiah D. MacCulloch. Adams was especially unhappy because he was leaving as "a servant of God" without any cash, and he blamed MacCulloch: Adams said MacCulloch, though well-to-do, would not give him money meant for him.[1]

MacCulloch, a doctor and pharmacist from Baltimore, had been ordained an elder during one of Adams's visits to that city the previous winter. After settling on Beaver Island in the spring, MacCulloch had opened a store with a fellow Baltimorean, Franklin Johnson. When he left on his mission, Adams ordered his new wife not to spend one cent at their store.[2] In a letter to Strang, Adams said: "The Dr. [MacCulloch] treated me mean, verry mean!! Dam mean!! Meaner than I was eaver treated by a Saint before." Adams warned Strang: "Oh! James, be wise, a thousand snares surround you—all are not true men that appear to be. God protect you—men will come to you with tales about me—yes! and women too—listen not to their slander—you know I am a true man but you don't realize how true I am and what I will do to serve you. . . . May my King live forever."[3]

According to Strang, one snare surrounding him had been set by Adams and his wife, Louisa. Strang said they were trying to ruin his reputation by falsely accusing him of having designs on one of Johnson's daughters, the elder of whom was then 15. The Adamses, Strang said, forged affidavits before Eri J. Moore, a justice of the peace, in an attempt to prove their accusation and then circulated them on the island.[4]

In mid-August, however, Adams was thinking about other sexual matters. Adams was beside himself with jealousy, imagining what might be happening to his wife, Louisa, whom he had left on the island. Adams had little trust in certain men there, and he wrote Strang, begging for information. "James!! I love!! Louisa!!! My Dear Wife!!!! Yes love her to MADNESS."[5]

Adams returned from his mission at the end of August, but within a month and a half, he would leave again—this time making a complete break with Strang and his church. Based mainly on Strang's published versions of where Adams and his wife went astray, the following events preceded his departure—at least on the surface. The story involving Johnson's daughter, however, appears to be more closely linked to Adams's exit than Strang admitted.

The previous winter Adams had been preaching in Boston when he was called home to Baltimore because Caroline, his wife of fourteen years, was thought to be dying. Ten days after the message, Adams finally arrived, accompanied by a woman whom he introduced as a rich widow. Adams persuaded Caroline, despite her precarious health, to travel alone to a town near Philadelphia.[6] In April 1850 Adams arrived on Beaver Island with the rich widow, whom he said he had married after Caroline died of consumption. In May it turned out that the reports of Caroline's death were greatly exaggerated. In a letter to one of the Saints on the island, she detailed her treatment at Adams's hands. The letter was read in public, and the troubles for Adams began.[7]

If the reports of Strang and his supporters can be believed, the rich widow, Louisa Cogswell, was in reality a prostitute from Boston. Louisa had a certificate of marriage to a man named Cogswell, in her own handwriting, but it was dated after her pretended widowhood. She had once lived with Cogswell, a store clerk who was still very much alive.[8]

According to Strang, Adams was subjected to progressive discipline until he lost his standing in the church.[9] But these actions—if taken at all—were not imposed until after Louisa Adams was punished by the church. Indeed, in an October 5 session of a church conference, Adams was unanimously sustained in his office after he apologized for "unpleasant feelings" that had arisen in his relationship to Strang and other members of the church. Adams categorically denied any opposition to Strang [10] and continued to sit at the right of the king. Reports of other ranking Mormons raise questions about whether Strang did in fact discipline Adams or whether Adams simply left the church and the kingdom. Mac-Culloch indicated a general reluctance to punish Adams on Strang's part and said Adams was never expelled from the church. [11] But there is little doubt that Louisa was excommunicated.

On October 10, 1850, Louisa Adams was found guilty by a Mormon court of "gross slander and personal insult" of Strang. That court, held at the tabernacle by Bishop James M. Greig, also found her guilty of conspiracy against the church and the kingdom and of breaking the covenant, which she had taken May 8. Nothing was said about Johnson's daughter in the official report. Louisa's sentence was the execution of "all the penalties, curses and maledictions" invoked by the covenant. One was that the gates of heaven would be closed against her. At the oath-taking, those who took the covenant said that if they violated it, "may disease rot my bones within me; parched and thirsty may I die without friends or succor; unloved of the good, cursed of evildoers." [12] It is revealing that Louisa was brought before the Mormon court not on charges of immoralities but on charges of slander and conspiracy. The threat to Strang and his kingdom apparently was perceived to be more harmful than any moral imperfections.

After the bishop's ruling, Adams continued to take part in the church conference until October 13, when Strang brought up the decision and asked for a motion of support. The conference, with one negative vote (was it cast by Adams?) sustained the ruling. In the afternoon session Strang remarked that Adams's position "is now vacant." Strang said Adams left "because the church would not countenance his wife in her devilish actions." [13]

Enraged by the expulsion of his wife, Adams left with her for Mackinac, vowing vengeance on the Mormons, especially Strang, and promising the extermination of all Strang's adherents. Adams took with him the curtains and fixtures he had used to put on theatrical productions in the tabernacle—and the Mormons accused him of stealing them. Among those accompanying Adams in his exodus were Eri J. Moore and his wife. The island's leading actor had moved with supporting cast and scenery for a new production, in which Strang would play the villain. Adams was promising an exposé.[14]

One of Strang's followers reported that Adams, on Mackinac Island, called Strang a "self-confessed imposter" who wanted him to get a couple of bottles of phosphorus, dress himself in a long white robe and make an appearance on Beaver Island's highest summit, called Mount Pisgah. Adams was to break the bottles there, make an illumination, and blow a trumpet before vanishing, so it would appear that an angel had paid the Mormons a visit.[15]

About a week after leaving for Mackinac, Adams returned with the county sheriff, Tully O'Malley, who carried a warrant charging Strang with driving Louisa Adams off the island by threatening her life. Strang evaded arrest on the island by chartering a schooner and setting sail for Mackinac with four other Mormons. There he requested an immediate hearing on the charge. Charles O'Malley, the justice of the peace who had issued the warrant, refused to start the proceedings without the warrant and the presence of Tully O'Malley, his younger brother. Strang took a room at a hotel and waited five days for the sheriff to arrive.[16]

A Mackinac resident said he saw Strang and his companions in Jillett's Tavern every evening playing cards and "otherwise conducting themselves unbecoming the followers of Christ." The Mormons, he said, were armed with heavy bowie knives and pistols, "more like a gang of pirates than any apostle of the Lord." He said he never saw more boldness mingled with hypocrisy and impudence.[17]

Mackinac was the seat of justice for Michilimackinac County, which covered the northern portion of the state and had long been the preeminent power in the Michigan northland. With its entrenched position as a center of trade, Mackinac Island had advantages over Beaver Island, but these were mainly military and traditional. Mackinac was originally settled because its high bluffs and location at the straits offered a commanding position for a fort. Fort Mackinac was built during the Revolutionary War, and for several decades fur trading was Mackinac's chief occupation. After the War of 1812, the island became the northern base of operations for John Jacob Astor's American Fur Company. But in 1834 Astor sold his interest in the firm, signaling the beginning of the end of that industry in Mackinac. Fishing was taking its place.[18]

As early as 1824, whitefish and "Mackinac trout" were being shipped from the island to Buffalo. By the 1850s the volume of fish traded had increased a hundredfold. At first the catches from 150 miles around were taken to Mackinac, where they were sorted, weighed, packed in barrels—each with a quarter barrel of salt— and shipped to market. The merchants of Mackinac outfitted fishermen on credit and took their fish in payment.[19] In the beginning the fisherman were Indians and Frenchmen, but by the time the Mormons began settling the Beavers, a few Americans and Irish were setting out their nets in the region. During the 1840s merchants and traders established themselves at several locations closer to the fishing grounds than Mackinac. Beaver Island, fifty miles to the west and in the heart of the rich fishing grounds of Lake Michigan, was one of these locations.[20]

Meanwhile, the rise of steam power on the Great Lakes meant boats needed more and more wood to burn; Mackinac, with its island forests depleted, had to import most of the cordwood it offered to the lake steamers.[21] Beaver Island had abundant forests: men simply had to get the wood chopped and transported to the docks. Beaver Island also had a natural harbor (as opposed to Mackinac's half-moon indentation), and increasing numbers of boats were finding it attractive to stop there. Beaver Island thus posed a direct economic threat to Mackinac.

The town of Mackinac had a population of about a couple of hundred, including Americans, French, half-breeds, and Indians. The town had a ragged look, with rickety, weather-beaten homes alternating with well-built but plain frame buildings. One of the town's two major streets ran around the harbor and led under the steep bluff mounted by Fort Mackinac. On the harbor's pebbly beach, wigwams generally could be seen, with the Indians' birch bark canoes nearby.[22] The pointed bow and stern of the canoes were replicated in the shape of the fishermen's craft, the twin-masted Mackinac boats. The other major street, on which the courthouse was located, was north of the first, extending west from the bluff to the shoreline. The two-story frame courthouse was one of the town's most distinctive buildings, featuring an eight-sided cupola with a like number of windows. The courtroom was on the second floor.[23]

On Saturday, October 26, Strang was arrested and brought

before O'Malley. The justice, who at thirty-six was a year younger than Strang, had been born in Ireland and educated as a priest. But after coming to this country when he was twenty, he became a merchant at Mackinac, where he held several county offices and served as state representative from the county. Adams's complaint now included the charge that Strang had threatened his life in addition to Louisa's. Strang pleaded not guilty. O'Malley then swore in Adams and his wife and began taking their testimony.[24]

Adams said the first threat against him came when Strang, who had been threatening Louisa, told him that if he "took her part," he "should leave the island or die." Adams testified that on at least two other occasions Strang said much the same thing when they were alone in the woods. Adams said Strang also warned him that if Louisa did not leave before the lake froze over for the winter, she would die with all who abetted her.[25] "Mr. Strang," Adams said, "said it would be easy, if any man of note should apostatize, to dig a hole in the sand under his house and put in a bladder of powder as that would leave no marks and would appear as a judgment from God." For this reason, Adams said, he and others watched his house the night before he left the island.

Louisa Adams testified at length about the covenant. Before taking it, she was told she could not get into the celestial kingdom without it. "After I came into the covenant, [Strang] told me the penalty for breaking the covenant is the sack, the stone and the lake." She said that frequently in the previous several months Strang had told her he would have her life unless she made a humble confession, apparently referring to her "gross slander and personal insult" of him.

According to the Mormon version of the examination, O'Malley asked leading questions and worked hard to make the evidence fit the accusation, to the point of suggesting amendments to testimony. O'Malley even allowed Adams to prompt his wife during her testimony. Strang objected, angering O'Malley. It was one of several objections and motions that were overruled.[26]

As Strang began to object, O'Malley interrupted and threatened to send him to jail for contempt of court. Strang responded, "I know the way."

O'Malley quickly ordered Strang jailed. "I'll let you know that you are not among your Mormon gang here."

"If I were," Strang said, "I should not see a justice of the peace under the mantle of magisterial dignity, blackguarding a prisoner at his bar. No Mormon is mean enough for that, Mr. O'Malley."

"Take him away," the justice told his brother, the sheriff, "don't keep him blathering here."

Strang was taken to jail, and Justice O'Malley continued the trial, swearing in several more witnesses. One witness said he heard Strang say that if Louisa Adams remained on the island until Christmas, she would be riding around Paradise Bay on a black horned ram, facing backward, for the boys to hoot at her. Whoever kept her company would share her fate. Other witnesses swore that they believed Strang to be a dangerous man and that there were forty persons on Beaver Island who would do just what he told them to, even kill a man.

In Strang's absence, O'Malley convicted him of threatening Louisa Adams and sentenced him to jail for six months.

Strang sought a hearing on a writ of habeas corpus in the contempt of court sentence. That night a friendly county judge ordered Strang released, citing several defects in O'Malley's actions. Strang sought another writ in the six-month sentence. Because the trial had been carried on in Strang's absence, that conviction was also set aside. A new trial was indicated. O'Malley's ignorance of judicial procedure was turning out to be Strang's best ally.

In spite of the judge's actions, O'Malley vowed he would return Strang to jail for two nights at least. Strang and some friends had gone to a saloon for oysters to celebrate his release. Just as the well-flavored delicacies were arriving, Tully O'Malley arrested Strang again and brought him before his brother. It was a few minutes before 9 P.M. on a Saturday, but Strang offered to go on with the trial, even though it was late. The justice, however, said he would not sit up nights to keep Strang out of jail. Strang was ordered back to confinement.

The jail was a log building with two very damp rooms, each about twelve feet square, built into the side of a hill. The front room had two grated windows without glass. The other room had no windows and was used as a toilet by the prisoners, who were denied access to the yard. The sheriff would not let Strang take his overcoat into jail, denied him a bed, blankets, or food, and refused him a clean plank to sleep on. At 10 P.M. another writ of habeas corpus was served on the sheriff, but he disregarded it, declaring that he would keep Strang prisoner until Monday morning.

But on Sunday evening the sheriff, having sought legal advice, released Strang. This gave Strang a night of freedom. On Monday morning he was arrested for the third time and brought to trial before O'Malley.

The justice began by making a concession of sorts to Strang: "We were rather heated at the former trial, and both used language doubtless which in our cooler moments we should regret. I hope all things will pass off smoothly now."

Strang was not in a mood to be conciliatory. "I am not aware that I was heated at all on that occasion. My language was quite proper. I have no apology to make, and am quite indifferent as to how things may pass off, perfectly assured that if I cannot be heard in my defense here, I have a sufficient defense in the blunders of this court."

This stung O'Malley. "Oh, I did not intend to make an apology. I am quite sure I did nothing which calls for an apology."

At one point in the new trial, George Adams testified that he had no wife but Louisa and had not had another wife for many years. When Strang began pressing Adams about Caroline, O'Malley abruptly asked the witness to step down.

O'Malley convicted Strang again, but he said he would release Strang if he could get two Mackinac residents to come up with a $2,000 bond each to assure that the peace would be kept for one year. When several persons offered to put up the bond, O'Malley added another condition. "Mr. Strang, as this is a very aggravated case, I shall require you to pay the costs."

"Mr. O'Malley, I shall pay no costs," Strang said. "Neither shall I give bail." And turning to the men who had offered to put up his bond, he said: "Gentlemen, I am under great obligation to you . . . [but] I beg you to sign no bond for me." To the justice, he added: "I am in your hands. Hitherto your ignorance has shielded me from your malice. . . . If you intend to commit me to prison, it is as well now as any time. But I will let you know that I am not to be treated in this manner with impunity."

Strang was committed to jail for the fourth time. But because his sentence was open-ended and because the proceedings appeared to be malicious on the part of the justice of the peace, Strang was freed again, without any requirement to pay court costs or put up a bond. He returned to Beaver Island a free man.

Because of the closeness of his trial to the November elections, how Strang had been freed was a subject of controversy. It was charged that Mormons gave their votes to the Democrats and a certain ticket in the county in return for Strang's release. Among those who were said to have helped free Strang in return for political favors was William N. MacLeod, who was running for prosecuting attorney on a ticket headed by John D. Irvine, a candidate for state representative.[27]

In the election the Mormons again demonstrated their clout and further antagonized their opponents, especially on Mackinac Island. Irvine's opponent, Edward Guilbault, was running on an anti-Mormon slate, while Irvine's ticket included three Mormons. Irvine won, 198 to 151, thanks to a 96 to 11 cushion from Peaine Township (the Beaver Islands). The election had mixed results for the Mormons, even though Irvine's team won. Henry Granger, an anti-Mormon, was elected sheriff, and Strang said Granger's name had been fraudulently inserted on Irvine's ticket so as not to be observed.[28]

Strang was not the only one who thought he detected fraud in the election. Backers of the Guilbault slate tried to have the returns from Peaine Township thrown out, which would have made the Guilbault slate the winner. The Guilbault backers claimed there were thirty to forty illegal votes cast on Beaver Island, which, they said, cast more votes than there were voters. They charged that Strang dictated the votes of his followers and that minors and women dressed as men cast ballots, with Strang threatening anyone who challenged the legality of a particular vote. This charge was taken to Lansing, the state capital, where the legislature found no reason to change the results.[29]

The 1850 census, taken on the island the month before the election, casts doubt on the claim that more votes were cast than there were voters. According to the census, about 180 men of voting age were on Beaver Island and about half of them appear to have been Mormons.[30] The potential vote thus exceeded the 107 votes cast there.

≥ ≥ ≥

After Strang's trial in Mackinac, newspapers in the Great Lakes region began taking an interest in King Strang and his island kingdom. The *Cleveland Plain Dealer* published a report that several persons on Beaver Island were guarding their homes with muskets, out of fear that Strang and his minions would slay them in the night. "Anyone who dares to disobey my laws," the article quoted Strang as saying in the tabernacle in October, "shall leave this island without a boat, or be a head shorter if he stays." The story added that Strang said that his laws were given by God and that the laws of the United States were of no account if they conflicted with his "higher law." This was similar to expressions in the covenant.[31]

For public consumption, however, Strang said that although God's law was above all human law, it forbade rebellion against governments and violation of their laws. When human and divine law conflicted, he said, members of the church were required to seek a change in the human law.[32] A reliance on a higher law was not unheard of in that time, for southerners frequently used the Bible to justify slavery, and northerners who ran stops on the Underground Railway cited moral reasons for their violations of the Fugitive Slave Law.[33]

Based on the principles of a higher law, Strang took from the Gentiles whatever he wanted, the *Plain Dealer* article charged. It said that after his tabernacle speech a party of Mormons entered a Gentile store and took fourteen barrels of pork and that property of another Gentile was burned, apparently referring to barrel staves belonging to Peter McKinley. The article reported that Strang told McKinley that he knew by revelation that the fiery judgment of the Lord was about to descend on him.[34]

Strang's press denounced these accusations as a "precocious mass of lies." The *Plain Dealer* reporter who wrote a story referring to Mormon misdeeds was called Mr. Plain Liar Jr. and challenged to show up within the dominion of the Mormon king. "We will assure him a good horse whipping, administered according to Mormon law, in the presence of a multitude of witnesses."[35] The Mormons also leveled charges of their own. They said that a Mackinac Irishman had broken into Johnson and MacCulloch's store and carried off some merchandise and that someone had broken into another Mormon store and stolen twenty barrels of pork and lard, which were found buried in the sand near the house of a Gentile near Whiskey Point.[36]

A Detroit newspaper reported that some who had followed George Adams to Mackinac had returned to Beaver Island to find their houses, furniture, and other goods in the hands of Mormons, who claimed possession by an "order of confiscation" issued by King Strang. One of those was Eri J. Moore, a former member of the church and nobleman in the kingdom. Moore and his wife had taken the covenant, which also had been administered to groups in his home, and the Mormon printing office had been built on his land. Now the Mormons were worried about gaining title to buildings they had built on Moore's property.[37] In explaining his falling out with Strang, Moore said that after he issued a process against a church member as justice of the peace, he was called before Strang and his privy council and given to understand that he must not do that again. Moore said he was told that Strang and the council concluded that he would have to be driven from the island.[38]

In responding to published charges, the Mormons tacitly admitted Strang's power on the island. The *Northern Islander*, Strang's new newspaper, said Strang "seldom makes a proposition but it is unanimously concurred in. We think another man cannot be found on earth so honest that all of his acquaintances will acknowledge him the standard of right, and so just that no one will open his house to one he has condemned."[39]

Faced with such unity and power, it is no surprise that many Gentiles, including some of the island's early settlers, were abandoning valuable homes and property to the Mormons. The population of the island that fall was about 500, two-thirds of whom were Mormon. Strang wanted the population to be all Mormon—or at least submissive to the Mormons.[40]

Meanwhile, Adams was playing royal roles before sparse theater audiences in the loft above a Mackinac store, knowing he had recommended much of what was reported to be taking place on Beaver Island. In the year before he left the kingdom Adams had written Strang about taking from the Gentiles. In a letter from Baltimore Adams said he had taught Johnson and MacCulloch the doctrine of consecration, which non-Mormons would later claim to be a euphemism for stealing from the Gentiles in the name of the church. "We are going into the gentiles with a Rush," Adams said. "We will send you—or I mean we will bring you some 'Rocks' so keep cool—all is good—all is straight—everything is going ahead."[41]

Adams had also advocated establishing a dominion for the kingdom by force. In another letter to Strang he asked how many men could be raised to fight for the kingdom. "Now if you can get twenty to twenty-five true men that will Be as true as steal you can take the kingdom and establish Peace on this Island." Adams said that even supposing as many as 300 men on the island, twenty-five disciplined men could whip 300 anytime. He recommended that Strang take action in December after the close of navigation. "We that are here are shut up from the Rest of the World for six months . . . the sooner the Blow is struck after the close of navigation the Better for we want time to Prepare and fortyfy ourselves against those without . . . if we take a Bold and Determind Desided stand and let our motto Be Victory or Death that the goverment will yield to our Request and let us alone."[42]

Along with Adams in Mackinac that fall, Moore was reported to be telling everyone who would listen about evil deeds of Strang and his followers. Moore said he was informed, probably by Adams, that as soon as the lake froze, it was the intention of the king and his privy council to massacre any Gentiles left on the island as well as any waverers among his own people.[43]

Moore charged that Strang or some of his followers had broken into his house and stripped it of his household goods, and even his justice of the peace docket and a set of lawbooks belonging to the state. The spoil, he said, was distributed to the "four winds." Two Mormon families were living in his home, he said. At the end of November Moore returned to St. James to demand his property back. According to Moore, Strang told him that he could not have any of it and that it would not be safe for him to remain on the island. Moore and his family were staying with Nicholas Bower, the township clerk at the time. Moore said Strang told Bower that if the Moores stayed with him more than twenty-four hours, he would blow up Bower's house and all that were inside. The two families kept a watch that night. The next morning the Moores moved across the bay to Peter McKinley's house. McKinley also had been threatened, Moore said, and a watch was kept that night, too.[44]

On December 2, on his way to Mackinac, Moore wrote to the governor, asking for protection because of threats Strang had made against him and others on the island. Moore added a new charge: that Strang was making counterfeit coins and that he had sent out bands of Mormons to pass bogus coins that fall. Moore said later that the Mormons were "loaded down" with counterfeit money, with one Mormon saying he had $1,400 in the roll of bills he was carrying. He said the Mormons had dug a cave on the island for minting operations.[45]

At the same time, after unsuccessfully trying, with Adams, to get the U.S. troops at Fort Mackinac to go to Beaver Island to arrest all the Mormons, Moore attempted to get Tully O'Malley to raise a posse, arrest Strang and "his band of robbers," and bring them back to Mackinac for trial. O'Malley, who was in the last month of his term as sheriff, apparently failed to raise a posse, but he did pay a visit to Beaver Island on December 7.[46]

According to the *Northern Islander*, O'Malley said the Mormons had "garrisoned the steamer Lexington, and mounted it with two heavy field pieces, and that the 'King of the Mormon Isles' had a guard or 'standing army' of 70 men, constantly under arms, and ready for action; and that by that means he had been prevented from serving legal process" on Strang and other Mormons.[47] McKinley stated it more simply: he said Strang collected seventy armed men to resist the sheriff.[48]

That night, between 7 and 8 P.M. on a farm about a mile south of the harbor, two vacant houses belonging to Thomas and Samuel Bennett were burned to the ground.[49] The *Northern Islander* said the Bennetts, who were Gentiles, had been taking "lawless liberties" along with other fishermen. "It is believed that the burning was incendiary, to revenge some of these supposed wrongs."[50] The suspicion pointed to the Mormons.

McKinley and Moore said Mormons had set fire to the houses to provoke non-Mormons to acts of violence. If any violence occurred, Moore said, the "Royal Army" could use that excuse for shooting the "mob" down. But the Gentiles stayed home to watch their own property. No one turned out at the fires.[51]

O'Malley, after a few days on the island, in which the Mormons said he kept out of sight, realized it would be useless to attempt to arrest Strang, and he returned to Mackinac. There he tried, also unsuccessfully, to enlist the U.S. troops at the fort to join his battle against the Mormon king.[52]

The *Northern Islander* was the successor to the *Gospel Herald*, and the *Islander's* first issue was December 12, 1850, about six months after the last edition of the Voree newspaper. A weekly, the *Islander* was the first and only newspaper in the Mackinac region and dealt frequently with the conflicts between Mormons and Gentiles, between Beaver Island and Mackinac Island.

In the same issue that reported Tully O'Malley's latest visit, the *Islander* sarcastically informed its readers that the "Standing Army of the Mormon King," consisting of a surveyor and twelve men, was opening a road from the harbor to Cable's Bay, about eleven miles south. "This company are fitted out as regular campaigners, each man having his knapsack and blanket, and armed with an axe. They eschew tents and despise houses, and altogether are a formidable looking body of men; a force that trees cannot stand against, and swamps cannot deter. . . .

"The 'King of the Mormon Isles' is enforcing the statutes for the construction and improvement of Highways on Merchants and Fishermen who have heretofore in such matters been to[o] good citizens to work or pay. Perhaps some of them will try to have him arrested and imprisoned for making them pay Highway taxes."[53] Under the Book of the Law, to be quietly published later that winter, the king had the right to appoint men to collect a tribute, from those who used the highways, for the construction and maintenance of the roads.[54]

McKinley and Moore had another view of the industriousness of the Mormons. In affidavits sworn to in December 1850 and January 1851, they accused the Mormons of a catalog of crimes and asked state and federal authorities for assistance. Their statements were published on February 1, 1851, by the *Detroit Advertiser*, a Whig newspaper that had no love for the Democratic leanings of Strang. Moore swore that Strang had told him the previous summer that the laws of the state "must be held merely as a tool to be used against the Gentiles," to injure them in every way possible. According to Moore, Strang said all of the offices on the island must be filled by Mormons or persons who would suit the purposes of the church.[55]

Also in February, Strang received a revelation, printed in the Book of the Law, that troops would be gathered against the kingdom. God commanded the Saints to "arise and thrash, for I will make thy power iron . . . thou shalt break in pieces many people, and shalt consecrate their spoil unto God, and their dominion to the Lord of the whole earth."[56]

At about this time, too, Strang received a warning that he was playing with fire on Beaver Island. His uncle had read of his imprisonment and a "terrible commotion" on Beaver Island, and he predicted, quite accurately, that "designing men will be creeping in and about your people & there will surely be a great breakup sooner or later and whatever curses may arise in the heated imaginations of the people may in some unlucky hour or Day be visited upon your head without even giving you any chance for a hearing."[57]

On February 18, 1851, the Mormons moved to arrest Moore, who they had learned was on Garden Island, a couple of miles north of Beaver and inhabited by a mixed race of Chippewas and Ottawas. According to Strang, Moore was selling whiskey to the Indians, a violation of state law. Strang said Moore brought his whiskey from Mackinac and sold nothing else.[58] In seeking to arrest Moore, a Mormon constable named Asa C. B. Field acted on a warrant signed by a Mormon who was a justice of the peace for Peaine Township.

Both the warrant and the complaint, filed by Samuel Graham, had been drafted by Strang. Worried that the Indians might defend Moore, the constable took a posse of eleven men.[59]

Early in the morning on the 18th, the posse crossed the ice to Garden Island and went directly to the Indian village, where they sat around the fire. They smoked and, through interpreters, talked with the Indians, but did not learn where Moore was. Later, while seven of the Mormons stood on the ice in Garden Island harbor, waiting for the constable to head for home, they saw a dog sled approaching from the direction of Mackinac. "There he is, there he is," someone cried. Moore had been walking behind the dog sled. Four of the Mormons headed for Moore. Moore then took a gun from one of the other men with the sled and ran back along the trail. The Mormons gave chase. Moore appeared to be heading for the protection of a group of men just stepping on the ice near a portage across Garden Island in the direction of Mackinac. The fastest Mormon, William Townsend, counted eighteen men in that group, which was about a mile from the village. "I was satisfied that it was no use for me to run up alone, so I stopped and waited for the constable," he said. The other three Mormons halted, too.

Meanwhile, three other Mormons had gone for the constable. Peaine, an old Chippewa chief, came out to talk to them. Two of the Mormons tried to talk to Peaine. Neither side could understand the other, but it was clear that Peaine was angry. An interpreter showed up, followed by Field, who asked the interpreter to tell the chief that he had papers to arrest Moore. Peaine refused to permit the arrest. He said there was an understanding that the Indians would protect Moore, and that when the Indians made a promise, they kept it. After their conversation with the chief, the Mormons talked among themselves about what to do next. While they were standing there, they heard two guns fired, saw a red flag raised where Moore had run, and heard balls striking in the bush. "The Indians were intoxicated," Townsend said, "and we had not gone there for a fight." The Mormons returned to Beaver Island.[60]

On the next day most of the Garden Island Indian men came to St. James harbor, where Strang was spending days and nights on board the steamer *Lexington*. The steamer, which had gone aground on another island and limped into Paradise Bay late in the fall, was iced in the harbor for the winter. On the *Lexington*, Strang was completing his translation of the Plates of Laban and was writing and proofreading for the coming publication of the Book of the Law of the Lord.[61]

About two-dozen Indians boarded the steamer to complain about the attempt to arrest Moore and to talk about relations with the Mormons. The topics included the burning of barrel staves belonging to McKinley the previous summer. The Indians also told the Mormons to come to their villages with smaller groups the next time, so as not to scare the women and children. When Strang asked if the Mormons might go to Garden Island the next day to arrest Moore, Peaine replied excitedly: "No! No!"[62]

On February 26 the Indians returned at McKinley's request and talked more intensively with Strang and his privy council. The Indians carried guns and tomahawks, had painted their faces with war colors, and followed a red flag. Strang said the Gentile traders on Beaver Island had "engaged the Indians to assume a hostile position toward the Mormons." He said there were about four chiefs and twenty braves at the meeting. The Indians were accompanied by about twenty white men, including McKinley, James Cable, and Thomas Bennett, and four women, including the interpreter, Mrs. Mary Davis. But it was the Indians who did most of the talking.[63]

In long speeches the chiefs detailed their attachment to the traders who supplied their wants and the fishermen who intermarried with them. They also talked about their bravery and cruelty in war. It was left to Peaine to give the key message. Peaine warned the Mormons of annihilation if they sued or attempted to arrest a non-Mormon, forced one to pay a highway tax, cut any steamboat wood unless it was purchased by McKinley, or extended their settlements beyond the present bounds. The warning, Strang said, was intended to induce the Mormons to give up their settlements and leave the island.[64]

Strang replied at length. When he came to the warning of war, he turned to the white men, took down their names, and read to them the laws concerning inciting Indians to commit crimes. He said he should prosecute them. Then, to Peaine, he said: "I am no child, and cannot understand you. Your voice is like a scolding woman. I will not hear you. March on." The white men were already moving away, and Peaine and the other Indians sullenly followed.[65]

None of this warning was printed in the *Northern Islander*, perhaps because Strang thought it would scare potential settlers. Strang would have enough bad news to keep him busy in the next few months without worrying about the Indians.

On March 16 the federal government became involved in the Mormon-Gentile dispute. George C. Bates, the U.S. district attorney for Michigan, wrote to John J. Crittenden, the U.S. attorney general, seeking instructions on complaints he had received against the Mormons. The complaints apparently were those from McKinley and Moore that had been published a month earlier by the *Detroit Advertiser*. Bates told Crittenden he was "credibly informed" that the Mormons had, "without purchasing any land, taken possession of nearly the whole island; that they are cutting and selling all the wood and timber." By that time it was an established principle that timber could not legally be cut from public lands, although enforcement of the law was erratic. Bates recounted Moore's charge that the Mormons had a "large establishment" for counterfeiting gold and silver coin. "An effort was made last fall to arrest some of them under the state laws for coining, but the sheriff was beaten off and failed to execute the process," Bates said. The only way to make arrests on the island, he continued, would be to have the secretary of the Navy order the warship *Michigan* to take the U.S. marshal there. "No vessel, except an armed one, could land there with a posse, as they avow their determination to resist all who come." Bates asked the attorney general for advice on indicting the Mormons on charges of cutting timber on federal lands, issuing warrants on counterfeiting charges, and calling on the officers and men of the *Michigan* to act as a posse.[66]

The net was closing around the Mormons, and although they probably were not aware of the federal threat, they were aware that something was afoot. On April 3, 1851, the *Northern Islander* noted the increased conflict between Mormons and Gentiles. The *Islander* said it had information about two threats against the Mormons. In one, a Gentile offered to help burn down the houses of twenty Mormons on Beaver Island. In the second, Thomas Bennett said he was determined to see Strang dead before fall.[67]

The Mormon newspaper reacted militantly. The Mormons, the editorial said, "will not huddle up like frightened sheep, and . . . should such an aggression be committed, the aggressors would be wiped off the face of the earth. . . . It is not safe to have such men left in our vicinity. They will forever be seeking to excite hostilities, and will never be at rest while their neighbors are at peace; and if suffered to remain among us will contrive by some means to put an end to the good feeling prevailing among the community here."[68]

The Mormons did not wait long for hostilities to be "excited" further. That same week, shortly after warmer weather had opened the lakes to navigation, Eri J. Moore obtained warrants from Justice of the Peace Charles M. O'Malley against thirty-eight Mormons, charging them with arson, robbery, burglary, and putting Moore "in fear of danger" when they tried to arrest him on Garden Island.[69]

The new anti-Mormon sheriff, Henry Granger, went to Beaver Island to arrest the thirty-eight, about one-third of the Mormon men on the island. The *Northern Islander*, in its report of the arrests, said Granger was backed by a posse of thirty intoxicated Indians and ten drunken Irishmen, armed with guns. The story was head-lined: "ANOTHER OUTRAGE—HUNTING MORMONS LIKE WILD BEASTS.—" The *Islander* said that to understand what happened, the reader would have to "imagine a tribe of wild savages, first made drunk, then provided with arms and ammunition, and then let loose upon the peaceable inhabitants of a town, with authority to make prisoners of all the town officers and principal publick men, have them whooping about your houses and swearing death against the men they are ostensibly sent to arrest." All of this took place, the *Islander* noted, even though there was not one act of resistance on the part of the Mormons. More than fifteen Mormons were arrested, and, according to the newspaper, they were beaten, abused, and threatened. One was surrounded by members of the posse, who told him that his father, who had been working in the woods, had been killed by those sent to arrest him; they showed him a portion of the father's clothing as proof. But this was just a deception meant to roil the Mormons.[70]

The posse wanted to arrest Strang, but he was nowhere to be found. The posse scoured the neighboring islands for him.[71]

Strang had gone to Hog Island, northeast of Beaver, to pick

up a large yawl lost from a steamer in the fall. The yawl, slightly damaged, had been trapped in icy shoals at the island, but a Mormon party had hauled it on shore two months earlier, to save it from being destroyed in the breakup of the ice in the spring thaw. With Strang were ten other Mormons. Some of them had come to help fix the boat, the rest to cut timber for oars.[72]

Two dozen men from the posse arrived at Hog Island while the Mormons slept on the evening of April 10. A little past midnight, the posse rushed the Mormon camp with Indian war whoops and Irish hurrahs. In the dark the Mormons, many of them without boots, broke toward their boat. But the posse had taken it. The Mormons evaded the posse and headed for the woods. Feeling their way through a deep swamp in the darkness, the Mormons, except for one member of their group, met on the opposite shore of the island, where they found an old leaky fishing boat, filled with ice and snow.[73]

The morning was frosty, and the lake was spotted with drift ice. The boat had neither sails nor oar locks, but it did have three oars. Even though the missing man had not shown up, the others pushed off to find a refuge. Many of them were half-dressed, and they had no provisions. According to Strang, for the next twenty-four hours the Mormons paddled west through the buffeting waves, skirting islands in the Beaver chain to avoid being seen. Early the next day, he said, they landed at Gull Island, a small, uninhabited island about ten miles west of Beaver.[74]

Meanwhile, on Hog Island, after searching at length for Strang, the sheriff took the clothing, tools, provisions, blankets, and cooking utensils the Mormons had left. The Mormons said they eventually got some of the supplies back, but most they never saw again. Among the spoils was a joiner's chest of tools, which had been taken to Hog Island to repair the yawl.[75] Those tools were later described by the Gentiles as "admirably suited for burglarious purposes."[76]

The sheriff took his prisoners back to Mackinac, where the prevailing topic at the Irish gin shops was Mormon lawlessness. O'Malley ordered the Mormons jailed. But when O'Malley learned that they were ready to put up bail, he dropped the charges against all except a few, who were let out on bond. At the next session of the county court, the charges against those few were also dismissed when no one appeared to give evidence against them. There are indications that Moore dropped his complaint against the Mormons after they agreed to allow him back on the island without fear of being arrested. Moore was on Beaver Island before the end of the month.[77]

On Gull Island the ten Mormons took refuge in the summer fishing settlement's best shanty, according to Strang's version of the events. Because they did not have an ax, they tore apart the other shanties for fuel. They found some provisions in the various shanties. To fix their leaking boat, they ingeniously shaped timber with fire and knives. With rocks, they hammered nails that they saved from the shanties they burned. Finally, after five days, the boat was ready for the lake, and the men returned surreptitiously to Beaver Island. Five days later, they made a trip to Hog Island to find the missing Mormon, who was still alive, having subsisted on rawhide oar straps, two quarts of frozen potatoes, and fish heads left from a dinner twelve days earlier.[78]

There was a conflicting report, however, about Strang's whereabouts at the time he said he was on Gull Island. Isaac Whicher, a resident of Mackinac, said he believed Strang had been with three men who passed counterfeit coins on the mainland a few days after Strang had fled Hog Island. A merchant on Grand Traverse Bay, about forty miles from Beaver Island, said that on April 16 the men had bought $40 in goods with bogus half-dollars. Whicher said that the three men were recognized as Mormons and that after the counterfeit money was passed, he and others gave chase, only to see those in the boat cock their guns.[79]

"It seems," Whicher wrote to Strang, "you are hard up for persecutions, first for religion, then for politics. [Yours] is an organization for doing mischief and cloaking the same under the sanction of religion."[80] Strang countered that Whicher had not mentioned him in an initial account of the affair that was published in the *Chicago Tribune*. In that version, Strang said, Whicher said he had no clue to the identity of the guilty parties or where they had come from.[81]

Sheriff Granger returned to Beaver Island to arrest Strang, who still could not be found. Granger raised funds for a reward and offered at least $25 for Strang's capture. With the reward as incentive, Strang said, he was being hunted by bands of Indians, half-breeds, and Irish. According to Strang, many of those searching for him believed that the sheriff's reward would legally justify killing him. "And there is not the slightest doubt that had they succeeded . . . [the] murderers would never have been prosecuted." A majority of the influential men of Michilimackinac County would have been glad to be rid of him "by any safe means, however unlawful," Strang said.[82]

Six weeks after the chase on Hog Island, Strang was still in hiding. Meanwhile, the complaints of those who sought Strang's arrest had taken effect in high places.

Chapter 9

The United States v.
James J. Strang

ON APRIL 30, 1851, President Millard Fillmore authorized legal action against the Mormons of Beaver Island. Because it was believed that Strang and the other Mormons would resist arrest, Fillmore gave the U.S. marshal in Detroit permission to use the U.S. steamer *Michigan*—the Navy's first iron-hulled warship—"to execute any process or order." [1]

The "Iron Ship," as it became known, carried 106 men, including a contingent of Marines. The 163-foot-long steamer was armed with one three-inch gun, an 18-pounder, in line with an agreement to limit the firepower of warships on the Great Lakes after the War of 1812. Following the pattern for steamships of that era, the *Michigan* was equipped with a full set of sails, for three barkentine-rigged masts, and had two paddlewheels, one on each side amidships. [2]

The *Michigan* had made an overnight visit to Beaver Island in August 1850, the ship's first stop there, and a portion of the crew had gone ashore. This time the warship would not be on a curiosity call. The *Michigan* arrived in Detroit on May 21 and received a party of federal officials on board, including U.S. attorney George C. Bates, U.S. marshal Charles H. Knox, and eight deputy marshals. [3] The *Michigan*'s departure for Beaver Island that afternoon was heralded in the *Detroit Advertiser* under the headline: "BEAVER IS-LAND.—'KINGDOMS TODAY ARE UPSIDE DOWN.'—" The article reported that the *Michigan* was sailing to "the seat of Empire of Strang the 1st" to arrest him. "His majesty has long set all civil authority at defiance, and he will now have a dire opportunity to try his spunk." [4]

Two days later the *Michigan* docked at Mackinac Island. The Marines were on deck as a show of force, part of the plan devised by

Bates, with the advice and cooperation of the ship's captain, Commander Oscar Bullus.[5]

Three men—Bates, the ship's first officer, and a deputy marshal—went ashore and proceeded to the courthouse. The May term of the court was to begin in four days, and James M. Greig, a Mormon from Beaver Island and a judge of the county court, was there in his shirtsleeves. The three men surprised the judge by walking up to his desk and asking him to come with them to the ship.[6] Greig, overcoming his shock, ordered his court officers, all Mormons, to arrest the three intruders for contempt of court. Bates then showed the judge a federal warrant for his arrest, which Bates threatened to use if Greig did not go with them on his own accord. He asked the judge to look out the courthouse window, so he could see that the warrant was backed with the power of the U.S. Navy. Greig was convinced. He walked to the Navy steamer, where Bullus, in full naval uniform, greeted him and escorted him to a small cabin below. It was clear to Greig that although he was not under arrest, he was a prisoner.[7]

The *Michigan* left Mackinac at 8 P.M. and steamed toward Beaver Island. Orders were given to slow the warship so it would arrive at the island at about 2 A.M., furnishing Bates time for the second phase of his plan—persuading Greig to help the federal officials arrest Strang.[8] The U.S. attorney went to Greig's cabin and recapitulated the crimes of which the Mormons had been accused, told of Mormon resistance to prosecution by the county authorities in Mackinac, and showed the judge a federal warrant for Strang's arrest. Bates said he was aware of the Mormon boast that Strang could not or would not be captured, that he would resist arrest by force or go into the swamps and morasses of Beaver Island where he could not be found. Greig was asked to write a message to Strang, stating the situation and urging him to give himself up, and to give directions on where Strang could be found. Greig refused.[9]

Bates then laid before Greig the orders to Bullus from the secretary of the Navy, putting the *Michigan* and her Marines at the disposal of the U.S. marshal. Bates warned Greig that he would "swing from a yardarm" if he did not cooperate. Greig appears to have become convinced that with the power of the federal government arrayed against them, Strang and the other Mormons would eventually be arrested. Greig finally agreed to write the letter—if the arrests would be made peaceably and apparently if Bates would deliver the letter alone. Bates agreed. He now had to calm the deputy marshals, who were eager to take Strang by force. The marshals were told to arm themselves and go to their hammocks below to await the call to action—a long roll on a drum. The *Michigan* again slowed. The marshals went to sleep.[10]

At 2:20 A.M. on Saturday, the Mormon Sabbath, the *Michigan* entered Paradise Bay and anchored off the beach. About ten minutes later, the ship's pilot rowed Bates ashore. The night was clear, and following specific instructions and a map penned by Greig, Bates proceeded to the house of Samuel Graham, Strang's top adviser. A light was glowing in an upper window of the hewn log dwelling.[11]

An oil lamp was burning by Graham's bedside. Graham was asleep, convalescing from a fractured skull and a broken arm he had suffered that month in a run-in with two Gentile fishermen. Graham had gone to Whiskey Point to talk with Sheriff Granger. Along the way Graham met the two fishermen, Richard O'Donnell and James Hoy. According to the Mormon version of the incident, Graham was walking past when one of the fishermen swung at him with a heavy cane; Graham blocked the blow with his arm, breaking it. Graham grabbed the man with his other arm, but the second fisherman took the cane and clubbed Graham's head, bringing him down. The fishermen then alternately beat him with the cane, crying: "Kill him, damn him!" Eventually the two fishermen were pulled away. Warrants were issued for the arrest of the pair, but the sheriff refused to act on them.[12]

Bates awakened Graham, whose arm was bandaged and who bore evidence of head wounds, and read him Greig's letter. Graham hesitated, but, after questioning Bates closely, he sent a messenger with the letter.[13]

A few days earlier, on May 19, Strang had been contemplating leaving his hiding place for Mackinac en route to the governor to discuss the "enormities which have been and still are practiced on us." In a letter to his wife, Mary, who was still on the island, Strang confided: "I don't feel at all well about going and had much rather have a fight & put my life in the scale, but I must take counsel. . . . I am no benefit here if I remain hid up & the counsel is against the issue of battle." Strang was worried about the Mormons on the island. He told Mary that he had intended to send his parents a barrel of fish, but changed his mind. "I am fearful that they [the fish] will be wanted here." He said Mary should keep the fish until she thought there was no danger of starvation.[14]

Several minutes after the messenger had left for him, Strang showed up at Graham's house and demanded to see the arrest warrant. Bates replied: "The papers are aboard, and if you will step aboard a few minutes, I will show them to you." Bates tried to persuade Strang that he could not avoid being arrested and could not escape from the deputies and Marines he had at his disposal. It would be best if he gave himself up promptly, Bates said. That may have been what Strang had in mind anyway.[15] Strang surrendered to Bates and, shortly before 3 : 30 A.M., climbed into the boat with Bates and the pilot. Before the sleeping deputies knew what had happened, Strang was on board the *Michigan*.[16]

On the warship Bates and Strang continued their discussion, joined by Knox, the U.S. marshal. Bates and Knox informed Strang that he and about thirty other Mormons were accused of trespass on federal land and other crimes. They told him that if the other Mormons would come on board to face a commissioner's inquiry, those who appeared to be not guilty would be discharged and the rest would be taken to Detroit to stand trial. Strang asked for a list of the accused and promised that they would allow themselves to be arrested. Bates eventually agreed to give Strang the names, against the advice of Knox, who said the list would warn those Mormons, who would run away. The list was sent ashore with a request from Strang for the men to come to the wharf. Within two hours, most of the thirty, and all of the men named who were on the island, had shown up.[17]

An awning was prepared on the deck of the *Michigan* for the commissioner's hearing. Then Peter McKinley, one of those who had filed complaints against Strang and the Mormons, said he would be unable to produce his witnesses for several days. The hearing was adjourned, and discussions began on what to do with the prisoners. Strang finally agreed to go with Bates to Detroit with three other Mormons if they were not jailed but only kept under surveillance until formally charged in court. Strang put up bail for four others. The rest were released, apparently pending further investigation.[18]

At 3 P.M. the *Michigan* weighed anchor and left Paradise Bay for Mackinac; it arrived there in four hours and twenty minutes—two hours less than it had taken the steamer to travel that distance under the slowdown.[19] Strang later said he believed himself to be the first "foreign potentate" on whom the United States "conferred the distinguished honor of bringing him into the country in a national vessel."[20] A day and a half later the *Michigan* docked at Detroit, then a city of 25,000 people. Strang and the three other Mormons were convoyed to the freshly scrubbed courthouse, where they were placed in the loose custody of a deputy marshal.[21]

On May 28 the case against Strang and the other Mormons went before a grand jury composed of men from the northern part of Michigan. In his charge to the jury, U.S. District Judge Ross Wilkins said Bates had informed him that Beaver Island had been "forcibly and unlawfully occupied by a lawless band, who have organized a government of their own, in opposition to the government of the state, and in open defiance of the laws of the United States. How far these misguided people have proceeded, or to what extent their conduct has reached, whether criminal or otherwise, is for you to inquire."[22]

George J. Adams, a key witness, testified on May 29. On June 2 the grand jury indicted Strang and two other Mormons on one count of counterfeiting—accusing them of minting bogus five-franc pieces (then legal tender in the United States) on June 1, 1850, and passing some to Adams on October 1. Strang was also indicted with nine other Mormons on twelve counts of trespass on federal lands, involving the cutting of timber on Beaver Island.[23]

On June 3 Strang was indicted with twenty-three other Mormons, some of whom also were accused in the other two indictments, on one count of obstructing passage of the U.S. mail. That day Strang and the other Mormons in Detroit were arrested and brought to court to be arraigned. All four pleaded not guilty. Strang gave bond of $3,000 and remained out of jail. The other three, being unable to put up bail, were jailed and would remain in custody for the next five weeks.[24]

The grand jury also weighed the evidence on a charge of treason but did not issue any indictments.[25] Judge Wilkins had pointed out that under the U.S. Constitution, treason "can only consist in the actual levy of war by arms or in adhering to the enemies of the government in time of war or rebellion."[26] No matter how questionable the actions of the Mormons were in relation to the government, the charge of treason did not seem to apply.

In its account of the case, the *Northern Islander* said the Mormons were accused of every crime from treason to "building a camp fire on a naked beach, with sticks of dry wood which grew on Congress land," the latter remark intending to belittle the federal charges of trespass on public land to cut timber.[27] The Mormons had been industriously cutting wood on the island since they had arrived. Since the Mormons never did buy much land on the island, it is clear that a substantial portion of the timber they cut was on federal land.

The *Detroit Tribune*, in December 1850, was among the first to publicly accuse the Mormons of any wrongdoing in the cutting of trees on the island. The *Tribune* charged that the Mormons were encouraged to "pillage government timber," to which the *Northern Islander* responded with a question: had the *Tribune* ever raised a similar point with its wealthy neighbors? "We believe other men are not called pilferers for cutting timber on government land, without permission."[28] Since 1831 it had been a felony to cut and remove timber from public lands without permission. Enforcement of the law, however, varied according to the section of the country and the size of the offense.[29] The grand jury indictment on charges of trespass on public lands specifically accused the Mormons of cutting 1,000 trees with a value of $1,000 and carrying away 5,000 logs, also with a value of $1,000, in each of twelve sections of Peaine Township.[30]

The Mormons claimed they could cut the timber because they were improving the land and intended to purchase it, though Strang seemed to discourage such intentions. The *Northern Islander* rationalized the cutting of timber by saying the preemption laws allowed such action.[31] What was not said was that the Pre-emption Act did not pertain to land settled after it was offered for sale. Once land was offered for sale, timber could only be legally cut by a settler who bought the land.

The government had been pressing this point, and its deputy marshals, including Peter McKinley, seized logs, timber, shingles, and staves. The *Northern Islander* called the marshals land pirates and said they even seized three pieces of loose plank on Johnson and McCulloch's pier. "Wherever you go through the woods and find a dozen staves remaining of a culled pile, look close and you will find 'U.S.' marked on the top one." In fact, the *Northern Islander* accused McKinley of going from cooper shop to cooper shop to seize staves and then employing all the workers he could find to make barrels of the staves in his own shop. "Wonder if the gallant Secretary of the Navy could not be induced to send the War Steamer Michigan up here to gather staves and hoop poles for Mr. Deputy McKinley's shop," the *Islander* asked. The paper said the seizures also frightened some poor Mormons out of their property: a Mormon "will not dare roll up his house body, after the U.S. Marshal has seized the logs, and then as winter comes on there will be a better prospect of driving off the Mormons."[32]

The seizures of timber-related products were a minor annoyance compared with federal prosecution. And while the seizures and the prosecution were part of the Mormon-Gentile conflict, the upcoming trial also could be viewed as a struggle between Whigs and Democrats. On the one side were Strang and his followers, who had almost unanimously backed the Democratic candidates in the last election. On the other was the federal government, led by the Whigs, from Fillmore to Bates. Bates himself later said that because the state government was being run by the Democrats, and the Mackinac County government was under the influence of the Mormons, it was left to the federal government to step in. Bates believed that state authorities were not vigorous in their efforts to bring Strang and his followers to trial because they felt the Mormon vote helped to keep them in power.[33]

For Bates, the trial was an opportunity to prove his abilities to the Fillmore administration, which was in the process of dispensing appointments in the new state of California. A number of Detroiters, including the president's brother, C. D. Fillmore, had recommended Bates for such California offices as judge and solicitor. Bates had been appointed U.S. attorney for Michigan by President William Henry Harrison, a Whig, in 1841. Bates held the job for four years, then was asked to resign when the Democrats took over the White House in 1845. When Whigs regained the White House with Zachary Taylor in 1849, Bates regained his job. A witty man, Bates was considered the equal of any in giving a political speech. With his bright blue eyes, light auburn hair, and captivating manner, he also was described as a favorite with the ladies.[34]

Judge Ross Wilkins was an active Democrat, who had been appointed to the Michigan Territorial Supreme Court by his friend, Andrew Jackson, in 1832. He was named a U.S. district judge in 1836, when Michigan was about to become a state. Widely respected for his intellect and lucid rulings, Wilkins also was credited with an overriding sense of fair play.[35]

Because of these political overtones, it was not surprising that Strang hired a lawyer who was a Democrat—"Colonel" Andrew T. McReynolds, one of the most popular men in Detroit. His main claim to fame was that he had been decorated for bravery as an officer in the Mexican War four years before. McReynolds had played a role in the organization of several state militia units and had risen to the rank of colonel in one. A former Whig, he had been elected to a term in the state Senate as a Democrat in 1846.[36]

The Detroit newspapers left little doubt about their sentiments. The *Detroit Free Press*, which represented the interests of the Democratic party, pooh-poohed the charges: it said the hue and cry against the Mormons was all moonshine. "Violations of the law may have taken place among them, and it would be strange, indeed, if they did not now and then occur in a community numbering some seven hundred souls." The paper said Strang would be taken at first sight "for one of those genuine American sovereigns, who till our soil and fell our forests, rather than the reigning king of a community in open rebellion against a government so powerful as the United States."[37]

The *Daily Advertiser*, a Whig paper, obliquely accused the *Free Press* of befogging and misrepresenting the charges against Strang and the Mormons. The *Advertiser* on June 6 printed the "original complaint" made against the Mormons—an April 9th letter from

Eri J. Moore to President Fillmore. It also published in that same issue an affidavit filed by George J. Adams, detailing some of the more salacious features of the kingdom, in particular the coronation and the oath of the Order of Illuminati. Adams said that Strang, after his coronation, ordered that his flag be raised "in defiance of the Stars and Stripes and all other flags of the world." Adams downplayed his own role, saying that Strang had crowned himself, instead of admitting that he had placed the crown on Strang's head. Adams also said he had often heard Strang teach that it was morally right to steal from Gentiles, burn their houses, and even take their lives—if it could be done without being discovered. Strang's former prime minister further swore that he had heard Strang say that Peter McKinley's barrel staves, of which there were about 50,000, should be burned, and that a few days later they were.[38]

Moore's letter stated—or overstated—the case against the Mormons even more strongly than Adams. Strang, Moore wrote, "organized several bands of his people to go out through the nation to burn cities and villages, to steal and plunder everything they can lay their lands on." Moore said the Mormons especially sought to rob as many guns and as much ammunition as they could. "They are all armed to the teeth with revolvers and Bowie knives, and with orders from said Strang to kill and slay every person that may come in their way."[39]

Moore's letter, although it gave an overly brutal impression of the Mormons' intentions, may have been an accurate representation of the rhetoric he had heard on the island. The Book of the Law contained similar statements, and three years later, a patriarchal blessing included the words: "Thou art destined for the Army of the Lord. And with the torch shalt thou light up the firmament. And on this continent shalt thou wield the sword. Thou shalt lay waste cities, towns and villages. Thou shalt go forth and tread down the wicked. Yea, thou shalt go even to foreign lands: And there shalt thou wield the two-edged sword with the vengeance of a destroying angel. And thou and thy brethren shalt dash in pieces the kingdoms of this world and rule them with a rod of iron. And thou shalt consecrate their dominion to the Lord of the whole earth."[40]

By printing these charges, without comments from the Mormons, the *Advertiser* was criticized by other Michigan newspapers.

Several accused it of attempting to sway public opinion against the Mormons and of thus making it more difficult to pick an impartial jury. Lansing's *Michigan State Journal*, for example, asserted that the *Advertiser* gave a "one-sided and bitterly prejudiced version" of the case and had convicted the Mormon defendants before their day in court, "a step grossly abusing the license of the press."[41] The reports in the *Advertiser* were such perversions of the truth, Strang said, that the paper would receive a severe condemnation from Judge Wilkins.[42]

In briefs filed in the case, Strang said he would prove that Adams was a notorious liar who had brought numerous malicious prosecutions against the Mormons and that Adams, his wife, Louisa, and Moore had perjured themselves. Strang accused Moore of claiming ownership of a new pier that had been built the previous winter by Johnson and McCulloch on a lot they had bought from Moore. Moore, Strang said, intended to take possession of the pier in a few weeks, thus giving an economic motive for his allegations against the Mormons.[43] The vindictive Adams, meanwhile, was giving lectures on the abuses of Mormonism in the Young Men's Hall in Detroit, an event that a sympathizer of Strang said was intended to fan the flames of religious and political prejudice.[44]

The trial was scheduled to begin on June 23. Strang was convinced that the public expected the Mormons to be convicted. In this atmosphere, on June 11, Peter McKinley arrived in Detroit from Beaver Island aboard the propeller *Pocahontas* with thunderous news: Thomas Bennett had been shot and killed on the island by a group of Mormons.[45]

That same day Bates dashed off a telegraphic message to President Fillmore: "Mr. Bennett has been murdered by the Mormons on Beaver Island. His Brother badly wounded. The Marshall has warrants to serve there on some twenty-five. The Steamer Michigan should be sent here forthwith. Great excitement on the Island and [deputy] Postmaster [McKinley is] here."[46] Bates followed the telegraphic dispatch with a letter the next day. "The truth is sir," Bates wrote, "that nothing but the interference of the Federal Government can put an end to the lawless violence which exists on that island. Our People are grateful to you for what has been done and they look to the exercise of the authority vested in the executive as the only means of arresting the course of these deluded people." Bates enclosed an affidavit from McKinley.[47]

McKinley had not seen the shootings, which occurred four days before he arrived in Detroit, but had seen the body of Thomas Bennett and the wound that shattered the right hand of his brother, Samuel. McKinley listed twelve Mormons who were reported to have been at the scene of the shooting—all were among those indicted by the grand jury. In the affidavit McKinley said that the non-Mormons on Beaver Island "have no protection from the laws of the state and that they are now compelled to ask, and do ask, the protection of the Federal Government." Without such protection, they and their property are at "the mercy of these lawless persons called Mormons."[48]

Fillmore, although willing to give Bates all the assistance he needed to arrest the Mormons for violations of federal laws, was not about to be stampeded into exceeding his authority. The president pointed out that he could "do nothing to arrest murderers of Bennett" because that was a violation of state and not federal law, but he did order the *Michigan* to assist Bates again in his case against Strang and the Mormons.[49] The *Michigan* would be needed to transport the remaining two dozen Mormons charged in the federal case from Beaver Island to Detroit, along with a large number of witnesses. Bates had requested the *Michigan* for this purpose "as a matter of economy." To charter a boat to do the job, he said, would probably cost the government $5,000.[50]

On June 12, the *Detroit Advertiser* published an inflammatory article based on details supplied by McKinley. Under the bold headline: "FURTHER OUTRAGES AT BEAVER ISLAND! BRUTAL AND DELIBERATE MURDER BY THE FOLLOWERS OF STRANG!!" the Advertiser stated that "the miscreants who have gathered themselves together on Beaver Island, under the title of Mormons, are making rapid and sure progress in the degrees of crime which lead from adultery, theft, arson, robbery to deliberate murder." Bennett, the paper said, had been forced to flee his brother's home, but that only a few rods away "he fell dead, pierced by five rifle balls and 40 buck shot!!" Referring to the "murder" of

Bennett, the *Advertiser* said: "We hope to see . . . the indictment of the miscreant Strang as an accessory before the fact. . . . It seems to us about time this gang of wolves was broken up."[51]

That same day, an apprehensive Strang wrote Governor John S. Barry to beg state protection for the "little settlement of Mormons, on Beaver Island, if indeed there is now any portion of it remaining." Strang feared that the settlement had already been annihilated, or would be before help could arrive. "You will forgive my anxiety," he wrote from Detroit, "I left a wife and children there. I do not expect to see either this side of the grave." Strang asked the governor to issue an order that the law should be obeyed and that the officers of the state should be respected, "without regard to religious denomination. . . . And do not fail . . . to show to the most obtuse, that the state holds a man an officer who is duly elected and lawfully qualified even though a Mormon." By that time rumors had reached Detroit that Bennett had been slain when he resisted arrest on a warrant issued by William N. MacLeod, the prosecuting attorney of Mackinac County. "For a long time," Strang said, "a set of lawless renegades . . . have defied the administration of the law there. . . . The law of the state is familiarly treated by these outlaws as 'Mormon Law,' and the civil Magistrates as 'Mormon Officers,' and resistance to the law is familiarly spoken of as a virtue."[52]

Two days later Strang's position was buttressed in Detroit with the assistance of the *Free Press* and Strang's allies in Mackinac, especially MacLeod and John D. Irvine, the state representative. They produced letters and documents that stated Bennett was killed after a posse had sought to arrest him for resisting an officer and after the Bennetts had fired at the posse, wounding a constable in the head. After an inquest, a coroner's jury reported that Bennett had been killed by a shot fired in an attempt to execute a warrant. The *Free Press* was not about to let the new information speak for itself. The paper leveled a blast aimed primarily at its rival, the *Advertiser*. "We would not defend the Mormons," the *Free Press* said. "We believe them a deluded and misguided people. But we are not prepared on that account, to invoke upon their heads the vengeance of laws they have not broken; nor to accuse them, because they differ from us in religious belief, of crimes so appalling as those with which they now stand charged. Let the legal tribunals search out the truth and visit upon the guilty the full measure of legal retribution. It should also be remembered that the Mormons are comparatively defenceless," the *Free Press* continued. "They have arrayed against them the prejudices of the entire community, and the popular ear is open to every tale of their transgressions. The press should stand between them and popular prejudice—not fan and inflame it."[53]

This advice did not deter the *Advertiser*. On June 16 it published incendiary statements about the autopsy conducted during the inquest on Bennett: "having been stripped, the body was cut in pieces . . . the heart was taken out, perforated by the bullet which did the deed, into which one of the gang thrust his finger, and holding it aloft, and twirling it around, called upon all to look upon the end of an enemy! Blood was then scooped from the cavity of the chest from where the heart was taken, and by the same hand was daubed in bitter derision upon the face of the corpse!"[54] Such reports were guaranteed to fan and inflame the popular prejudice.

The day the *Advertiser* printed those heart-twirling words, the *Michigan* arrived in Detroit. On June 17 the warship left for the north, carrying Bates, the deputy U.S. marshal and several of his assistants, the U.S. commissioner, and James J. Strang, along with his attorney, Colonel McReynolds. They were headed for Beaver Island to take depositions in the federal case against the Mormons.[55]

Early in the afternoon of June 18 the *Michigan* docked at Mackinac in a light rain and picked up more passengers, including H. D. MacCulloch and Samuel Graham. They had been in jail, having been arrested in the killing of Bennett. During the five-hour trip to Beaver, MacCulloch and Graham probably filled Strang in on what had happened on the island since he had left with Bates more than two weeks before. The one big event, of course, was what Strang had heard described as the cold-blooded murder of Bennett. Samuel Bennett already had given his version of the shooting in a Mackinac courtroom before Charles M. O'Malley.[56] The Mormon version was markedly different.

Relations between the Mormons and the Bennetts had always been difficult, but in the six months before Strang's arrest they had become inflamed. After the burning of the Bennetts' two vacant farmhouses, the two fishermen were accused of assaulting a "damned

Mormon" and threatening to kill him. When a Mormon constable tried to arrest them, they fought him off and escaped. The Bennetts later gave themselves up and pleaded guilty to the charge, according to the *Northern Islander*. They were fined $10 each by a Mormon justice of the peace.[57]

Samuel Bennett said Strang had told them that even though they were non-Mormons they would have to comply with the laws of the kingdom and pay tithes. (Even the *Northern Islander* said the law of tithing applied to the stranger dwelling among the Mormons as well as to the Mormons.)[58] Thomas Bennett told Strang they would not pay anything except what they were required to pay under the laws of the country. To which Strang was said to have responded: "Well, Bennett, if you do not pay the tithe, mark my words, that you will be sorry."[59]

The shooting of the Bennetts was the culmination of the incident in which Samuel Graham suffered a broken arm and a fractured skull. Warrants had been issued for the arrest of Richard O'Donnell and James Hoy, the two fishermen accused of beating Graham. But Sheriff Henry Granger had refused to execute the warrants.[60] Reports varied as to why.

The first warrant had been issued by Mackinac County Judge James M. Greig. The *Northern Islander* reported that Granger refused to execute that warrant because it did not have the county seal, even though the *Islander* said such warrants never had them. Another report claimed that Granger said the warrant should have been issued by a justice of the peace. A justice of the peace, Marvin M. Aldrich, issued the second warrant. Granger refused to act this time because, the *Islander* said, Aldrich was a Mormon and the complainant, Graham, also was a Mormon. Another report said Granger refused because he recognized no civil authority on Beaver Island.[61]

The Mormons then asked the county prosecuting attorney, William N. MacLeod, a friend of Greig's, to have O'Donnell and Hoy arrested by constables from Mackinac and taken there for trial. MacLeod instead came to Beaver Island, to vindicate the integrity of the law on the spot, as the *Islander* put it.[62]

Acting on MacLeod's advice, Aldrich issued another warrant, charging O'Donnell and Hoy with assault and battery and intent to kill. A Mormon constable, William Chambers, accompanied by three men, all unarmed, went to the Cable's Bay area to arrest the pair. As they neared Samuel Bennett's house, the Bennetts—with guns in their hands—stopped the constable and his men and forced them to retreat. The Bennetts told Chambers that the fishermen had agreed that none of them would be arrested by a Mormon officer. About sixty fishermen, they said, would rally at the signal of three gunshots and kill any man who attempted to arrest any of them.[63] Samuel Bennett later said that they had not offered any resistance to the constable, but even he admitted that they had told Chambers it was no use for him to try to execute "Mormon laws" there.[64]

Chambers reported back to Aldrich, who issued a warrant for the arrest of the Bennetts on a charge of resisting an officer. Armed with the warrant, Chambers tried to form a posse but found the men reluctant to go. He went to MacLeod, who told him to try again and to put down the name of every man who refused to join the posse and he would prosecute them. This time Chambers met with success. He gathered a posse of thirty to forty men (Samuel Bennett said sixty) armed with muskets, rifles, and pistols. Three days after the first incident with the Bennetts, Chambers and his posse again traveled to the Cable's Bay area.[65] Since the death of his wife and children in a storm on the lake, Thomas Bennett had been living with his brother near the Gentile fishing settlement there.[66]

Leaving most of the posse slightly behind, Chambers approached Samuel Bennett's house. The Bennetts, who saw him coming, shut the door. The constable spoke to them through a window, telling them he had a warrant for their arrest and urging them to give up peaceably. Samuel Bennett said they were told that if they did not surrender, they would be taken dead or alive. Once again the Bennetts were tenacious about what they perceived to be their rights and unyielding to what they saw as high-handed measures by the Mormons. They responded with oaths and threats. They said they would not obey Mormon law, King Strang's law, or any other law but the law of the country.[67]

It is unclear exactly what happened next.

The Mormons say Chambers went back to his posse and, followed by the other Mormons, approached the house again. As he came within range, three shots were fired from the house, the third wounding Chambers in the head, bringing him down. The posse returned the fire, aiming through the window and the door. Samuel Bennett said he and his brother managed to keep out of the way of the balls until the Mormons broke in the door. Then a fusillade soon ended all resistance.[68] In the stillness, Thomas Bennett lay dead, hit by several rifle or musket balls and riddled by a charge of shot. Samuel was hit by one ball, which shattered his right hand.[69]

Three days later, in court, Samuel Bennett said the Bennetts had fired only one shot—by accident—and that it could not have hit anyone. He said that after the posse talked to them, he had picked up his double-barreled shotgun, and his young wife, Julia, "who was very much alarmed and excited," grabbed the gun in an attempt to take it away from him and the gun discharged. After it went off, the Mormons began firing and trying to break in. Bennett also accused the Mormons of coming in, dragging his brother outside, and then firing at him. "During the time they fired at him, he raised his hands and implored them in the name of Almighty God to spare his life."[70] However, McKinley, in his affidavit, swore that he was informed and believed that both were shot in the house. The Mormon version at least had a consistency that the Gentile versions lacked.

Meanwhile, Hoy, one of the original targets for arrest, escaped into the woods. O'Donnell tried to escape by sea. He put out in a boat, pursued by part of the posse in another. As the posse's boat gained on his, O'Donnell produced a rifle and threatened to shoot if the posse came any closer. Three rifles drew a bead on O'Donnell from the second boat, which continued to close until a man in the bow grabbed O'Donnell's gun by the barrel and O'Donnell surrendered. The rest of the fishermen never showed up in response to the gunfire.[71]

Thomas Bennett's body was dragged (by the hair of his head, McKinley said) to the beach and placed in his own boat. Samuel Bennett and his wife were compelled to get in, too, and the Mormons put up the sail and headed for the harbor.[72]

A coroner's inquest was held at Troy, under the direction of Aldrich, who asked H. D. MacCulloch, the only physician on the island, to conduct a postmortem examination. Rather than wantonly cutting Bennett's body, twirling the heart, and daubing blood on the victim's face, as reported in the *Detroit Advertiser*, MacCulloch said the examination was conducted with decorum and propriety, "in the most public manner." MacCulloch's version of propriety could easily have been misinterpreted, however. He said he found three bullet wounds—in the shoulder, the neck, and the chest. The first two were deemed not fatal. MacCulloch said that "upon the examination of the wound in the chest it became necessary to open the body to determine its nature and extent. Upon cutting back and laying back the sternum, or breast bone, the cavity of the chest was found filled with blood, giving immediate evidence of the penetration of the heart, and that organ was raised from its ordinary appendages to exhibit to the jury the passage of the bullet through its structure." MacLeod, one of the twelve members of the coroner's jury, assisted in the examination because he had formerly been in the medical profession, MacCulloch said. MacLeod "passed his hand into the chest for the purpose of ascertaining where the ball lay; he was not successful, and the necessary incisions were closed with care."[73]

The *Detroit Advertiser* said MacCulloch had admitted that he was a member of the posse, and the paper found it curious that a member of the posse that shot Bennett would perform the postmortem. The jury was composed of six Mormons and six Gentiles, including MacLeod, the prosecuting attorney who was doing double duty as a juror. MacCulloch said all of the jurors agreed that Bennett was killed while resisting a constable carrying a valid warrant. Three of the Gentiles refused to sign that verdict, solely on ground that the constable was not an American citizen, MacCulloch said. McKinley said the three Gentiles felt the shooting was premeditated murder.[74]

Bennett was buried without ceremony in a plain coffin near the lakefront. His grave was covered with a pile of stones as a warning to other Gentiles. Nothing was said about any further action against Samuel Bennett on the warrant for his arrest. According to the *Advertiser*, there was a "fearful excitement" among the Indians and Gentiles of that area over the shooting. But they were restrained by McKinley, Moore, and others, who persuaded them to await the execution of the state law in the matter.[75]

Samuel Bennett filed complaints against many of the Mormons, accusing them of murder. In the meantime, MacCulloch and Graham had gone to Mackinac and were arrested and jailed. About twenty others were arrested on Beaver Island in the Bennett case. On the arrival of the *Michigan* in Mackinac, however, MacCulloch and Graham, along with a half-dozen other Mormons, were apparently released into the custody of the federal officials and returned to Beaver Island to give depositions for the federal trial. The other fourteen were kept in jail in Mackinac, where they would remain in custody for eleven weeks before being discharged after a grand jury refused to indict them.[76]

The *Michigan* arrived at Beaver Island on the evening of June 18, with its cargo of federal officials, witnesses, and the Mormon king and his lawyer. Both sides in the case had agreed to take depositions there from witnesses and that these depositions would be filed in open court during the trial. To oversee the process, William D. Wilkins, the newly appointed clerk of the U.S. District Court in Detroit and son of Judge Wilkins, had gone along to serve as U.S. commissioner.[77]

The depositions were taken over two days, in the *Northern Islander* office. About fifty witnesses appeared, mostly on the side of the Mormon defendants.[78]

Only one person gave testimony to support the allegation that Strang and two other Mormons had counterfeited coin of the United States. The man, a former Mormon named Daniel S. Wheelock, said Strang asked him to pass counterfeit money on October 9, 1850, the morning after a George Adams theatrical production, *Pizarro*, in the tabernacle. Strang's wife, Mary, who suddenly had been taken ill, had remained there overnight, and the next morning, Wheelock returned to the tabernacle to get an umbrella and saw Strang there.[79] "He wanted men to go off on a consecrating expedition and a-passing counterfeit money," Wheelock said in his deposition. "Showed me three half dollars, and said he would make more as soon as he could get materials. They were American half dollars. Only had one in my hand. He told me they were bad." Wheelock said Strang never said anything in his presence about counterfeiting at any other time, and he said that he had never seen tools for manufacturing counterfeit coins in Strang's possession.[80]

Several Mormons testified that they had been at the tabernacle that morning but had heard no conversation between Wheelock and Strang. They said Strang was busy attending to his wife and that everyone was told to be silent.[81]

Three weeks earlier one young man had told federal officials that the Mormons were carrying on extensive counterfeiting operations in a cave they had dug in Mount Pisgah, on the western side of the island. The youth claimed he had been asked to join the operation and had seen the counterfeiting taking place in the cave. But when the youth was asked to point out the location of the cave in a legal proceeding, he admitted that his tale was false and burst into tears. Strang said it appeared as if Adams had persuaded the youth to tell the tale.[82]

Some persons still concluded that the Mormons had something to hide at Mount Pisgah, and they went there. But a thorough search yielded nothing. They decided the counterfeiting cavern must be somewhere else. Strang said the idea that it was nowhere did not occur to them.[83]

In the deposition-taking, Bates concentrated much of his time on issues that, while substantial, did not appear to relate to the three charges against the Mormons: counterfeiting, obstruction of the mails, and trespass on federal lands. One of his prime topics was the covenant; McReynolds wondered what these questions had to do with counterfeiting. Bates asked many of the Mormon witnesses if they had taken an oath in which they renounced allegiance to all laws, powers, potentates, presidents, or governors except the laws of Strang or those of the Mormon church. Some said they had not; others said they had, but added that they could recollect nothing that bound them to support their Mormon brethren against the Gentiles or to give testimony backing their brethren.[84]

MacCulloch's memory was fuzzy when Bates asked him about the covenant. He admitted he had taken it and said Adams had administered it to him. But MacCulloch did not remember the covenant as Bates described it and could not recall the language, saying he had never read it.[85]

Reuben Field, Elvira's father, said he had taken the covenant. "There is nothing in the covenant as I consider it requiring me to violate any law of the United States or of Michigan." He admitted that Bates's summary of the covenant was substantially correct, but maintained that the language related to church affairs only.[86]

Bates contended that the Mormon witnesses would swear to anything for Strang and that the only way to impeach their testimony was through making them testify to their belief in the prophetic power of Strang. After MacCulloch's wife, Sarah, was examined by McReynolds for her deposition, Bates pulled a chair near her and sat down. What follows is Bates's perhaps fanciful description of his cross-examination.[87]

"Mrs. MacCulloch, you are an educated, accomplished lady, born in Baltimore, and reared in the very best society. Can it be that you are a Mormon?"

"Yes, sir, I have that honor, sir," she said, her eyes flashing.

"Can it be possible, madam, that so accomplished a lady as you are can believe that that fellow Strang (pointing contemptuously at him) is a prophet, seer and revelator?"

"Yes, Mr. District Attorney, I know it."

"Perhaps we do not comprehend each other, madam. What do you mean by a prophet?"

"You know well enough, Mr. District Attorney. I mean one who foretells coming events, speaks in unknown tongues, one like Isaiah and the prophets of the Old Testament."

"Ah, madam, how do you know that Strang speaks in unknown tongues and foretells coming events?"

"Because I have heard him—and witnessed those events thus foretold."

"Can it be possible, Mrs. MacCulloch, that you are so blind as to really believe that that fellow who sits there beneath you—that Strang, is the prophet of the Lord, the successor of him who bore his cross among the jeers and sneers of of Mount Calvary?"

Mrs. MacCulloch rose in anger and shook her fist in Bates's face. "Yes, you impudent district attorney, and were you not such a darned old fool, you would know it, too!" The Mormons cheered, and the federal officials and the rest of the crowd laughed.

At 4 A.M. on Saturday, June 21, the *Michigan* left Beaver Island for Detroit, carrying all of those it had brought up, plus a half-dozen other Mormon defendants and thirteen witnesses for the defense and the prosecution. The warship arrived in Detroit late on Sunday.[88]

The groundwork for the trial began Monday in the courtroom in the Government Building at the southwest corner of Griswold Street and Jefferson Avenue. Jefferson was the finest street in the city, with brick and stone sidewalks, and the Government Building, originally a bank, was the city's first structure of dressed stone. Bates and the U.S. marshal had their offices there.[89]

The selection of the jury had been completed on Thursday when Strang made a motion for a separate trial. Judge Wilkins rejected his motion, and the jury of ten Whigs and two Democrats was sworn in.[90]

Wilkins exercised his usual firm control over the proceedings—even if he was not always literally on the bench. A handsome and graceful man with features compared to Byron and Poe, Wilkins was a restless judge, frequently moving in his chair as he studied papers and other evidence. Often he would stand up, and while still paying strict attention to the proceedings, go to the back of the courtroom and fill and light his immense pipe. He would smoke as he walked around, letting the two sides argue the case.[91]

Bates had spared little expense in the case. The *Northern Islander* claimed the prosecution cost the government $30,000, enough to buy most of Beaver Island. This estimate may have been high, but the expenses related to the trial were huge for that time. The known fees charged by the court clerk and the marshals alone approached $1,000, and this was only the beginning.[92] Added to this would have to be the time and expenses of the attorney's office, the judge and jury, and the value of the Navy's services for furnishing the *Michigan* and her crew.

Likewise, Strang said, the prosecution took a heavy toll on the Mormons in time, property, and money, more than $15,000 worth. The property of the Mormons on Beaver Island and their existence as a settlement, he said, were in imminent jeopardy, with some families in danger of starvation. Strang said that in alleviating the needs of the poor, he had expended all his available means and was unable to provide bread for his family from day to day.[93]

When the trial began in a courtroom crowded with spectators, it became clear that Bates was pinning the prosecution's hopes on the charge of obstructing the U.S. mail and assaulting the carrier with dangerous weapons. Bates said he thought the evidence was quite clear against the Mormons on that indictment.[94] For the first two days Bates read into evidence the depositions of several prosecution witnesses, including Peter McKinley, Richard O'Donnell, Peaine, and two mail carriers, John B. Dorry and Augustus Gould, also called LeBlanc. With one key exception, the prosecution witnesses told essentially the same story.[95]

In mid-February 1851 McKinley, the deputy postmaster on Beaver Island, had given the mail to LeBlanc for carrying to Mackinac. LeBlanc put the mail in a canvas bag and left Beaver Island in a dog sled with Dorry. (During the winter in the upper region of Michigan, mail was delivered about once a month by dog sled.)[96] LeBlanc and Dorry stopped for the night at Garden Island, where they met Eri J. Moore and his wife, who wanted to travel with them to Mackinac to spend the rest of the winter.[97]

The next morning, with Moore walking and his wife riding in the sled with the mail, LeBlanc and Dorry took the portage over Garden Island and headed across the ice for Hog Island, the first reference point on their snowy route to Mackinac. A short while later three men ran toward them on the ice. Since those with the dog sled did not know who the men were—and thought they might be Mormons in pursuit—LeBlanc whipped the four dogs, and they hurried on. One of the pursuers called Dorry's name, but still the dog sled continued. The three men had been sent by McKinley, who said he had asked them to warn the carriers that some men intended to rob the mail. Being outdistanced by the dog sled, the three men—Richard O'Donnell, Jacob Mathes, and Henry Larraway—came upon Indians spearing fish near Hog Island and sent them after the sled. Two or three miles after the pursuers were first spotted, two Indians closed the gap with the dog sled, called out, and swung their hats. The sled stopped near Hog Island.[98]

"We heard [the Mormons] were going to take Mr. Moore and take the mail away from us," Dorry said. Inexplicably, they then turned back toward Garden Island, where they would be closer to the Mormons, and on the way met several other Indians and O'Donnell, Mathes, and Larraway. The latter trio and the Indians trailed the faster dog sled toward Garden Island.[99]

As they approached Garden Island, those with the sled said they saw a dozen men come out of an Indian village. That group spotted the dog sled, stopped for a moment, then began heading to intercept it. This caused apprehension at the sled; Moore was frightened, correctly fearing that the men were Mormons. "We told Moore he had better run back" toward O'Donnell's group and the Indians trailing them, Dorry said. LeBlanc gave Moore a pistol, and Moore ran off, retracing their tracks in the snow.[100]

The Mormons saw Moore break away from the party, and Dorry heard them say plainly, "There he is, there he is." About half of the Mormons started running after Moore, the rest apparently continuing toward the sled and LeBlanc, Dorry, and Moore's wife. Dorry said he heard one of them say, "They must have the mail there."[101]

The dog sled party was outdistancing the Mormons over the remaining quarter mile to the village when a number of Indian men and boys ran out on the ice, Peaine among them. Peaine saw the chase, put his hand to his mouth, and gave a whoop. The Mormons stopped, looked around, and gathered in a cluster. At about the same time, two guns went off in the bush near the portage where Moore was headed. The Mormons who had closed to within a quarter mile of him also stopped, then walked back to where the rest of the Mormons were being approached by Peaine. One Mormon went out to meet the Chippewa chief and sought to shake hands with him, but Peaine refused.[102]

Peaine said he and the Mormon spoke to each other but neither understood the other's language. Peaine said he asked: "What brings you here, why don't you go home and mind your business?" After a few moments, the entire Mormon party headed back across the ice for Beaver Island. The mail, by this time, had been hidden in one of the Indian houses by a squaw, at the request of LeBlanc.[103]

On key points, some testimony from the Gentiles aided the Mormon defendants. One of the men McKinley sent to protect the mail testified that the dog sled carrying the mail was forced to turn back because the ice was broken up beyond Hog Island. The mail, Jacob Mathes said, "could go no further."[104] On the accusation that the Mormons had carried dangerous weapons, Dorry said he saw the handle of a knife among the Mormon party but no guns. If this was the case, the Gentiles had more guns than the Mormons did. Le-Blanc said there were two pistols in the dog sled, including the one he gave Moore. Mathes said Larraway also was carrying a pistol but that he did not know whether Larraway had fired it. Peaine said the shots that were heard from the bush had been fired by Indian boys who were hunting.[105]

After the reading of the depositions by the prosecution on Friday, Micajah Drown testified that he had heard Strang and other Mormons say they intended to control the mail to "stop the damned Pseudoes from writing to the public what occurred on the island."[106] Strang had often said he wanted the post office moved from Whiskey Point to the Mormon side of the harbor to make it more accessible to the bulk of the island population and because the Gentiles on Whiskey Point abused Mormons seeking their mail.[107]

On Saturday, June 28, George Adams took the stand. He remained there all day. After telling about his background in the church, Adams testified to threats by Strang involving the mail. The previous fall, Adams said, Strang told him a number of things he intended to do on the island that winter. Adams said he argued against the plans and told Strang the people would write letters about them. According to Adams, Strang said the mail would not leave Beaver Island after winter closed in, that he would prevent it.[108]

"I asked Strang how he would detain the mails. He said he had good faithful brethren of the kingdom, that had bound themselves by the covenant of the kingdom to do anything he said." Several of the Mormons, Adams testified, had said they would take the mail if Strang told them to do so. Adams said that he asked Strang what he would do if the mail carrier resisted and that Strang replied that it would be "very easy to cut a hole in the ice, and a bag with a stone [and] a man in it would soon find their way to the bottom, and dead men told no tales."[109]

"I told him when spring came these things would find their way to Mackinac, and elsewhere, and bring ruin upon him and the people. He said he had plenty of good covenant brethren who would swear to anything he instructed them to—he also said they would think it no wrong." Adams also testified that Strang had made comments about the mail in a meeting of his privy council, saying he "would have control of the mail, and that communications should not leave there unless he knew what they were, and from where they went."

Adams's cross-examination began in the morning and continued throughout the afternoon. It did not appear to alter his testimony, but it did seem to impugn his motivation. Time after time, Adams denied specific accusations involving threats that persons, not all of them Mormons, said they had heard him make against Strang and the kingdom.

Question: Did you while in Mackinac last winter, say in the presence of surgeon Theodore Gregg, while you were theatrically connected with him, that you would have revenge on Mr. Strang? Adams replied that he had no recollection of saying anything of the kind. He also denied that he had said he would produce another Nauvoo breakup in connection with the Mormons on Beaver Island because of the excommunication of his wife. He denied that he had said in the fall that he would raise a mob and have the Mormons driven off the island by spring and that he would wash his hands in Strang's heart's blood and that he would lead the people.

Did you say in the Mormon tabernacle that Strang was the best man, the most just man, the most righteous man that you ever knew or ever lived on earth? Answer: "Never said anything of the kind, may have said something similar to some of the expressions in sarcasm."

McReynolds also questioned Adams about threats he allegedly made against the Gentiles on Whiskey Point. Question: At a meeting in the tabernacle in May 1850, did you say that you would burn McKinley's house because of the treatment the Mormons had received at the hands of the Gentiles on the Point, especially at the post office? Answer: Never said anything of the kind.

Adams said that some Mormons had told him the burning of McKinley's house had been decreed by Strang and that one Mormon, Phineas Wright, wanted him to try to talk Strang out of it. "If these things go on, it will destroy us all," Adams quoted Wright as saying. Wright, however, accused Adams of saying he was going to the Point under the guise of making friends and preaching, and after gaining the confidence of the Gentiles, he would make the Point a smoking ruin. According to MacCulloch, Adams said he would whip any man who would not go along and that he even had picked out a spot to apply the match, some wood shavings near a cooper shop.

The final witness for the prosecution was Eri J. Moore, whose accusations were in large part responsible for the indictment of the Mormons on charges of obstructing the mail and assaulting the carrier with dangerous weapons. In a March 8 letter to the governor and in his April 9 letter to President Fillmore asking for state and federal action, Moore had written about Mormon conduct that could be considered obstruction of the mail.[110]

Moore had written the president that in February, while on Garden Island, he and his wife decided to return to Mackinac with the mail carrier, LeBlanc. "After starting and going some six or eight miles, we were overtaken by two Indians, who were sent post haste after us, to inform us that James J. Strang has sent fifteen or twenty men after us, all armed with revolvers and Bowie knives, to intercept and rob the United States mail, and to kill whoever should be found with said mail, and especially myself, after being so informed, we returned immediately back to Garden Island."[111]

His account changed significantly at the trial. On the stand on Monday, June 30, Moore said the only weapon he saw during the incident was a large, ugly cane with a heavy iron spike on the lower end. He said he saw this "weapon" in the hands of one of the Mormon defendants. Moore also said he was one of three persons who had custody of the mail. Dorry and LeBlanc earlier had indicated that they alone had been entrusted with the mail.[112]

After Moore's testimony McReynolds moved that the case against Strang and four other Mormons be dismissed because of a lack of evidence. Strang had produced an affidavit that he was nowhere near the dog sled on the date in question and that there was no attempt against the mail, simply an attempt to arrest Moore. Strang asserted that the posse met the mail unexpectedly and passed by without paying any attention to it or the person having charge of it. The judge agreed to dismiss the charges against two of the Mormons but refused to do so for Strang and the others.[113]

McReynolds opened the defense's case by saying that the location of the alleged mail obstruction, in full view of an Indian village, was the last place the Mormons would have chosen. Adams's testimony was false, McReynolds said, adding that the very offenses Adams sought to fasten on Strang were the ones that Adams himself had proposed to commit. McReynolds then obtained permission for Strang to address the jury.[114]

Strang said he once had a smattering of legal lore but did not appear as a lawyer. He wished to say something about the system of "higher law"—divine law—on Beaver Island. He said the Mormons had a divine law to govern them but denied that it was above all civil law. Their law, he said, taught obedience to rulers and magistrates and all in authority.[115]

Referring to the rancor and bitterness of religious animosity, Strang said religious persecution of the Saints had caused rivers of blood to flow in the past. He said a certain book, the Book of the Law, had been referred to in testimony for the purpose of affecting the public mind and the jury. The character of this book and the covenant had been misrepresented, he said. It was alleged, he said, that because the defendants had taken a certain covenant, they were bound to commit overt illegal acts, to rob the U.S. mail, and to repudiate the laws of the country. The defendants, he said, believed in the doctrine that God established this nation and government for the final gathering of the children of God and the reestablishing of his church upon the earth. The Book of the Law taught nothing at variance with the laws of the country and good moral and religious society, Strang said.

Then Strang spoke with great vehemence, as he turned to Adams and the other witnesses against the Mormons. He asked the jury why, if a Mormon was not to be credited, those not fit to belong to the Mormon church were to be believed. The main witnesses, he said, were cast-off members of the church. Adams, Strang said, had shown through his testimony that he was the second in command of the church and its chief spokesman and religious teacher. He said Adams had shown that through the covenant of the church and his teachings, he had so corrupted the people that they were ready to commit all kinds of depredations, even to robbing the mail. Adams had shown, Strang said, that as a teacher of the church he had, through the covenant, taught his followers to disobey all laws but those of the kingdom and had heard them declare their willingness to violate the laws of the land, state and national. Adams had taught these doctrines, Strang said, and now he appeared as the pure and immaculate witness to punish them for doing things that he, as a religious teacher and apostle, had instructed them in.

Strang then sat down, leaving the case once more in McReynolds's hands. McReynolds began by reading a procession of depositions of Mormon witnesses, who said they thought both Adams and Moore had a bad reputation on the island for truthfulness and that they would not believe them under oath.[116]

Members of the Mormon posse that had been sent to arrest Moore then testified that there had been no attempt by anyone to stop the dog sled, that the Mormons who appeared to be chasing the sled were also going to the Indian village, and that the Mormons were trying to find the constable to arrest Moore. They also said they never heard the mail mentioned while they were there. Curiously, none of the Mormons in the posse who testified ever saw the warrant for Moore's arrest, nor did any know why he was being sought. Two of them testified that one or two members of the posse had a pistol and another, a cripple, had the "ugly cane."[117]

Samuel Graham said he had been entrusted by McKinley with carrying the mail from Beaver Island to Mackinac both before and after the Moore incident. On cross-examination, even McKinley admitted that after he recovered the "obstructed" mail, he sent it to Mackinac on a ship owned and operated by those he had accused of mail robbery.[118] The federal case was unraveling.

The trial continued until July 8, a red-letter day in Strang's life. Strang made his closing arguments, in which he said he told the jury he was being prosecuted for religious reasons. He compared Bates and his accusers to the lawyers and Pharisees who persecuted Christ.[119]

In his charge to the jury that evening, Wilkins, a Methodist, made it clear that the law opposed prosecution of anyone for religious beliefs, no matter how absurd one might think they are. The *Free Press* described Wilkins's charge as exceedingly able and luminous. "After listening to his examination of the testimony bearing upon the case, no one entertained a doubt as to what the verdict must be." For once, the *Advertiser* agreed.[120]

The case against Strang and ten other Mormon defendants was submitted to the jury that night, with instructions to issue a sealed verdict. After only a short consultation, the jury made its decision, which was announced at 9 A.M. the next day. The verdict, to almost no one's surprise, was not guilty. Strang had won. And the decision, in effect, overthrew the entire prosecution against the Mormons.[121]

Surprisingly, after devoting several columns of its daily news space to testimony in the trial, the *Advertiser* reported the verdict in a two-paragraph story and then dropped it.[122]

The *Free Press* seized the opportunity to drive home points it had tried to make throughout the course of the trial. It pointed out that the Mormons had been assumed guilty at the outset: "without one particle of proof they were branded as felons and murderers—as being so sunk in infamy and crime, as to be without the pale of human sympathy, or common justice." The evidence in the case, the *Free Press* continued:

> was of the most dim and shadowy nature. Most of it related to anything else than the charge of obstructing the mail, and seemed designed rather as a general exposé of Mormon credulity and the peculiarities of the Mormon faith than as testimony upon which a prosecuting officer could seriously ask conviction by the jury. There was little evidence of the obstruction of the mail; but the testimony was full and voluminous upon the question of King Strang's gifts prophetical—upon binding covenants, books of the law, and church discipline and management generally. That the Mormon defendants were Mormons was the only crime fully substantiated.[123]

The remaining indictments against the Mormons were put over to September 15 and the court's fall term. The prisoners in those cases, meanwhile, were out on bail. On September 29 those indictments were quietly dropped.[124]

Shortly after the verdict Strang and several other Mormons took the steamer *Wisconsin* back to Beaver Island. The friendly captain of the ship "made a little display" in their behalf as the ship entered the harbor past Whiskey Point. A "considerable number" of persons had gathered there, some swearing that Strang would never land alive, but he was not molested.[125]

One of the first things Strang did after he got ashore was to change his mailing address. Because of the Mormons' problems with the post office at Whiskey Point, Strang asked his correspondents to direct letters to the post office in Mackinac. After the lengthy and expensive court case involving the mail, Strang deemed it "less trouble and delay" to go fifty miles to pick up his correspondence. No letter, he decided, was safe at the post office on Beaver Island.[126]

Chapter 10

Gentile Exodus

W HILE THE MORMON TRIAL was winding down in Detroit, Strang's ranking adviser, Samuel Graham, was urging him to abandon Beaver Island. During the trial, Graham had left Detroit to return to Parma, his former home, west of Jackson, Michigan. He was joined there by his wife, who was about to have a baby and had been anxious to leave the island. Graham did not want to go back.[1]

On July 8, 1851, the day the jury was deliberating, Graham wrote Strang that the sooner the Mormons left the island the better. "I think it unsafe for eather of us to go there. . . . I had rather go to Salt Lake than live in a continual strife," he said, adding that he was "worn out with persecution." Graham also was upset about the work ethic on the island. "I have stayed there and been growled at by lazy loungers as long as I will," he wrote in another letter to Strang, "and in saying this to you I don't want you to think that I complain of any thing that you could have done." Then he added a revealing comment about life in the kingdom: "But James, we must have men that will work and not steal if we would build up a kingdom or church."[2]

According to one apostle, Graham and his family eventually were cut off from the church after he "grew faithearted when he saw the Saints enforcing the laws of the kingdom."[3] Ironically, Graham testified in Detroit that he had been Strang's assistant in translating the Plates of Laban into the laws of the kingdom. And one former follower of Strang said Graham later claimed that he and Strang had fabricated those eighteen plates.[4]

No matter how intimate an adviser Graham had been, after his break with the island kingdom he was unable to remove his household goods and team from the island. In asking Strang why, Graham pointed out that he had invested more than $2,500 in Beaver Island and that all he expected to take off were the team and goods.[5] As the months passed, communications between Strang and

Graham turned increasingly bitter. Graham must have made an accusation involving his wife and Strang, for Strang responded: "I am sorry you should put so low an estimate on your wife's virtue merely to give me an unvalued compliment." In another bit of spiteful one-upmanship, Strang added, "You forget that I stand a head and shoulders above those you strain your vision to look up to."[6]

The loss of Graham, hard on the heels of Adams's stormier exit, weighed heavily on Strang. In a letter to his brother, he asked soulfully: "shall I ever have one friend, true and unchanging?"[7] In a letter to Graham, Strang admitted: "I have loved you more than I have loved any other man save one; more than the love of women. In sorrow and shame I confess I love you yet."[8] The "save one" undoubtedly was Benjamin Perce.

Another separation touched Strang even closer to home. Shortly after his arrest in May, Strang had written his wife, Mary, ordering her to leave the island. The order seems to have been made less out of fear for Mary's safety than that Mary was jeopardizing Strang's hold on his followers. Strang had made Mary a member of his privy council in April, but he apparently suspected that she was working against him and the church while he was in Detroit. Graham defended Mary, saying that she had not opposed Strang or the church and that she was the victim of some influential enemies.[9] By this time, however, Graham was an uninfluential friend, as far as Mary—or anything—was concerned. Even though he had ordered her from the island, Strang evidently still had feeling for her. Within weeks, he was worried that the break would be total, that her heart had turned from him. Graham doubted this. "I think she will yet meet you and be to you all that she ever was if you ever git on a place where peace reigns."[10]

Graham was right. Mary had gone to Illinois to visit her brother, William, and she ended up staying there with her children for more than a year. But by late 1852 she and their children had moved to the Voree area, where she decided to remain and where Strang visited her. Strang later claimed he was "as much at home" there as he was at Beaver Island, although he considered the latter his residence for political reasons.[11] With Strang's headquarters gone and the contingent turmoil absent, Voree would serve as the "Garden of Peace" Mary was seeking.

During the spring and summer of 1851 turmoil was the operant word on Beaver Island. Charges relating to the federal case and the shooting of Thomas Bennett were not the only ones Mormons had faced. A number of Mormons had been arrested on other criminal charges. Strang said the total of Mormons arrested during that period was ninety-nine. He said that he had had to face forty different allegations himself and that he had been jailed six times in the previous year.[12] No Mormon was found guilty of any offense, however. And when Strang returned to the island in the middle of July, the only Mormons who had not been set free were the fourteen still chafing in custody in Mackinac on charges of murdering Bennett. They would be released and return home before the end of August.[13]

At one time, for nearly a month, three-fourths of the men on the island had been away, either as defendants or as witnesses in criminal cases, leaving only twenty-four Mormon men on Beaver. The farm work, meanwhile, had fallen mainly on the women, who cultivated the crops needed to save the settlement from starvation the following winter. The *Northern Islander* said the enemies of the Mormons had openly vowed to continue the arrests until they had taken all the men off the island and then driven off their families.[14]

The outcome of the federal trial reversed the Mormon fortunes. After the verdict, the *Islander* said that "a few weeks ago every body, except a few of the faithful, believed we should be obliged to leave this place immediately. Now the blindest can see that we have an entire victory . . . that the day of mobbing the Mormons here has gone by." Three months earlier, the paper pointed out, armed men were hunting the prophet. "Now he sits quietly in his own house, without keeping one of his trusted friends by to assist him, and dispenses the law to these same men as a Justice of the Peace; and when business requires, goes alone and unarmed in the midst of them, without molestation or danger."[15]

Strang had been elected a justice of the peace in the spring but had been unable to perform the duties until after his trial. He immodestly wrote of himself later that "so great was the advantage of transacting business before one who was well versed in law, and would swerve from no duty, that before fall his most violent persecutors became suitors before him. . . . in some instances appeals were taken from his judgments, but none were reversed."[16]

Despite the calmer atmosphere on the island, there still were periods of intense confrontation. In September, after the remaining Mormons had been released in the Bennett shooting, a bench warrant was issued in Mackinac for the arrest of H. D. MacCulloch on the charge of murder, apparently a holdover from the Bennett case.[17] MacCulloch, who had been arrested in the case initially, had been released from jail at Mackinac along with Samuel Graham to give depositions at Beaver Island in June.

On September 20 a deputy sheriff arrived at Beaver Island to arrest MacCulloch, taking him prisoner at the harbor. At that moment, according to Eri J. Moore, Strang and other Mormons rushed out of a meeting in the printing office and surrounded the deputy, threatening him and telling him that he could not take MacCulloch or anyone else. MacCulloch got away.[18] (He would not be brought to trial in the case, and Strang and two others would be indicted in June 1852 on a charge of feloniously helping MacCulloch escape.)[19]

The night after the MacCulloch incident, Moore saw Strang, with a sword buckled at his side, heading for Marvin Aldrich's house. The Mormons were said to be assembling there under arms to await the return of the sheriff from Mackinac with a posse to arrest MacCulloch. The sheriff did not show. At about midnight, Moore said, several Mormons threw stones through the windows of his house, where Moore and his wife were staying with the Austin and Bower families.[20]

In a by now familiar refrain, Moore said the Mormons made his family feel like they had to be on guard all the time. The Mormons, he said, also harassed the Gentiles with petty lawsuits, which often were heard before Strang as justice of the peace. In an unsuccessful request for assistance from the governor, Moore claimed that Strang had said the Gentiles or the Mormons had to leave the island. Moore said a long box had been brought onto the island that he presumed contained guns and lead. "Winter is a coming on when there will be no way for us to git any help nor git a way. There are but a few of us here," Moore told the governor.[21] The *Northern Islander* said the Mormons outnumbered the Gentiles on the island that winter by about 1,000 to 20.[22]

Moore pointed out that his means were "all use up and these Hell hounds at my heals." According to Moore, Strang said that "if

166

I would give him a deed of some propperty that I have that I could
live here & by a little exertion I could remain here & do business,
but I [k]new a nought of this people to [k]now that I could not live
with them unless I was on good terms with them."[23]

For his part, Strang maintained that as winter approached,
those who had been most hostile to the Mormons attempted to get
a group together to winter on Whiskey Point and prepare for a fight
with the Mormons. But the prospect of battle—which would have
been conducted with long odds if the *Islander's* population figures
were correct—frightened off many, Strang said.[24]

One Gentile resident of that period said that about twenty
non-Mormon families spent the winter of 1851–52 on the island,
at Cable's Bay.[25] The Gentile presence was withering, and perhaps
the best indication was that Peter McKinley had relinquished any
claim to his Whiskey Point land in October 1851 and left. Early in
1852 a Mormon named Dennis Chidester took over the job of Beaver Island postmaster from McKinley. Dennis was the brother of
Edward Chidester, one of the publishers of the *Northern Islander*.[26]

Meanwhile, Strang was solidifying his hold on the choice
property at the harbor. Late in 1851 he bought thirty-three acres,
on which his new home and the still uncompleted tabernacle were
located.[27] Work on the tabernacle had been halted while the Mormons were defending themselves in court and devoting their ener-
gies to subsistence. Strang's home no longer was the rude log dwelling he had lived in when he was crowned king, though his new
quarters were still not pretentious.

The "King's Cottage" was a sturdy two-story frame home with
a porch across the length of the front. Massive doors at the front and
rear were connected by a hallway through the center of the home.
There was a large room on either side on the first floor, with two
bedrooms and closets upstairs. The house was built in a grove of
hardwoods and scattered evergreens on a level area just below the
bluff where the log house stood. There was a view of the harbor and
Lake Michigan beyond. A white picket fence surrounded the yard.[28]

On the home front, Strang added a second polygamous wife
seven months after he had sent Mary away. On January 19, 1852,
he quietly married Betsy McNutt, a thirty-one-year-old spinster not
noted for beauty. At a social gathering at St. James, she was being

teased about being an "old maid" when she responded that there was only one man on the island that she would consider marrying. That one man, it became evident, was King Strang, who was made aware of Betsy's comment. Although not completely enamored of the idea, Strang offered himself to her in marriage, out of a sense of gallantry.[29] With Mary gone, his household now consisted of two wives and Elvira's child.

Their trial over, the Mormons began to feel more secure about publicly expressing their feelings about polygamy. In March 1852 the *Northern Islander* supported the right of any religious group to practice polygamy. The *Islander* was reponding to reports that the Utah Mormons were openly avowing the practice. "Does not the constitution of the United States guarantee freedom of religion to all citizens? The law of polygamy is a part of the religious faith of the Brighamites. The practice of it according to their faith, is escential to the salvation of the great body of mankind."[30] The *Islander* article continued, "If the people of Utah think polygamy a wholesome institution, and choose not to condemn it as a crime, whose business is it? In that Democratic country, have not the people a right to make such laws as they think fit for their own government? . . . nothing can be found in the common law against polygamy; nothing in the civil law; nothing in the Old Testament against it. But . . . the Brighamites who are so far behind the times, as to follow the example of God's chosen servants of the olden time, are, forsooth dangerous and rebellious citizens."[31]

Normally vitriolic in referring to the church of Brigham Young, the Strangites had begun to sympathize with it, but not with its leader. The *Islander*, continuing the Strangite tradition of sniping at Young, referred to him as a corrupt, cowardly man. The particular reference was to information, which the paper would not vouch for but printed anyway, that Young had left Salt Lake for California "with a strong guard, and an immense amount of treasure." The *Islander* said it had no doubt that Brigham was capable of such treachery. "By his folly and wickedness he has blown up a storm that he cannot ride out. . . . His deluded followers will be abandoned by him to their fate. Some better man [did the paper mean Strang?] will vindicate their right to live on the earth."[32]

Later, the *Islander* admitted that the report about Young was false. "We are glad of it. Brigham is a bad fellow, but he is lied about because he is a Mormon," said the Mormon newspaper that had helped spread those lies.[33] In another instance, while predicting the total failure of Young's plans—"if indeed he has any plans"—Strang himself commented: "As it is natural for Charlatans to ever busy themselves with predicting evil on all who are in their way, Brigham and the host of elders with which he has flooded the country, have from the beginning of my ministry, poured out a perfect deluge of predictions of dire calamities upon me, and my speedy downfall."[34] The same could have been said about Strang and his comments about Young.

≈ ≈ ≈

At the beginning of 1852 Strang owned about 100 acres on Beaver Island, and he wrote his brother that he had his eye on another 100 that would give him a total of about a mile and a quarter of frontage around the harbor, even though Strang told his brother that he had too much property.[35] In the same month Strang wrote this letter, actions were taken that indicated which 100 acres Strang had his eye on. The sequence of events also was revealing about Strang's way of doing business on the island. A judgment had been declared against Eri J. Moore's property, and in order to pay the judgment, the sheriff seized the land and put it on the auction block. The three parcels affected totaled ninety-nine acres.[36]

The ninety-nine acres included forty near the harbor that Moore had bought on July 14, 1851, perhaps betting that Strang would not return to the island after the Detroit trial—or at least that his influence would be diminished. When Strang did return, Moore probably realized his mistake—especially when it became clear two months later in the MacCulloch incident and the stoning of his house that the Mormons were unbowed by their legal experiences. On Strang's return, one of Moore's allies was quick to sell. Nicholas Bower relinquished his rights to an acre on the harbor.[37]

The auction of Moore's land was held on April 22 at Mackinac. William N. MacLeod bought the property for $360 and two months later sold it to Strang for $400. Moore got something for his land, however. On August 10 Moore relinquished all claim to sixty-two acres of the land to a Detroit-area land speculator for $500.[38]

The sheriff also had seized thirty-nine acres on Whiskey Point once owned by Peter McKinley and 140 acres about a mile south of the harbor that once belonged to Thomas Bennett. This land was put on the block in another sheriff's sale. On August 6 Strang bought the Bennett land for the bargain-basement price of $71.70 and the McKinley land for $54.[39] With the Whiskey Point acquisition, Strang and the Mormons had taken control of almost all of the harbor area.

There were complaints about the Mormon dealings. One man in Mackinac accused the Mormons of selling his personal property. The Mormons explained that the man and his partner had been assessed taxes for land and goods they owned in the township and that when the men left the island and the taxes remained unpaid, the township sold their merchandise to meet the tax bill. The Mormons said this was done according to law under the direction of the township supervisor—who at the time happened to be James J. Strang—and the township treasurer, George Miller. Miller, a Mormon, also was a deputy sheriff and involved in the sheriff's sales of land.[40]

One Gentile from Mackinac maintained that it was a "successful trick" among the Mormons "to levy an incidental tax of some kind upon their Gentile neighbors within their jurisdiction, and when payment was demanded [the sum of which would often amount to half the value of the property taxed], and the Gentiles refused [to pay], a suit was brought, judgment rendered, execution issued, and the whole sold to some good Mormon for a mere trifle. No appeal was ever allowed." McKinley was one of those affected by such procedures, the Gentile said, adding that McKinley was defrauded of a "handsome property" and forced to leave the island penniless.[41]

Strang had been named supervisor, the highest office in the township, at the annual Peaine Township meeting in the same month that Moore's property was put on the block. Mormons were named to fill all the township offices, as they had been in 1851. Strang continued as a justice of the peace. At the meeting four ordinances were adopted, including ones that designated Whiskey Point as a quarantine ground and as a hospital site for persons having smallpox and other diseases.[42] The Mormons apparently considered those two uses appropriate for that land, given the Gentile history of the Point.

≈ ≈ ≈

That spring saw an influx of fishermen and traders on the island, but for many, the stay was short. One steamer landed fifty persons at Whiskey Point, but the buildings there were so rundown and the prospects so unpromising that most left in the same boat, Strang said. Of the men who remained, two began selling whiskey to the Indians.[43]

Although supplying liquor to Indians was a violation of state law, for decades liquor had been traded to the Indians for fur and fish. Traders also did a big business selling it to Indians and other fishermen. In 1851 a state law was amended to require a bond from traders before they could sell liquor. The bond was designed to cover damage that could be blamed on alcohol. Peaine Township, run by teetotaling Mormons headed by a king who had been a temperance advocate since he was twenty-one, enforced the law strictly. Strang said no trader on Beaver Island could come up with the required bond, making it easy for the authorities there to take action.[44] The bond was at least $500, with at least two sureties who were residents of the respective county and approved by the local township board.[45] With the Peaine Township board controlled by Mormons, it is not surprising that no one there could meet the requirements. As a precaution, Strang assembled every man who could have served as a surety, and after "full consultation," they pledged not to become a surety for a liquor dealer.[46]

As for the two traders selling whiskey to the Indians on Whiskey Point, Strang said that within a week the pair found themselves fined $20. They escaped further prosecution, he said, by shipping away all their liquor and promising to reform. The pair then went into partnership with a Mormon in the fishing business. One day, Strang said, one took a boat belonging to the Mormon and went to Mackinac, where he boasted that he had stolen enough to make good his fines. Mackinac considered this an excellent joke, Strang said.[47]

The liquor law was generally condemned throughout the region, Strang noted. The collection of the fines by constables, he said, was spoken of in newspapers as acts of robbery. One of those fined was James Cable, who ran a trading house on Cable's Bay. Cable paid a judgment of $50 levied by a Mormon justice of the peace. Cable had been trying to sell his holdings for a year, and he finally sold his property in October 1852 to two Mormons. While Cable was selling out, a number of Mormon families formed a settlement, named Galilee, on Cable's Bay.[48]

By the end of the summer of 1852, six fines involving violations of the liquor law on Beaver Island had been paid, with another case pending. Strang also served notice that traders on small sail vessels would find themselves a target of the law if they did not stop selling liquor. Strang said the township officers were firm in their duty and the result was a marked improvement in the sobriety of the people in and around the Beaver Islands, especially among the fishermen. The Mormons continued to be upset about the sale of liquor to Indians elsewhere and asked why the liquor law was not being enforced at Mackinac, where they said the Indians were in a "continual state of intoxication."[49]

The *Islander* said the white fishermen were rapidly leaving the Beaver Island area and Indians were taking their places, a change the paper deemed favorable. "There is less of vice and dissipation among the Indians than among the whites of the borders. Separate from the influence of vicious white men, the Indians are moral, industrious, honest and peaceable."[50] The Mormons had been putting out the welcome mat for the local Indians in several ways. The township had ordered that a small Indian burial plot on the harbor near the dock be enclosed and cared for, an action the *Northern Islander* hailed as a first for protecting ancient burial grounds from civilization.[51]

The Indians had another reason to be thankful to the Mormons. During the previous winter, which was a severe one, the twenty-seven Indian families on Garden Island were destitute, Strang said. The Mormons, to whom the Indians had been hostile, furnished provisions to the Indians on credit. "They paid promptly, and have been fast friends to the Mormons ever since," he remarked.[52] "They have surrounded me as so many children, eating at my table, and sleeping in my house . . . as though they were members of my family" whenever they visited St. James. "But there is no vagrancy—no vagabondism among them. They are careful, unsolicited, to bring as much as they use."[53]

In the next year and a half, the number of Indians there nearly doubled, Strang said, because the "more sedate and orderly" of other bands in that area joined the Garden Island group. Strang said that Indians, from fifty miles around, when injured by a white man, came to him for redress. Chiefs, he said, went out of their way to express their gratitude for his kindnesses to the Indians and their confidence in him. Strang wrote that "the Catholic priest from Cross Village [on the mainland], when making his annual visit to the Beaver Island Indians [in 1852], charged them, last of all, that if they got into any difficulty they should go to Strang; if anybody cheated them they should go to Strang; if anybody came among them selling whisky they should go to Strang; but they must not go to hear Strang preach."[54]

     🐦 🐦 🐦

At sunrise on July 8, 1852, about ninety Mormon men brought sacrifices to a spot in the woods near Font Lake. The occasion was King's Day, the anniversary of the coronation of King Strang, a day set aside by the Book of the Law of the Lord for feasting and celebration.[55] The king, however, spent the first anniversary of his coronation awaiting a verdict in Detroit with many of his fellow Mormons. The 1852 celebration was the first.

In the prescribed ceremonies, as a thank offering to God for giving a kingdom to the Saints, the king was to offer a heifer "without blemish." And the Book of the Law said: "After this manner shall all the children of the kingdom sacrifice: every man a heifer or a lamb or a dove. Every man a clean beast or a clean fowl, according to his household."[56]

At noon, Strang preached on the fate of apostates: "The Lord

shall blot out his name from under heaven." That sermon was followed at 1 P.M. by the feast for 488 persons—the families of those
who offered sacrifices.[57]

A few days after that holiday feast, the *Green Bay Spectator*
reported that within the previous few months several families had
been "driven from Beaver Island, in a state of destitution and misery, by the so-called 'Latter Day Saints,' because they refused to
affiliate with Mormondom, and refused to be participators in the
crimes and enormities which have signalized the course of the followers of James J. Strang, and shocked the moral sense of the entire
country." The Whig newspaper added that "for such open and un-
disguised violators of the Laws of the Land, there can be no punishment too severe—no penalty too adequate. The time is coming
when a collision will take place, unless they abandon their nefarious
practices, and abominable crimes."[58]

To the charge of driving families from Beaver Island, the
Northern Islander responded with something less than a denial: "If
there was one word of truth in this, it would but be the beginning
of the fulfillment of that scripture which says, 'reward her as she
rewarded you.' . . . if there are any persons who have been driven
from here in poverty and want, they came to want by drunkenness,
and by spending their time and money in trying to drive off the
Latter Day Saints. The pit they dug for us they have fallen into, and
there has been no driving except by sending officers of the law to
arrest them for their perjuries and their thefts. If this is driving men
off, we intend to keep at it."[59]

The *Spectator* also accused the Mormons of plundering fishermen in that region, and the *Islander* produced a similar reply: "If
there was one word of truth in this accusation, it would be but the
law of reprisals which prevails." And the *Islander* asked if it were
not a little puzzling that "just at the moment a Mormon colony
landed here all the fishermen for hundreds of miles around, among
whom previously thieving was a daily occurrence, reformed and became perfectly honest?"[60]

Strang accused the fishermen of plundering the Mormons, including regularly helping themselves in their gardens—to the point
of cleaning out some remote fields of potatoes and turnips. Some of

the guilty parties were detected and prosecuted, with the Mormons recovering damages. Others put up bail and then left the area.[61]

In one instance, Strang said, Henry VanAllen, the keeper of the Beaver Island lighthouse, had hid eighteen nets belonging to B. G. Wright in the lighthouse. A short time later the buoys for twenty-four new nets VanAllen had set out were pulled underwater by a strong current pushed by high winds. VanAllen could not locate the nets and suspected the Mormons of stealing them. He made the mistake of proposing to Mormon leaders that he return Wright's nets in exchange for his. Meanwhile, VanAllen's buoys popped to the surface, and his men took in his nets, filled with fish. VanAllen was arrested but forfeited his bail by fleeing. With his departure, affairs on Beaver Island were entirely in the control of Mormons, Strang said.[62]

Included in the outcry in the papers of Great Lakes ports was an article in a Buffalo daily called *Rough Notes*. The paper reported that it had received many complaints—"especially from fishermen"—about a "gang of men" at Beaver Island who "have now driven off all the fishermen from the island, stolen most of their property, and make a business of appropriating whatever they can lay hands on belonging to the boats which call there." *Rough Notes* added: "It would seem that the narrow escape some of them had about a year ago from the halters of justice has not produced a good effect on them, but on the contrary made them more annoying and paved the way for fresh crimes and outrages. . . . Something should be done to check the high-handed proceedings of this piratical band of desperadoes before they become any more troublesome."[63]

The *Islander* replied sarcastically: "It astonishes us that such things should occur in a civilized and christian country; more that it should happen so near us, and we hear nothing of it." The *Islander* said the people "have itching ears to hear something against the Mormons. No matter what occurs, if it is ill done it is laid to them."[64]

Strang said that during that summer there were at least fifty accounts published of "Mormon depredations on the property of others." He added that not one of them would have been credited for a single moment, had it been asserted about any other people.

Each account, Strang said, contained glaring absurdities and im-possibilities. Yet they were "repeated from mouth to mouth un-doubtingly by those who in other matters are not over credulous. It is clear enough if any reliance can be placed on newspapers and legends, that the Mormons have a most plenary power of miracles in mischief-making, and if not preserved from destruction by the Almighty, are wonderfully and supernaturally strengthened in vil-lainy and protected from punishment by the Devil."[65]

At the end of the summer, the *Islander* said that for six weeks almost every sailboat that arrived at St. James from the fishing grounds had brought the report that the fishermen were about to destroy the Mormons. But the reports were erroneous. And in mid-September another group of settlers arrived—thirty-three persons from New York state—giving evidence the Mormons were becom-ing more firmly entrenched.[66]

In the fall of 1852 all of the Gentile families had moved out except eight, including that of Walter Whitney, a carpenter who had built Strang's newest house. According to Whitney's daughter, Elizabeth, the Gentile traders were long gone. Peter McKinley had moved his family to Mackinac. James Cable had gone to Indiana. Alva Cable had come with a boat and taken a group of Gentiles to Pine River on the mainland.[67]

Elizabeth Whitney later wrote of her family's last days on Bea-ver Island.

> One morning about the first of November a messenger came to every Gentile family with a letter from the king, saying every Gen-tile family must come to the harbor and be baptized into the Church of Zion or leave the island within ten days. Within 24 hours after receiving the notice, every Gentile family had gone but ours. They had taken what they could in fish boats. Our boat being small, father thought best to wait for a vessel to come and take us away.
>
> The fourth day no vessel had come. Father feared the message to the captain of the vessel had not been delivered [by an Indian family]. . . . Our goods were packed, and every day some Mormon men could be seen walking along the beach, each carrying a gun, but none ever spoke to us. They were anxious days to us, watching and waiting for a sail. Father had made up his mind if the vessel did

not come we would take what we could in our small boat and go to the Indians for protection until we could get to the main land. The evening of the ninth day had come and no welcome sail in sight."

Then, in the darkness of the early morning of the tenth day, the boat came. The goods were carried to the shore, and the captain and a man named John were loading the yawl. "Our pets had all been put on board, our clothing and most of our bedding was loaded. Mother and I had gone to the vessel. All was loaded except a few boxes and two large trunks. When father and John started to go back to the shore after them several men were standing beside the goods and each had a gun in his hands. This was enough. Father knew the rest of our goods must be left."[68] The sails were quickly hoisted, the anchor raised, and soon they were sailing east toward Pine River, later to be named Charlevoix, where the sun was just coming up.

Chapter 11

The King as Legislator

WITH THE ISLAND under his thumb in 1852, Strang sought a larger sphere of influence as he mapped a maneuver to fulfill his youthful dream of being a legislator. The key to his plan involved confusion over the state's 1851 reapportionment of legislative districts.[1] In the confusion, the Mormons of Beaver Island voted twice and helped elect two state representatives.

Although Beaver Island, which Strang considered to be part of the unorganized county of Emmet, was attached to Mackinac County for judicial purposes, Emmet was included with Newaygo County in a legislative district comprised of roughly the northern half of the Lower Peninsula. But according to Strang, almost everyone assumed Beaver Island was in the Mackinac district for the election of a state representative.[2] The Mormons did not disabuse them.

The Mackinac district—along with the other Upper Peninsula districts—elected their representatives on September 28; the rest of the state elected theirs on November 2. On September 28 Peaine Township had a choice of two Mackinac men, Alexander Toll and Charles M. O'Malley, for state representative from Mackinac County. The vote indicated the Mormons were not enthralled with either candidate, but Peaine Township favored Toll, 86 to 56. Toll was elected. The vote in Mackinac County was described as light because of the confusion over election districts. Although there were 142 votes cast in Peaine, the *Northern Islander* indicated there were about 240 eligible voters there, among an estimated 1,700 residents.[3] A month later the bulk of the state would elect state representatives, and the Mormons would vote again—for Strang.

Strang the candidate had known bitter disappointment in elections. On March 9, 1834, in the Town of Hanover, New York, Strang had unsuccessfully sought to be elected constable, even though he was two weeks too young to hold office, a fact he neglected to mention. And three years earlier he had to be satisfied with being fourth corporal of the local militia because he had refused to "buy men's votes with rum."[4]

The election for constable left him particularly upset. Strang called the whole process unequalled for folly and corruption, apparently overlooking the folly in his quarter. Although 472 votes were cast in the town meeting, more than 500 were counted for almost every office. One man who had run on two tickets received 711 votes, and both candidates for one office had an even higher total. Except for the corruption, Strang thought he might have won. He had the most votes of any in his party, but he could not challenge the decision because he was underage and thus vulnerable himself.[5]

On Beaver Island, Strang's followers were attentive to political matters, a reversal of their Voree stance. At Voree, the *Gospel Herald* had admonished the Saints as late as 1848 to "keep perfectly clear of politics. Cast no votes. Attend no elections." The *Herald* said politicians "may make you fair promises, but they will never do you any good."[6] However, on Beaver Island, Strang and the Mormons saw advantages in political activity, and they were on a political roll.

In the election of county officers in Mackinac County on September 28 the Mormons scored an important victory. A Mormon, George Miller, was narrowly elected sheriff in a three-way race with 114 votes. Another Mormon, Dennis Chidester, lost by two votes to J. P. King of Mackinac for probate judge. Chidester also had 114 votes, an indication of bloc voting by the Mormons; King had 116.[7]

For the November 2 election, Strang's name had been quietly nominated for state representative in the Newaygo district, and Strang received all 165 of the votes cast on Beaver Island for that office. Getting those votes canvassed was a more difficult matter. The canvassers met in Newaygo, north of Grand Rapids. The *Islander* said Newaygo was not only hundreds of miles away by any traveled route but it was only "barely possible to get the returns there in season to be canvassed." Nevertheless, before the board of canvassers met in Newaygo, the *Islander* was confident that Strang had been elected.[8]

The representative of the unorganized counties on the board of canvassers was Dennis Chidester. When Chidester arrived in Newaygo, officials there had no intimation that Strang was in the race—or even that Beaver Island was in that legislative district. Chidester succeeded in satisfying the canvassers on both counts, and on November 16 Strang was certified the winner of the election. There were 200 votes split among four other candidates, and Strang's nearest rival, James Barton, had 52 votes.[9] The king, who had been elected justice of the peace, then township supervisor, was now the elected representative for one-fourth of the area of the state.

The bloc voting of the Mormons carried through to the other races, too, from president on down. No Whig candidate received more than one vote on Beaver Island, while those on the Democratic side—including the electors for Franklin Pierce—got at least 154. The *Northern Islander* said the Beaver Island results presented "a unanimity probably no where else seen." The paper reported that it was the fear of persecution by the Whigs and not any great liking for the Democrats that caused the one-sidedness of the vote: the knowledge that the Whigs "had persecuted us as a party measure, and the absence of any assurance that they will not do it again, lost them eighty or 100 votes."[10]

Strang regarded his election as a great triumph, and yet, in the next breath, he said he did not value the office. "I would sooner resign today if I could get the same things done which I believe I can accomplish by being in the House," he wrote in a candid letter to his brother three weeks after his election. "Frankly, brother, I intend to rule this country [an apparent reference to the Beaver Island region]; and it will be a hard struggle if I do not make myself one of the Judges of the [state] Supreme Court within one year."[11]

The *Islander* said that "the only thing that could possibly induce Mr. Strang to leave home at that season of the year is the preeminent necessity of a Representative who is acquainted with the intrests of this section of the country, and who will faithfully attend to them."[12] Strang said the pay, $3 a day for a forty-day session, was not equal to what his time was worth, "and I prefer quiet and household comforts, to the noise and confusion of publick life."[13] This from a man who was a lightning rod for controversy.

In savoring his victory, Strang's thoughts went back to his youth, where one of his goals was to be a member of the state legislature. In his youth, he said, many "trod on me as ruthlessly as though I had been a worm of the dust. . . . And this is my revenge;—to triumph in the forums of the same publick where they sought and well-nigh accomplished my ruin." [14]

As for his youthful goal of fame, Strang wrote that he was convinced it depended on God's calling and not on any office man could bestow. "I have made my mark upon the times in which I live, which the wear and tear of time . . . shall not be able to obliterate. Like Moses of old my name will be revered, and men scarsely restrained from worshiping me as a God. . . . George C. Bates and Charles H. Knox have secured to themselves a niche in the Temple of Infamy, by their connection with my persecutions, which will remain when it is forgotten that Millard Fillmore, their master was ever President of the United States." Fillmore was a forgettable president, but Strang's megalomania seems to have sprouted new leaves with his pronouncements about the "infamy" of Bates and Knox.

Perhaps this was a symptom of mid-life crisis as Strang was approaching his fortieth birthday and keeping track of his accomplishments with a prejudiced eye. "We are but middle aged men; in the very prime and vigor of life," he wrote his brother, and he remarked at how fast the world had grown up before their eyes. In his expansive mood, he urged his brother, who had never been north of Detroit, to come for a visit. "Come up here in the mild weather of summer and I will take a boat and carry you any where, every where, just where the breeze and our pleasure direct us, and you shall enjoy health and happiness to your hearts content." This Strang felt he could deliver: he was the king.

His election victory behind him, Strang indicated he wanted to avoid unnecessary disputes. "I seized the flood tide, but do not intend to follow the ebb. I am content with having outrun the waves [and] lived out the storm, and will seek calm waters." A man who has nothing could afford to be "at war with all the world, for he is no worse off for being plundered," but Strang said he was no longer poor.

While Strang was writing of happiness and of seeking calm waters, some citizens of Mackinac, upset that he had been elected to the legislature, were hoping to prevent him from taking his seat. The plan, Strang learned, was to arrest him on an old indictment when he stopped at Mackinac on his way to the state capital at

Lansing. The old indictment was the charge resulting from the aborted arrest of MacCulloch in September 1851. The indictment, accusing Strang and two other Mormons of "corruptly, feloniously, and with force and arms" helping MacCulloch escape, had been made early in June 1852, two months after Strang was elected township supervisor.[15]

Strang said the Mackinac County grand jury had trumped up the indictment in an effort to frighten him into leaving Mackinac and thus prevent him from taking his seat with the county board of supervisors, which met there. One of the grand jurors had even mentioned the indictment to Strang before the warrant was issued, saying he had better leave to avoid arrest. But Strang did not leave town—and hours later he was arrested. He refused to give bail, but because there was no jail fit for use in Mackinac County at that time, the officials there had a problem. After being in loose custody for several days, Strang eventually was released, and he left for Beaver Island. Later, Strang continued to visit Mackinac on public and private business without being molested.[16]

Two weeks after being arrested, Strang was on such a visit to attend a county board meeting, and he made a motion that a new county jail be built behind the county courthouse. The motion passed. The jail, although built, would never house Strang. His days of imprisonment at Mackinac were over, and the latest plan to jail him was foiled—at Mackinac, at least—when he decided to travel to Lansing via Green Bay.[17]

Lansing had been the state capital since 1847. That year the legislature, then meeting in Detroit, had located the capital in a "hole in the woods" in Ingham County's Lansing Township. A two-story capitol building was constructed in time for the first session of the legislature there in 1848. The white-frame structure, with green shutters and topped by a plain cupola, housed the legislative halls, supreme court room, state library, and several offices. The building was noted for bad ventilation, and during the legislative season its rooms often were smoke-filled.[18]

In Lansing Strang stayed at the Benton House, the city's best hotel and its first brick building. The three-story hotel had about sixty rooms and a large hall for dancing and other functions. It was the center of social activity in the city of about 2,000 people as well as a political headquarters.[19]

On January 5, 1853, the legislature convened its first biennial session under the new state constitution. At 10 A.M. the House of Representatives was called to order, followed by a roll call of the counties. Member-elect James J. Strang answered the call for "Newaygo and the counties thereto attached."[20] Strang had an unusual announcement to make, but it would have to wait until organizational business had been handled.

First, the seventy members of the House took the oath of office. And in the afternoon, with Democrats dominant by more than a 2 to 1 ratio, the House elected a speaker, then moved to the selection of other officials. Strang voted with the Democratic majority.[21]

The legislative agenda began with notice that a bill would be introduced to construct a ship canal and locks at the falls of the St. Marys River at Sault Ste. Marie. Another major piece of legislation slated for consideration was a general railroad bill.[22]

But first Strang had some House business of a more personal nature. Strang informed the members that he had been arrested that morning at the Benton House. The arrest was made by C. W. Tuttle, the undersheriff of Wayne County, on a warrant issued in Mackinac County. The old indictment had pursued him to Lansing. When arrested, Strang insisted that he could leave only with the permission of the House. When Tuttle made it clear that he intended to take him—by force, if necessary—before the House met, Strang said he would treat any such action as an unprovoked assault. And when his claim of privilege was disputed, Strang said: "I will put my neck in a halter upon that."[23]

To the House, Strang repeated that the arrest raised a question of privilege, and he asked the House to take the action it deemed required under the circumstances. Strang attributed the arrest to malice, and even the press reported that there was a powerful prejudice against him. The matter was tabled, and the next morning a legislator presented a communication from Tuttle asking permission of the House to remove Strang, who was being kept under surveillance since his arrest. Tuttle's request was referred to a select committee of five members, who met that afternoon and issued a report the next day.[24]

The committee rebuked those in Mackinac who had prompted the arrest and implied that they had attempted to turn the law into a vehicle for oppression and persecution. Tuttle, the select panel said, was only following orders. The warrant had been placed in Tuttle's hands on Monday, with instructions to arrest Strang on Wednesday before the session began. The committee concluded that the arrest was designed to deprive Strang's constituents, and the House, of his services. The panel recommended that the House adopt a resolution finding the arrest of Strang to be an infraction of its privileges. The report and the resolution were adopted unanimously, and Strang was free to continue his duties as a legislator.[25]

Although he had not yet been appointed to any standing committees, the next day he would be named to the committee on mines and minerals, one of the least prestigious assignments. In his first week he also was busy taking care of district affairs. He introduced his first bill—to organize Emmet County for judicial purposes, an important bill for the Mormons because it would effectively separate Beaver Island and the rest of the county from Mackinac County and create for Emmet its own county government. The bill was referred to committee.[26]

Meanwhile, another threat to Strang's future in the legislature had appeared. On January 7, the same day that Strang's arrest was ruled out of order, the man who had finished second to Strang in the election filed a petition contesting Strang's right to hold the seat. Barton's petition was referred to the House elections committee.[27]

Barton was represented before the committee by Charles H. Taylor, a former Michigan secretary of state and state representative. Strang represented himself. Taylor claimed that Strang was not a resident of the Newaygo district and that Peaine Township (the Beaver Islands) was not part of the district under the 1851 reapportionment. Strang argued that Peaine was part of Emmet County, which was expressly included in the Newaygo district.[28]

A three-member majority of the committee of five decided that Beaver Island was not part of Emmet County and that Strang thus could not have been elected to represent the Newaygo district. The majority concluded that Barton was entitled to the seat. The remaining two members of the committee sided with Strang, declaring that the Beaver Islands had been part of the county then known as Emmet since 1840, when Tonedagana County was organized; Tonedagana had been renamed Emmet in 1843.[29] (The maker of an 1852 map of Michigan also appeared to back the minority report. He colored the Beaver Islands in harmony with Emmet County.)[30]

Debate in the full House on the contested seat was set for 2 P.M. January 11. Taylor argued Barton's case at length, and he was followed by Strang, once again in the role of the underdog.[31] Strang, however, possessed qualities that had allowed him to overcome handicaps before.

As the legislature was finding out, Strang could be companionable and yet magnetic. Two keys to that magnetism were his eyes, described as "a dark brown color, rather small but very bright and piercing, giving an exceedingly animated expression to his whole countenance."[32] A former Mormon said Strang's eyes seemed "as though they could bore right through a person." The eyes were particularly effective when Strang was practicing his oratorical skills, which were described as being "of the fervid, impassioned sort that would carry his audience with him every time. His words came out in a torrent; he could work himself into emotional spells at will, the sincerity of his words being attested by tears when necessary to produce that effect, or by infectious laughter when his mood was merry."[33] That afternoon, before the House, he would begin in a sober and humble manner.

> Mr. Speaker, rising for the first time in my life to address a legislative body, I am quite sensible of my inability to do justice to this question, in which not myself, a humble individual among the sands of society, but democracy and the right to self-government have so deep an interest. . . . I deeply regret that any matters merely personal should have become mixed in the discussion. My religious faith is between me and the Eternal. To him and to him only will I answer. If I am elected to represent the Newaygo district, I am the representative, though my faith be unpopular. And if I am not elected, I am not the representative, though my faith be as pure as that of the angels.

. . . [Taylor] proceeded to show the great power of the House in the premises, its omnipotence in judging of the election of its members, and has made a clear case that from your judgment there is no appeal. But, he has not shown that you have a right to judge wrong. He has not shown that you have a right to reject the member who is elected for the purpose of receiving one who is not elected. He has not exonerated you from the obligations of that oath you have all sworn by the name of the great God, requiring you to judge right even in the case of those who have no appeal."[34]

At 5 P.M. Strang paused to let the House take a break. At 7 he resumed his arguments until 9:30, when the House adjourned until the next day. The next night, Strang concluded his speech. Taylor followed with his final arguments, apparently unconvincing, for after a few comments from members, the House voted 50 to 11 to allow Barton to withdraw his petition. Strang had retained his seat.[35]

Strang said that some of the ablest members of the House stated on the floor that not only were they persuaded by his arguments but also their prejudices were removed. One of these was Epaphroditus Ransom of Kalamazoo, a former governor and chief justice. Strang's reasoning ability, energy, and eloquence also gave him high marks from the press. The *Jackson Citizen* said: "'King Strang' plead his right in a masterly and convincing manner. He is a talented man, equal to any other man in debate and general information." The *Pontiac Jacksonian* said: "The Prophet . . . in a speech of much strength, shrewdness and tact, maintained his right to be enrolled among the Honorables of Michigan."[36]

By the fifth week of the session, the legislature had adopted four bills that Strang had introduced on the organization of counties and townships.[37] Three of the bills weakened the control Mackinac exerted over the northern Lower Peninsula and thus made his trip to Lansing worthwhile.

One act ordered the organization of Emmet County and scheduled an election of county officers, who would take over county affairs from the officers of Mackinac County. Under the act, which passed the House on a 50 to 7 vote, Beaver Island was split into two townships, Peaine on the north and Galilee on the south, and a separate mainland township of Charlevoix was absorbed into Emmet. The first township meeting of Charlevoix Township was to be held at the home of a Mormon. Strang said it was understood by the legislature that nearly the entire population of Emmet was Mormon and that the administration of its affairs would be in Mormon hands.[38]

The act quadrupled Emmet's area, which now included all of the northwestern corner of the Lower Peninsula north of Grand Traverse Bay plus Beaver and the other islands north of that bay. The main fishing grounds of Lake Michigan were within the county, and to the *Northern Islander* it was apparent that St. James was destined to be the center of trade and the seat of county business.[39]

Emmet took in all of the Mormon settlements in the region except one being started at Drummond Island, an island about twice the size of Beaver just off the easternmost edge of the Upper Peninsula. Drummond was roughly fifty miles east of Mackinac, while Beaver was the same distance west. Strang acted to solidify the fledgling Drummond settlement through a bill to organize that island into a township as part of Chippewa County. The first meeting of the new township was to be held at the home of a Mormon family there.[40]

The legislature also adopted two other bills introduced by Strang that completed the dismantling of the sway Mackinac held over the unorganized counties of the northern Lower Peninsula. The county of Cheboygan was organized, on an enlarged basis, and the organization of Grand Traverse County was completed. The unorganized counties in the region were either absorbed or attached to these counties for judicial purposes, thus ending the similar ties they had had to Mackinac County. Strang also saw to it that the legislature corrected situations in which Newaygo, Oceana, and Grand Traverse counties did not have a circuit judge by establishing those three counties, as well as Emmet and Cheboygan, in judicial circuits.[41]

With his regional house in order, Strang was free to turn his attention to affairs of the whole state. He found himself in the thick of legislative battles on issues that ranged from the trivial to the most momentous.

On the more mundane side, Strang stirred up a fuss over a bill to provide each school district in the state with a copy of Webster's unabridged dictionary. About 3,000 copies were expected to be needed, at a cost of up to $4 a copy. During the debate it was asserted that a large publishing house in the East had a great interest in selling the book, to the point of having an agent in Lansing who was instrumental in getting the bill introduced and was logrolling it toward passage. Strang denounced the book itself, saying it was an imperfect dictionary, which contained 1,000 words spelled contrary to its own rules for spelling. Strang attempted to supplant Noah Webster's work with another dictionary. The House decided not to go along with Strang's proposed switch, but the bill to buy Webster's eventually was defeated, with Strang in the majority.[42]

On more weighty legislative matters, Strang pricked pomposity and proposed commonsense changes. This was particularly true in debate on the general railroad bill.

Under the state constitution, a general law was required before railroad companies could organize—on their own—to build routes. The general laws were designed to free the legislature from the pressures of enacting special laws for companies wishing exclusive privileges, but the various railroad interests were at the legislature in force, competing for advantage under the general railroad bill. Critics of the bill said it would allow monopolies over routes for a pittance.[43]

Strang was an opponent of the general railroad bill, as drafted, and he played a prominent part in the debate. When one proponent of the bill, in cataloging his experience in railroad law, unwittingly fell into the role of a straight man, Strang pounced. Heman B. Ely, the representative of Marquette and Chippewa counties on Lake Superior, said he had "considerable experience in this matter of railroads." In fact, Ely and three brothers were building a railroad from what would be the city of Marquette to the iron ore mines inland. Ely told of his familiarity with railroad laws in other states and with the history of railroads in Michigan.[44]

"I have been over some of the routes where [rail]roads are now on foot," Ely said. "I have slept out nights and have been over various parts of this state, in ways that would almost appear incredible. . . . In coming down from the north, I was obliged to travel through seventy miles of snow on foot, and that occupied me six days' time, and I have during my travels often slept in the snow, and if I have not had some experience, I would ask who has."[45]

Ely pointed out that the House and Senate versions of the bill were essentially alike, even though, he said, they were drawn up without consultation. The House bill was drafted with great care from the best of the precedents on the subject, he said, and he argued for keeping the bill free of amendments, unless they were obviously needed.

In response, Strang admitted that he had not had "a very large experience" in railroad matters. "I have occasionally traveled in the forests, and at times slept out in the woods with the howl of wolves for my lullaby, and the snowbank for my bed, as well as the gentleman from Chippewa." Then he began to wield his debater's scalpel to expose Ely's argumentative flaws. "But in all that peculiar experience, I have learned nothing of the laws by which railroad companies are organized. . . . What little I have learned of the laws . . . , I have learned somewhere else besides in slumbering in a snowbank, and by some other voice besides the howls of wolves and forests," Strang said to howls of laughter and much applause in the House chamber.

Earlier, Strang proved he could cut to the quick and reduce an opposing argument to absurdity. To get back at him, the proponents of the general railroad bill often made personal allusions to his background by saying something about Beaver Island or the Mormons. Strang's old nemesis, the *Detroit Advertiser*, said the proponents of the bill took this religious tack "to neutralize his able arguments against a loose and unguarded bill being passed. . . . There is no one of the advocates of a general law able to measure swords with Strang in debate, and they all know it, so they fight him outdoors and in, by low insinuations about Beaver Island. Such a mode of dealing with one who ever treats every member like a gentleman, without intruding . . . his peculiar religious views, is not exactly 'on the square,' but he is able and will take care of himself."[46] Strang, in his debate with Ely, used the fact that he was called a prophet in a reference to Ely's comment about the Senate and House versions of the bill being so nearly alike, though drafted without consultation. He also took notice of Ely's comment that the bill had been drawn with great care.

Now, it may be that the bill before us has been drawn with a great deal of care. I do not doubt, that if two gentlemen succeeded in drawing two bills exactly alike, without any consultation with each other, so that, from section 1 to section 53 of the bills, there is no material difference, that they, at least, have been guided by some such inspiration that they ought to claim to be prophets, or the sons of prophets. . . .

I have discovered a certain kind of care used in drawing up this bill, that railroad companies may be organized under it—that they shall be possessed of legal franchises, which they shall hold in the nature of contract, and therefore not subject to repeal. I have discovered that there has been care used in drawing this bill, that a company once organized should not be easily dissolved—that its corporate existence should not be easily forfeited, and that its functions should not be easily taken away; but there are two kinds of care, that, with the little wisdom of which I am possessed, I have not been able to find in the bill. . . . I have not found one single word to guard the state against liability for breaches of these contracts which it has made, and to which it had bound itself by past actions. . . . All the care that is used is to provide for the corporations, not for the people. . . .

Now, I acknowledge myself that without being an especial enemy to corporations, I am not particularly friendly to them, but I regard them as one of those things without which it is difficult to transact the business of the country, but nevertheless as things that we should institute and suffer to exist only when we find a real public necessity for it. It is so natural that a corporation once sprung into existence, and without a soul to be judged at the bar of him who judgeth hearts, should be a little inclined to overreach—to get advantage of men, that we ought, at least, to be cautious about producing such things. . . .

The bill which is before us is a bill providing that anybody that pleases . . . may build a road wherever he thinks proper. [Strang said it cost $20,000 per mile to build a railroad line.] . . . and what are men required to pay to secure a route? . . . only $25 per mile. . . . and though they should neglect to do their work, make their surveys, pay their installments, and complete their road, their franchises are not thereby lost. They are entitled to those franchises until by the judgment of a court, they are taken away from them; so that unless we are to employ attorneys to litigate them out of existence, they remain . . . spread over all the state to stand in the way of any future legislation. . . .

But I said that with all the care used in drawing this bill, there was no care used for the citizen. Now where is your right, the right of your neighbor, your constituency? . . . No question of public necessity is made. No guards surround the rights of property. Not one single provision is incorporated in this bill—not one single word do you find written in it to say that your property shall not be taken away by mere rapacity, when there is no public necessity. Not one single word is found in this bill, drawn up by Divine inspiration [he said to laughter], to protect the rights of the citizen. . . .

There is a provision in the constitution that provides that private property shall not be taken for public use except in a particular manner, and that manner provides not only for securing the right of a citizen to his property, but his full compensation for it; but it provides further for the manifesting of that necessity—for the making of that necessity apparent. . . . Although I have never slept upon a snowbank over this bill, I think I am warranted in saying that it does not contain the provision that no property shall be used except the Legislature have declared the necessity. . . . this bill not only provides nothing of the kind, but it does not provide that any court, judge, commissioners and jurors shall declare the necessity. It is simply a question between the rapacity of one man and the injury of another.

Strang concluded his speech, which a *Detroit Advertiser* correspondent called one of the most powerful and elegant of the session, by saying:

It is true that I have bestowed but very little time upon the matter. It is true that I have had but little knowledge of law, and that a great while ago; yet I believe that these are the true positions in law.—But whether I have, or have not, erred in the principles of law, certain it is that the people of the state of Michigan are not prepared to give every rapacious speculator the right to go and lay his road wherever he pleases, not only across their fields, their yards, their houses, and over the graves of their children, just because they can make money out of it. . . . if the state was going to lay roads for public purposes, any such power would be surrounded with guards to prevent the desecration of everything we hold sacred.

Four days later all of the amendments proposed to the general railroad bill in the House's committee of the whole came before the House for a vote—one vote. The speaker ruled that the amendments would be voted on as a group. The pressure apparently was on for passage of the bill without delay. Strang objected, asking for a division of the membership on the speaker's ruling. The speaker declared Strang out of order. Strang persisted in his objection for several minutes. He explained that while he had moved many of the amendments to the bill, he also had strenuously opposed others, and he would stultify himself by voting against those he had moved and for those he had opposed. Strang insisted on his right to record his vote for some of the amendments and against the others. He told the speaker that such was the practice in deliberative assemblies, that it was a well-established parliamentary rule, and that under similar circumstances during the session he had called for a division, or a separation of the membership, and it had been ordered without hesitancy. Under the rules, Strang said, a request for a division is a right of any member and must be granted without a vote. The speaker replied that his request was out of order.[47]

On a vote of 35 to 28, the amendments were approved. The next morning the *Journal of the House* made no mention of the speaker's decision or of Strang's call for a division. Strang called the attention of the House to the omission, and the speaker said a correction would be made. The general railroad bill was given final approval by the House on February 8, in a 41 to 29 vote, with Strang in opposition.[48]

A few days later the House voted to censure the correspondent and editor of the *Detroit Advertiser* for a report charging the speaker with "iniquitous decisions" during the passage of the general railroad bill. The *Advertiser* referred in particular to the decision on Strang's call for a division. The vote on the censure was 49 to 6, with Strang among the six.[49]

Although in the minority on the railroad bill, Strang and other opponents would be able to claim eventual victory on the legislation. In the Senate, as one newspaper put it, the bill was "quietly put to sleep" by being tabled as the session wound to a close.[50]

Other major legislation did make it through, including bills to authorize construction of a mile-long canal with two locks at Sault Ste. Marie. The canal would be completed within two years with the aid of a federal land grant to the company that built it. This legislation, considered of primary importance for the state, provided an indication of the high regard for Strang in the House. He was named chairman of a conference committee that met with its Senate counterpart to resolve the final differences between the two bodies over the bill. The conference report was approved without change by the House.[51]

A bill to prohibit the manufacture and sale of intoxicating liquor proved that Strang's vote could not be predicted. The passage of a prohibition law in Maine had fueled support for a similar "Maine law" in Michigan, and the legislation received what was said to be an unprecedented show of support through petitions. A teetotaler, Strang would be expected to vote for the bill, but he opposed it, mainly for civil rights reasons. He said that the bill, which passed the House 57 to 12, would institute dangerous rules on the admissibility and competency of evidence and that its provisions against handling appeals in the usual manner were equivalent to a denial of justice, at least in the case of poor defendants.[52]

The bill included a provision for an election in June to determine whether it should take effect that year. Strang said the referendum amounted to delegating legislative power to the people, which he maintained was unauthorized by the state constitution, which had no referendum provision.[53] The courts would side with Strang's position, ruling the law unconstitutional.[54]

The *Jackson Citizen* blasted the legislature for shirking its responsibility on the liquor law, but it mentioned Strang as one of at least seven members in the House who had "met their responsibilities direct, with honor to themselves, their constituents and the state."[55] The most wide-ranging accolades for Strang came from the *Detroit Advertiser*, once his most bitter foe among the press. In their opposition to the railroad bill, Strang and the *Advertiser* found themselves allies. The *Advertiser* said Strang's "course as a member of the present Legislature has disarmed much of the prejudice which had previously surrounded him. "Whatever may be said or thought of the peculiar sect of which he is the local head," the *Advertiser* noted, " . . . throughout this session he has conducted himself with a degree of decorum and propriety which have been equalled by his industry, sagacity, good temper, apparent regard for the true interests of the people, and the obligations of his official oath." [56] The paper said Strang's "standing for influence, tact, intelligence, ability and integrity, was second to none" in the legislature. [57] This was heady praise from a paper that had once labeled him a miscreant and one of a pack of wolves.

The *Temperance Advocate* called Strang the most talented debater in the House. "He seems equally ready on any subject, political, commercial, financial, judicial, educational, or anything else in the range of legislation." The paper added that "from his social position as 'King of Beaver Island,' he is the lion of the House, and is always pointed out to the ladies visiting the Capitol." [58]

With good reviews of his performance as a legislator ringing in his ears, Strang set out to gain a higher office. Once again, he was thinking big and willing to be the focal point of a confrontation—once again, with his longtime, long-distance adversary, Brigham Young. With the backing of a petition signed by the Democrats in the legislature, Strang began soliciting a federal appointment to replace Young as governor of the Territory of Utah. The territory had been formed in 1850, and Young had been appointed by President Fillmore as its first governor. Young's appointment was due to expire in 1854. The *Battle Creek Journal* said it would be "a delicate matter to attempt to dethrone Governor Young; but the King is competent to any emergency. Bold, energetic, and cunning; and as he has rendered the party good service, and is reliable under all circumstances, he will probably be appointed." Young, however, would not be replaced as governor until 1857 [59]—and then not by Strang.

Chapter 12

Battle of Pine River

WHILE STRANG HAD HIS MIND on the mountaintops of Utah, he had to live through the valleys of the relationship between the Beaver Island Mormons and their neighbors. The first hint of an embattled 1853 came at a meeting of the Mackinac County board of supervisors on February 3. With Strang absent in the legislature in Lansing, the board ruled that George Miller, the Mormon who had been elected sheriff in September 1852, had failed to meet filing requirements. The board declared the office vacant and ordered a new election for April 4.[1]

Even though the *Northern Islander* said Miller had indeed met the filing requirements, the issue appears to have been moot. With Emmet County being organized, Miller would no longer be a resident of Mackinac County. Emmet elected its own sheriff, Miller's son, Joshua, on May 3. In that same first election for Emmet County, Mormons also were elected to fill the other county offices.[2]

With the Mormons in command in Emmet, Strang boarded the steamer *Morton* the week after the county election. En route to Buffalo, the *Morton* stopped at the Mackinac wharf for a few minutes, long enough for some on shore to learn that Strang was a passenger. A deputy sheriff boarded the steamer to arrest him.[3] The old indictment had apparently been dusted off again.

Strang claimed that the attempted arrest was an attempted kidnapping and that the deputy vowed to "serve him as they did old Joe" (a reference to Joseph Smith). But the deputy, Ben Rice, could not find Strang immediately, and the boat left the dock, with Rice on board. Strang had locked himself in his stateroom, where he even ate his meals.[4]

When Rice traced Strang to his room, he called on passengers to help him make the arrest. With the help of a passenger 'posse,' Rice forced open Strang's door, but, gun in hand, Strang threatened to shoot the first man who entered. The passengers scattered, and

Strang barricaded the doorway. Rice nailed the door shut, figuring he had his prisoner boxed in and would get help at the boat's next stop.

This state of siege continued until the steamer docked on the Canadian shore north of Detroit to take on wood. Learning this from a fellow Mormon named Pierce (probably one of the Pierce brothers, either Isaac or Jonathan), Strang broke open his door and sprang for the rail. Rice grabbed him by the collar as he was climbing over the side. Pierce stepped up, pulled a revolver, and told the deputy to let Strang go or he would shoot.

Deputy Rice drew his pistol and, aiming at Pierce, pulled the trigger—but the gun misfired. (The Mormons later claimed the deputy had had buck fever and forgot to cock his pistol. They said the bursting of a cap that the deputy thought he heard was only the thumping of his heart.) Strang jerked himself loose and jumped ashore. Soon he was swallowed by the wilds of Canada. Pierce followed.

ਇਹ ਇਹ ਇਹ

Meanwhile, the Mormons were making the most of their control of the governmental machinery in their area. They issued a warning about the sale of liquor by trading vessels on the Lake Michigan waters of Emmet County. "If the trade is persisted in," the *Islander* said on May 12, "the Sheriff will go out with sufficient force and make arrests in all such cases. The law will be enforced whatever the cost. He is a fool who at this day thinks he can defeat it by crying pirates, robbers. That cry has been raised once too much."[5]

That provocative message literally prompted alarm bells in Mackinac. On May 16, four days after the warning was published, the following was posted throughout Mackinac:[6]

NOTICE

The citizens of Mackinac county and all others interested in the matter are requested to meet at the C House to-morrow (Tuesday) evening at the ringing of the bell, to devise ways and means of protecting themselves against the felonious depredations of the Mormons.

The notice was signed by J. P. King, the local township supervisor, and five others, including two officials who had been friendly to the Mormons—John D. Irvine, the district attorney for the Upper Peninsula, and William N. MacLeod, one of four justices of the peace who signed. A large number of people attended the meeting; Irvine was named chairman. MacLeod made an eloquent and spirited speech, which he concluded by moving a series of resolutions. These were unanimously adopted.[7] One resolution took notice of the new boundaries of Emmet County and the organization of Drummond Township and said these factors, "taken in connection with the avowed determination of the Mormons to make forcible arrests under color of law, is highly dangerous to the rights and interests of the citizens of Mackinac."[8] Mackinac was feeling the point of the whittling Strang had done in the legislature. It had had a measure of control over one-quarter of the state, but now, except for its own county, its domain had been sliced away.

Apparently MacLeod and Irvine were also feeling the impact of those changes. They had enjoyed the backing of the Mormons and owed their elections to them. Now the Mormons were in another voting district, and, as supporters of the Mormons, MacLeod and Irvine were in the minority in Mackinac. As Strang put it, "These men professed to be our friends, solely from a regard to the right, and at the expense of their interest at home." Now with the organization of Emmet County, they found themselves in an uphill struggle to carve out a new political constituency. "If they were . . . hypocritical friends," Strang said, "they would now seek the favor of their old opponents by being first and loudest to cry out against the Mormons."[9] And they did.

In the Mackinac meeting, references were made to thefts and arsons on Gull Island, on the northern shore of Lake Michigan, and at Pine River and Grand Traverse. The crimes were blamed on the Mormons. The manifesto from the meeting stated that in the recent "outrages" was recognized "a spirit, which if not quelled by the strong arm of the law, must eventually lead to the most determined resistance." A committee was appointed to seek the aid of the president and governor, to call public meetings, and to take "such measures as may seem conducive to the public safety."[10]

John W. McMath, the secretary of the meeting and a justice of the peace, sent a recapitulation of the session to the Detroit papers along with a covering letter. In the letter he wrote that "much excitement has prevailed" at Mackinac because of the "frequent and daily recurring instances of robberies, burglaries, and other depredations committed by the Mormons of Beaver Island upon the fishermen along the shores and upon the waters of Lake Michigan. It appears the Mormons are becoming more daring than formerly. Heretofore, they were satisfied with robbing the poor fishermen of their boats, nets and fish, stealthily, doing every thing possible to avoid detection; but now, seeing the utter impossibility of being brought to justice, they carry on their piratical trade with scarcely any regard to concealment."[11] McMath pointed out that it was nearly impossible for a fisherman to guard his property because of the nature of the business. The fisherman's gill nets had buoys attached that could be seen a mile or two away, but the nets often were set eight or ten miles from his dwelling, too far off to be seen. According to McMath, the Mormons—who had three ships in their "navy," the schooners *Dolphin*, *Emmlin* and *Seaman*[12]—would soon learn the location of the nets, "and when the wind is fair, sail out to them . . . , take them up, then shifting their sails, are soon far away on the water, leaving no trace by which to be detected. In the night they make their descent upon the land, steal, rob and burn what they can find, then with oars and sail they glide away. . . . The only reason that can be assigned for these acts is (as they have openly declared) that they intend to monopolize these fishing grounds, and appropriate the same to the service of the Lord and His 'Saints.' "[13]

One Gentile called the Mormon enforcement of the liquor law "an excellent ruse" by which the Mormons could board every small vessel and enter every trading house and fisherman's hut to confiscate (or rob) goods and imprison violators. The Mormons could thereby harass the Gentiles in their business, "all under legal color, and for the temperance cause."[14] McMath said one reason for the Mormons' boldness was that northern Lake Michigan was in Emmet County and all offenses committed there were under the jurisdiction of that county's "Mormon tribunals, with good Mormons for witnesses and jurymen."

The *Northern Islander* responded that some of the alleged crimes were committed in Mackinac County, under the jurisdiction of "Mackinac tribunals, with good Mackinac men for witnesses and jurymen," but that nothing ever came of those charges, even though there was said to be proof against the Mormons.[15]

Strang also pointed out that although there were Mormon justices of the peace on Beaver Island, the circuit court had yet to meet in Emmet County. "The tribunal has not been organized, the jurymen have not been empannelled, nor the witnesses brought into Court." He called the whole reference to Mormon tribunals, witnesses, and jurymen gratuitous.[16]

The *Islander* added that no one county had exclusive jurisdiction over crimes committed on the waters of Lake Michigan: "all the counties contiguous to the Lake have concurrent jurisdiction of offenses committed on the waters within the State. If the Mormons affect secrecy no longer, fill the courts of the Lake counties with prosecutions, but not the newspapers with lies."[17] The only question at issue, the *Islander* said, was whether the state liquor laws would be enforced. "The officers of Emmet County are conscientiously doing their duties . . . and the officers of Mackinac [are] engaged in . . . unblushing violation of their official oaths [to enforce the law]." According to Strang, the liquor trade was suppressed throughout the Beaver Island group, except for Gull Island. The *Islander* said Mackinac was finding "its right to violate the law by trafficking in liquors trampled upon; and its interest in making money at the expense . . . of the Indians endangered."[18]

Liquor had been big business at Mackinac, ever since it was used to purchase furs from the Indians during fur trading's heyday. The *Islander* said Mackinac had more people selling liquor than any village of the same size in the state. According to Strang, as many as twenty "groggeries" in Mackinac were open constantly during the fishing season, and the boarding houses there generally had well-patronized bars. But the big money in liquor, he said, was made in the fishing grounds, where most of the liquor was sold and where most of the liquor sold was "Indian whiskey."[19] The recipe for Indian whiskey was two gallons of alcohol to thirty gallons of water, plus enough tobacco to make the mixture intoxicating and enough cayenne pepper to give it sufficient strength to justify the name "firewater." This adulterated concoction, more intoxicating than pure liquor, cost about six cents per gallon to make and was sold for twenty-five cents a quart, or as little as fifty cents a gallon in bulk. The high profit margin for liquor, the *Islander* said, probably netted Mackinac more income in the fishing grounds than the other trade articles combined.[20]

At the same time the Mormons were threatening the export of Mackinac liquor to the fisheries, the Mormon port of St. James, with its natural harbor and its prime location in the midst of the best fishing grounds, was becoming more of a threat to Mackinac's stake in the fishing business. This provided another incentive for Mackinac to act against the Mormons, Strang said. "Mackinac is too much used to being all, and in all; and too little able to bear competition, to be willing to see any other place of business in her vicinity."[21]

On June 30, 1853, the *Northern Islander* concluded its response to the resolutions from Mackinac by stating: "'Let words cease and deeds begin.' We prefer peace; but if war must come, let it be upon us and not upon our children. We shall not yield a step to the threats and are ready today for the blow."[22] It would come within two weeks.

                           ❧ ❧ ❧

Midway between Grand Traverse and Little Traverse bays on the Lower Peninsula, a quarter-mile-long river entered Lake Michigan. The stream, the Pine River, along with a small round lake and another shorter stream, formed a waterway to a fourteen-mile-long inland lake known as Long Lake. This large lake was surrounded by timber, making the area attractive to settlers. And Pine River emptied into a Lake Michigan bay that made a passable harbor for fishermen.[23]

It was to this place, twenty-five miles southeast of Beaver Island, that many Gentiles had gone when they left the Mormon kingdom. Among the first at the Pine River settlement had been Alva Cable, who built a large house on the south bank of the river. Cable added a cooper shop that employed several men and a store that supplied the settlement with basic provisions and a few dry goods. Among the more recent settlers was the Walter Whitney family, who had left Beaver Island for a fresh start in November of 1852.[24]

Earlier that November Sheriff George Miller had carried warrants to Pine River seeking men accused of stealing nets on Beaver Island. The *Northern Islander* reported that no arrests were made because "almost the entire population" took to the woods when Miller arrived. Miller went on to visit Grand Traverse, and when he stopped at Pine River on his way back to Beaver, some of those he sought took to their boats and fled, even though there was a severe storm on the lake. "The Pine River settlement is little else than a band of vagabonds and thieves," the *Islander* said, "and the sight of an officer of the law sets them all in a twitter."[25]

While fishing ostensibly was the main business of the settlement, Strang implied that thievery was. He said that men from Pine River occasionally stole from Mormons on Beaver Island and that they prowled about the region, robbing others and blaming the thefts on the Mormons.[26] The Pine River settlers were just as vehement that in their charges that it was the Mormons who were stealing.

In November 1852 the *Northern Islander* had expressed doubts about the future of the Pine River settlement, saying it was "entirely destitute of provisions and winter supplies."[27] The settlement survived the winter, though, and late in April 1853, the *Islander* touted the location's advantages, including good farmland and fishing. The paper said a "considerable body" of Beaver Island settlers intended to go there in May, news that probably did not sit well in Pine River.[28]

In the first part of May, Galen B. Cole, a Mormon and the newly elected supervisor of Charlevoix Township, the mainland portion of Emmet County, conducted tax assessments at Pine River to the consternation of the settlers there. After he left, according to the *Northern Islander*, some men lamented that they had not killed him. The settlers at Pine River sent resolutions to Mackinac saying that if the "law was not put in force, they would take the matter in their own hands."[29]

These resolutions and those adopted later at Mackinac apparently dissuaded anyone from Beaver Island from settling at Pine River that spring, except for two disaffected Mormon families. One was headed by an elder named William Savage, and the other included a·young man named Hull and his widowed mother. When they left the kingdom, they pretended to be moving to the new Mormon colony on Drummond Island. As soon as their boat was out of sight of Beaver Island, they headed instead for Pine River, where they sought the protection of the settlers there.[30]

The Pine River settlement continued to grow with Gentiles that spring. By one count it included more than twenty-five families. Strang said that by summer the settlement had about seventy men, many strident opponents to the imposition of what they termed Mormon law in their area.[31] What appeared to be a relatively routine judicial matter for a few Pine River residents would touch off an explosion there in July.

On the evening of July 12 Emmet County Sheriff Joshua L. Miller left St. James, the county seat, to summon jurors for the session of the circuit court to be held there on July 19. His boat had a crew of five men, and they stopped overnight at Galilee before setting out for Pine River the next morning. At Galilee, Miller had learned that new threats had been made at Pine River to kill any man who attempted to serve any papers there. Miller decided to take another boat and nine more men, making a total of fifteen men in two boats.[32]

The presence of that many men, Miller thought, would prevent any violence until his mission could be explained. After the explanation, no objection was expected. After all, the Gentiles had complained about Mormon justice, and here the Mormons were trying to get non-Mormons to serve on juries in what was described as a Mormon county. Serving summonses on three prospective jurors should present no problem.[33]

But the Mormons did not realize the impact of a May 19 letter sent by the Mackinac committee of safety, headed by William N. MacLeod. In an "Address to the Inhabitants of Pine River," which offered sympathy and unspecified support, the committee also urged them to take action against the Mormons.[34] "We feel that the time has come when something must be done . . . to resist their practices, pretensions, to punish their outrages and if need be to banish them from the land. It is a strife in which there can be no reconciliation and no compromise; it may require violent measures, and may terminate in bloodshed. But there is no other alternative and you must count the cost and be prepared. . . . These people are rapidly increasing and it will be easier to crush the serpent in its weak infancy than to wait until years add to his venom and strength." In other words, Mackinac hoped the Pine River hotheads would take on the Mormons at the first opportunity. The committee also gave the inhabitants detailed instructions on how to prepare for the Mormons. They were told to "organize a company of reliable men who can be depended upon in any emergency. Admit none but those who are prepared to go to all lengths when called upon. . . . Arm yourselves as well as you can for the present, let your guns be always loaded and convenient for immediate action." [35]

The residents were advised to keep a guard near their boats throughout the night and to agree on a signal at which they would rally in an instant. Two months later, these instructions would be followed almost exactly. In the meantime, according to Strang, the Pine River men had been furnished guns by Mackinac. [36]

za za za

July 13th was a clear, bright day at Pine River. Women were holding a quilting party at one of the fishermen's homes near the south bank of the river. From the high bluff nearby, someone spotted two objects on the lake in the direction of Beaver Island. With the aid of a spyglass, it could be seen that the objects were fishing boats being rowed toward the mouth of Pine River. As the boats neared the mainland, a rush of excitement went through the crowd of women. Mormons were coming! The women knew their men had made up their minds to fight if necessary. [37]

As the Mormons approached the beach, they saw numerous armed men running about. Guns were being fired, apparently as a signal. The Mormon party supposed this show of strength was to prevent any arrests of Pine River men. Since Sheriff Miller had no warrants to arrest anyone and was there only to summon jurors, the commotion was not the cause of any great uneasiness among the Mormons.[38] At about 2 P.M. the Mormon boats landed side by side on a narrow beach next to a dense growth of timber and bushes just south of the river. A short distance away on the beach, a group of fishermen had gathered, expecting trouble. The Mormons walked over to them and stated their business. Although several fishermen had gathered with menacing words and manner, they appeared at least partially satisfied with the sheriff's explanation.[39]

The Gentiles were suspicious of any civil process issued in St. James, however, and they became more so when they learned the names of the men who were wanted as jurors. Two of the three men being summoned were Savage and Hull, the disaffected Mormons, and the third was David Moon, who had gotten into several scrapes on Beaver Island. The Gentiles believed that Strang wanted these men for something other than jury duty and that the summonses were a pretext to get the men to Beaver Island.[40]

Moon was an especially dark character. In the 1840s, the *Northern Islander* said, Moon's Indian wife had died from wounds suffered when he beat her with an ax, and a few years later he and three other men took turns raping another squaw. In the more recent history of Beaver Island, the paper said, Moon had exhibited double-dealing by selling the same quantity of barrel stave bolts to two different persons. He was paid two barrels of whiskey by one of the buyers. When he brought the whiskey to the Beaver Islands and began selling it to Indians, he ran afoul of Mormon enforcement of the state liquor laws. He paid a $20 fine and costs, but when he threatened the Indian who made the complaint, his stay in custody was prolonged. Then both men who had bought the bolts filed legal action against Moon. He fled the islands and eventually located in Pine River.[41]

According to the Mormons' published version of events, that day at Pine River the Mormons went ashore unarmed to serve the summonses. The Gentiles said the Mormons carried arms and insisted on taking the three men right then, dead or alive. Eventually the Mormons admitted that they did take four guns, which they hid under some coats in one of the boats.[42]

Sheriff Miller read his authority for summoning the three men. To the men of Pine River, the language sounded more like that of a warrant. They told the Mormons that no one would be taken and advised them to return to Beaver Island immediately. Meanwhile, Alva Cable and two other men had gone down to the Mormon boats. When they returned to the Pine River group, one was heard to say: "They have no guns."[43]

Things were getting uncomfortable for the Mormons, who could see armed men gathering on the bluff. The sheriff and the rest of his party began heading to their boats. About thirty Pine River men, carrying guns, filed down a narrow path through the trees and bushes to the beach, where they formed a row.[44]

A half-hour after they had arrived, the Mormons began to shove off. There was confusion. Threats were exchanged. Suddenly, a shot echoed along the beachfront, and a young fisherman named Lewis Gebeau slumped to the ground. Gebeau, who had lived for a time on Beaver Island and was Elizabeth Whitney's half-brother, said he was walking toward the Mormons to talk to some former acquaintances. He said he had stopped to examine his gun when he was shot, by a Mormon, the Gentiles said. Gebeau claimed that he learned later that the shot was fired from a horse pistol by Jonathan Pierce, described as one of Strang's "hard-fisted men." Pierce was said to have exclaimed: "We are running away like a set of damned cowards; I'll let them know I am not afraid."[45]

Gebeau was hit in the calf of his leg, and the wound was not serious. But the men of Pine River said they thought he had been killed and they began firing. Later the Gentiles claimed that both sides were firing shots.[46]

The Mormons said none of them had fired a shot and that their last man was just climbing aboard his boat when a murderous fire broke out from the beach and from the bluff. The Mormons had to stand up in full view to push off by using their oars as poles. Balls were raining on them like hailstones, the *Northern Islander* said. Strang, who was not present, said more than 100 shots were fired, all at short range. Some fishermen, he said, stood on the beach and fired at the Mormons as if they were target shooting.[47]

Six Mormons were wounded, three seriously. One Mormon

poled his oar with one arm, the other dangling because a shot had broken both bones below the elbow; he collapsed from the loss of blood. Another steered his boat even though a ball had entered at his hip and passed down the thigh to lodge near his knee. A third was hit just below the shoulder by a ball that cut an artery. Jonathan Pierce was slightly wounded.[48]

As the Mormons rowed out of range, the Pine River men gave chase. A heavy fishing boat with twenty-five men aboard led the way. Two smaller boats followed, trailing about a mile back. With their lighter boats, the Mormons had a good head start. About ten miles out, however, the heavy, eight-oared fishing boat began closing the gap.[49]

The situation was bleak. The Mormons were outgunned and outmanned. Every able-bodied man was rowing, but the pursuing boat was nearly within range. Then the Mormons saw a ship—the bark *Morgan*, en route to Chicago, lying becalmed. Could they make it to the ship? The Pine River boat closed within range, and once the fishermen aboard realized where the Mormons were heading, they resumed firing.[50]

The captain of the *Morgan*, E. S. Stone, was eating dinner in his cabin when he heard the shots. He rushed on deck and spotted the boats. "A brisk firing was kept up from the stern boat upon the two others," he wrote in his log. "The two boats ahead were endeavoring to get clear from the more powerful assailants in the larger boat, which was fast gaining on them—keeping up a brisk running fire without receiving a shot in return."[51] The two Mormon boats, Stone wrote, "approached within hailing distance of us and begged us to take them on board and afford them protection," which he did when the two boats came around the *Morgan* to shield themselves from the Pine River boat. One Morman brought his rifle on board, saying: "Now we will give it to them." But Stone disarmed him and the other Mormons.[52]

The men from Pine River, about fifty rods away, ceased firing and lay on their oars. Stone said they "hailed us, forbidding my receiving the cursed Mormons on board—that they were pirates, deserved death and should die." They told Stone that if he protected the Mormons, they would fire at the bark. Stone mildly replied that he would not allow them any nearer the *Morgan* in their "excited state." The men discussed the situation and then rowed back toward Pine River.[53]

Stone noted that "rifle balls had shattered and riddled the boats in picturesque style," but that as far as the boats' crews were concerned, the shots had "miraculously escaped taking effect in immediate vital places." An oar pulled by one man had been hit three times, and yet the man was unhurt. The Mormons said that more than 200 shots had been fired at them. The boats were spattered with blood, and the water in the bottom of them was red.[54]

The Mormons were fed aboard the ship. After nightfall the *Morgan* took them to Galilee, where they went ashore in their own boats. The next morning H. D. MacCulloch was summoned to Galilee to dress the wounds. Sheriff Miller had not been hit, nor had two other prominent Mormons involved, Franklin Johnson and L. D. Hickey.[55]

Later that day, the *Northern Islander* published a broadsheet extra about the Pine River incident under the headline: "MURDEROUS ASSAULT—ATTACK ON SHERIFF MILLER—SIX MEN WOUNDED." The story included something for the residents of Pine River to think about: "A large number of the attacking party were recognized, and measures are being taken to bring them to justice. There would be no difficulty in fitting out a party from here who would make the Pine River settlement as bare as the palm of a man's hand; but the moral effect of sending a half dozen to State Prison is worth more than the death of them all. Legal remedies are better than violent ones." At Mackinac this message evolved into a report that the Mormons were threatening to go to Pine River with 600 men and "sweep the land."[56]

At the circuit court session at St. James the next week, David Moon and others were indicted for shooting at the sheriff. When an officer went to Pine River to make arrests, the settlement was deserted. The settlers had fled, some to Little Traverse Bay and to Grand Traverse. Many of the fishermen had found refuge on Washington Island, on the west side of Lake Michigan at the entrance to Green Bay. The fishermen at Gull Island, another hotbed of opposition to Strang, had also abandoned their settlement. There were no white men at either place. None of those indicted in the Battle of Pine River was ever arrested.[57]

The Mormons lost the battle but won control over the Pine River area. In the spring of 1854 the Mormons again made plans for settlements there, and the first Mormon settlers arrived in May.[58]

Meanwhile, on Beaver Island, more settlers arrived in 1854 than in any previous year, according to the *Northern Islander*.[59] One attraction was cheap land, for none had to buy it in the legal sense. No land was bought from the federal government or sold by any form of deed on Beaver Island for the three-year period starting in the summer of 1853. Except for areas at or near the harbor and at Galilee, the island was government owned and for sale. But the Mormons, who owned less than 1,000 of the 33,000 acres of land on the island, had built homes, established farms, and cut timber over much of the island.[60] They had been assigned their land by Strang as an inheritance, after paying a tithe. There was no legality to the procedure, however, and the settlers were squatters.

Another attraction was the availability of jobs. The *Northern Islander* of July 13, 1854, said hundreds of additional men could find steady employment there. "An industrious man with a good span of horses, can do better at teaming than he can in the learned professions elsewhere." The paper claimed that "every kind of business is prosperous at this place. Money was never as plenty as at this time." In the fall of 1854, the *Islander* said laborers were so scarce that one employer was on a trip to hire help.[61]

As soon as settlers got off boats, the men could always find work chopping cordwood. With an average of three steamers stopping at the island each day during the season, the demand for cordwood outstripped the supply. Three wharves were selling steamboat wood at St. James and one at Galilee.[62]

Beaver Island had become the main stop for steamboats between Detroit and Wisconsin, with more boats landing there than at any place north of Milwaukee. Recognizing the island's importance, Congress had appropriated money for construction of a lighthouse at St. James. The rise of Beaver to the preeminent spot, as far as shipping through the straits was concerned, came at the expense of Mackinac.[63]

Shipping was not the only area in which the Beaver Islands were surpassing Mackinac. In 1854 the state census listed Emmet County with a population of 4,971, as opposed to a stagnant 1,639 for Mackinac County. The Beaver Island chain boasted a population of 2,608. While the population of Beaver Island itself had been slightly more than 500 in 1850, it claimed 2,000 in 1854, or a quadrupling in four years. The *Islander*, always thinking big, said there was room for 50,000 without crowding.[64] The message from the census was clear: the new kingdom was flourishing while the old king of the straits was wheezing.

The census reported that the predominant occupation in the Beaver Islands was fisherman: 170 of 442 men listed that trade. There also were eighteen coopers, eighteen sailors, and five boat builders; thus about half of the men had jobs relating to fishing. After fisherman came laborers (with 74 men, probably mostly wood choppers) and farmers (with 73).[65]

Mackinac and Emmet counties were the state's two leading producers of barrels of fish. But Emmet was number one, packing 33,863 barrels in the previous twelve months to Mackinac's 19,011. The Beaver Islands alone packed more than Mackinac County, with 20,864 barrels. At $7 for each 200-pound barrel, the islands' fish trade amounted to nearly $150,000. Strang claimed that the islands' annual export trade in fish, plus cordwood and potatoes, amounted to $325,000.[66]

Before the Mormons took control of the Beaver Islands, some of the fish caught by fishermen there had been sent to Mackinac to be packed and shipped. By 1854 not only were all of the fish caught by Beaver Island fishermen being packed in barrels at Beaver, but also Mormon trading with Mackinac had all but ended, as a consequence of the Mackinac crusade against the Mormons.[67] The Mormons were trading instead with other ports on the Great Lakes, and their business was not inconsiderable since the Mormons imported many of the provisions they needed. Although Beaver Island no longer dealt with Mackinac, Mackinac still sought to deal a blow to the Mormon kingdom. One opportunity would occur in the 1855 legislature, in the drive to dismember Emmet County and contain the Mormons on the Beaver Islands.

Chapter 13

The Drive to Dismember Strang's Empire

WHEN STRANG WAS FIRST ELECTED to the legislature, his opponents questioned whether he was living in the Newaygo district. Upon his reelection on November 7, 1854, he was accused of vote fraud. The opponents' suspicions were aroused by the Mormon vote, which was not only one-sided but also unanimous. Emmet County cast 695 votes in the race, and Strang received every one.[1]

Even with that huge vote, Strang took no chances on losing his seat. The Emmet County board of canvassers provided an apparent fallback position. The board, with Strang as chairman and including three other Mormon officials, met at St. James on November 14 and declared him elected without regard to the results in the rest of the Newaygo district. The board's reasoning: under the reapportionment act of 1851 the county now had enough people to be entitled to a separate state representative.[2]

The Mormons need not have worried. Ten days later the Newaygo district's board of canvassers, with H. D. MacCulloch as chairman of the four-member board, certified 1,374 votes for state representative in the district; Strang's 695 from Emmet County alone were more than a majority. He also tallied nineteen of the twenty votes in Cheboygan County for a total of 714.[3]

The candidate in second place was Albert Tracy Lay, a lumberman from Grand Traverse County, who received 367 of his 368 votes from his home county. John A. Brooks was third, with 261, almost all from Newaygo County. The remaining thirty-one votes were split four ways.[4] Either Lay or Brooks would have had enough votes to win the election in 1852, when Strang's winning total was 165, but the Mormon settlements in Emmet County had grown dramatically since then. The question was: had they grown enough to cast 695 legal votes?

Looking ahead to the new legislative session shortly after the election, the *Detroit Advertiser* said Strang would "doubtless" be contesting with five other representatives for the Democratic leadership in the House. Calling Strang a shrewd manager, the *Advertiser* paid Strang high respect as a politician, saying that he "wields more political power than any other one man in the state."[5] If the *Advertiser* were talking about ability to control votes in one's district, it may have been right; but if the paper were talking about clout in the state at large, or even in the House alone in 1855, it was guilty of gross overstatement. The political winds had shifted, against the Democrats and against Strang.

At one point, there was a question about whether Strang could even survive what he termed a "powerful demonstration" to unseat him. It was charged that Emmet County had overvoted by enough to assure Strang's election, and the *Detroit Tribune* reported that Lay would contest Strang's election on the ground that Strang had not received more than 250 legal votes to Lay's 368.[6]

The *Northern Islander* said a caucus of the Fusionists (or Republicans) had decided to send for Lay to fill the Newaygo seat: "the caucus determined to assume that Mr. Lay was duly elected, and give him Mr. Strang's place, 'without wasting time on it,' in other words, to judge the cause against Mr. Strang without evidence, and refuse to receive it." The "opportune appearance" of an article in the *Michigan State Journal* in Lansing, the *Islander* said, shamed the Republicans out of that plan.[7]

The *State Journal* described the allegations against Strang as "thoroughly malicious and utterly unfounded." Strang, the paper said, had frequently been accused "of exercising an undue influence over the electors in Emmet. . . . If there is any force in the argument, . . . the candidates are all in the same boat." The article pointed out that although the vote for Strang was unanimous in his home county, the vote for Lay and Brooks was nearly so in their home counties. "If the unanimity of the vote raised the slightest suspicion against Mr. Strang, it does precisely the same against Messrs. Lay and Brooks."[8]

An in-depth analysis of the 1854 state census taken that summer in Emmet County indicates that the county did cast more ballots than there were legal voters. The Emmet census, conducted by

Strang and other township officials who were Mormons, reported 839 males of voting age (twenty-one and above) in the county. But official township lists of the males "over 21" contain only 662 names, plus notations that the names of seventy-four persons could not be ascertained or were unknown, for a total of 736, or more than 100 shy of the 839 males "counted" of voting age.[9] It seems likely that the seventy-four anonymous persons tallied in the summer remained anonymous in the fall and thus did not vote. The nameless ones could have been transient fishermen who were in the area only for the peak fishing season. Eliminating the anonymous as potential voters leaves 662, and if all of them voted, the total would be thirty-three fewer than Strang's election total.

A check of the names shows that, based on known ages, at least five would have been too young to vote. The lists also appear to have at least seventy-one duplicate names. Nine persons appear to make the lists three times, and one four. The whimsy of the census taker in Peaine Township is apparent. After the name Napoleon Bonaparte is the notation "(not the emperour)." Charles Douglass, Strang's first polygamous wife, is on the list of males.[10] Eliminating apparent duplicates and ineligibles reduces the probable number of eligible voters to 585.

On the lists also are about 135 names of Indian men, who were eligible to vote if they were "civilized" and not a member of any tribe, the change in the state constitution that William N. MacLeod had proposed in 1850. Ascertaining tribal membership was difficult, as was making a definite judgment on whether an Indian was civilized. Strang wrote in 1854 that of the main body of Indians in his area, the only ones who could speak English were children: a majority of the Indian men could read and some could write, but only in their own language. In a legislative report filed in 1855 by a committee that Strang headed, he wrote: "there is no standard of civilization, by which to determine who are entitled to the elective franchise. In some parts of the state those only are regarded as civilized who have an English education, and are principally employed in professional, agricultural or mechanical labors. In others, the vices of whites are satisfactory badges of civilization."[11]

It would have been to Strang's advantage to consider as many Indians as possible to be civilized and thus eligible to vote. But even if all of the Indians listed were considered voters and indeed voted, Strang's vote total was probably inflated by at least 100. Strang did say that after the census was taken that summer, the arrival of new settlers expanded the county population. However, because of a three-month residency requirement, any settler who arrived after the first part of August would not have been eligible to vote in November unless he had previously been a resident of the state.[12]

Emmet was not the only county in the district to have a suspiciously high turnout in the election. Grand Traverse, which counted 375 males of voting age in the census, cast 374 votes, and Newaygo, with a census count of 337 men twenty-one and older, cast 285. Statewide, the turnout was 66 percent of the census figures, while Emmet County's was 83 percent. Newaygo's was 85 percent, and in Albert Lay's home county of Grand Traverse, it was 99.7 per cent. "After a great flourish of trumpets," Strang said, the challenge to the seat "looked so bare faced, Mr. Lay shrank from the exhibition."[13]

Emmet County may have given its unanimous support to Strang, a Democrat, but the county, which generally supported Democrats on the state ticket that year, went for the Republican candidate for governor, Kinsley S. Bingham, over Democrat John S. Barry, 650 to 45. Barry had been governor during the Mormons' legal difficulties in 1851, and they felt he had given the people of Mackinac his tacit support.[14]

Perhaps it was no coincidence that the state's leading Democrat, U.S. Senator Lewis Cass, once the party's presidential nominee, visited Beaver Island aboard the warship *Michigan* in August and paid his respects to Strang at the "Court of St. James." The *Northern Islander* said the "kindest expressions" passed between Cass and the king.[15] If Cass were trying to shore up the Mormon vote for Barry, he was unsuccessful. The loss of the Mormon vote was not crucial, however, as Barry and many other Democrats were inundated in a Republican tidal wave.

The Republican party had been formed in 1854 in part as a reaction against the Kansas-Nebraska Act, which provided for "popular sovereignty," the right for settlers to decide whether a new state would permit slavery. The Democrats had supported the act, and Republicans sought to prevent the extension of slave territory. In Michigan, Bingham's entire Republican ticket was elected, and Republicans outnumbered the Democrats by about two to one in both houses of the legislature.[16]

During the legislative session Strang again lived at the Benton House, and this time he apparently was accompanied by his first wife, Mary. His sister wrote that James was taking Mary and his six-year-old daughter Harriet to Lansing, while the older children stayed with his father and mother, who had moved to Voree.[17] Another legislator at the Benton House was Jacob A. T. Wendell, a twenty-eight-year-old merchant from Mackinac.[18] Wendell, although a fellow Democrat, would seek to undo much of what Strang had accomplished in the last session.

The session began January 3, 1855, and for the first time since 1841 the Democrats did not control the House. Indeed, it was a chamber of many strangers and few familiar faces for Strang: only five of the House's seventy-two members had been reelected. Almost by default, Strang became a member with high seniority, with a front-row desk. Despite the Republican control, he was named chairman of the Indian Affairs Committee. Wendell, in what would prove to be an ominous move for Strang, was named to the Towns and Counties Committee.[19]

During the first few days of the session, Strang served notice that he intended to be a busy legislator—even as a member of a minority party. He began the process for bills to organize counties, bills to construct roads, and a bill to create a new judicial district.[20] Strang again was working hard—and was again in the midst of controversies.

On January 8 Strang set off a furor by seeking an investigation of the state prison at Jackson to see if state officials had established a counterfeiting operation there.[21] (A month later, the committee that investigated the prison reported that it had found numerous deficiencies, including a convict who said he had been hired to counterfeit coin.)[22]

Also on January 8 he presented the petitions of several Negroes seeking the right of suffrage. Strang told the House that in "looking for the man, he looked not in his face to see the color of the skin, but to the soul." In reporting this quote, the Democratic *Detroit Free Press* thought Strang was ready "to fuse"—or join the Republicans, a fusion of Whigs and Free Soilers.[23] It is known that Strang's party ties that session were weak: he did not attend Democratic caucuses, claiming he had too much legislative work to do.[24]

Strang's views on slavery had long been closer to those espoused by the Republicans than to those of the Democrats. In 1849 he had expressed his opposition to "slavery in every form."[25] And in an hour and a half speech on January 24, Strang echoed Governor Bingham in denouncing the Fugitive Slave Law.[26] Later, he was one of several Democrats who voted with Republicans to pass a rights and liberties law that provided protections for fugitive slaves.[27]

The legislation that kept Strang the busiest that session was aimed directly at him and his budding empire—the plan to dismember Emmet County. The plan was designed to prevent the Mormons from settling anywhere except on Beaver Island and the other islands in that area.[28]

Mackinac Representative Jacob Wendell, more commonly known as Theodore, was the key promoter of the dismemberment plan. To the Mormons, Wendell had originally been one of the good people in Mackinac. Just five months earlier, in describing "deeds of villainy" against the Mormons, the *Northern Islander* concluded that the more respectable citizens of Mackinac either approved of those anti-Mormon actions or were indifferent to them; Theodore Wendell and his brother were the only known exceptions.[29]

The stand of the Wendells did not go unnoticed in Mackinac. The *Islander* reported that competitors had put up a large sign in front of their own store, pointing out that the Wendells had refused to join the crusade against the Mormons and asking the fishermen to trade with them, as "constant and reliable enemies of the Mormons." The Wendells' only offense, the *Islander* said, was "refusing to join in deeds of lawlessness against us."[30] Perhaps the sign did prove costly to the Wendells' business, for during the next legislative session, Theodore Wendell clearly was on the side of those working against the Mormons, and he would prove a formidable adversary.

On January 25 and 26 Wendell presented two petitions, one

from residents of Emmet County and the other from A. S. Wadsworth and 150 other residents of Grand Traverse and Antrim counties, asking that the mainland portion of Emmet County be detached from the Beaver Islands.[31] At one time Wadsworth had a speculative interest in the Pine River area of mainland Emmet. He had also been accused of prying into Strang's affairs.

While in Lansing for the previous session of the legislature in 1853, Strang had obtained a land office map of the Pine River area. A Mormon settlement had been projected there, and Strang used the map to mark the lands targeted for the settlement. One day, when Strang was out of his hotel room, Wadsworth leafed through Strang's papers and found the map, according to the *Northern Islander*. Wadsworth then went to the land office, the *Islander* reported, and entered the marked lands for himself.[32]

Since 1852 Wadsworth had been selling lots in Elk Rapids, a village he laid out about thirty miles south of Pine River; he claimed that he had begun purchasing the Pine River land even before he arrived in Lansing. After filing for 214 acres at Pine River himself, Wadsworth relinquished half to Charles P. Bush of Lansing on February 17, 1853. A year later—and after the Battle of Pine River in July 1853—Wadsworth sold his remaining half for $2,000 to C. A. B. Pratt. Bush, a state senator, later sold his half for $2,000 to John S. Dixon and his wife, Phoebe, who was Pratt's sister.[33]

In the spring of 1854 Mormons George T. Preston and Galen B. Cole settled near the land owned by Dixon and Pratt. Dixon, a thirty-five-year-old Lansing teacher, had bought the land after deciding that a change of climate and occupation would improve his poor health. During that same spring he and his family left Lansing for Pine River, but at Mackinac he was persuaded not to settle his land in the face of the Mormon settlement. They instead passed the year at Old Mission, opposite Elk Rapids on Grand Traverse Bay.[34]

During the 1855 legislative session Dixon was back in Lansing, attacking the Mormons and lobbying for legislation designed to prevent Mormon settlements on the mainland and to limit the official control Mormons possessed in that region to the offshore islands.[35] Dixon met with more than moderate success. Wendell, with the unanimous support of the Towns and Counties Committee, reported out several bills that met Dixon's objectives. "Your committee is of the opinion that a peculiar state of facts exists in that portion of the state, requiring possibly legislative intervention," Wendell said. "Without deciding where the fault principally lies, it is evident that a feeling of deep distrust and repugnance, approaching warlike hostility exists between different classes of people inhabiting the islands and the mainland."[36] The committee recommended bills that would create a separate township and county organization for the Beaver, Fox, and Manitue islands and that would reorganize Emmet County to include only mainland townships.[37]

Strang moved to reject the bills. Their object, he declared, was to open the liquor traffic, further the ends of certain land speculators, and injure the Mormons. Strang said he hoped the good order of the last three years in that area would be investigated.[38] Wendell said Strang was wrong about the bills' intentions, and that he hoped Strang would preach good order less and practice it more. Strang's motion was rejected. The bills were read the first and second times and laid on the table.[39]

One observer noted the House actions and said it appeared "the King's friends have had enough of him, and are turning the cold shoulder. Words, words, words seem to constitute his majesty's weapons, and they are always ready, and so far, I believe no one has been injured bad."[40]

The *Jackson American Citizen* laid Strang's problems to a changing political climate. "He has not the Legislature of two years ago to deal with and his projects and hopes are vanishing away. He some time ago brought in a bill to establish a new judicial district upon the lake shore, with the ultimate object of placing himself on the bench, but this Legislature will never sanction such an outrage. . . . He is a dangerous man to tamper with—of good habits, intelligent, persevering and extremely energetic, yet ambitious, restless, domineering, and possessed of great cunning. His influence here, however, is very limited."[41]

On February 5 the bills were ordered to a third reading, and Strang made several minor changes in the bill creating Beaver Island

County, plus one major one, changing the name of the new county to Manitue, later spelled Manitou, after the Indian name for the Great Spirit. On February 6 the House passed the bill organizing a new Emmet County, 60 to 4, with Strang in a decided minority. On February 8 the bill creating Manitue County was approved 60 to 1 in the House, with only Strang opposed.[42]

Should the Senate concur, the *Detroit Advertiser* said, Strang would be "'monarch of all he surveys' on the islands, but he cannot command on the mainland."[43] And with minor changes the Senate did concur: the dismemberment was complete. The legislature also decided that the new county would have a state representative to itself, assuring the Mormons of a voice in future legislatures but preventing Beaver Island Mormons from representing mainland areas.[44]

The act reorganizing Emmet County divided it into five townships, and in all of the townships except Charlevoix, which included Pine River, township meetings were set for May 1. That day came and went with no meetings, and thus no officers were elected. The meeting in Charlevoix Township was set for May 29. According to the act, the meeting was to be held at the home of John S. Dixon, who had no home in the township at the time the legislation was approved. Dixon did build a temporary dwelling after he arrived at Pine River on May 11 with his wife, their three children, a prospective business partner, and a hired hand.[45]

As election day approached in the township, a majority of the legal voters were Gentiles, although about thirty Mormons had settled in the township within ten days of the town meeting, giving them a majority of the population. The election was viewed as a referendum on Dixon's actions; he had spent the winter in Lansing seeking to separate the township from a Mormon-dominated county. Dixon, a candidate for supervisor, justice of the peace, and school inspector, was made clerk of the election.[46]

Ten persons voted in the election, and Dixon was handed a stunning rebuke. The men who were elected township officers included both Mormons and Gentiles, headed by Galen B. Cole as supervisor and George T. Preston as clerk. Cole and Preston, both Mormons, also were two of the four men elected justices of the peace. Dixon was not elected to any office. He had received only one vote—his own—for supervisor, and the highest number he received for any office was two, his own vote and that of his hired hand.[47]

According to the *Northern Islander*, the scene at the election needed but one thing to make it perfect: that those legislators who were so anxious to cut up Emmet County to get a part of it out of Mormon jurisdiction could have been there to see how grateful the people were. The legislators "could have not looked more blank than Dixon did. Poor fellow! he thought they were voting for him, and never dreamed that his election was doubtful till he counted the votes."[48] The county reorganization not only failed to prevent Mormons from settling there but also had legalized their control over the township.

On June 5 an interim election of Emmet County officers was held, and the results were little different as far as Dixon was concerned. A slate of officers, a majority of them Mormons and the rest friendly to the Mormons, was elected without opposition. Preston was elected clerk.[49]

A month later the Mormons would make a more indelible impression on the Gentile settlers of Pine River. But first they took care of business—some pleasant and some not so pleasant—on Beaver Island. On July 8, during a church conference there, the Mormons celebrated the fifth anniversary of Strang's coronation with sacrifices and feasting. Three days later the conference removed two of the church's top leaders.[50] Samuel P. Bacon, the successor to Samuel Graham as president of the Twelve, was stripped of his office. A resolution stated that he had "corrupted himself" and gone among the enemies of the church. Warren Post, who presented the resolution, later wrote that Bacon had "denied the work being done was the inspiration of God" and had called it "human invention."[51] Franklin Bevier, the president of the Seventies, had taken up residence among the Gentiles and "utterly neglected" his office; he was removed, too.[52]

To fill vacancies, five men were ordained as apostles—Anson W. Prindle, Edward Chidester, Isaac Pierce, Lorenzo D. Tubbs and James C. Hutchins. They joined Post, L. D. Hickey, Ebenezer

Page, and Phineas Wright as members of the Twelve, which still had three vacancies.[53]

Two days after the conference had ended, Strang and fifty other men and women sailed to the mainland in fishing boats and camped near Pine River. On the next day the group went up Pine River to Long Lake or, as the Mormons called it, Lake Mormon. The Mormon party traveled about five miles southeast on Lake Mormon to the lake's south arm, then two miles south to a small island, which they named Holy Island. There they spent the night. On the following day the Mormon boats gathered up the settlers in that area, and the Mormons held a conference, at which they thanked God for delivering them from civil war and threatened persecution.[54]

When the Mormons returned to Pine River on the next day, Dixon's wife noticed that some of the boats were towing long pieces of timber and that most of the Mormon party was walking along the path on the bank. She suspected mischief and decided to investigate. Some of the men were dragging timber out of the water on the south side of the river; one was carrying a spade; the rest were standing in a group, with Strang in the midst, on the bluff. When she asked what they were doing, she was told they were about to erect a gallows, to hang all those who had violated their laws. Frightened, Mrs. Dixon returned home.[55] After the Mormons left, the gallows was found standing, with four roughly carved images of men hanging by their necks. On top of the frame was sketched a coffin, drawn with red chalk, and three men walking away from it; the inscription read: "Dixon in his dying hour abandoned by his friends." One of the suspended images had a sign: "Dixon, successor of the Pine River murderers—may his days be few."[56]

The Mormons denied that they had hung Dixon in effigy on the gallows. The *Northern Islander* said the hanged men had attacked two boatloads of Mormons in the Battle of Pine River two years earlier. The *Islander* later described those men as "refugees from justice, who, indicted for their crimes in this region, have gone to seek sympathy in other places, as victims of Mormon atrocities."[57]

During that summer four more Mormon families moved to that area, settling at the eastern end of Lake Mormon. By summer's end Dixon had become thoroughly discouraged: he felt unable to oppose the Mormons and unable to protect his property against thievery. He had lost a new lumber wagon, three sugar kettles, and a boat; a neighbor had lost some planking. Dixon claimed that most of these items were found on Beaver Island or in the area of Mormon settlements on the mainland.[58]

Responding to Dixon's charges, the *Northern Islander* related that Dixon also had told of a theft at Mackinac when he had changed boats there in the spring. Dixon said his cow was stolen, on a main street, in broad daylight. He searched for the cow in vain. After several hours' delay and annoyance, an Irishman drove the cow back to Dixon and apologized: "I thought you was a Marman."[59]

Dixon wrote Theodore Wendell early in the fall, asking for advice. Wendell said he "would not move an inch," even if it meant exterminating every "skulking Mormon," but he did not offer assistance beyond moral support. Dixon decided to leave: his family left for Northport, on the western side of Grand Traverse Bay, and he followed a few weeks later, after disposing of his potato crop.[60]

During that fall the *Islander* reported a "steady tide" of emigration from Beaver Island to the Pine River area.[61] New townships were in the works, due to the efforts of Mormon officials.

The annual meeting of Emmet County's board of supervisors was held on October 22. Since Charlevoix Township had elected the only supervisor in the county, Galen Cole constituted the county board, which proceeded to create four new townships in the county, including two bordering Lake Mormon in the area of Mormon settlements. Cole, as chairman of the board, and George Preston, as county clerk, certified that the acts creating the townships had been passed by a "majority" of the board.[62]

At a special election in November the Mormon presence in the county hierarchy was diluted as about forty residents elected a more non-Mormon slate of county officials. And late that month the Mormons suffered other losses.[63]

The settlement at Pine River had needed supplies for the winter, and Preston had hired a small vessel, the *Maid of the Mist*, to transport goods from Beaver Island to the mainland. After the boat, captained by Jonathan Pierce, one of Strang's "hard-fisted" men, was loaded on November 25, a storm came up with snow, rain, and

KING OF BEAVER ISLAND

an adverse wind. Preston, eager to return to his family, would not wait for the weather to improve. The boat, without passengers, was later found near the mainland shore. Preston, Pierce, and two other Mormon men who had been aboard were presumed drowned. The kingdom lost two of its leaders.[64]

Chapter 14

Consecration and Thievery

I N THE FALL OF 1855, after years of public denials and private practice, Strang came close to an open admission that he had more than one wife. His comments were prompted by an article in a Detroit area newspaper, which accurately stated that Strang's first wife resided in Wisconsin while "he has particular favor to two women [on Beaver Island], by whom he has children."[1]

Strang, in the *Northern Islander*, responded first to the "implication" that his first wife was a "runaway wife" or a "separated woman." He said he had a 760-acre farm in Walworth County, Wisconsin. "Mrs. Strang, or, if you please, my first wife, stays there most of the time to take charge, occasionally spending a winter with me at the Capitol, or on this Island."[2] While there is corroboration for the statement that Mary spent the previous winter with Strang in Lansing, there is none that she had been on the island after the Detroit trial in 1851. The cunning king was apparently mixing prevarication with truth again.

As for the two other women, Strang wrote in the *Islander*, he was quite willing for readers to believe that he had "particular favor for two, four or ten women, whom I provide for, and who bear children to me, and whom I would marry if the law permitted me. If they imagine that in this I violate any law of this State they are mistaken. As to the question of morals I am prepared to justify it. And upon any question of morals, until the law interposes, I have a right to judge for myself."[3]

As late as June 8, 1854, the *Islander* had been equivocal on polygamy. After printing a defense of the Utah doctrine on plural marriage, the paper added: "we do not subscribe to its entire soundness." But with Strang's switch to a defiant stance on polygamy, there could be little public doubt that he was a practitioner.

On Beaver Island, couples were bound under God's law for time and eternity—for their life on earth and for their life in the hereafter. The Saints believed that the family existed forever and that a man's station in heaven would be directly related to the number of wives and children he had.[4] To Strang, polygamy was one more vehicle to achieve lasting fame.

In his expanded version of the Book of the Law of the Lord, printed in 1856, Strang wrote that "polygamy elevates man, by giving him more blessings in well doing, a higher reward for a faithful and virtuous life, a more numerous posterity to perpetuate his fame, and inherit his honors." Many of the "most eminent statesmen and scholars of modern times," he said, "have died childless, or left only bastard children of degraded women, and slaves; who, had Polygamy been reputable, would, like the Patriarchs, have transmitted their virtues and their greatness to a numerous posterity."[5]

In 1855, as if to underscore his belief in polygamy, Strang took his fourth and fifth wives—two nineteen-year-old cousins, who were both intelligent and pretty. The first was Sarah Adelia Wright, the daughter of apostle Phineas Wright. Sarah was married to Strang over the objections of her father, who told her he would not forbid the marriage, but said: "My daughter, I would almost as . . . see you buried [as] marry into polygamy. I am afraid you will not be happy."[6] Sarah took the chance. She thought that since Strang was the Lord's chosen prophet, everything would be all right. They were married by one of the apostles on July 15, during the Mormons' visit to Holy Island near Pine River. Three months later, on October 27, Strang married Phoebe Wright, also over the opposition of her father, B. G. Wright.[7]

According to Elvira Field Strang, polygamy never received general favor on the island: some men simply could not afford to practice it; others opposed it in principle. By the end of 1855, she said, it became the cause of much dissatisfaction. Although some elders took additional wives in an attempt to popularize the practice, Elvira said this did not give the people "sufficient confidence in their opposition to and disobedience of the civil laws of the land in regard to the taking of more than one wife."[8] The *Islander*, however, professed to be unaware of any law prohibiting polygamy, even though Michigan had one. That law made polygamy punishable by a fine of up to $500 or as many as five years in prison, depending on the severity of the offense.[9]

Elvira said there were no more than twenty polygamous marriages in the kingdom. Strang had the most wives—with five. L. D. Hickey had four, George Miller three, and the others two. B. G. Wright and Phineas Wright each had two wives, despite opposing their daughters' involvement with polygamy.[10]

Decades later, Sarah talked about her life with Strang. She said the wives all lived with him in the same house but each had separate rooms. The wives met together with Strang for prayers and ate at the same table. "We had no quarrels, no jealousies that I know of . . . he was a very mild spoken, kind man to his family, although his word was law."[11] Strang also said that he never knew of a quarrel between his wives.[12]

A distinct division of duties existed among Strang's first two polygamous wives, according to their skills. Elvira wrote and copied letters for him, and she also kept meteorological records for the Smithsonian Institution. Betsy was the head cook and housekeeper.[13] The house had expanded with the household. By the end of 1855, Elvira had three children, two sons and a daughter. Betsy also had had two sons and a daughter, but one of the sons died as an infant. An addition was erected behind the "palace" and connected to the main house by a covered walkway.[14]

In the summer of 1855 John H. Forster, an engineer assigned to a lake and shoreline survey party, spent a season on Beaver Island, providing an extended opportunity for an outsider to observe life there.[15] Forster reported years later that he had called at Strang's house on business and that Strang was seated at his dinner table with his wives and children. "He had the air of a well-to-do patriarch but . . . did not extend to us the hospitalities of his table. Perhaps his religion forbade him giving salt to the Gentiles. The king had an office downtown, where he said he would prefer to meet us." There, in the printing office, Forster found Strang to be more genial.

He was shrewd enough to extend us the freedom of the island. . . . We complained that we found the saints, scattered over the island, very reticent, disobliging, if not hostile. They would give us no information. Living upon unpaid for or stolen lands, these saintly people thought, doubtless, that our purpose there was to spy out the land and report the state of affairs to the government. Of course . . . their suspicions were unfounded. King Strang excused his people, said they were ignorant, and that he would rectify matters. He was as good as his word and we had no further trouble, except from the unkindness of young 'saintesses,' who incontinently fled to cover every time we meandered their pleasant country roads."

Strang often joined the lake survey crew in their camp and drank tea there. Forster said Strang also "refused not to partake liberally of certain stores in our medicine chest. He became quite jolly and delighted us with his free and easy stories about the saints. . . . He praised his wives lavishly, declared that they were fond of him and the institution of polygamy." [16]

For Strang to partake of such items would be contrary to his church's stance against tea and alcohol. The general abstinence of the Beaver Island Mormons contrasted with the situation among the Mormons in Utah, where those drinks were in common use. In 1833 Joseph Smith had announced a revelation, known as the Word of Wisdom, that advised the Saints to avoid alcohol, tobacco, and hot drinks (tea and coffee). The advisory, however, was just that, and there is evidence that even Smith did not follow it strictly. It was widely ignored until the mid-1860s, when Brigham Young decided to revive it, and it eventually evolved into a test of faith. [17] On Beaver Island, even though the public stance was unyielding, there were instances of use. One "respectable lady" furnished "intoxicating liquors" for a party of young people, and the *Islander* lamented that no one had objected, and added: "in spite of our utmost efforts, a few among the most influential men will occasionally drink on board steamers and at public places." [18]

Officially, no betting or gaming was allowed on the island, but the rules were apparently liberal on other amusements. Dancing, theatrical productions, and even card playing were permitted, although some Saints thought the latter gave them a bad name. The *Islander* was proud that the Saints presented "an example of honesty and good order among themselves without parallel in all the State . . . so exemplary in their every day life that . . . there is not a prisoner, a pauper, a drunkard, and scarcely a Sabbath breaker." [19]

Despite proclamations of virtue, there were chinks in the character of the Beaver Island Mormons, and Romeo Strang was among those who paid a price for them. Romeo was King Strang's nephew, and while living in the Voree area he had gone to Racine in the fall of 1855 to seek work on the railroad. He said he talked to a conductor with some prospect of success until he mentioned his name was Strang. "To my surprise that broke it all up and he would hardly converse with me afterwards. I . . . can lay it to nothing else than a prejudice against the Mormons," Romeo wrote his father, David.[20] Romeo Strang had another reason to be angry at his uncle, who had just left the Voree area after a short visit. During the visit, Romeo had proposed to continue farming there on shares for another year. The farmland involved was owned by his uncle, and his grandfather, Clement Strang, was living on it.[21] (Although they had moved to Voree, Strang's parents had not become Mormons. They would remain Baptists for the rest of their lives.)

His uncle had raised no objections to the farming proposal, Romeo said, but refused to let him continue to work the quarry on the land. According to Romeo, his uncle also said he might let someone else farm the land the following spring; Romeo said his uncle told him that "his children to enjoy his favor must become Mormons."[22] Romeo was not only Strang's nephew but also his son-in-law, for earlier that year he had married Strang's oldest daughter, Netti (Myraette Mabel), his first cousin.[23]

Romeo received the impression that his uncle was trying to force him to move to Beaver Island by making it impossible for him to live in Wisconsin. "I see plainly that I must be a Mormon or leave here and as I do not chose to become one nor engage with them in stealing and destroying the Gentiles I must not depend on business here."[24]

The "stealing" would be alluded to decades later by Strang's son, Clement, who was only a year old when Romeo made this comment. Based on long conversations with his mother, Elvira, Clement called "consecration" one of "Three Horrible Blunders" that Strang made in the kingdom. The others were polygamy and the totalitarian nature of the government there. Clement said that as a youngster he remembered the term consecration being used in a sub rosa manner, leaving the impression that it was "some practice that was taboo to the average Christian conscience; something that our parents and near relatives wished had never happened." As the years passed, he said, questions about consecration were answered frankly, "though with deep regret."[25]

Among Joseph Smith's Mormons, the Law of Consecration referred to the deeding of land and goods to the church for a communal system, the United Order of Enoch. Some Mormons, however, perverted the interpretation to include plunder. In the late 1830s the leader of a Mormon group called the Danites was quoted by Smith as secretly telling his captains that "it is written, the riches of the Gentiles shall be consecrated to my people, the house of Israel; and thus you will waste away the Gentiles by robbing and plundering them of their property; and in this way we will build up the kingdom of God."[26]

Among the Gentiles near Beaver Island, the term consecration was a synonym for stealing. And according to the *History of the Grand Traverse Region*:

> So complete and perfect were the arrangements for carrying on an extensive system of thievery and robbery, that immense quantities of "consecrated" goods were, from time to time, brought to the island, and converted to Mormon use. On this point the concurrent testimony of persons who lived there from the early days of the colony up to the time of Strang's death, and who were in positions to know the facts, is conclusive. The plunder seen by them, and portions of which some of them used, consisted of dry goods, leather, fishing nets, horses, cattle—anything, in short, of practical value, that could be purloined with comparative safety.[27]

One Gentile offered an explanation on why the Mormons sought to banish others from an island that was ample for five times its population. The island being a "secluded place, they want to make it a depot for plunder—a refuge for those who they send out to rob, steal and pass counterfeit money, with no witnesses on the island."[28] When a Mormon left the island, as in the case of Samuel Graham, his goods often remained behind and were consecrated. And if an alienated Mormon could not afford to lose all, he would stay, a seed of discontent below the surface of the island society.[29]

In addition to his comments on consecration and other "blunders" of the kingdom, Clement Strang aimed an arrow at the heart of the Strangite church, saying that he thought his father was an atheist. This belief, he said, was based in part on Strang's immersion in some of the writings of Thomas Paine.[30] Curiously, Paine had a telling comment that would apply to "prophets" who were atheists.

In the *Age of Reason*, Paine wrote that "infidelity does not consist in believing, or in disbelieving; it consists in professing to believe what he does not believe. It is impossible to calculate the moral mischief, if I may so express it, that mental lying has produced in society. When a man has so far corrupted and prostituted the chastity of his mind, as to subscribe his professional belief to things he does not believe, he has prepared himself for the commission of every other crime." Even, perhaps, consecration? Paine went on: "He takes up the trade of a priest for the sake of gain, and in order to qualify himself for that trade, he begins with a perjury. Can we conceive of any thing more destructive to morality than this?"[31]

In 1855 charges of thievery and other depredations swirled afresh around the Mormons of Beaver Island. Some of the specific charges appeared unfounded. Early that year, in a Brighamite paper, the *St. Louis Luminary*, an elder accused Strang of sending his missionaries to rob and plunder. The elder said three stores in Lapeer were broken into and robbed, and the men caught in the act. "One was Strang's first counselor. His name is Hix or Hickey. He gave them leg bail. The others were awaiting their trial." The *Northern Islander* roundly denounced the charge and said Hickey had never been arrested there or anywhere else.[32]

In the summer of 1855, the *Pontiac Gazette* asked whether the Mormons of Beaver Island were horse thieves after five or six horses were stolen in the Pontiac area and a propeller reportedly unloaded eleven horses at the island shortly thereafter. An Oakland County sheriff's officer investigated. En route he met Strang, who gave him letters to some of the principal men of the island, saying that any service done for the officer would be considered as done for him. Upon arriving at the island, the officer was "shown every hospitality, and piloted whithersoever he wished to go.—But no horses could be found. . . . But at about every half mile he would encounter a Mormon. He was not out of sight of a Mormon, in all probability while he remained on the island."[33]

One soon-to-be-infamous islander, Thomas Bedford, later related that Strang did indeed give the officer every assistance—including furnishing the thieves to join the search. On the first day, at Strang's direction, one-half of the island was searched, and on the next day the other half. Bedford said the horses were moved from one end to the other during the night. Team horses and working oxen were much in demand on the island, and Bedford said that at one time eight of the thirteen teams of horses on the island had been stolen elsewhere.[34]

The *Islander* challenged the *Gazette's* accusation and added that in St. James there were no police, "the law affording ample security to property. So ample is this security, that the houses are without locks, and valuable stores in which no person sleeps have only common padlocks on." Strang's house only had a wooden latch, even when he and his family were away. "And his house is forty rods from the nearest building, surrounded by a thick set grove, affording perfect concealment, and only two hundred feet from the lake, where boats could load from the house and depart unseen. . . . It is hardly probable that a band of outlaws, such as the Gazette persists in calling the Mormons, have been congregated together for the purpose of stealing & c., and yet so honest that none will steal from another."[35]

After the *Islander's* exercise in logical argument, the *Gazette* withdrew part of its statement but indicated that it still had doubts about the Mormons. "We doubt not that among themselves, there cannot be found in the State of Michigan a more quiet, industrious community than that on Beaver Island. But we insist these facts prove nothing positively to the credit of these men before God. We do not believe that a band of thieves and robbers, if isolated from the world, forming a community for a common purpose, would steal from each other."[36]

Two months later the debate resumed. The *Islander* reported that the horses had been found in Milwaukee, a predominantly Catholic city. "We suppose the Gazette will now withdraw all its hard words, and charge the people of Milwaukee with being a den of Roman Catholic thieves."[37] Far from it. The *Gazette* responded that the fact the horses were found in Milwaukee "would naturally corroborate the charge that they were first landed at Beaver Island—since publick attention having been called to the circumstances, and publick officers of the law being on the watch, it is natural to suppose the horses would be secretly taken from the Island, and wonderfully discovered in another place." The *Islander* then asked whether that logic worked both ways. "If they had been found here, would you hold that conclusive evidence that they wert stolen by Catholics of Milwaukee?"[38]

The Mormons often said that if anything untoward occurred on the lakes or in shoreline communities near Beaver Island, the tendency was to blame them. An article in the *Chicago Journal* illustrated their point. In a story by a correspondent from Grand Traverse, the *Journal* reported that in August "two of the Mormon fraternity visited the house of a Mr. Ladd, and he being from home, took his child, telling its mother they would make a king of him. Mrs. L. called for help, when a plaster was put over her mouth. Three Indians, however, hearing her cries, proceeded to the house, when the Mormons decamped." The *Islander*, overcoming a reluctance to honor the story with a response, asked a few pointed questions: "What do the Mormons want to steal children for? With their dozen or twenty wives apiece, can't they raise as many children as they want? If they wanted more, could not they get them at the Chicago poor houses at half the expense of stealing them?"[39]

There were other reports of "Mormon outrages" in Michigan throughout the fall of 1855. A mill was burned; a store was robbed of barrels of sugar; another store lost goods valued at $1,600; and a tannery was robbed of leather and hides worth $500. All of these incidents were blamed on King Strang's men, even though some took place more than 200 miles from Beaver Island.[40]

With these depredations, the talk of possible bloodshed increased. A reporter for the *Lansing State Republican*, after a stop in Mackinac, said he was "really surprised at the deep and determined feeling which has taken hold of every person in that community . . . [and which] pervades that entire region. . . . We are told on all hands that the Mormons are the authors of all these robberies and crimes. . . . unless the unfortunate differences existing between the Mormons and the 'gentile' population are soon amicably arranged, the most serious and deporable consequences will unquestionably be the result."[41]

The *Grand Rapids Herald* said it was "forced to believe that there is a body of men among the Mormons who are no better than thieves and desperadoes of the most dangerous description. If they are not countenanced by Strang, he should take active measures to have them brought to justice; if they are, the people of Michigan should take the matter in hand with a will."[42]

The *Islander* took note of this "general and simultaneous assault" on the Mormons by the press and said there appeared to be a "reasonable prospect" of renewed government prosecutions, similar to those of 1851. "The thing is not pleasant, but still we say, let it come. We are better able to stand persecution now than we were then. And now, as then, the press have repeated every false and ridiculous tale until the public have taken up the old proverb— 'There cannot be so much smoke, without some fire.' " As for the threat of revenge, the *Islander* told the Lansing paper to "come just when you get ready, and you need not take pains to give us notice." The *Islander* said that the Mormons could not be thrown out of the area. "They will satisfy you on that question whenever you wish to 'try it on.' " In a prescient note, the *Islander* added, "We have known for years what the editors seem so anxious to impress on us, that when the public vengeance is waked up the law will not protect us, and that among an angry people innocence is no shield. We do not expect Governor or President to protect us against mobs. We live in the continual assurance that any one of us might be murdered in a neighboring county and not a magistrate could be induced to issue process against the murderer."[43] Within a year, these comments would be proven prophetic for Prophet Strang.

Chapter 15

The Conspirators

THE WINTER OF 1856 set a standard for cold throughout the nation. For more than seven weeks ice bridged Lake Michigan between Beaver Island and the mainland, allowing teams to cross with loaded sleds. Spring arrived on the calendar, but there was still no open water in the northern part of the lake, and the ice stretched farther south than anyone, even the oldest Indian, could remember.[1]

On April 1 the weather broke. The temperature rose to 48 degrees, the warmest on the island since November 14. On that day the *Northern Islander* published its first "daily" edition. Also on that day—and more consequential for Strang—Thomas Bedford visited Johnson and MacCulloch's store, where he chatted with a young man who had crossed the ice from Garden Island.[2] The tenor of the conversation indicated that Bedford had become quite uninhibited in his tales of Mormon activities.

A small, dark-complexioned man, Bedford had married a daughter of George Miller sometime after the Miller party arrived at Beaver Island in the fall of 1850. The daughter, Ruth Ann, had taken the covenant that same fall, when she was fifteen years old. Bedford, a farmer-fisherman, was twenty years older. Although Bedford had married a Mormon woman and had joined the church, he was not considered a "strong professor." An inveterate smoker, Bedford riled the Mormons by disregarding the church's ban on the use of tobacco.[3] And this was not the only matter in which Bedford—or his wife—ran counter to the rules of the church and king.

In 1855 a major rebellion had arisen over the bloomer costume, and the Bedfords were in the forefront. At a July church conference, Strang ordered all Mormon women to wear the costume, declaring that any woman who disobeyed him would do so over his dead body. Even so, some women did not wear the costume, and among those who resisted were the wives of Bedford, H. D. MacCulloch, Franklin Johnson, and Alexander Wentworth.[4] With the wives of MacCulloch and Johnson at odds with Strang, it was no minor tempest.

The basis for the bloomer rule was the Book of the Law of the Lord, which required the Saints to dress in a manner "seemly and convenient." In his 1855 decree, Strang said this meant women were to wear full-length calico pantalets, covered by a matching, straight-waisted dress reaching down to the knees.[5] (Strang was not the only Mormon leader to have problems enforcing a dress code. Brigham Young designed a similar "Deseret costume" for the Utah women, but it was not a success and soon disappeared.)[6] By 1855 some Mormon women, most notably Elvira Field Strang, had worn the bloomer costume for more than five years. In 1852 the *Islander* noted that the bloomer style was being worn by a majority of the island's "respectable women," though some had never adopted it. "Besides a few very excellent persons who never liked it, a number of individuals hanging on the skirts of society are ever ready to display themselves before strangers with long dresses."[7]

The *Islander* subsequently seized opportunities to praise the convenience of the bloomer costume and to ridicule other fashions. It declared that the bloomer style was especially handy for traversing muddy roads, because it freed both hands from maneuvering a skirt. It pointed out that hoop skirts, eighteen feet in circumference, were being worn by ladies elsewhere. "Who will be the first in this fashionable city to put them on?" the *Islander* asked sarcastically. "To those who have itching eyes for Gentile customs, we suggest that they make speed, or they will be too late." Now and then, the *Islander* said, a lady deemed it "beneath her dignity to wear a Mormon dress. Who are these dignified ladies? What has been their past life, that they will not demean themselves by stooping to Mormon styles?" It described one such woman as a thief and an adultress, and then added: "It is right that such a one should not wear a Mormon dress. . . . But is it not a little curious to see them put on airs about it? Who keeps such company? Look and see, and judge them by the company they keep."[8]

Those families whose women did not keep company with the bloomer costume were subjected to what at best could be called church discipline. At worst it could be called harassment. Bedford, for example, became the target of lawsuits and attachments based on claims of debts. He said Mormons in good standing also refused to pay him money they owed him, costing him about $70. Bedford added another accusation: that Mormons had robbed him of a span of horses, two fishing boats, and ninety nets.[9]

The Mormons had given Bedford cause to be outspoken on that mild April day. And talk he did. Bedford was overheard telling the Garden Island visitor that on orders from Strang, some men had stolen a boat from Gull Island. The boat's owner had offered a reward of $50, and Bedford said that if he wanted to make $50, he would go to Mackinac and provide information on the boat's whereabouts. Several other persons were present in Johnson and MacCulloch's store, and Bedford's friends were apprehensive because of his temerity.[10]

That evening, after dark, a messenger came to Bedford's house and told him that Brother Strang wanted to see him at the printing office. Bedford found it full of men, but Strang was not there. Dennis Chidester was. He told Bedford: "You've been betraying us, telling about stolen property, and we're here to make it right. We have been ordered to shut you up by giving you forty lashes, save one." The men had a rawhide horsewhip and several switches made of blue beech, also called ironwood, that had been twisted and toughened by heating. Bedford said the men were going to take him into the woods, but after going about fifty yards, he refused to go farther and told them: "There's plenty of room for this job right here, so whip away." The men did not remove any of Bedford's clothing, his outer garment being only a light jacket. When the men had given him the thirty-nine lashes, Bedford asked if there were anything else to account for, as he would like to take all the whipping due him right then. But the score seemed to be settled and the men let him go.[11] On the whipping of Bedford, one Mormon, Wingfield W. Watson, said he heard Strang say: "Whatever you do, let it be done quickly." Watson said it was apparent that Strang knew something would be done.[12]

Mormons later circulated the story that Bedford had been whipped after being caught in the act of adultery. Sarah Wright Strang said Bedford's fishing partner, David Brown, had returned home to find Bedford in bed with his wife. Soon after that, Sarah heard that Brown and several other men "caught Tom and tied him up and whipped him." Sarah said she never heard of anyone else being whipped.[13] The latter comment lends credence to the "stolen boat" version of the whipping. For on April 3 the *Northern Islander* reported a "flogging" that week in which a man was "called to account" for "lying, tale-bearing, and endeavoring to incite to mischief and crime."

Immediately after the whipping, Bedford said, he decided to kill Strang. He returned home, took down his double-barreled duck gun, and without telling his wife what had happened, started to go out. Mrs. Bedford, fearing that he had been persuaded to do some unlawful work, asked: "You are not going to do anything for Strang?" Bedford replied: "I'll do for Strang, if I get hold of him." Bedford went to Strang's house, which had a light in a window. He stood near a fence in front of the house for about fifteen minutes, then remembered that there were two men with Strang that evening. Bedford said he realized that it would be foolhardy to make an open attempt on the king's life at that time. He went home.[14]

The big thaw continued the next day, when, according to the *Islander*, the man who had been flogged went around "bragging that it did not hurt him, and proposing his readiness to take another.[15]" Bedford said he went to the printing office and met Strang, who asked him: "Were you whipped last night?" "You know I was," Bedford said he replied, "for there is none of this deviltry done unless you give the orders for it. But I want you to understand that you have licked a full-blooded Englishman this time." Strang defiantly bidded Bedford to do his worst. Bedford responded that he would not do his worst; he then left the office. He said he never spoke to Strang again.[16]

On the following day, the *Islander* reported, the "whipped loafer" took the beeches he had been flogged with and showed them around, "asking sympathy of the tender hearted." The "greatest curiosity," the paper said, "was to see a lady, who used occasionally to beat a black servant girl with an iron poker, bigger than any of them [beeches], exhibiting one of the sticks and thinking it was too cruel."[17]

Bedford said that after the whipping, he went around armed, hoping for a chance to murder Strang. He said that at first he was alone in this determination, but later was joined by H. D. Mac-Culloch, Franklin Johnson, and Alexander Wentworth.[18] Wentworth needed little prodding to join in the conspiracy. He had a serious grievance against Strang.

Wentworth was seventeen when he arrived on Beaver Island in the summer of 1850, in time to witness the coronation. Earlier that year he had been boarding with the Nathan Foster family in Koshkonong, Wisconsin, about forty miles west of Voree. Wentworth probably had joined the church as a result of the efforts of Hiram P. Brown, who had been preaching in the Koshkonong area since 1847. Foster became the presiding elder over a branch that numbered twenty-two persons. In a letter of August 29, 1850, Brown asked Strang to "have a watchful eye on my boy Allek Wentworth."[19]

At about that same time Strang accused George Adams and his wife of trying to ruin his reputation by saying he had designs on one of Franklin Johnson's two daughters. Johnson's elder daughter, Phebe, was then fifteen. A Gentile resident of the island said later that Strang wanted to marry one of the Johnson girls, but that she had a lover, Wentworth, who eventually married her. The girl was Phebe.[20] According to a younger brother of Sarah Wright Strang, Wentworth was "rather dressy and nice appearing" with his fair complexion, blue eyes, and dark hair. And yet Sarah's brother said some islanders "thought it queer" that Phebe had married Wentworth.[21]

At first Wentworth was a faithful subject. He appears in the Strang papers on November 26, 1852, when he, along with Elvira Field Strang and others, signed a petition seeking a pardon for Nathan Foster, who had been imprisoned in Jackson for refusing to testify against Strang in the 1851 trial in Detroit. The next summer, Wentworth was among those sent on missions and among those wounded in the Battle of Pine River.[22]

According to Watson, the "wasp that stung Wentworth" landed after Wentworth had been talking loudly against polygamy. Strang referred to Wentworth's comments in a meeting and said it came with ill grace from a man "whose father was his grandfather and whose mother was his sister." Watson said that when the meeting was over, a few of the men sought the meaning of Strang's curious remark. The mystery was soon solved.[23]

ả ả ả

On April 7, 1856, the biggest news in the Manitou County election was that H. D. MacCulloch was not returned to office. Edward Chidester was elected clerk and register of deeds, the post MacCulloch had held for several terms.[24] The election indicated MacCulloch's fall in the kingdom.

For confirmation of MacCulloch's loss of status, one only had to read the *Northern Islander*. It contained numerous accusations against MacCulloch the official, including that he refused to turn over records to his successor, suppressed records of land ownership, and falsified records. "If he discloses any pretended crimes of the Mormons," the *Islander* said, "they will believe him as guilty as any one."[25] Realizing the sensitive position MacCulloch had held, the Mormon leaders apparently compiled a list of allegations to discredit testimony that he could give.

For almost six years MacCulloch had held a prominent position in church and island affairs. He was a judge of the highest tribunal in the church and a member of the king's privy council. But, according to the *Islander*, a problem lingered in the background: alcohol. On joining the church he promised to reform; still, the paper reported, there were frequent lapses.[26] In public office MacCulloch was not without ability. In 1854 he was supposed to have run for state representative, to succeed Strang. But, according to the *Islander*, he had been getting drunk more often; most lake boats had a bar, and when they stopped to wood at St. James, MacCulloch tipped the bottle too frequently for his own good.[27] Because of his drinking, the *Islander* said, MacCulloch was dropped from consideration for state representative. Mormon leaders feared he "would bring disgrace on a people who were well spoken of for little but their temperance." Told the reason for the decision, MacCulloch again promised to reform. He then was reelected county clerk and register of deeds; Strang was reelected state representative.[28]

In 1855, the *Islander* reported, "it began to be whispered

around freely among strangers who traded here, that [MacCulloch] was no longer a believer, and was only holding on for a chance to make a 'big pile' out of the Mormons and be off to distant parts." The paper also declared that MacCulloch had long been accused of short-changing his customers, including using false weights and measures, but that no action was taken until the charges were made by men of the highest respectability. After a hearing, MacCulloch was removed from the church councils. Bedford later asserted that drunkenness was not a factor in MacCulloch's removal, but that he had been ousted because a "jealous" Strang feared MacCulloch might supplant him.[29]

ða ða ða

With the warmer weather of April, the snow disappeared rapidly and robins and pigeons appeared in abundance. The earliest of flowers brightened the awakening countryside. On April 10 open water could be seen from the southwest side of the island, and on the 11th the ice began breaking up between the island and the mainland. The first wild geese passed overhead on the 15th, bringing northward with them the first thunder of the year. The Beaver Island lighthouse was lit on April 21, and on the 26th the ice broke up in St. James harbor. With the disintegration of the ice, the fishermen headed for their stations with their gill nets. The first ship of the season would be arriving soon, and with it the first of the elders returning from the winter missions. Spring had arrived at Beaver Island.[30]

On April 27 the steamer Superior, from Chicago, became the season's first ship to dock at St. James. In Mackinac on the 28th a passenger, George Leslie, penned a letter to the editors of the *Chicago Tribune*. He reported that at Beaver Island he had had:

the pleasure of seeing the Prophet and High Priest Strang, as well as several of the other dignitaries of the place. They gave the population of the place at 1,500, and state that it is rapidly increasing. The whole settlement, so far as we could see, has an aspect of thrift and neatness about it which shows that the community must be industrious. They have got three piers at the harbor, with several thousand cords of wood, got out for the purpose of supplying boats. They possess one grist and one saw mill. . . .

They print a daily and a weekly paper, . . . [in which] the doctrine of polygamy is not openly avowed but only defended with mediocric ability. We have heard it reported from a reliable source that Strang has got nine wives: a statement which, if true, would go far to prove that his practice is even more distinct and efficacious than his profession.[31]

The *Northern Islander*, in printing this letter, added: "A letter from Mackinac, speaking well of the Mormons, is a rarity. Mr. Leslie must allow us to correct him in a portion of his letter. He has made the wharves and mills too few, and Mr. Strang's wives too many. And what distinguishes him from most publick men is, that he has nobody's wife but his own."[32]

&ab; &ab; &ab;

The opening of the lake to navigation allowed H. D. MacCulloch to head for Lansing, via Chicago, with Dr. J. Atkyn, a daguerreotypist who had set up shop in St. James. In Chicago, MacCulloch was said to have held up a bullet that he declared would kill Strang.[33]

Reporting the May 6th departure of the two men from the island, the *Northern Islander* commented: "Two doctors left here yesterday, and today two or three ignorant persons say they are on an errand of mischief. After taking a drink, they may be such fools, but they are likely to do more mischief to themselves than anybody else. Getting up a new persecution would be an uphill business at this time."[34]

The *Islander* had little good to say about Atkyn—he was a "universal dead-head and common sponge . . . [who] when other men wanted instruments of their revenge, for want of better, they took him." The paper said Atkyn had first appeared on the island in 1850, when he was put off a steamboat for refusing to pay his passage. He "obtained a precarious subsistence a few weeks by going back and forth between Mormons and Gentiles, and offering his services to each as spy upon the other."[35] He soon disappeared, returning briefly in 1852. In the summer of 1855 Atkyn stopped at the island a number of times and eventually set up a daguerreotype business, backed by a loan from a Mormon businessman for the necessary equipment. He spent the winter of 1855–56 on the island.[36]

The *Islander* said Atkyn was generally intoxicated when he was working. "He soon drank up all his stock of alcohol, laid in for the work, and spent the balance of the season in lounging about telling tales, and making himself a nuisance generally."[37] In possible references to MacCulloch and Johnson, the paper said that a couple of other men had private supplies of alcohol totaling about sixty gallons, "and a nest of apostates ripening on bitterness, guzzled over it till the stock ran out, creating a little misery, and breeding much for the future."[38]

Shortly after MacCulloch and Atkyn left for Lansing, two Mormons had a legal skirmish in Mackinac that once again indicated the strength of the anti-Mormon feeling there. The Mormons, Alden and Charles Hale, were the keeper and assistant keeper of the lighthouse at Skillagalee Rock. While they were in Mackinac with their boat, a man filed a complaint that the boat had been stolen from him the previous summer. A warrant was issued, and the Hales were arrested.[39]

The *Islander* said the case went to trial even though "numerous persons" identified the boat as the government one assigned to the lighthouse. The Hales went before a magistrate, who, seeing that the case against them could not be sustained, released them. The Hales immediately left in the boat for the lighthouse; however, they were pursued by a boat containing four men. Both boats were running against a head wind and once came within thirty feet of each other. At that moment one man in the second boat pointed a rifle at the Hales and said that unless they gave up the boat, he would shoot. But Charles Hale pulled a revolver, and in a standoff the boats slowly separated. The propeller *Dunkirk* came by, and the Hales headed for it, with the boat from Mackinac fleeing. "Had the pursuers been armed with any kind of authority, they would have gone aboard and made their arrests," the *Islander* said. "Having none, the presence of a disinterested party alarmed them."

The incident involving the Hales provided more fodder for the conflict between Strang and Theodore Wendell, who had been squabbling almost continuously since the 1855 legislative session. The *Islander* said Wendell, as the collector of Mackinac, had furnished the boat to the Hales and could have convinced his neighbors that the boat was not stolen. It appeared, the *Islander* maintained, that the prosecution was instigated by Wendell to get the Mormon lighthouse keepers removed, enabling him to secure replacements. Another reason Wendell wanted the Hales removed, the paper said, was that they were not paying a $50 "tax" that the collectors at Mackinac had imposed on lighthouse keepers for "good will."[40]

Earlier in May the *Islander* had accused Wendell of suggesting that a group of mainland Indians kill Strang after they inquired about a rumor that Strang was bent on taxing them. Wendell, whom the *Islander* took great delight in calling the "Emperor of the continent of the Great Turtle" (a reference to Mackinac Island), also was faulted for not informing the Indians that the rumor was unfounded.[41]

Meanwhile, in Lansing MacCulloch was seeking state action against Strang. According to the *Islander*, MacCulloch and Atkyn made "laborious efforts to get up a commotion."[42] Michigan's governor, Kinsley S. Bingham, was said to have had a secret agent on the island—probably Atkyn—and based on the agent's reports, corroborated by MacCulloch, the state government withheld the school money that had been apportioned to Manitou County, apparently because of enrollment fraud. The Beaver Island group had about 1,000 children of school age, according to Strang's allegedly inflated reports for the 1854 state census, which would have entitled the islands to about $500 in per-pupil aid.[43]

The state authorities were not reluctant to act against Strang, but their legal options were limited and MacCulloch soon realized that his chances of getting state support to overthrow Strang were small. Two weeks after he had left, he returned to the island, resolved to ensure the desired result himself. MacCulloch brought back several pistols, which he distributed among his fellow conspirators.[44]

At that same time the *Islander* was downplaying a report from the captain of the propeller *Oriental*, who said MacCulloch had "devoted his life to revenge" on the prophet. "Don't believe a word of it," the *Islander* said. "It is natural that those who turn from the truth, should seek the life of the Prophet. Such is the common course. But when Dr. Atkyn last winter told a similar tale on [MacCulloch], he repelled it with indignation. Possibly when he and [the captain] were both badly 'shot in the neck,' they talked foolish bravery. But they who fear the assassination of the Prophet may as well reserve their fears awhile." The *Islander* did refer to "two individuals possessed of wealth and prominent standing" (apparently MacCulloch and Johnson), as the "leaders of the disobedient and rebellious." The pair, the paper said, raised the "howl," because "all private right and publick interest was not made to bend to their private interests, piques, and prejudices. . . . What has come of it? Nothing. There is no mob. We don't know who expects one."[45]

The warnings were there for Strang. But so, too, was the feeling that the king had survived so many attacks that he must be impervious to the slings and arrows. Earlier in 1856 Stephen Post had written his brother Warren that the "notion exists on the island that God will take care of the prophet, no matter what he does, we have nothing to say about it."[46]

The storm clouds on Beaver Island paralleled thunderclaps on the national scene. In word and in deed, each lightning bolt striking the public sensibilities seemed to spark another as the country sorted itself into opposing camps before the Civil War. Mob rule became almost routine.[47] In the Kansas Territory, free-state and proslavery forces battled for national advantage. On May 21, 1856, hundreds of heavily armed proslavers—accompanied by artillery pieces—descended on the free-state town of Lawrence after the arrests of free-state leaders there. By the time the smoke and dust cleared, two newspaper offices and a hotel had been destroyed. In their almost leaderless condition, the people of Lawrence had offered no real resistance. Two days later the abolitionist John Brown avenged the sacking of Lawrence and other perceived crimes against free-staters. Brown led a party of seven men who, without warning, brutally slaughtered five proslavers with short swords.[48]

Not all of the violence was on the frontier. In Washington, D.C., that same week, Charles Sumner of Massachusetts rose in the Senate to deliver a speech called "The Crime Against Kansas," a sweeping indictment of slavery interests. One official he singled out was an absent South Carolina senator, elderly Andrew Pickens Butler, whom Sumner accused of paying homage to the "harlot" slavery. Two days after that speech, Butler's nephew, Representative Preston Brooks, called Sumner's remarks a libel on South Carolina and his uncle; like John Brown, he exacted his own retribution, cornering Sumner at his desk on the Senate floor and beating him senseless with a cane. Sumner would not be able to resume his senatorial duties for three years.[49]

Meanwhile, on Beaver Island, the conspirators needed a way to escape Mormon retribution after the assassination. In Mackinac Thomas Bedford and Alexander Wentworth obtained a boat, which they surreptitiously sailed to Beaver Island and hid. During the next five days, while keeping out of sight themselves, they practiced with their pistols. For five nights, they watched for a chance to shoot Strang, but did not get a suitable opportunity. Finally, Bedford and Wentworth feared that the boat would be discovered and suspicions aroused. On the morning on May 30 they took the boat out into the lake, turned it around, and sailed into St. James harbor, as if they had just returned from Mackinac. The *Northern Islander* reported that the boat was suspected as stolen. "Who has lost one? Don't lay the theft to the Mormons, but come and get the boat." A few nights later the boat was seized by Mormons, filled with stones, and sunk in the harbor.[50]

≥● ≥● ≥●

In dense fog the U.S.S. *Michigan* docked at St. James late in the morning of June 2. Thomas Bedford loaded his double-barreled shotgun with buckshot, eighteen to twenty in each barrel, and stationed himself along the route to the dock, waiting for Strang to pass by to pay a courtesy call on the ship's captain. Strang did stroll down to the ship, but he was arm-in-arm between two friends. Bedford could not get a safe shot.[51]

The *Michigan* had changed since its 1851 visits to Beaver Island. Its rigging was topsail instead of barkentine, and a larger captain's cabin, complete with bathtub, had been built over the poop deck. While the *Michigan* was in port during the next two foggy days, a number of islanders took their complaints against Strang to the captain, Commander Charles H. McBlair, a thirty-three-year veteran of the Navy who had been in command of the warship for eight months.[52]

McBlair wrote that a "great disturbance" was prevailing on Beaver Island because of the withdrawals from the church of "two of the most intelligent men," MacCulloch and Johnson. Those two, he said, gave such "frightful accounts" of conditions that he felt it his duty to receive affidavits to present to Governor Bingham. On June 6, after the *Michigan* had docked in Chicago for an eight-day stay, McBlair mailed the statements to the governor. By the time they reached Bingham's office in Lansing, however, the governor apparently had left for the Republican national convention in Philadelphia.[53]

In the affidavits, Strang was accused of robbery and frauds related to the 1854 state census on Beaver Island. McBlair told Bingham that he had "every reason to believe that the greater part of the community has been for a long time engaged in a system of plunder" on fishermen and others in that region. Strang, he said, exacted a tithe from the booty. McBlair said he based his comments about plunder on information he received from "persons of apparent respectability" during his visit to the island. The information was "given very cautiously and with a lively apprehension of dangerous consequences, if their disclosures should become known." McBlair said it was also alleged that Strang had padded population figures in the 1854 state census to nearly four times the actual number for his own "sinister objects"—apparently to substantiate the burgeoning Mormon vote and to obtain a larger share of school funds from the state. Christopher Scott and Franklin Johnson enumerated the families to McBlair by name, coming up with ninety-five on Beaver Island and eight on Gull Island. They estimated an average of five in each family, making a total of 515 inhabitants, compared with the 1854 count of about 2,000 on the island.[54] (Decades later, one of Strang's most devoted followers, Wingfield W. Watson, estimated the settlement on Beaver Island at seventy families in 1856 but noted that some of the families were large.)[55]

In his letter to Bingham, McBlair wrote that there were ten to twelve persons "who have more or less openly seceeded from the church and are exposed to all the consequences of Strang's resentment. It is said there are a number of others who at heart are opposed to Strang but suppress their feelings from fear." McBlair said MacCulloch and Johnson simply wanted to wind up their business affairs and leave the island; the two families believed that their open split with Strang threatened not only their property but also their lives. They were seeking prompt and vigorous protection by the state.[56]

Bingham drafted a reply to McBlair on July 1, after returning from Philadelphia, where the Republicans nominated John C. Frémont for president and attacked "those twin relics of barbarism—polygamy and slavery." (The Utah Mormons were the focus of the party's antipathy to polygamy. The Republicans argued that if popular sovereignty were extended to other territories besides Kansas and Nebraska, the territory of Utah would vote to allow polygamy.) Bingham told McBlair that he would submit the affidavits to the state attorney general and said that if there were any way that Strang and the other "offenders" could legally be brought to justice, it would be done. "I regret to say however," Bingham wrote, "that the shrewdness of 'King Strang' in procuring a separate County organization for the Beaver Islands has made it almost an impossibility to bring them to trial." The governor added that in the next legislature he would recommend that Manitou County be attached for judicial purposes to Kent or Mackinac counties. "Then I think there will be no hindrance to the regular administration of Justice."[57]

At the time he sent the governor the affidavits, McBlair told his superior, Secretary of the Navy James C. Dobbin, what he had done and added an intriguing comment about his future plans in relation to the Mormons: on the *Michigan*'s way back to its home port of Erie, Pennsylvania, he planned to stop at Beaver Island and render "such assistance to those citizens threatened by the hostility of Strang as I can consistent with a cautious regard for the laws of the State and my public duties."[58]

On Friday, June 13, the *Michigan* left Chicago; it arrived in

Milwaukee early that evening. For the crew, including thirty Marines, the stop was routine. They busied themselves "keeping the ship's arms and furniture clean and themselves in tolerable trim. The officers were lounging around, the cook was getting dinner. The crew were some of them braiding hats, and some mending their breeches and swearing at each other. And one of the mariners was on guard aft, watching the capstan."[59]

The only excitement at Milwaukee occurred when the *Michigan* left on Sunday. It ran aground and remained stuck for some time.[60] There would be more excitement ahead, on Beaver Island.

Chapter 16

Assassination

O N BEAVER ISLAND, assassination plans had again been laid. The timing depended on the arrival of the *Michigan*, which was to provide the escape route for the assassins. At 12:50 P.M. on Monday, June 16, 1856, the warship took its place at the dock in front of Johnson and MacCulloch's store. The drama could begin. The weather was clear and pleasant, with the temperature in the mid-50s and a light breeze from the south. Symbolically, for Strang, it would cloud over by late afternoon.[1]

A number of islanders visited the *Michigan* during its first few hours in port, and some of the ship's officers conferred with H. D. MacCulloch at his home, near the dock. Commander Charles H. McBlair learned that conditions had changed little on the island: the "party of seceders" was still small, and MacCulloch and Franklin Johnson said that Strang and his followers had begun to plunder their property through "trumped up" judgments. They asked McBlair for assistance, and he decided to send for Strang, "to induce him to abandon his schemes against them."[2]

Late in the afternoon Alexander St. Bernard, one of the ship's civilian pilots, was dispatched to find Strang.[3] He first went to the tabernacle, where construction had resumed after more than five years. The building, with some of its wood decaying, had become dilapidated, and Strang had called on the Saints to repair and complete the structure.[4] At the tabernacle, St. Bernard was told that Strang had just gone home. There, Strang was sitting with his four wives, and he received the pilot cordially. Several times, on visits to the *Michigan*, Strang had met St. Bernard, a veteran of thirty years on the Great Lakes and a familiar figure in his blue uniform with brass buttons.[5]

When Strang heard St. Bernard say the captain wanted to see him "on business," he put on his plug hat and accompanied the pilot. The pair linked arms and chatted amiably as they walked the quarter-mile to the ship. Meanwhile, on the front porch of the F.

248

Johnson & Co. store, Thomas Bedford and Alexander Wentworth had joined a group of forty persons, including MacCulloch, Johnson, and some Marines from the ship.[6]

Strang and St. Bernard turned off the road and headed toward the narrow passageway between the high piles of cordwood on the dock, about sixty feet from the store. At that instant Bedford and Wentworth came off the porch and quickly stepped up behind the men. Unseen by Strang or the pilot—and just as a boy standing near the *Michigan* cried out: "Brother Strang, they are going to shoot you!"—Bedford and Wentworth fired, almost simultaneously. Bedford's shot passed through the back of Strang's hat and hit him on the head. Wentworth's struck Strang in the small of the back. Strang crumpled to the dock on his left side and turned his head to see who had shot him.[7]

Wentworth bolted for the *Michigan*, but Bedford, who had only a single-shot pistol, ordered him back to finish off Strang. Wentworth returned. From point-blank range he fired another shot—at Strang's head—wounding him on the right side of his face. Wentworth again ran. Bedford remained to club the king repeatedly, one report said seven times, on the head with the butt end of his long horse pistol until the weapon broke. Then he, too, ran for the *Michigan*.[8]

Weapons in hand, the pair of assassins ran aboard. "That damned rascal is out of the way," Wentworth cried.[9]

"Who?" asked a crewman who had heard the shots. "Strang, the damned son of a bitch," was Wentworth's reply.

According to the *Northern Islander*, in its surprisingly dispassionate account of the shooting in its final issue, the assault was committed in view of several officers and crew members on the deck of the steamer, as well as those on the porch of the store, "and no effort was made to stop it."[10] Bedford said he thought McBlair saw the whole thing.[11]

Once on board the *Michigan*, Bedford and Wentworth asked for protection. McBlair said the pair "avowed the act," and he "immediately had their persons secured." It was 6:50 P.M. The prisoners were not put in chains but simply placed under the care of an officer, who supplied whatever they needed for their comfort.[12]

Meanwhile, Mormons rushed to the scene to find their king

lying in his blood, apparently dying. A few Mormons and officers from the ship carried Strang to apostle Anson Prindle's house nearby.[13]

McBlair dispatched the ship's surgeon, Dr. James McClelland, to see if he could be of assistance. McClelland began probing the wounds. The first shot had hit near the top of Strang's left ear, then glanced along the skull nearly two inches, cutting an artery. One of the Mormons hovering attentively over Strang would press his finger on the severed artery for the next several hours, until the bleeding stopped.[14]

The second shot lodged in Strang's right cheekbone about an inch from the eye, and the third entered his back on the lower left side near the spine. McClelland could not locate the latter two bullets, but he did not probe deeply, for he thought either wound was mortal. Besides the bullet wounds, Strang's face was disfigured by the pistol-whipping, which left contusions angling from above the right eye across the nose to the chin. McClelland dressed the wounds and remained close by.[15]

Outside the Prindle house, Mormons huddled in intensely excited groups. Others stood guard. McBlair feared that the Mormons might be plotting vengeance, and he sent a detachment of Marines ashore to protect those who could be considered in danger. The families of Bedford and Wentworth knew nothing of the shooting until 9 P.M., when an officer and Marines from the *Michigan* arrived to help them carry possessions to MacCulloch's house, where Marines were posted.[16]

Late that evening Mormon leaders met in the printing office to discuss how to press their legal claim for Bedford and Wentworth. Early on the 17th, Sheriff George Miller sent a note to McBlair requesting a conference with him at the printing office. McBlair later wrote that he did not wish to meet with the Mormons because he did not wish to complicate the situation. He parried the request, informing Miller, via letter, that Bedford and Wentworth were in his custody and that it was his intention to surrender them to civil authorities at Mackinac. "If you desire at any hour after ten a.m. to confer with me, you will find me on board," McBlair wrote.[17]

Miller did not show up. He later wrote that the Mormons were reluctant to board the ship. "We had previously heard that if he could decoy any of us on board, he intended to confine us and take us away, having us dealt with as outlaws."[18]

Surrendering the prisoners to the Mormon authorities, McBlair wrote three months later, "would have been giving them up to the rage and fury of a rabble of religious fanatics whose revenge would not have stopped short of their immediate destruction. . . . It seemed to me that my duty was very simple and plain. I had only to convey the prisoners to the nearest point in the state where they could be given up without danger to their lives from popular fury."[19] As if to buttress that impression, St. Bernard was warned to be on his guard, because many Mormons thought he had led the king to the assassins.[20]

The Mormons thought they knew what would happen if the prisoners were taken to Mackinac. Wingfield W. Watson, one of the first Mormons on the scene after the shooting, wrote within hours of it: "They will be freed, set at liberty at Mackinac. They will be applauded and extolled."[21]

Late in the morning of the 17th, Commander McBlair, with some of his officers, visited Strang and expressed sorrow that the shooting had occurred while the *Michigan* was docked at St. James. Strang was alert enough to demand the prisoners, a demand rebuffed by McBlair, who would later deny that there had been any such request.[22]

In a heavy rain McBlair walked back to the ship. About 1 P.M. the Michigan cast off from the dock and steamed for Mackinac, carrying seven island families, including those of the prisoners and MacCulloch and Johnson. In all, about thirty persons left the island with some of their effects. The *Northern Islander* said the *Michigan* carried off "all the persons supposed to be complicated in the affair, thus affording military protection to murderers and overthrowing the sovereignty of civil law."[23]

At 5:40 P.M., the *Michigan* docked at Mackinac, and an hour later the prisoners were delivered to Sheriff Julius Granger of Mackinac County. Bedford and Wentworth were treated as heroes, and there was great excitement and rejoicing. They were escorted by the sheriff and officers from the ship to the jail, where a spontaneous ovation greeted them.[24] The pair of assassins held an open house at the jail. Residents flocked in with congratulations and offers of assistance. One brought a bed and some tobacco and pipes. Another brought a bottle of brandy. Cigars and whiskey were passed out. As had been the case aboard the *Michigan*, everything necessary for their comfort was provided.[25]

Some residents talked in French to the thirty-year-old sheriff, who later told Bedford and Wentworth that the residents had warned him that if he locked them up, they would tear the jail down. The doors remained open and unlocked.[26] King Strang apparently was dying, and his assassins were kings of Mackinac. Before nightfall the residents left the jail, and the prisoners followed them out the door. The sheriff took Bedford and Wentworth and their families to his boardinghouse, where he kept them for a week, without charge. Bedford said that on his earlier visit to Mackinac he had informed the sheriff, whom he knew well, what he intended to do to Strang.[27]

After three days of such treatment, Bedford and Wentworth were taken before a justice of the peace. The hearing lasted less than an hour, and the prisoners were discharged. It would be the only trial they ever would have. The justice, however, solemnly announced in court that he would have to charge them $1.25 each in court costs—but added that, under the circumstances, he would trust them for the amount. Bedford doubted that he ever paid the $1.25, even though one day someone on the street in Mackinac handed him a $5 bill without saying what it was for. Although it would be rumored that he received large sums of money in connection with the shooting of Strang, Bedford said the $5 was the only money that could be put in that category.[28]

ﻬ   ﻬ   ﻬ

The Indian scrambled ashore at the fishing camp on Gull Island, giving passing interest to beaching his canoe. "Big man shot!" he cried. "Big man shot!"[29]

Black Jack Bonner, with the stunning report still echoing around the camp, pushed off in his boat to find out more about the situation on Beaver Island. He was the first Irishman to reach the island after the shooting, but there would be more as the news spread and the Gentiles mobilized.[30]

On June 20 the *Islander* printed the Mormon account of the shooting and added: "In consequence of the laying up of Mr. Strang with his wounds, and the disarrangement of affairs growing out of the occurrence, the Daily Islander will be suspended." It was the *Islander*'s final issue.

On that same day, the *Detroit Advertiser* reported the assassination attempt, apparently based on reports from crewmen of the *Michigan*, which had docked at Detroit the day before.[31] The article concluded with these prescient comments: "Strang was heart and soul as well as intellect of the Mormon gang and it is to be strongly hoped that his death will break them up and scatter them abroad. There remains no man among them capable of wielding Strang's influence or of supplying his place." Although prophetic, the article was premature in its use of the past tense for Strang.

Also on June 20 George Miller mailed a letter from Milwaukee to Lewis Cass, the U.S. Senator from Michigan. In the letter, written June 18, Miller told Cass what had happened and complained strongly about McBlair's refusal to turn over Wentworth and Bedford to the authorities at Beaver Island. That refusal, Miller said, was "one of the most daring, high-handed aggressions of civil jurisprudence." Miller asked Cass to find out if McBlair's actions were sanctioned by the government, especially the Navy Department. Miller wrote that a day or two before the arrival of the *Michigan*, the Mormons had heard threats by MacCulloch, Johnson, Wentworth, Bedford, and others that "they would show Strang that he had not all power in his hands" when the *Michigan* arrived. According to Miller, those men said that Strang ought to have been killed long before, that the federal government had taken up their controversy, and that when the *Michigan* came, the Mormons' "time would be short."

৯ৎ   ৯ৎ   ৯ৎ

Nine days after the assassination attempt, Strang was still alive, but his legs were paralyzed from the bullet near his spine and his face was horribly swollen and blackened from the bullet wound near the eye. The Saints continued to pray for his recovery. And realizing that Strang represented their best hope of staving off raids by the

Gentiles, the Mormons let it be known that their king was indeed alive and that they thought he would recover. Meanwhile, their enemies were plotting their destruction.[32]

On June 24, another steamer, also named the *Michigan*, a commercial vessel about the same size as the Navy warship, stopped at Beaver Island en route from Buffalo to Green Bay. The passenger ship, also a side-wheeler, normally stopped at Mackinac, Beaver Island, and Washington Island, at the mouth of Green Bay. Mac-Culloch, perhaps scouting the temper of the Mormons, was spotted on board the steamer at St. James harbor, but nothing untoward happened, and the *Michigan* continued on its way.[33]

The *Michigan* had other passengers besides MacCulloch. Two were the sheriff of Mackinac County, Julius Granger, and his deputy and father, Lyman Granger. They were gathering a posse to help arrest some of the leading Mormons at Beaver Island. The charges, based on complaints made at Mackinac since the shooting of Strang, involved arson, theft, and other offenses. The *Green Bay Advocate* reported that the sheriff came to Green Bay for recruits for the posse, amid talk of plans to drive off the Mormons or "exterminate" them. "We shall expect to hear of a bloody fight soon," the paper said. "Kansas matters will be left in the shade." At Washington Island the posse was increased to about thirty men.[34]

On June 26 the *Michigan* headed back across the lake for Beaver Island. The steamer docked at 4 P.M. at Galilee, to take on wood. There the posse arrested two men, one of whom was Samuel Wright. Wright, described as a large man "with a countenance indicative of untamed and brutal passions," drew a revolver, which was taken from him after a struggle. He was hustled aboard the *Michigan*. Two other men were pursued to the woods: several shots were fired, but they escaped.[35]

The *Michigan* then steamed for St. James, docking at about 6:30 P.M. near MacCulloch and Johnson's store. There the Mormons learned that not only was MacCulloch aboard but also Wentworth and Bedford, returning with three other apostates, Franklin Johnson, Christopher Scott, and Conrad Steinhelber.[36]

The Mormons were caught by surprise. On landing, several members of the posse who were unknown to the Mormons walked very indifferently along the dock—to surround Mormon targets, some of whom were making fast the boat, others quietly watching the docking. One Mormon was arrested as he came for the mail.[37]

MacCulloch, Bedford, and Wentworth then appeared. Three Mormons saw them and ran back along the dock only to be cut off by the rest of the posse. One of the Mormons jumped into the harbor and soon was forced to grab the pier to save himself from drowning. Lyman Granger, who was sixty-three years old and weighed about 335 pounds, reached down and caught the Mormon by the hair and "flopped him up on the pier as if he had been a bass," Bedford said.[38]

After a struggle the other two Mormons gave themselves up. Several shots were fired by the posse, but no one was hurt. Two or three persons who had professed to be Mormons apostatized and boarded the steamer. The posse also threatened to take Strang aboard, dead or alive, when a group of Saints began to gather to see what the uproar and the shots were about. The *Michigan* set off for Mackinac.[39]

A correspondent of the *Green Bay Advocate* was aboard the *Michigan*. He wrote:

> You would pronounce us a very brave and warlike people, re-turning from the seat of war with our prisoners and spoils, our stacks of arms and our loud boasting of feats performed, and threats to be executed. I assure you, in all soberness, matters are becoming desperate hereaway and it would be no seven days' wonder if all our Mormon friends at the Beavers were . . . completely routed and 'cleaned out'. . . .
>
> The plan now is to return this week if possible, with at least 150 men, properly armed and equipped, and just clear every Mormon from the island—peaceably if possible—but if they won't do that, then at the range of a rifle. And judging from today's manifestation, I have little doubt but that they will carry their plans out to the letter. God help them if half their wrongs and grievances be true. The Mormon kingdom then richly deserve such a fate.[40]

Considerable excitement was reported at Mackinac, and at Washington Island, with armed companies fitting out at both places.[41]

The posse's foray heightened Mormon fears that another attempt would be made on Strang's life, and church leaders decided that Strang should leave on the first boat south. He would be taken to Voree—the City of Refuge, the Garden of Rest.[42]

For years Strang had advised the Mormons to keep their weapons ready to defend their lives and their island. Now he was literally paralyzed and realized that an armed conflict would be disastrous for his people. After he was carried on board the propeller *Louisville* for the trip to Voree, Strang gave an order to Edward Chidester: "Tell Anson [Prindle, one of the apostles] to tell the brethren in a quiet way that I think we will have to draw off before our enemies." The king's directions for the Mormons were for "every man to take care of his family" and do the best he could until shown what to do. This was taken to mean that it would be best for the Saints to scatter in small groups that would not attract much attention or opposition until anti-Mormon passions subsided and Strang regained his health. Strang recommended that the leading men—those who were the most obnoxious in the minds of the Gentiles—leave the island. And a large number did, with their families.[43]

The *Louisville* departed on June 28, with Strang and several of the Saints. Also leaving for Voree, in boxes filled by elders, were 1,500 unbound copies of an expanded version of the Book of the Law of the Lord. The 336-page book had been printed and folded for several weeks, awaiting a bookbinder. One had been sought, without success.[44]

On the night of July 1 the *Louisville* landed at Racine, and Strang was carried on a couch to the train depot for the trip to Burlington. The railroad line to Burlington had been completed the year before.[45] Strang was first taken to his parents' home in Voree, a stone dwelling just west of the White River and on the north side of the road from Burlington. Strang's mother took one look at his wounds and exclaimed that she had seen him in that condition in a dream years earlier. After a few days, Strang was moved to a house just east of his father's.[46]

Two days after Strang left the island, the exodus for Voree and points nearby swelled to about 200 when several families departed on the *Iowa*.[47] The kingdom was disintegrating.

Meanwhile, on tiny St. Helena Island about thirty miles northeast of Beaver Island, an anti-Mormon expedition was being mustered from fishing stations in that area. The force of about sixty well-armed men was being organized under the leadership of Archibald P. Newton. Newton, a merchant-fisherman, and his brother, Wilson, had a huge investment in St. Helena, including a store, a dock, and a cooper shop, and they claimed they were about to go broke because of Mormon raids that had cost them fish and fishing equipment.[48]

Particularly vexing to Archibald Newton, however, was the loss of a pair of oxen. After that theft, he said, he took an armed search party to Beaver Island. He did not find the oxen but claimed he did find their hides, hung up to dry. Newton then vowed to clear the island of Mormons. And after the shooting of Strang, according to one report, he put up $1,200 to hire men to fulfill that vow. All of the Mormons were not guilty of robbery, Newton acknowledged, but he said the laws of the Mormons made it the duty, and therefore the practice, to shield the guilty. Any attempt by an outsider to enforce the law against a Mormon was futile, he said.[49]

When word reached St. Helena that Strang had left St. James, the expedition set off for Beaver Island, ostensibly to recover lost property of merchants and fishermen—but also to drive off Strang's followers. About fifty men sailed on the schooner *C. L. Abel*, chartered from Mackinac. A dozen others followed in fishing boats. Among those in the group was Lewis Gebeau, the Gentile youth who had been wounded in the Battle of Pine River.[50]

On July 3 the expedition invaded the northern part of the island, split into six companies, and cautiously advanced toward St. James, expecting strong resistance. Instead, the Mormons were thoroughly disorganized. When the invaders realized there would be no concerted opposition, they dispatched patrols to order the Mormons in outlying farms to gather at the harbor with their possessions. As soon as a boat arrived, the Mormons were told, they would have to leave. Sheriff Julius Granger had come with warrants to arrest some of the leaders of the Saints but soon learned that the leaders had left; the warrants were never served.[51]

Wingfield W. Watson gave a graphic description of the actions of the invaders.[52] Watson had gone from his home in the center of the island to the harbor to see what was happening and get some supplies. On his way home he was met about a half mile from the harbor by two men, armed with rifles, pistols, and bowie knives. The men had just come through a gate from Marvin M. Aldrich's house, where they had been threatening Aldrich's wife and family and ordering them to leave, just as they had done at various other houses that afternoon.

"Where are you going?" one asked Watson, then twenty-eight.

"I am going home."

"Where do you live?"

"I live about six miles up on the island."

"Well, get your things down here to the harbor by 1 o'clock tomorrow, or your house will be burned over your head."

Watson said he told the pair that his wife had just given birth to their second daughter two days earlier and that he did not want to leave the island because she was in no condition to travel.

"That's a God damn pretty fix you've got into now," one of the men responded. He repeated the order for Watson to get his things down to the harbor.

"That's pretty hard," Watson remarked.

The pair said that if Watson called that hard again, they would tie him to a small cherry tree by the roadside. "We will whip you while we can stand over you."

Watson saw by the flush of their faces that they had been drinking, and he concluded that remonstrance was useless. He decided he had better move on.

At home Watson's wife said that if those men wanted her to go, they would have to carry her, because she was not able to walk to the harbor by herself. Later his wife agreed that she would have to leave, and that by going very slowly, she might be able to make it.

The next morning Watson again walked down to the harbor, to hire a team to transport the possessions they felt they could not do without. He had no luck and headed home expecting that they would have to leave almost everything behind. However, his brother-in-law, James Smith, later procured an ox team for them and sent a young man out with it.

At 9 A.M. Watson put his stove, a few boxes of goods, and some bedding aboard a wagon. He carried the baby in his arms, and walking very slowly, he and his family managed to get down to the harbor.

The beach on the west side of the harbor "seemed here and there like an open fair, or marketplace, with cattle, tents, fires, smoke, furniture, and household goods of every description; all waiting, according to the dictates of the mob, to be off on the boat's arrival." And it had become clear that the expedition was, indeed, a mob, as it sacked St. James.

The unfinished tabernacle was burned. Those who tried to defend themselves and their homes were routed into the street and their houses burned. The contents of two stores of general merchandise—J. M. Wait's and Aldrich's—were plundered. And the mob forced some Mormons, at gunpoint, to remove stones from Thomas Bennett's grave.[53] The Saints, as a matter of custom, had been piling stones on Bennett's grave "with a muttered curse" in the five years since his death.[54]

To show its spite against Strang, the mob shot up his house and other belongings. His large poultry yard was a special target. His extensive libraries, at home and at the printing office—including many rare books—fell into the hands of the mob. Some of the books were thrown into the street and tramped in the mud. At the printing office, church-related pamphlets were tossed into the street and lay fluttering in the wind. After taking possession of the printing office, the mob set and printed a manifesto that was circulated among the Mormons and the Gentiles. The manifesto was crudely printed, but its message was clear:[55]

EXTRA—ISLANDS REDEEMED—The dominion of King Strang is at an end. The band of marauders, once occupying the Beaver group of Islands . . . have fled at the approach of the Sheriff. The land is redeemed, a kingdom no longer exists upon the borders of one of our most populous states. . . . The institutions of our country secure protection to all her citizens, especially to their religious freedom; but when its tenets are criminal and directly antagonistical to our laws and subversive of our constitution, we as citizens would prove recreant to our duties to permit a longer continuance of the evil.

It should be a matter, therefore, of public rejoicing to all persons living contiguous to the lakes that this nest of banditti have been exterminated, and we would take this occasion to caution the citizens of Wisconsin against many of them who have fled within her precincts. . . . Of this sad condition of things we are now happily set free—and we say again we have reason to congratulate ourselves and rejoice that the state has been relieved of an excrescence that had recently become intolerable.

Few islanders escaped the effects of the mob. While awaiting a boat to take them from the island, Watson and his family had stopped at James Smith's house when MacCulloch came by to have a chat with Smith. In an adjoining room, Watson could hear them speculating about who could stay on the island and who could not. Watson overheard MacCulloch say: "Watson is too good a Mormon to stay."[56] Elvira Field Strang later said the Mormons who showed a disposition to renounce their beliefs were left undisturbed, while those who would not change their ideas to suit the mob were ordered to leave immediately. She and the other wives had apparently left before the mob arrived.[57]

One Mormon, J. S. Comstock, said one leader of the mob was Alexander Toll, a Mackinac merchant who had served with Strang as a state representative in 1853. Comstock said Toll threatened to burn his house down over his head if he did not leave. When asked what authority he had to give such an order, Toll replied with surprise and indignation: "You presume to ask for my authority. This is my authority," he said, clasping his gun. Comstock added that the men of the mob claimed that Governor Bingham had encouraged them to act. Comstock had come to Beaver Island in the spring of 1855. He had a house and lot in St. James, for which he had paid $300. He also had a farm of 160 acres, crops in the ground, cattle, and farm equipment—all of which the mob claimed. He estimated that his forced departure cost him at least $2,000.[58]

On the afternoon of July 7 the steamer *Buckeye State*, after stopping at Mackinac en route to Chicago, arrived at Aldrich's dock on the south side of the harbor. With the arrival of the steamer, the bustle reached a frantic pitch.[59]

James Smith had made plans to leave on the *Iowa* a few days later and had only a few of his things packed. But Archibald Newton and one of the men who had stopped Watson earlier spoiled these plans, just as Smith and Watson's family were about to sit down for supper.[60]

"Why ain't ye getting yer things aboard?" Smith was asked.

"I was waiting for the *Iowa* to come in," Smith said.

"God damn ye, get yer things aboard," Newton said, slamming him with an open palm across the side of his face, whirling him around, and then jamming a revolver into his chest. "Get yer things aboard."

"MacCulloch told me I could stay till the *Iowa* came in," Smith said.

"God damn MacCulloch," Newton said, "we'll play hell with him pretty soon."

Newton's partner began throwing water in the stove. He jerked the bed clothes off one of the beds, nearly pulling Watson's six-day-old daughter onto the floor. Watson's wife cried out just in time.

All of those living and camping near Aldrich's dock were hustled on the *Buckeye State*. The Mormons were driven on like cattle—worse than cattle, because the mob saw to it that most of the cattle stayed. Watson lost a heifer.

Watson loaded most of the belongings he had brought to the harbor aboard the ship. But his brother-in-law saved next to nothing. What Smith had worked for thirty years to accumulate was swept away in an hour. Smith had built a large sawmill on the island and had shipped in machinery of various kinds. He had a blacksmith's shop, turning lathe, and belting. He pleaded that he was innocent and that no charges had ever been brought against him, but he never got a penny out of the thousands he had invested in the island. He was a "God damn Mormon."

Watson's wife was one of the last to board at Aldrich's dock. Watson walked ahead of her with their baby in his arms. His wife rather feebly followed. A companion of Newton's walked behind her, gun in hand. She was not moving fast enough. "God damn ye, move on," he said.

The *Buckeye State* then steamed up to MacCulloch and Johnson's dock. When the lines were made fast, the same procedure was followed for those camped there. The little property the Mormons were allowed to take with them was mainly luggage and household effects. Most of the more expensive property was seized. Horses and mules were taken, as well as boats, fish and fishing supplies, and large quantities of furniture, provisions, and household goods.[61] According to Watson, the mob's grand scheme was to persuade the Mormons to get their belongings down to the harbor, to be shipped on the first boat. "But in reality it was simply that they might rush us all aboard in as great hurry and bustle as possible and then retain our cattle and goods as a booty while the boat shoved off."[62]

The booty was divided among the invaders, as best as they could agree, to reimburse them for losses they claimed to have suffered through Mormon robberies. A press report said "oxen, horses, boats, fishing tackle, barrels—in fact all sorts of property . . . had been stolen by [the Mormons] and secreted upon the islands" in an "abundant variety and astonishing amount."[63] Bedford was given a span of Aldrich's horses to replace the pair he said had been stolen from him.[64]

At 7 P.M. the 282-foot *Buckeye State* had taken aboard as many Mormons as it could hold. It carried 350 passengers, about 100 more than normal. The lines were cast off, and the steamer, captained by L. Chamberlain, headed for Chicago by way of Green Bay and Milwaukee. The boat had been chartered by H. D. MacCulloch, and the passage for the Mormons was paid by goods appropriated from Aldrich's store.[65]

Earlier that day the propeller *Prairie State* had arrived in Detroit with fifteen Mormon families from Beaver Island. Of the situation on the island, the *Detroit Tribune* said: "Chaos reigns there. The charm that bound the heterogeneous mass together is broken and the singular state of society falls to pieces of its own innate weakness or corruption."[66] The new "authorities" on the island had fixed a deadline for the Mormons to leave, after which "no quarter" would be shown.[67]

With the departure of the *Buckeye State*, twelve families were left waiting to get off the island; they were sent on the next boat, apparently the propeller *Louisville*. It arrived in Detroit on July 10 with some Mormons.[68]

The Gentile mob had swept the Beavers clean. The kingdom was no more. A mob had nurtured Strang's dream of royalty in 1844, and twelve years later a mob had turned it to ashes.

After years of harsh talk about how they would deal with a Gentile invasion, why didn't the Mormons resist? Sarah Wright Strang said that the king never told them to. But, in addition, the Mormons on the island were mainly helpless—and leaderless. Most of the leaders had fled before the mob arrived. Sarah doubted that the Mormon remnant was well armed. "I don't think there was 50 firearms on the island," she said.[69]

                                                                       *** ***

Meanwhile, in Voree, on the very day the *Buckeye State* was loading up on the island, Strang's eyes brightened, his "countenance lit up," and he appeared to be a great deal better. His wife Sarah, after getting off the island, had stopped to see him, but left almost immediately to go live with her father, Phineas Wright, elsewhere in Wisconsin.[70] Five months pregnant with her first child, she felt obliged to go with her father rather than stay with her husband. "I had no other way to live, only with my father."[71]

Despite his apparent improvement, Strang told Edward Chidester that "the active part" of his life was ending and that "the bearing off of the kingdom" must devolve on others. Although Strang said he felt his ministry as chief was done, he did not name a successor.[72]

In the spring of 1844 Joseph Smith had made startlingly similar comments. Smith told the Council of Fifty that he was "weary and tired" with the burden he had so long carried. "And in the name of the Lord, I now shake from my shoulders the responsibility of bearing off the Kingdom of God to all the world," giving that job to the council.[73]

As at Nauvoo, internal dissensions had contributed to Strang's downfall. Indeed, in March 1856 Stephen Post had written his brother Warren that "we cannot consistently support [any] king in the church but Jesus. Whilst living under the laws of the United States we are bound to obey the laws.—No man can serve two masters. You cannot serve a temporal king and a Republican government at the same time. The thing is preposterous."[74] And yet such a system had survived on Beaver Island for six years.

Six weeks earlier, the period from July 5 to 9, 1856, had been set aside for a church conference at St. James. On July 8 "solemn sacrifices" were to be offered "as thank offerings to God for giving us the kingdom." On the 9th, God was to be praised with music and dancing.[75] Instead, the mob was holding a "conference" on Beaver Island. There were no thank offerings from the Mormons and no music and dancing. By then, the kingdom had been taken from them, and the exodus was completed. No Moses had appeared to lead the Saints to a new promised land.

On July 8, the sixth anniversary of the coronation of King Strang, about ninety refugees of that kingdom were deposited at Green Bay by the *Buckeye State*. The *Green Bay Advocate* described their condition.

> They are all in the most destitute circumstances, having neither money nor provisions, and not even clothes, save the shabby habiliments on their backs. All of their moveables, except a scanty supply of bedding, they were compelled to leave behind. . . . According to the statements given to us by persons of the party which is now here, the doings of the mob were without even a shadow of authority. . . . [Newton's] only excuse for violence against these unfortunate and misguided people was that they had stolen an ox from him. . . . It is one of the most pitiable cases we have recorded in a long time.[76]

Also on the coronation anniversary, in Voree, Strang was failing. According to Edward Chidester, "It seemed as though he just wilted away."[77] The wounds on his head were practically healed, but not so the one on his back. It was feared that a kidney had been pierced by the shot there.[78]

Chidester asked Strang if he were "going to leave us." Strang said yes. Chidester then again asked Strang if he were going to appoint a successor. A tear formed in Strang's eye, and he said: "I do not want to talk about it."[79]

That night Chidester took care of Strang until 2 A.M., when Lorenzo Dow Hickey and one of his wives, Adeline, got up. Chidester finished a letter he was writing. At about daybreak Chidester helped turn Strang and make him comfortable, and then took a nap himself, at the foot of the bed. An hour and a half later, Chidester awoke; there was no one else in the room, except Strang. Chidester got up and discovered that Strang was dying. For about an hour he nursed Strang. When he saw the end was near, Chidester sent for some of the neighbors, who would have included Strang's parents. Chidester asked Strang if there were anything he wished to say.[80]

"Yes," Strang replied, but that was his last word. Chidester closed Strang's eyes at 9:45 A.M. Besides Chidester, the Mormons at his deathbed were Hickey, Hickey's wife Sarah, George Miller, and two of Strang's wives, Betsy and Phoebe, and Betsy's children.[81] Strang died on July 9, 1856, one day after the sixth anniversary of the establishment of his kingdom and exactly twelve years after he claimed to have received the letter of appointment. He was forty-three.

Strang was buried at 2 P.M. on July 10 at the Saints' cemetery in Voree. Hickey opened the funeral service with prayer, and according to Chidester, "such a prayer I never heard except from the Prophet himself, it seemed as though the earth trembled, the wagon where he stood did at any rate, he had the Spirit to such a degree that he never had it before, at least he says so. Bro. B. G. Wright then attempted to preach, but it was only an attempt, Bro. Hickey had the Spirit." In as grand a style as possible for the Voree area, Strang was laid to rest. Chidester paid $20 for the coffin, which was said to be worth $35. The funeral shroud was of the finest silk flannel and had cost $4.77. Chidester said: "I considered him worthy of the best, and therefore I gave it to him." A number of other Saints, including George Miller and his family, and a "respectable congregation of Gentiles" were present. None of Strang's immediate family, or that of his first wife, Mary, was mentioned.[82]

After the *Buckeye State* had dropped off 150 Mormons at Milwaukee on July 9, there were still 100 Saints aboard when the steamer stopped at Racine on its way to Chicago. At Racine a son of B. G. Wright delivered the news that Strang had died that morning at Voree. Many of the Mormons were thunderstruck, for they had expected Strang to recover.[83] After all, the Saints had been taught to believe that Strang was called by God to complete the work of Joseph Smith. Were those revelations a sham? Who would take Strang's place?

On July 10 the *Buckeye State* docked at Chicago. The *Chicago Tribune* reported that the 100 Mormons were "utterly destitute." Their church had been burned, crops destroyed, and they "are homeless wanderers. Those here are without means of any kind, and are entirely dependent upon charity for support."[84]

The Mormons stood on the dock at Chicago, with the summer sun beating down, wondering what to do, where they were to spend the night. While curiosity seekers stared at the Mormons, one man cursed the leaders of the mob for sending the Mormons to Chicago and for robbing them. The man shoved open some large warehouse doors and told the Saints: "Come in here out of the heat and rest yourselves till you can find places to go." This was the first kind word the Mormons had heard from an outsider since the exodus had begun.[85]

Sketch of Strang's house on Beaver Island. *Clarke Historical Library.*

Ruins of corduroy road built by Mormons on Beaver Island. The harbor, Paradise Bay, is in the background of this 1940s photograph. *State Archives of Michigan.*

Mormon printing office on Beaver Island. The building, which now houses a historical museum, is the only Mormon structure remaining on the island. *State Archives of Michigan.*

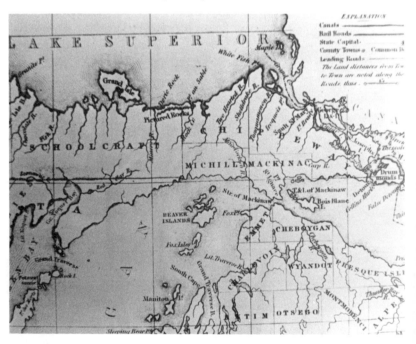

The Beaver Island region, as shown on an 1850s map of Michigan.

The old state Capitol building, the one in use in 1853, when Strang
became a member of the House of Representatives. *State Archives of
Michigan.*

A view of Lansing, taken from the Capitol cupola, in 1857. *State Archives
of Michigan.*

Home of H. D. MacCulloch, one of the richest Mormons on Beaver
Island. *State Historical Society of Wisconsin.*

Ruins of a more typical Beaver Island Mormon home, built of squared
logs. Harbor is in background. Neither of these houses exists on the island. *State Historical Society of Wisconsin.*

Johnson and MacCulloch's store. The assassination of Strang was launched
from here by Thomas Bedford and Alexander Wentworth. *State Historical
Society of Wisconsin.*

Thomas Bedford, assassin of
Strang. *Burton Historical Collection,
Detroit Public Library.*

Ruth Ann Bedford refused to wear
bloomers. *Burton Historical Collection, Detroit Public Library.*

DAILY
NORTHERN ISLANDER.

VOL. I.   SAINT JAMES, LAKE MICHIGAN, FRIDAY, JUNE 20, 1856.   NO. 33.

THE DAILY ISLANDER.
COOPER & CHIDESTER,
PRINTERS AND PUBLISHERS.
TERMS:

The Daily Islander will be furnished to subscribers ... times a week from the opening to the close of navigation, and once a week from the close of navigation till the opening, at six dollars a year.

Those subscribing for less than a year, will be charged, during the season of navigation, at the rate of two dollars a quarter.

The Weekly Islander will be furnished to subscribers once a week from the opening till the close of navigation, and once a month from the close till the opening, at two dollars a year.

TERMS OF ADVERTISING

Advertisements will appear in the Daily Islander at the following rates:

8 lines, 1 year, $8 00
"   1 quarter,   2 00
"   a less period, first insertion,   50
"   every subsequent insertion,   25
Advertisements in the directory, on the first year, 1 year,   2 00
"   1 quarter,   1 00

Advertisements in the Weekly, one dollar per square for three insertions, and twenty-five cents for every subsequent insertion.

Notices of births, marriages and deaths, in both papers, 25 cents.

All other notices inserted once at 10 cents a line.

MURDEROUS ASSAULT.

On Monday last the U. S. steamer Michigan entered this harbour at about 1 o'clock, P. M., and was visited by the inhabitants promiscuously during the afternoon.

At about 7 o'clock Capt. McBlair sent a messenger (San Barnard, the Pilot) to Mr. Strang, requesting him to visit him on board. Mr. Strang immediately accompanied the messenger, and just as they were stepping on the bridge leading to the pier in front of F. Johnson & Co.'s store, two assassins approached in the rear, unobserved by either of them, and fired upon Mr. Strang with pistols. The first shot took effect upon the left side of the head, entering a little back of the top of the ear, and rebounding, passed out near the top of the head.

This shot, fired from a horse pistol, brought him down, and he fell on the left side, so that he saw the assassins as they fired the second and third shots from a revolver; both taking effect upon his person, one just below the temple, on the right side of the face, and lodged in the cheek bone; the other on the left side of the spine, near the tenth rib, followed the rib about two inches and a half and lodged.

Mr. Strang recognized in the persons of the assassins Thomas Bedford and Alexander Wentworth. Wentworth had a revolver, and Bedford a horse pistol, with which he struck him over the head and face, while lying on the ground. The assassins immediately fled on board the U. S. steamer, with pistols in hand, claiming her protection.

The assault was committed in view of several of the officers and crew from the deck of the steamer, also Dr. H. D. McCulloch, Franklin Johnson, and others, and no effort made to stop it.

Mr. Strang was taken up by a few friends, and some of the officers of the boat, and carried to the house of Messrs. Prindles, where the surgeon of the steamer made an examination of his wounds, and declared recovery hopeless.

Process was taken out for the apprehension of the assassins, and the Sheriff of the county called on Capt. McBlair for their delivery. The Capt. refused to give them up, saying that he would take them to Mackinac, and deliver them into the hands of the civil authorities of the State there.

The steamer left the next day, carrying off all the persons supposed to be complicated in the affair, thus affording military protection to murderers, and overthrowing the sovereignty of civil law.

Hopes are entertained of Mr. Strang's recovery.

Our exchanges, especially those of the Republican stamp, are filled with accounts of the atrocities committed in Kansas, under the pretence of enforcing the laws of the Missouri invaders. Kansas is effectually overrun, if not conquered, and but for the fact that the Mormons, when in Missouri, were served the same way, and for precisely the same reasons, and the invaders justified by the publick, north as well as south, we should expect the rising indignation of the free States to drive out the invaders. As it is, we presume in three or four years the robberies, murders and banishments will be forgotten by those northern communities, now so much excited on the subject. If the doctrine of popular sovereignty had been allowed unrestrained force in Kansas, those who now oppose it in the north, would have justified it in the end it will become the bulwark of freedom; not of slavery.

We learn by a letter from an old, tried, unwavering Democrat, that at the caucus in Mackinac last May, to send delegates to the State convention, Wendell made a rally to send himself as delegate, by circulating a call for a general rally to devise means to expel the Mormons. This would do for a Know Nothing. A pretty Democrat Wendell is.

In consequence of the laying up of Mr. Strang with his wounds, and the disarrangement of affairs growing out of the occurrence, the Daily Islander will be suspended.

A Fair Start.—The list of contributors to make Kansas a free State stands as follows:
Z. Chandler, $10,000. Eber B. Ward, $10,000, S. S. Barnard, $1,000, Charles Merrill, $1,000, Shubael Conant, $1,000. Twenty-five thousand dollars is not a bad start for one day in a one horse city like Detroit. We want to hear from Chicago. —Detroit Advertiser.

WISCONSIN AND MICHIGAN LAND GRANT.

The Wisconsin Railroad Land Grant, just made by Congress, is to aid in the construction of a railroad from Fond du Lac, on Lake Winnebago, northerly to the State line of Michigan, 155 miles; and also from Madison or Columbus, via. Portage city, to the St. Croix River or Lakes, between townships 25 and 31, (near St. Paul, Minnesota,) about 250 miles; thence easterly to Bartield, on Lake Superior, about 60 miles. The grant to Michigan is for a road from Little Noquet Bay, on Lake Michigan, to Marquette, on Lake Superior; thence to Ontonagon; also from Ontonagon and Marquette southerly, to the State line of Wisconsin.—Plain Dealer.

There is also a grant to Michigan for railroads in the Lower Peninsula, providing for two roads from the existing railroads north to the Straits, and northwest to Lake Michigan.

INTERESTING FROM UTAH—MOVEMENT FOR THE FORMATION OF THE STATE OF DESERET.

St. Louis, Tuesday, }
May 27, 1856. }

The Salt Lake mail has arrived here bearing dates to the 26th of March.

A convention for forming a State Constitution met at the Council House on the 17th of March, and organized by the election of the Hon. J. M. Grant, President.

Committees were appointed to draft a constitution. They had a conference on the 24th, and unanimously reported a Constitution for the State of Deseret. Chief Justice Kinney dissented from the report, but only on one point, viz: that he preferred to have the Judges elected by the people rather than by the General Assembly.

The Republican to-day publishes the Constitution of the State of Deseret, recently formed and ratified by the people in gen-

---

Front page of last issue of the *Northern Islander,* on June 20, 1856, gives the details of the shooting of Strang in a surprisingly dispassionate account. *Yale University Library.*

The U.S. Navy's first iron warship, the steamer *Michigan,* had orders to assist in the arrest of Strang and played a key role in the escape of Strang's assassins. From painting by Charles Robert Patterson. *Dossin Great Lakes Museum.*

A view of Mackinac Island street in 1856, with Fort Mackinac and the county courthouse (with the cupola) in the background. Both the fort and the courthouse building, where Strang was put on trial, still exist on the island. *Mackinac Island State Park Commission.*

Strang and his third polygamous
wife, Sarah Wright Strang. *Clarke
Historical Library.*

Marker on Strang's grave in Burlington, Wisconsin. *State Historical
Society of Wisconsin.*

Epilogue

A FEDERAL INQUIRY was conducted into circumstances surrounding the assassination of James Jesse Strang, but basic
questions remain unresolved. The inquiry, remarkable for
its lack of vigor, grew out of George Miller's complaint to Senator
Lewis Cass about Commander Charles H. McBlair and the *Michigan*. Cass forwarded the complaint to the Navy Department, with a
note that appeared to exempt the Navy from any blame. "As to
[Miller's accusation of] interference of the government in bringing
about the unfortunate occurrence . . . of course the suggestion
needs no contradiction from you," Cass wrote Secretary of the Navy
James C. Dobbin. "But the letter contains statements which I think
are proper for consideration by the Navy Department." [1]

The department received the note on June 30, 1856, and informed Cass that an inquiry would be made. McBlair, however, did
not learn about Miller's complaint until two months later. He requested copies of any papers relating to it, so he could respond, to
relieve himself from "injurious impressions." [2] Copies of the Miller
and Cass letters were sent to McBlair, and only then did the department suggest that he submit a report on the assassination and
its aftermath. "The propriety of offering an explanation will be
apparent to you," wrote Charles W. Welsh, then acting secretary of
the Navy. [3]

McBlair wrote Welsh that the "first intimation" he had of the
assassination attempt was the appearance of Bedford and Wentworth
on board his ship. Despite the evidence to the contrary, McBlair
said there was no demand for him to surrender the pair to the authorities on Beaver Island. "Where there was no demand," he said,
"there could be no refusal. . . . The tenor of the whole letter of
Miller . . . conveys covertly the insinuation that this vessel was
more or less implicated in the crime itself. It will hardly be thought
necessary or even worthy of me to notice seriously a charge so hei-
nous, sustained by no evidence and proceeding from a source so

infamous," describing Miller as "one of the band of thieves and pirates" at Beaver Island.[4]

Welsh sent Cass a copy of McBlair's explanation on October 2, with a perfunctory note.[5] The matter apparently was considered closed.

Another opportunity for an investigation—this time involving the dispersion of the Mormons—was treated as cavalierly.

Early in 1857, in its first session after the assassination of Strang and the dispersion of the Mormons, the Michigan legislature received a petition from forty-eight residents asking that J. S. Comstock's property on Beaver Island be restored to him or that he be paid for it. The petition was referred to committee, where it died. Comstock had also presented the petition to Governor Kinsley S. Bingham but said the governor did not even send him back his extra postage stamp.[6]

Comstock did not let his request end there. Late in 1859 he wrote a new governor, Moses Wisner, that members of the "lawless mob" were unmolested by the government, even though they were living in Mormon houses and had appropriated Mormon goods.[7] Wisner replied that Comstock wrote as if a mob had invaded his rights and suggested that Comstock appeal to the laws in his own county. "I doubt not the courts of that county will protect and afford you all the redress necessary." Comstock responded that he felt his case was "too much like insurrection to Justify the Gov. in referring us to County Court, where the mob is a vast majority."[8]

The latter comment was close to the mark. If members of the "mob" were not in control on Beaver Island in the years after the dispersion, it is apparent that enemies of the Mormons were.

In the fall 1856 election for Manitou County, the first since the dispersion, the names on the ballot read like a roll call of anti-Strang forces. Among the candidates were H. D. MacCulloch, Alexander Wentworth, and Thomas Bedford, who had returned to the island with their families. They were all defeated, however. In the race to succeed Strang as state representative from Beaver Island, MacCulloch lost to Peter McKinley, 43 to 18. In the contest for county treasurer, Wentworth lost, by a similar margin, as did Bedford in a bid to be fish inspector.[9]

The low vote totals indicate that only a couple of hundred

persons were living on the island. Most were fishermen and other Gentiles who had moved into abandoned Mormon homes at St. James. A few one-time Mormon families had remained on the island, including those of Tobias and John McNutt. The McNutts were brothers of Strang's wife Betsy, and their farms bordered on Round Lake, about six miles from St. James. After the excitement of the dispersion died, the McNutts moved into two of the abandoned houses at the harbor. Some new arrivals bought land and built homes out of dismantled Mormon structures.[10]

A couple of years after the dispersion, Walter Whitney and his wife moved into Strang's home for two years. They became the first persons other than Strang's family to live in the house, which Whitney had helped build. Later the home became the target of souvenir hunters. What was left eventually burned and went to ruin before the turn of the century. Strang's first island home, a hewn log cabin, was still standing then, but like the other houses the Mormons built on the island, it does not exist today.[11]

In the first fall after the dispersion, almost every farmhouse on the island was deserted. Weeds competed with flower beds. Chickens scuttled about empty barns. James O. McNutt, a son of Tobias McNutt, said in his diary that the Mormons had planted their crops before they were driven off. "Families that came on the island had a picnic, for they could go where they pleased and get the crops for nothing, only the work of harvesting them."[12]

Wentworth had a good team, and he transported potatoes to the dock, where they were shipped to market. One day, James McNutt said, Wentworth had his three-year-old daughter with him while he was hauling potatoes, and she fell off the load. Before he could stop the team, the hind wheel of the wagon ran over her, killing her instantly.[13]

Among the former Beaver Islanders who returned after the dispersion were James Cable as a merchant, Whitney as a carpenter, and Eri James Moore as a merchant and wood salesman. By 1860 Julius Granger had settled there as a fisherman, and his father, Lyman, who had been the lighthouse keeper before McKinley took the job, was running a boardinghouse. The Mormon printing office was converted into a hotel. The liquor sellers returned.[14]

There were 499 persons on the island at the time of the 1860 census. Although the Mormons were no longer there, the vestiges they left were a subject for official comment. The census taker found twenty-one unoccupied dwellings on Fox Island and noted: "Good dwellings, formerly occupied by Mormons, who departed these islands, thank God."[15]

After losing the election for county treasurer, Wentworth and his family moved to Janesville, Minnesota, where they lived with the Franklin Johnson family.[16] But Wentworth returned to the island for a couple of visits before the start of the Civil War. Elizabeth Whitney Williams said Wentworth came back "to see how things were prospering." During the last of his visits, she said, he boarded with her and her husband for several weeks. "He was a fine looking and intelligent man, very quiet in his manner," Mrs. Williams said. "We had several other boarders at the same time, people who came to see King Strang's Island. Alec, as they always called him, was their guide to show them the best fishing streams and take them to hunt ducks and wild pigeons. I often talked with Wentworth about the shooting of Strang, asking him if he had any regrets about what he had done. He said, 'I have never yet regretted what I did. The Mormon life was bad, and there was no good in it as I can see and I would not live it over again for anything.'" After that visit, Wentworth never came back, and Mrs. Williams said she never heard from him again.[17]

Nine months after the start of the Civil War, Wentworth joined Company F of the 5th Regiment of the Minnesota Infantry as the company was being organized at Fort Snelling, Minnesota. He enlisted as a corporal, and was promoted to first sergeant on August 25, 1863. Six days later, at Camp Bear Creek, Mississippi, he died of chronic diarrhea. He was thirty years old. His record declared him a "good soldier and competent [non-commissioned] officer."[18]

Unlike Wentworth, Bedford remained on the island for several years after the dispersion. In the fall of 1856, shortly after he lost his race for fish inspector, the Mackinac County Board of Supervisors paid him $12.25 on account 484, which was not identified. Sheriff Julius Granger was paid $144 on accounts 486 to 489, and Granger's father, Lyman, was paid $13 on account 490, all of which were also unidentified. One board member present that day was

Archibald Newton, the supervisor of Moran Township.[19] Was it just
a coincidence that those four individuals were involved in the dispersion of the Mormons? A suspicious mind might wonder whether
taxpayers helped foot the bill for the outfitting of the mob.

Bedford lived on the island until 1864, when he sold his forty
acres to his wife for $75. His wife promptly mortgaged the land for
$300 to pay for Bedford's defense against a charge filed in Mackinac
County. Bedford was accused of murdering William Gallagher.[20]

Before a trial was held, Bedford, at age forty-nine, joined the
Union Army for the last year of the Civil War. He never returned
to the island, instead settling near Eaton Rapids, south of Lansing.
His wife remained on Beaver Island, however. In the 1880 census
for St. James she listed herself as a widow—perhaps to help Bedford
avoid prosecution, for he was still alive. In 1882 Bedford's wife was
reported to have occasionally visited him at Eaton Rapids, the last
time within the previous year. During that visit it was understood
that Bedford was to return with her to the island, but he did not.[21]

Perhaps one reason he did not was a Cheboygan newspaper
article, published after an interview with him was printed in the
Detroit News. In the July 7, 1882, article in the News, Bedford
detailed his role in the assassination of Strang. Two weeks later the
Cheboygan Democrat said Bedford had forgotten to mention that
when he left the island it was in the hands of the sheriff, charged
with the slaying of Gallagher: "He broke out of jail at Mackinac
Island and got off clear, since which time the officers of Mackinac
County have been unable to learn of his whereabouts"—that is,
until the News interview was published. Gallagher's daughter, the
Democrat said, was still alive "and it is said that even at this late day
it would be easy to convict Bedford, and it is not impossible that
he may yet be called to account for the murder."[22] There is no
record that he was, however. And this may not have been the only
other time Bedford was accused of killing someone. Strang's
son, Clement, described Bedford as a triple murderer.[23]

On July 5, 1889, Bedford died in Eaton County of Bright's
disease, a kidney disorder. His age was listed as seventy-six.[24] He
had lived thirty-three years after the assassination of Strang.

The assassins of Strang, despite predictions to the contrary,
also drained the lifeblood from Strang's church. The Green Bay Ad-

vocate, after the Mormons of Beaver Island had been scattered, assessed their future positively: "Their history, whatever may have
been their faults, is one which will excite sympathy everywhere,
and it will be contrary to all experience if it does not enlist new
supporters to their cause, and new converts to their religion. . . .
however wild and baseless a religious creed may be, persecution will
bring it followers when nothing else will . . . and . . . we shall
expect to hear from [the Strangite Mormons] in some new home
increased in numbers and strength."[25]

That prediction has not come true. Even in the first months
after the dispersion, it was apparent that the strength of the church
had died with Strang. Many Saints were left in a state of mingled
doubt and disappointment. Their "true prophet" had died, and, one
by one, members left the church. There were those who tried to
keep the faith, however. Warren Post said some of the apostles had
called a church conference for October 6, 1856, but few had attended and little was accomplished. Another conference was set for
December 6, 1856, but bad weather and the poverty of the Saints
prevented much from being done then, too. On February 10, 1857,
five of the apostles—including Post and Lorenzo Dow Hickey—
met near Racine, Wisconsin. They prayed and communed all night.
"We became satisfied," Post said, "that the twelve could not lead
the church without a prophet." In line with the directive issued by
Strang after he had been shot, the apostles decided to take care of
themselves and their families until the word of the Lord guided
them on "other duties."[26]

Strang, with his goal of a sizable posterity, left twelve children, including one born in Wisconsin to each of his four plural
wives after he died. Four years after his death, Strang's first wife,
Mary, was still living with their three children and working a valuable farm near Voree. Mary, like Betsy and Phoebe, never remar-
ried. Elvira and Sarah did, but not to Strangites.[27]

As the years passed, Strang-related memories and memorabilia
became neglected. At one point after the dispersion, Sarah Wright
Strang became sick and was told by her doctor that she would not
recover (although she did). "I told my people to gather up all James'
books and papers and burn them up," she said. Sarah feared that
her son might try to follow in his father's footsteps. "I thought if

the Lord wanted my son to do any work, he was abundantly able to tell him without any old books or manuscripts of his father's."[28] Today none of Strang's descendants is involved in the church he headed.[29]

At Voree the Mormon cemetery where Strang was buried turned into a cow pasture. In 1876 Strang's daughter Netti (Myraette Mable) had his remains moved to a lot at the Burlington Cemetery. There the grave stayed unmarked for a half century before a marker was erected. The simple headstone gives his name and the years of his birth and death.[30]

Today the Strangite church has approximately 200 members, with about one-third living in the Burlington, Wisconsin, area, and another third in New Mexico. There are about a dozen Strangites in Michigan but none on Beaver Island. The church is led by three high priests. It has not had another prophet—or another king.[31]

To this day, the debate continues about James Jesse Strang. Was he a scoundrel, twisting religious means to suit his ends? Was he an imposter who filled psychological needs through the emotional support of gullible followers?[32] Was he a prophet of circumstance, tapped by an angel to lead God's people?

In 1858 a former follower, Stephen Post, wrote that Strang was an imposter, a scoundrel, and the leader of a band of robbers. "He made lies his refuge. . . . No wonder he did not want to talk about a successor, he felt, of course, that is if he was not past feeling, that such an unholy kingdom ought to be dissolved."[33]

Strang, however, may have understood that the kingdom was of Strang, by Strang, and for Strang. Without him, there was no reason for it to exist. And no need for a successor.

If Strang was not a prophet of God, what motivated him to claim he was? The most credible explanation is that after the death of his daughter in 1843, Strang realized his life span was limited and his goals might never be accomplished. However, when he viewed the power and promise of Joseph Smith and the Mormon church, his dreams of royalty and empire were rekindled. With Smith's assassination Strang saw his opening and, in a bold bid, presented himself as Smith's successor. In debater's terms, he assumed the affirmative position of prophet and presented his proof: the letter of appointment, the visit by an angel, the brass plates, the testimony of witnesses—the latter three with precedents in Smith's career. Based on the evidence, it is probable that Strang—or someone under his direction—manufactured the letter of appointment and the brass plates to support his claim to be a prophet and to sell land ,at Voree.

If this scenario is correct, Strang's advocacy of himself as a prophet was more than suspect, but no psychological delusion. Strang undoubtedly was carrying psychological baggage, but when viewed in the context of his socially turbulent era, with its doctrine of Manifest Destiny and with the formation of such groups as the communal Oneida community, he may not appear as unbalanced as he would in today's world. Strang also did not appear to act in a deluded manner, despite his uncommon role as prophet and king: he kept his feet on pragmatic ground in his skillful dealings in politics and in the courts. He knew where one world ended and the other began.

A believer in Strang as a prophet has to accept—on faith— several major incongruities. First, that a man who was a self-proclaimed atheist at nineteen would maintain, at thirty-one, that he had been ordained by an angel as ruler of God's people. Second, that the same God who, in the letter of appointment, had said the Saints "shall not be mooved" from Voree would, through Strang, point out a new church headquarters, Beaver Island. Third, that a prophet who had said God cursed polygamy would later learn that polygamy was God's way.

As a practical matter, both polygamy and the island setting helped Strang maintain his hold on his followers by making it more difficult for a disgruntled family to pack up and start a new life elsewhere. But it was the pervasiveness of Strang's hold on his followers that eventually led to rebellion—and his assassination.

Even though he died without a successor, Strang succeeded. He had realized his kingdom. He had tasted power. He had found a market for his intellect. He had gained lasting notoriety. And through time he has survived. Long before his death, he had said that kingdoms could decline and fall, that "all the works of man are destined to decay. . . . And fame, fame alone of all the productions of man's folly may survive."

Notes

The following abbreviations are used in the notes and references:

Ancient: James J. Strang, *Ancient and Modern Michilimackinac* (rpt. ed. Mackinac Island, Mich., 1959).

Beinecke: James J. Strang Papers, Western Americana Collection, Beinecke Rare Book and Manuscript Library, Yale University, New Haven, Connecticut.

Burton: James J. Strang Papers, Burton Historical Collection, Detroit Public Library, Detroit, Michigan.

Clarke: James J. Strang Papers, Clarke Historical Library, Central Michigan University, Mount Pleasant, Michigan.

DA: *Detroit Advertiser*, 1836–1862, Detroit, Michigan.

Diary: Diary of James J. Strang, 1831–1836, Beinecke.

GH: *Gospel Herald*, 1847–1850, Voree, Wisconsin.

Navy: Correspondence of Secretary of Navy, Record Group 45, National Archives, Washington, D.C.

NI: *Northern Islander*, 1850–1856, St. James, Michigan.

VH: *Voree Herald*, 1846, Voree, Wisconsin.

ZR: *Zion's Reveille*, 1846–1847, Voree, Wisconsin.

In the quotations from letters and other manuscripts, the original wording, spelling, and punctuation are retained.

Chapter 1. Opportunity

1. William R. Hamilton, statement in *History of Hancock County*, ed. Charles J. Scofield (Chicago, 1921), pp. 845, 846.

2. Ibid.

3. Ibid.; *History of the Church of Jesus Christ of Latter-day Saints*, ed. B. H. Roberts (Salt Lake City, 1957), 6:602, 606; 7:142.

4. Scofield, ed., *History of Hancock County*, pp. 709, 845–47 (a diagram of the jail floor plan is given between pages 840 and 841); Roberts, ed., *History of the Church*, 6:616–19; 7:101.

5. Journal History of the Church of Jesus Christ of Latter-day Saints, June 10, 1844, Library-Archives, Historical Department, Church

of Jesus Christ of Latter-day Saints, Salt Lake City (hereafter referred to as the Mormon Church Archives); *Nauvoo Expositor*, June 7, 1844; Roberts, ed., *History of the Church*, 6:487–91; Donna Hill, *Joseph Smith* (New York, 1977), pp. 392, 393.

6. *Warsaw Signal*, June 12, 19, 1844; Roberts, ed., *History of the Church*, 6:486–91, 577–80; 7:122–25.

7. *Warsaw Signal*, June 29, 1844; Roberts, ed., *History of the Church*, 6:548–61.

8. Roberts, ed., *History of the Church*, 6:553–74. The justice of the peace and captain was Robert F. Smith.

9. J. H. S., statement in Scofield, ed., *History of Hancock County*, pp. 846, 847; *Chicago Democrat*, July 10, 1844; Roberts, ed., *History of the Church*, 6:606.

10. J. H. S. statement.

11. Roberts, ed., *History of the Church*, 6:574, 607, 608, 617; 7:103.

12. Ibid., 6:617–20.

13. Ibid.

14. Ibid., 618–20; 7:103–5.

15. Ibid., 6:618–20; Hamilton statement.

16. Roberts, ed., *History of the Church*, 6:617–21; 7:104–6.

17. Hamilton statement.

18. Ibid.

19. J. H. S. statement; Hamilton statement; Roberts, ed., *History of the Church*, 6:621–25; 7:108–10.

20. "Chronicles of Voree," copy in State Historical Society of Wisconsin, Madison, pp. 10–12. This church history, "A record of the establishment and doings of the stake of Zion called Voree—Wisconsin, made by scribes appointed to that office," apparently was begun after June 27, even though it covers a period beginning five months earlier.

21. Elvira and Charles J. Strang, "Biographical Sketch of J.J. Strang," copy in Strang Papers, State Library of Michigan, Lansing.

22. Fawn M. Brodie, *No Man Knows My History* (New York, 1946), pp. 362, 363; *Times and Seasons*, Mar. 15, 1844; Robert B. Flanders, *Nauvoo: Kingdom on the Mississippi* (Urbana, Ill., 1965), pp. 38, 39, 322; Glen M. Leonard and T. Edgar Lyon, "The Nauvoo Years," *Ensign* 9 (Sept. 1979): 11, 12.

23. *Times and Seasons*, Jan. 1, 1844; *St. Louis Daily Evening Gazette*, May 9, 1844; Leonard and Lyon, "Nauvoo Years," p. 12; Roberts, ed., *History of the Church*, 6:287.

24. "Chronicles of Voree," p. 6; Brodie, *No Man*, pp. 293, 294; *St. Louis Daily Evening Gazette*, May 11, 1844.
25. Hill, *Joseph Smith*, p. 279.
26. Henry Adams, "Charles Francis Adams Visits the Mormons in 1844," *Proceedings of the Massachusetts Historical Society* 68 (Boston, 1952): 286.
27. *Warsaw Signal*, Feb. 14, June 19, 1844; Hill, *Joseph Smith*, pp. 45, 374–76, 387.
28. "Chronicles of Voree," pp. 6, 7.
29. *Warsaw Message*, Feb. 7, 1844; Hill, *Joseph Smith*, p. 387.
30. "Chronicles of Voree," p. 7; Journal History, Feb. 23, 1844.
31. "Chronicles of Voree," pp. 7, 8.
32. Ibid., pp. 8, 9.
33. *Milwaukee Commercial Herald*, July 5, 8, 1844.
34. "Chronicles of Voree," pp. 1, 9; "letter of appointment," Beinecke.
35. "Letter of appointment."
36. Ibid.
37. Roberts, ed., *History of the Church*, 7:132–33; Hill, *Joseph Smith*, p. 374.
38. *Times and Seasons*, Oct. 1, 1844; Hill, *Joseph Smith*, p. 374, 421, 422; Leonard Arrington, *Brigham Young: American Moses* (New York, 1985; Urbana, Ill., 1986), pp. 111, 112. For a discussion of the precedents or authority for eight possible methods of succession, see D. Michael Quinn, "The Mormon Succession Crisis of 1844," *BYU Studies* 16 (1976): 187–233.
39. Roberts, ed., *History of the Church*, 7:132, 175.
40. "Chronicles of Voree," pp. 12, 13; *NI*, Nov. 2, 1854.
41. *GH*, June 14, 1849; Journal History, Aug. 5, 1844.
42. "Chronicles of Voree," p. 13.
43. *The Record of Norton Jacob*, ed. C. Edward and Ruth S. Jacob (Salt Lake City, 1949), p. 7.
44. "Chronicles of Voree," pp. 13, 14.
45. Crandell Dunn to Elder Appleby, Aug. 4, 1846, in *Latter-day Saints' Millennial Star* (hereafter referred to as *Millennial Star*), Oct. 15, 1846.
46. *NI*, Nov. 2, 1854.
47. "Chronicles of Voree," p. 9, 10.
48. Ibid., p. 14.
49. Roberts, ed., *History of the Church*, 7:223–30.
50. Ibid.

51. Ibid., 132, 228–42; Arrington, *Brigham Young*, pp. 113–16.
52. *GH*, June 14, 1849; Jacob, ed., *Record of Norton Jacob*, p. 7.
53. Hill, *Joseph Smith*, p. 424; Quinn, "Mormon Succession," pp. 191, 216.
54. Strang to Louisa Sanger, Dec. 5, 1844, Journal History.

Chapter 2. Dreams of Royalty

1. Charles A. Strange, "The Strangs of Westchester," *New York Genealogical and Biographical Record* 98 (1967): 199–204; 99 (1968): 8, 169, 170; 100 (1969): 162; 101 (1970): 28; 102 (1971): 92.
2. Family records of Clement Strang family, copy in Henry E. Legler Papers, State Historical Society of Wisconsin; Strange, "Strangs," *New York Genealogical and Biographical Record* 101 (1970): 28; 102 (1971): 92; James Jesse Strang, uncompleted autobiography, Beinecke, pp. 1, 2. Strang began the autobiography in 1855, and it was broken off—in mid-sentence—with Strang writing about his ancestry and his life from birth until he was twelve. The seven-page manuscript was reprinted in *Michigan Historical Collections* 32 (1903): 202–6.
3. Strang, autobiography, p. 1.
4. Ibid., pp. 3, 4.
5. Whitney R. Cross, *The Burned-over District* (New York, 1950), p. 57; Strang, autobiography, pp. 4, 5.
6. Strang, autobiography, p. 3.
7. Ibid.
8. Ibid., pp. 3, 6, 7.
9. A former follower, Wingfield W. Watson, gave this account in a letter to Henry A. Chaney, undated, Beinecke.
10. Strang, autobiography, p. 7.
11. James Jesse Strang, Diary, Beinecke, p. 16 (12). The diary was transcribed, with coded sections deciphered, by Mark A. Strang in *The Diary of James J. Strang* (East Lansing, 1961). In my notes the page numbers of Mark Strang's diary will be given in parentheses after the page numbers for the original diary. In some cases Mark Strang made minor errors in deciphering the coded sections. Where these errors are a factor in this history, they are pointed out.
12. Ibid., pp. 15, 16 (12, 13).
13. Ibid., p. 15 (12). Mark Strang's translation omits the "a" before "part of myself."

14. Ibid., p. 16 (12).
15. Records of Fredonia Academy, Historical Museum of Barker Library, Fredonia, N.Y.
16. Ibid.
17. Myraette (Strang) Losee to "Friend Dennison," Feb. 1878, Strang Papers, State Library of Michigan; Diary, p. 16 (12); records of Fredonia Academy.
18. Diary, p. 16 (12).
19. Ibid., pp. 5, 15 (5, 11, 12).
20. Ibid., pp. 15, 17 (11–14).
21. Ibid., pp. 6, 7, 19, 22 (6, 15, 17). Mark Strang's translation makes both "government and countrie" plural.
22. Ibid., pp. 19, 22, 23 (15, 17, 18).
23. Ibid., pp. 1–6, 14, 15, 18 (4–6, 11, 14).
24. Ibid., p. 5 (6).
25. Ibid., pp. 23, 24 (19).
26. Ibid., p. 60 (34).
27. *The Life and Adventures of Henry Thomas* (Philadelphia, 1848), pp. 87–141.
28. Diary, p. 29 (22).
29. Ibid., pp. 44, 45, 55 (27, 28, 32); E. and C. Strang, "Biographical Sketch," p. 1.
30. Diary, p. 45 (28).
31. Ibid., p. 35 (24).
32. The Doctrine and Covenants, p. 144.
33. Diary, p. 55 (32).
34. Myraette Losee to Dennison, Feb. 1878; Andrew W. Young, *History of Chautauqua County* (Buffalo, N.Y., 1875), pp. 427–28; *VH*, May 1846.
35. Cross, *Burned-over District*, pp. 3, 55, 56, 75; Diary, pp. 2, 21 (4, 16).
36. *VH*, May 1846.
37. Diary, p. 10 (8).
38. Ibid., p. 14 (10, 11).
39. Ibid., p. 25 (20).
40. Ibid., pp. 24, 29 (19, 21).
41. Ibid., p. 25 (20).
42. Ibid., pp. 86, 87 (44, 45).
43. Ibid., p. 69 (38).
44. Ibid., pp. 1, 17, 23 (4, 13, 18).

45. Ibid., p. 48 (29).
46. Strang to Peter L. Fraser, June 27, 1836, Beinecke; Diary, pp. 77–79 (41, 42).
47. Diary, pp. 78, 79 (42).
48. Ibid., pp. 73, 77, 85 (40, 41, 44); Myraette Losee to Dennison, Feb. 1878.
49. Diary, pp. 91, 92 (47).
50. Ibid., p. 89 (46).
51. Ibid., pp. 92–94 (48, 49).
52. Ibid., p. 98 (50, 51).
53. Ibid., pp. 97, 98 (50, 51).
54. Ibid., pp. 100, 101 (52, 53).
55. Ibid., pp. 101–3 (53, 54).
56. Ibid.
57. Ibid., pp. 103, 104 (54).
58. Ibid., pp. 104–8 (54–56).
59. Ibid.
60. Ibid., p. 88 (45).
61. Ibid., pp. 100, 108–10 (52, 56, 57). In 1835 speculation fever was rampant in the nation. See Paul Wallace Gates, "The Role of the Land Speculator in Western Development," in The Public Lands, ed. Vernon Carstensen (Madison, 1968), pp. 349–54.
62. Diary, pp. 100 (52).
63. Ibid., pp. 108, 109 (57).
64. Strang to Wealthy Smith, Sept. 10, 1836, Beinecke.
65. Diary, pp. 109, 110 (57).
66. Ibid., pp. 108–10 (57).
67. Strang to Wealthy Smith, Sept. 10, 1836.
68. Diary, pp. 113–18 (59–61).
69. Ibid.
70. Ibid.
71. Ibid., pp. 118, 119 (61).
72. Ibid., p. 121 (62).
73. Strang to Wealthy Smith, Sept. 10, 1836.
74. History of Racine and Kenosha Counties (Chicago, 1879), pp. 293, 471; GH, June 14, 1849.
75. GH, June 14, 1849.
76. Diary, p. 121 (62).
77. Ibid., p. 118 (61).
78. Ibid., p. 121 (62, 63); Strang to W. L. Perce, Sept. 22, 1836, Beinecke.

79. Diary, p. 95 (49).
80. Ibid., p. 122 (63); E. and C. Strang, "Biographical Sketch," p. 1; Strang letter of June 12, 1836, Beinecke; Strang to Peter Fraser, June 27, 1836.
81. Strang to John W. James, Dec. 29, 1836, Beinecke; John P. Downs, *History of Chautauqua County and Its People* (New York, 1921), p. 428.
82. Strang to Wealthy Smith, Sept. 10, 1836.
83. Strang to W. L. Perce, Sept. 22, 1836.
84. W. L. Perce to Strang, Oct. 10, 1836, and Strang to Benjamin Perce, Feb. 23, 1837, Beinecke. Mary Perce's father has often been described as a Baptist clergyman. In 1825 he apparently was (see *GH*, June 14, 1849), but a decade later, at the time of Strang's marriage, he was in the candling business. Whether he also was a minister then is not known.
85. Family records of Clement Strang family.
86. Strang to Benjamin Perce, Feb. 23, 1837.
87. Ibid.
88. Ibid.
89. See the letters of the period in the Strang Papers, Beinecke.
90. Strang to Mary Strang, Dec. 8, 1836, Beinecke.
91. Strang to Mary Strang, Dec. 5, 1836, Beinecke.
92. Strang to Mary Strang, Dec. 5, 8, 1836.
93. Mary Strang to Strang, Jan. 25, 1837, Beinecke.
94. See also other letters of the period, Beinecke.
95. Strang to Mary Strang, Jan. 20, 1837, and Mary Strang to Strang, Jan. 25, 1837, Beinecke.
96. Strang to "Amanda," Feb. 25, 1837, Beinecke.
97. Strang to Mary Strang, Feb. 20, 1837, Beinecke.
98. See the letters of the period, Beinecke; E. and C. Strang, "Biographical Sketch," p. 1.
99. E. and C. Strang, "Biographical Sketch," p. 2; land records, Chautauqua County, Mayville, N.Y.; certificate of commission as postmaster of Ellington, signed by Postmaster General Amos Kendall, Beinecke. The appointment took effect Nov. 24, 1836.
100. *Strang Family Newsletter*, ed. Janet Strang Shott (La Canada, Calif., Apr. 1980), p. 12.
101. Myraette Strang to Strang, May 16, 1840, and to Mary Strang, May 24, 1840, Beinecke.
102. *VH*, May 1846; Downs, *History of Chautauqua County*, p. 376.
103. Myraette Losee to Dennison, Feb. 1878; see also letters of the pe-

riod, Beinecke. Strang appears to have had control of the paper for only a few months.
104. *VH*, May 1846.
105. *History of Walworth County* (Chicago, 1882), pp. 332, 333, 890, 897, 902; *History of Racine and Kenosha Counties*, pp. 319, 472.
106. E. and C. Strang, "Biographical Sketch," p. 2; Ellen Perce to Mary Strang, July 11, 1841, Beinecke.
107. Henry E. Legler, *A Moses of the Mormons* (Milwaukee, 1897), reprinted in *Michigan Historical Collections* 32 (1903): 180–224 (p. 183).
108. Myraette Losee to Dennison, Feb. 1878; *Strang Family Newsletter*, Apr. 1980, p. 12.
109. E. and C. Strang, "Biographical Sketch," p. 2.

Chapter 3. The Rajah Manchou Plates

1. "Chronicles of Voree," pp. 14, 15.
2. Ibid., pp. 15–18.
3. *VH*, Jan. 1846.
4. Ibid.
5. Ibid.
6. Ibid.; "Chronicles of Voree," p. 29; Strang to Mrs. Corey, Sept. 26, 1854, reprinted by Strang as the pamphlet *The Prophetic Controversy* (St. James, 1856).
7. "Chronicles of Voree," p. 30; *VH*, Jan. 1846. Many historians have incorrectly spelled Manchou's last name as Manchore.
8. Brodie, *No Man*, p. 42 (reproduction of the characters said to have been copied from the gold plates).
9. "Chronicles of Voree," pp. 29, 30.
10. Strang to Mrs. Corey, Sept. 26, 1854.
11. *Southport Telegraph*, Sept. 30, 1845.
12. *Southport American*, Oct. 11, 1845.
13. *Racine Advocate*, Oct. 7, 1845.
14. *Southport Telegraph*, Oct. 21, 1845.
15. *VH*, Apr. 1846; *Warsaw Signal*, Aug. 18, 1846.
16. Stanley Hirshson, *The Lion of the Lord* (New York, 1969), pp. 6,7, 243–45. Exactly when Strang grew his full beard is in doubt. It is known from daguerreotypes that he had one a decade later, and he apparently had one in 1846. The April 1846 issue of the *Voree Herald* refers to his letting "his beard grow long."
17. *VH*, Sept. 1846.

18. "Manuscript History of the Anti-Mormon Disturbances in Illinois 1845," Thomas C. Sharp Papers, Beinecke, pp. 24, 25; Scofield, ed., *History of Hancock County*, pp. 854, 855; Hill, *Joseph Smith*, pp. 433, 434; Roberts, ed., *History of the Church*, 7:446, 447.

19. Scofield, ed., *History of Hancock County*, pp. 854, 855; Arrington, *Brigham Young*, pp. 124, 125; Hirshson, *Lion*, p. 65; Hill, *Joseph Smith*, p. 434.

20. "Chronicles of Voree," pp. 33, 34.

21. Dale L. Morgan, "A Bibliography of the Church of Jesus Christ of Latter Day Saints (Strangite)," *Western Humanities Review* 5 (1950): 50; *VH*, Jan. 1846.

22. Morgan, "Bibliography," p. 50.

23. "Chronicles of Voree," pp. 34, 35, 49–51.

24. Ibid.

25. Ibid., p. 57.

26. Ibid., p. 54.

27. The letter is in Beinecke. There was precedent for Smith's naming a successor without a public announcement. He had done so with David Whitmer in 1834, but Whitmer, one of the three witnesses to the existence of the gold plates from which the Book of Mormon had been translated, had been excommunicated in 1838. See Quinn, "Mormon Succession," pp. 193–99.

28. Reuben Miller to Strang, Feb. 15, 1846 (letter is dated 1845, but it was written in 1846), Beinecke.

29. "Chronicles of Voree," p. 49; an account of this mission is given in Smith's obituary in *GH*, June 14, 1849.

30. "Chronicles of Voree," pp. 58, 59; *GH*, June 14, 1849.

31. "Chronicles of Voree," pp. 58, 59; *GH*, June 14, 1849.

32. Testimony relative to the "crimes and heresies of the Twelve" at Nauvoo (Apr. 6, 1846), Beinecke. For a discussion of the origins of the whittling societies, see Thurmon Dean Moody, "Nauvoo's Whistling and Whittling Brigade," *BYU Studies* 15 (1975): 480–90.

33. Legler, *Moses*, p. 188; *VH*, Aug. 1846.

34. Journal History, Feb. 4, 1846; Russell R. Rich, *Ensign to the Nations* (Provo, Utah, 1972), pp. 3–5, 20–22.

35. *VH*, May 1846.

36. Ibid.

37. *GH*, June 15, 1848.

38. *Millennial Star*, May 15, 1846.

39. *GH*, June 14, 1849.

40. Miller to Strang, Feb. 15, 1846.

41. *VH*, June 1846; *Warsaw Signal*, Jan. 7, 1846.
42. Strang to Emma Smith, Feb. 22, 1846, Chicago Historical Society, Illinois.
43. The first letter in the correspondence apparently was written by Bennett on Feb. 24, 1846. It is in the Library and Archives, The Auditorium, Reorganized Church of Jesus Christ of Latter Day Saints (hereafter referred to as Reorganized Church Archives), Independence, Mo.
44. Thomas Ford, *History of Illinois* (Chicago, 1854), p. 263.
45. Morgan, "Bibliography," p. 52; Journal History, July 25, Oct. 4, and Dec. 16, 1840.
46. Journal History, Feb. 1, 3 and 4, 1841, and Apr. 8, 1841.
47. *Times and Seasons*, Oct. 15, 1842; Roberts, ed., *History of the Church*, 5:36, 37; Flanders, *Nauvoo*, pp. 261–63; Brodie, *No Man*, p. 309.
48. *New York Herald*, May 16, 1842; Journal History, May 7, 11, 17, 1842.
49. Roberts, ed., *History of the Church*, 5:35, 36.
50. Flanders, *Nauvoo*, p. 261; Leonard J. Arrington and Davis Bitton, *The Mormon Experience* (New York, 1980), pp. 69, 197; Brodie, *No Man*, p. 310.
51. *Times and Seasons*, Aug. 1, 1842; Flanders, *Nauvoo*, p. 265.
52. *Wasp* extra, July 27, 1842.
53. *Times and Seasons*, Aug. 1, 1842.
54. *Millennial Star*, July 1, 1845.
55. Bennett to Strang, Mar. [25], 29, 1846, Beinecke.
56. Bennett to Strang, Mar. 31, 1846, Beinecke.
57. Bennett to Strang, Apr. 7, 1846, Beinecke.
58. *Times and Seasons*, May 2, 1842; Hill, *Joseph Smith*, pp. 192–94; Brodie, *No Man*, pp. 170–71.
59. *VH*, June 1846. One of Joseph Smith's sisters would charge decades later that her name was forged to a document supporting Strang that purportedly was signed by Smith family members. Katherine Salisbury's accusation appeared in the *Saints' Herald*, Apr. 26, 1899.
60. Bennett to Strang in early 1846 (no date), Beinecke.
61. *Times and Seasons*, July 15, 1842; Roberts, ed., *History of the Church*, 5:269, 271; *Among the Mormons*, ed. William Mulder and A. Russell Mortensen (New York, 1958), pp. 126, 127; Journal History, Oct. 14 and Dec. 3, 1844; John Hardy, *History of the Trials of Elder John Hardy*, Mormon Church Archives.

62. *Times and Seasons*, Aug. 15, 1843.
63. Journal History, Oct. 14, 1844.
64. Ibid., Dec. 3, 1844, and Apr. 10, 1845.
65. *Times and Seasons*, Apr. 15, 1845.
66. *Millennial Star*, May 1, 1846; *Times and Seasons*, Dec. 1, 1844; Nov. 1, Dec. 1, 1845.
67. *New York Times*, Mar. 20, Aug. 19, 1867; Roberts, ed., *History of the Church*, 6:349; Peter Amann, "Prophet in Zion," *New England Quarterly* 37 (Dec. 1964): 478. Amann's article details Adams's colorful history in his later years.
68. Robert P. Weeks makes this case in "The Captain, the Prophet, and the King," *Mark Twain Journal* 28 (Winter 1975–76): 9–12. One of Adams's biggest cons was his ill-fated attempt to establish a colony in the Holy Land in 1866–67.
69. Adams to Strang, Mar. 27, 1846, Beinecke.
70. Strang to Adams, May 5, 1846, Beinecke.
71. Bennett to Strang, Apr. 7, 1846.

Chapter 4. Stirrings of a Royal Order

1. Bennett to Strang, June 2, 1846, Beinecke.
2. *VH*, Apr., July, and Sept. 1846.
3. Ibid., Sept. 1846.
4. *New Era*, Jan. 1847. This dissident newspaper was printed in Voree, copy in Reorganized Church Archives.
5. *VH*, Apr. 1846; Benjamin Chapman to Strang, Mar. 24, 1846, Beinecke.
6. *VH*, May 1846.
7. Land records, Walworth County, Elkhorn, Wis. After selling the 650 acres, Perce left Voree for New York state, where he was killed in the fall of 1847 in a construction explosion. Details of Perce's death are in a letter from J. Williams to J. N. Bacon, Apr. 12, 1848, Beinecke. Several Perce parcels were sold at Voree at prices approaching $50 per acre before the end of 1847, with Strang involved in the agreements as a witness.
8. *VH*, May 1846.
9. Ibid., July 1846. For details on the timing of Bennett's arrival and the revelation, see Reuben Miller's pamphlet, *James J. Strang, Weighed in the Balance of Truth, and Found Wanting* (Burlington, Wis., Sept. 1846), pp. 18–20, Mormon Church Archives.

10. Ritual of the Order of Illuminati, Beinecke.
11. Covenant book, Beinecke; Miller, *James J. Strang*, p. 20; *DA*, June 6, 1851.
12. Covenant book.
13. Ritual of Order of Illuminati.
14. Bennett to Strang, Aug. 11, 20, 1846, and proposed "diploma," all in Beinecke.
15. Bennett to Strang, Aug. 11, 1846.
16. Roberts, ed., *History of the Church*, 6:260, 261; *NI*, Aug. 23, 1855; *Saints' Herald*, Jan. 27, 1904; Ford, *History of Illinois*, p. 321. For a perspective on Strang's royal roots and the Smith connection, see Klaus J. Hansen, "The Making of King Strang," *Michigan History* 46 (1962): 201ff. Five members of the Council of Fifty later joined Strang's church: George J. Adams, William Marks, George Miller, John E. Page, and William Smith. Other studies of the Council of Fifty and its influence include Hansen's *Quest for Empire: The Political Kingdom of God and the Council of Fifty in Mormon History* (East Lansing, Mich., 1967); D. Michael Quinn's article, "The Council of Fifty and Its Members, 1844 to 1945," *BYU Studies* 20 (1980): 163–97, which downplays the role of the council; and Andrew F. Ehat's "'It Seems Like Heaven Began on Earth': Joseph Smith and the Constitution of the Kingdom of God," *BYU Studies* 20 (1980): 253–79.
17. *VH*, June 1846.
18. "*Chronicles of Voree*," pp. 82, 102; *VH*, Sept. 1846.
19. *VH*, Aug., Sept. 1846.
20. *Millennial Star*, Oct. 15, 1846.
21. *VH*, Aug. 1846.
22. Ibid., Apr. 1846.
23. Ibid., Aug. 1846.
24. Ibid., Sept. 1846.
25. Ibid.
26. *Warsaw Signal*, Aug. 18, 1846.
27. *St. Louis American*, Oct. 1, 1846.
28. Strang to Mrs. Corey; *Millennial Star*, Oct. 15, 1846.
29. Strang to Mrs. Corey.
30. Young, letter of Jan. 24, 1846.
31. In his diary entry of Mar. 20, 1833, Strang wrote about the throne of the Spirit of Nature, "who veils his face in light."
32. This conclusion also was reached by Charles Eberstadt, "A Letter

That Founded a Kingdom," *Autograph Collectors' Journal* (Oct. 1950): 4.

33. Dale L. Morgan makes this statement on p. 27 of his typewritten notes in his catalog of a portion of the Strang Papers in Beinecke.
34. Eberstadt, "A Letter That Founded a Kingdom," p. 5.
35. Ibid.
36. The postscript was not included in the copy of the letter in the "Chronicles of Voree," pp. 1–6, nor in the copy published in *VH*, Jan. 1846.
37. Strang to Mrs. Corey.
38. Ibid.
39. *Saints' Herald*, Dec. 29, 1888. The land on which the plates were found was owned by Perce. Barnes would buy land nearby within two years. See land records, Walworth County.
40. Myraette (Strang) Losee to Strang, July 29, 1845, May 5, 1846, Beinecke.
41. W. L. Perce to Strang, Jan. 29, 1850, Burton; Lydia Perce to Mary Strang, Sept. 20, 1846, Beinecke.
42. Myraette Losee to Strang, May 5, 1846.
43. Wealthy Smith to Strang, Nov. 1, 1846, Beinecke.
44. Myraette Losee to Strang, Aug. 20, 1846, Beinecke; *Mayville Sentinel*, Mar. 19, 1846; *VH*, May 1846.
45. Bennett to Strang, June 2, 1846; *VH*, May 1846.
46. *VH*, May 1846; Strang to David Strang, June 13, 1846, Clarke; Myraette Losee to Strang, Aug. 20, 1846, May 13, 1847, Beinecke; R. B. Clark, bill to Strang, from Feb. 11, 1843, with interest to May 20, 1853, Beinecke.
47. *ZR*, July 8, 1847.
48. *GH*, Nov. 11, 1847.
49. Ibid.
50. *ZR*, Feb. 25, 1847.
51. Ibid.
52. Miller, *James J. Strang*, pp. 1, 3.
53. Reuben Miller, *Truth Shall Prevail* (Burlington, Wis., 1847), p. 6, Mormon Church Archives. The January 1846 issue of *VH* mentioned a "charge," but not an anointing. The "Chronicles of Voree" detail the anointing, but the earliest portions of it were written much later than the events they describe; how much later is an unanswerable question.
54. *VH*, Oct. 1846.

55. "Chronicles of Voree," p. 132; Richard L. Anderson, "Reuben Miller, Recorder of Oliver Cowdery's Reaffirmations," *BYU Studies* 8 (1968): 284.
56. Miller, *James J. Strang*, p. 21.
57. *Mormon Doings*, Mormon Church Archives; minutes of High Council meeting called by Aaron Smith, Oct. 4, 1846, Beinecke.
58. *ZR*, Dec. 1846.
59. Louisa (Sanger?) to Strang, July 15, 1846, and another letter, undated, but written in 1846, Beinecke.
60. "Chronicles of Voree," p. 84; *VH*, Oct. 1846; minutes of High Council meeting, Oct. 4, 1846.
61. "Chronicles of Voree," pp. 105, 106, 119.
62. Ibid., pp. 98, 122; *Mormon Doings*.
63. *Mormon Doings*; *ZR*, Nov. 1846.
64. *Mormon Doings*.
65. "Chronicles of Voree," pp. 123, 124; *ZR*, Nov. 1846.
66. *ZR*, Nov. 1846.
67. *The New Era*, Jan. 1847.
68. *ZR*, Nov. 1846.
69. Ibid.
70. *GH*, June 22, 1848; *The New Era*, Jan. 1847; Lester Brooks to James M. Adams, Jan. 12, 1847, Beinecke.
71. *ZR*, Jan. 14, 1847.
72. *GH*, Dec. 23, 1847; John W. Crane to Strang, Sept. 26, 1847, Beinecke. Strang's house was described as being a rude log dwelling in *GH*, Oct. 26, 1848.
73. *GH*, Dec. 23, 1847, Aug. 17, 1848.
74. Ibid.; *History of Walworth County*, p. 903.
75. *GH*, Aug. 17, 1848.
76. Ibid., Dec. 23, 1847, Jan. 4, 1849; "Chronicles of Voree," p. 152.
77. *GH*, Dec. 23, 1847.
78. *"Chronicles of Voree," p. 151; ZR*, July 8, 1847.
79. Morgan, "Bibliography," p. 53.
80. A. Tewksbury to Strang, Apr. 3, 1847, and resolutions of Boston branch, Feb. 1, 1847, Beinecke.
81. Resolutions of Boston branch; Alden Hale to Strang, Dec. 2, 1848, Beinecke; *GH*, Feb. 22, 1849.
82. *ZR*, Aug. 19, 1847.
83. *GH*, Feb. 22, 1849.

Chapter 5. Beaver Island

1. *VH*, Oct. 1846.
2. *ZR*, Dec. 1846.
3. Miller, *James J. Strang*, p. 20.
4. *ZR*, Dec. 1846.
5. Elizabeth Whitney Williams wrote that Strang told her father that he was forced to take shelter at Beaver Island while on a steamer trip back to Wisconsin in 1846. See her book, *A Child of the Sea* (Ann Arbor, Mich., 1905), p. 61. While Mrs. Williams's book is unreliable in its history of the Mormons on Beaver Island, her account of certain events in which she or her family was involved is credible and dovetails with known facts. For Strang's inquiries about other islands, see letters of Feb. 1847 in Burton.
6. Terry Hart, "The Religions of Beaver Island," *Journal of Beaver Island History* 1 (1976): 103–6.
7. Helen Collar, "The Pre-Mormon Settlement on Beaver Island, 1837–1852," *Journal of Beaver Island History* 2 (1980): 10, 11.
8. John Fisk to Strang, Feb. 5, Apr. 29, 1847, Burton.
9. *Acts of the Legislature of the State of Michigan* (Lansing, 1850), pp. 82–85; *NI*, Apr. 22, 1852; Strang, *Ancient and Modern Michilimackinac* (rpt. ed., Mackinac Island, Mich., 1959), p. 38. This history of the Beaver Island region includes Strang's propagandist version of the conflicts between the Mormons and Gentiles in that area. It was first published at St. James in 1854.
10. *Ancient*, p. 40.
11. Ibid., pp. 41, 79.
12. *ZR*, July 8, 1847; *Ancient*, pp. 38, 39; *New York Tribune*, July 2, 1853. The Indians would soon move to Garden Island, see *Ancient*, p. 39.
13. *ZR*, July 8, 1847; *GH*, May 24, 1849.
14. *ZR*, July 8, 1847; *Ancient*, p. 93; Fred W. Foster, "The Beaver Islands," *Michigan History* 39 (1955): 386–88.
15. *ZR*, July 8, 1847.
16. *Ancient*, p. 41; *ZR*, July 8, 1847; *NI*, July 24, 1851.
17. *ZR*, Aug. 19, 1847.
18. *GH*, Dec. 28, 1848.
19. *ZR*, Aug. 19, 1847.
20. *GH*, Dec. 2, 9, 1847.
21. *ZR*, Feb. 4, Aug. 19, 1847.
22. *GH*, Nov. 25, 1847.

23. *Ancient*, p. 41.
24. Helen Collar, "Mormon Land Policy on Beaver Island, *Michigan History* 56 (1972): 89.
25. Benjamin H. Hibbard, *A History of the Public Land Policies* (New York, 1924), pp. 158–70.
26. Collar, "Mormon Land Policy," p. 89; *ZR*, Aug. 19, 1847; *GH*, Dec. 21, 1848.
27. Beaver Island land records, Charlevoix County, Charlevoix, Mich.; Collar, "Mormon Land Policy," p. 94, 97.
28. Collar, "Mormon Land Policy," pp. 91, 92, 95, 96.
29. Ibid., pp. 92, 93; *DA*, July 1, 1851; deposition of Randolph Dinsmore, *U.S. v. Strang*, Burton.
30. Beaver Island land records; Collar, "Mormon Land Policy," p. 93.
31. *Ancient*, p. 41.
32. *GH*, Apr. 19, 1849.
33. Ibid.
34. *Ancient*, p. 43.
35. *GH*, Jan. 3, 1850. According to *GH* (June 21, July 12, Sept. 20, 1849), sixty-five of the new settlers came in three groups from Voree.
36. *Ancient*, pp. 42, 43.
37. Diary of James Oscar McNutt, State Historical Society of Wisconsin, p. 3 (hereafter cited as McNutt diary); *ZR*, July 8, 1847; Williams, *Child of the Sea*, p. 90; Wingfield W. Watson to Milo M. Quaife, Jan. 21, 1919, Beinecke.
38. *ZR*, July 8, 1847; *GH*, Dec. 7, 1848; Ivan H. Walton, "Developments on the Great Lakes, 1815–1943," *Michigan History* 27 (1943): 83–86.
39. McNutt Diary, p. 2; Watson to Quaife, Jan. 21, 1919.
40. *Ancient*, p. 42; *GH*, Sept. 20, 1849; Collar, "Mormon Land Policy," pp. 99, 100.
41. Collar, "Mormon Land Policy," p. 99; Beaver Island land records.
42. John Fisk to Strang, Apr. 4, 1849, Burton.
43. Rich, *Ensign*, pp. 20–22, 87–94.
44. *ZR*, Jan. 14, 1847.
45. Ibid., Feb. 25, 1847.
46. Journal History, Dec. 22, 1846.
47. Ibid., Jan. 29, 1847.
48. Rich, *Ensign*, p. 95.
49. Ibid., pp. 99–101.
50. Arrington, *Brigham Young*, pp. 143–46.

51. Ibid., p. 146; Ray Allen Billington, *The Far Western Frontier* (New York, 1956), p. 200.
52. Arrington, *Brigham Young*, pp. 153–56; Hirshson, *Lion*, pp. 87–89; Billington, *Far Western Frontier*, p. 200.
53. Hirshson, *Lion*, p. 96.
54. *GH*, Aug. 3, 1848.
55. Journal History, Nov. 25, 1847.
56. *GH*, Feb. 17, 24, 1848.
57. Ibid., Aug. 3, 1848, Nov. 29, 1849.
58. Ibid., Aug. 3, 1848.
59. Watson to Quaife, Jan. 21, 1919.
60. "Chronicles of Voree," p. 178; Land records, Walworth County; *GH*, Feb. 3, 1848.
61. *GH*, Feb. 3, 1848.
62. Ibid., Dec. 28, 1848, Feb. 8, Mar. 22, 1849; report of committee on clothing and orders adopted by the association, Sept. 23, 1848, Beinecke.
63. *GH*, Dec. 28, 1848.
64. Ibid., Jan. 11, 1849.
65. Ibid., Aug. 23, 1849.
66. Ibid., Aug. 30, 1849.
67. B. G. Wright to Strang, Feb. 14, 1850, Beinecke; E. and C. Strang, "Biographical Sketch," p. 4; *DA*, July 8, 1851. Strang appears to have patterned the Order of Enoch after Joseph Smith's United Order of Enoch, which had problems similar to those experienced by Strang. See Brodie, *No Man*, pp. 106–8, 115, 116, 120–22, 141, 142, 220–22.

Chapter 6. Elvira and Charlie

1. Arrington and Bitton, *Mormon Experience*, p. 197. For an analysis of the origins and development of Mormon polygamy, see Lawrence Foster, *Religion and Sexuality: Three American Communal Experiences of the Nineteenth Century* (New York, 1981; Urbana, Ill., 1984).
2. *GH*, Jan. 11, 1849.
3. Statement that Strang said was dictated by Willard Griffith, Oct. 23, 1846, Beinecke.
4. *ZR*, Feb. 4, 1847.
5. Ebenezer Page to Strang, Jan. 17, 1847, Beinecke.
6. *ZR*, July 22, 1847.
7. Ibid., Aug. 12, 1847.

8. Ibid.
9. *GH*, Aug. 24, 1848.
10. Ibid.
11. Four locks of hair, presented in Jefferson County, N.Y., June 23, 1847, Beinecke.
12. Wingfield W. Watson, in interview by Milo M. Quaife, apparently on Dec. 11, 1918, said Strang told this to him and two or three others. Notes from this interview are in Beinecke.
13. Clement J. Strang, Elvira's son, in interview by Milo M. Quaife, Feb. 12, 1921, Beinecke.
14. John Cumming, "Lorenzo Dow Hickey," *Michigan History* 50 (1966): 65.
15. Clement Strang interview.
16. Memorial booklet prepared and published by Elvira's son, Charles J. Strang, after her death in 1910, copy in State Library of Michigan.
17. Ibid.
18. Samuel Graham to Strang, Jan. 13, 1848, Beinecke.
19. Milo M. Quaife, *The Kingdom of Saint James* (New Haven, Conn., 1930), p. 101. Quaife's version was apparently based on information from Clement J. Strang, including an interview by Quaife and a letter to Quaife of Oct. 11, 1920, Beinecke.
20. Strang, The Book of the Law of the Lord (1851), hereafter cited as Book of the Law.
21. Memorial booklet; Clement J. Strang to Quaife, Aug. 13, 1920, Beinecke; *GH*, Aug. 23, 1849.
22. *GH*, Aug. 2, 9, 1849. The land was purchased on July 20; see Collar, "Mormon Land Policy," p. 99.
23. Gilbert Watson to Strang, Oct. 7, 1849, Beinecke.
24. *GH*, Aug. 9, 1949.
25. Ibid., Nov. 15, 1849.
26. Ibid., Sept. 27, Oct. 11, 1849.
27. Ibid., Nov. 8, 15, 1849.
28. Cumming, "Hickey," pp. 52–55; *ZR*, Feb. 4, Mar. 11, 1847.
29. *GH*, Oct. 26, 1848.
30. "Chronicles of Voree," pp. 186, 187, 192; *GH*, Sept. 27, 1849.
31. *GH*, Nov. 15, 1849.
32. Lester E. Bush, Jr., "Mormonism's Negro Doctrine: An Historical Overview," *Dialogue* 8 (Spring 1973): 25.
33. *GH*, Nov. 15, 1849.
34. "Chronicles of Voree," p. 80.

35. *GH*, Feb. 17, Sept. 21, Nov. 2, 1848.
36. Ibid., Nov. 15, 1849.
37. Ibid.
38. Ibid.
39. Ibid.; *GH*, Nov. 1, 1849; "Chronicles of Voree," p. 174.
40. The events described in this and the subsequent paragraphs are taken from *GH*, Nov. 22, 1849.
41. Ibid.; *GH*, Dec. 27, 1849.
42. *GH*, Dec. 27, 1849.
43. Ibid.
44. Lorenzo Dow Hickey to Strang, Dec. 6, 1849, Beinecke.
45. Hickey to Strang, Dec. 24, 1849, Beinecke.
46. Marvin M. Aldrich to Samuel Graham, Nov. 23, 1849; Hickey to Strang, Dec. 6, 1849, and Strang to Hickey, Dec. 10, 1849, all in Beinecke.
47. *GH*, Nov. 11, 1849; Gilbert Watson to Strang, Feb. 11, 1850, Beinecke; Cumming, "Hickey," pp. 58, 59.
48. Peter Hess to Strang, Nov. 22, 1849, and John Ursbruck to Strang, Nov. 17, 1849, Beinecke.
49. Strang to Amos Lowen, Nov. 21, 1849, Beinecke.
50. Hess to Strang, Nov. 22, 1849.
51. James Canny to Strang, June 16, 1850, Beinecke.
52. *GH*, Dec. 27, 1849.
53. Samuel Graham to Strang, Dec. 15, 1849, Beinecke.
54. Mary Strang to Strang, Nov. 4, 1849, Jan. 4, 1850, Beinecke.
55. Mary Strang to Strang, Jan. 9, 1850, Beinecke.
56. Mary Strang to Strang, one letter with no date (apparently the end of Dec. 1849), Jan. 4 and Jan. 9, 1850, Beinecke.
57. Abigail Strang to Strang, May 1850, Beinecke.
58. Strang to Mary Strang, Jan. 25, 1850, Beinecke.
59. *GH*, Mar. 7, 1850.
60. Strang to Bennett, Jan. 25, 1850, Beinecke.
61. "C. J. Douglass" to Strang, Feb. 4, 1850, Beinecke.
62. A. J. Graham to Strang, Jan. 22, 1850, Beinecke; Clement Strang interview; Covenant book.
63. *GH*, Mar. 28, 1850.
64. Ibid.; W. L. Perce to John Davis, Jan. 29, 1850, Burton.
65. *GH*, Jan. 11, Nov. 8, 1849.
66. Abigail Strang to Strang, May 1850.
67. *GH*, June 6, 1850.

68. Morgan, "Bibliography," pp. 63, 64; *Journal of Senate* (Washington, D.C., 1850), pp. 398, 399, and Records of Committee on Public Lands, Records of U.S. Senate, both in Record Group 46, National Archives, Washington, D.C.

Chapter 7. The Coronation

1. *Ancient*, p. 44.
2. Ibid.
3. James M. Greig to Strang, Feb. 28, 1850, Beinecke.
4. *Ancient*, p. 44.
5. Ibid., p. 38; *GH*, May 23, 1850.
6. *Ancient*, p. 44.
7. Ibid., pp. 44, 45; *GH*, Apr. 25, May 2, 1850.
8. *Ancient*, p. 45.
9. Ibid.
10. Ibid.
11. Ibid., pp. 45, 46.
12. Ibid., pp. 44, 46.
13. Charles O'Malley to Strang, Apr. 25, 1850, and Tully O'Malley to Strang, May 2, 1850, Beinecke; Strang to Charles O'Malley, Apr. 30, 1850, Burton; *Ancient*, p. 46.
14. Charles O'Malley to Strang, Apr. 25, 1850.
15. *Michigan Biographies* (Lansing, 1924), 2:63, 159.
16. William MacLeod to Strang, May 1, 1850, Burton.
17. Strang to William Johnston, May 7, 1850, Burton.
18. Election results of Michilimackinac County, Records of Mackinac Island State Park Commission, Lansing.
19. Strang to William Johnston, May 7, 1850.
20. Judge Hezekiah G. Wells made that assessment in the *Michigan Historical Collections* 3 (1881): 40; see also ibid., 21 (1894): 399, 400.
21. William MacLeod to Strang, July 21, 1850, Burton.
22. Ibid.
23. *Michigan Historical Collections*, 3:39.
24. Book of the Law, pp. 1, 2, 5, 7.
25. *GH*, Mar. 1, 1849.
26. George Adams to Strang, Feb. 18, 1850, Beinecke.
27. Book of the Law, pp. 2, 5.
28. Ibid., pp. 8, 35.
29. M. Strang, *The Diary*, p. xliii.

30. Samuel Graham to Strang, July 20, 1850, Beinecke.
31. *Ancient*, p. 46.
32. *GH*, May 30, 1850.
33. Bennett originated the Plymouth Rock chicken and wrote a book on poultry raising. See Morgan, "Bibliography," p. 53.
34. Bennett to Strang, May 29, 1850, Beinecke.
35. Stephen Post, "Journal of trip to Beaver Island for a conference in 1850," Stephen Post Papers, Mormon Church Archives, pp. 1, 4.
36. Post, "Journal," pp. 4, 5.
37. Bill of sale, July 9, 1850, Burton.
38. Post, "Journal," p. 6.
39. Ibid., p. 7.
40. *DA*, June 3, 1851.
41. Post, "Journal," p. 7.
42. Ibid., pp. 7, 8.
43. *GH*, May 23, 1850.
44. Post, "Journal," p. 8.
45. Stephen Post to Warren Post, Sept. 12, 1850, Clarke.
46. Post, "Journal," pp. 9, 10.
47. Covenant book.
48. Deposition of Reuben Nichols, records of *U.S. v. Strang*, Burton; *DA*, June 6, July 3, 10, 1851.
49. Deposition of William J. Clark, *U.S. v. Strang*, Burton; *DA*, July 3, 1851.
50. Deposition of Smith Ketchum, *U.S. v. Strang*, Burton.
51. Deposition of Hiram Beckwith, *U.S. v. Strang*, Burton.
52. Post, "Journal," p. 10.
53. Ibid.; *Detroit News Tribune*, Nov. 7, 1915.
54. Post, "Journal," pp. 10, 11.
55. Ibid.
56. Ibid.; notes of speeches in conference on Beaver Island, July 3, 1850, Beinecke.
57. Notes of speeches.
58. Eri J. Moore, affidavit, Jan. 2, 1851, Executive Office Correspondence, State Archives of Michigan, Lansing.
59. Post, "Journal," p. 11; *Ancient*, p. 44.
60. Post, "Journal," pp. 11, 12.
61. Ibid.
62. *Ancient*, p. 46.
63. Post, "Journal," p. 13.
64. *Ancient*, p. 47.

65. Ibid.
66. Collar, "Pre-Mormon Settlement," pp. 15–18.
67. *Ancient*, p. 47.
68. Post, "Journal," p. 13; *Ancient*, p. 48;
69. Post, "Journal," p. 13.
70. Ibid., p. 14.
71. *Ancient*, pp. 48, 49.
72. Post, "Journal," pp. 15, 16.
73. Ibid., p. 14.
74. Ibid., pp. 14, 16, 18.
75. Record of the organization of the kingdom, Beinecke; Post, "Journal," pp. 17, 18.
76. Post, "Journal," p. 17; *Saints' Herald*, Nov. 10, 1888.
77. Post, "Journal," p. 17, 18; *Saints' Herald*, Nov. 10, 1888.
78. Post, "Journal," p. 18.
79. Book of the Law, p. 35.
80. Clement Strang interview; Clement J. Strang, "Why I Am Not a Strangite," *Michigan History* 26 (1942): 460; deposition of David R. Whipple, *U.S. v. Strang*, Burton; *DA*, June 6, 1851.
81. Post, "Journal," p. 18; *DA*, June 6, 1851.
82. Post, "Journal," p. 19; *DA*, June 6, 1851.
83. Post, "Journal," p. 19. For an account of the development of polygamy on Beaver Island, see David R. Lewis, "For Life, the Resurrection, and the Life Everlasting: James J. Strang and Strangite Mormon Polygamy, 1849–1856," *Wisconsin Magazine of History* 67 (Summer 1983): 274–91.
84. The date of birth was Apr. 6, 1851. See *Strang Family Newsletter*, Apr. 1980, p. 12.
85. Post, "Journal," p. 19; Amos Lowen to Strang, Dec. 7, 1850, Beinecke.
86. Book of the Law, pp. 71–73.
87. Some of the those who defected became key leaders in the founding of the Reorganized Church of Jesus Christ of Latter Day Saints. See Quaife, *Kingdom of Saint James*, pp. 113, 114.
88. Abigail Strang to Strang, May 1850.
89. Strang to unnamed married woman (no date), Beinecke.
90. Post, "Journal," p. 20; Book of the Law, p. 50; *NI*, Dec. 12, 1850.
91. Book of the Law, pp. 50–52, 58.
92. Post, "Journal," p. 20.

Chapter 8. *"Hunting Mormons like Wild Beasts"*

1. George Adams to Strang and to Louisa Adams, Aug. 1, 1850, Beinecke. Writers generally have spelled MacCulloch's name McCulloch, but he signed it MacCulloch.
2. *GH*, May 23, 1850; *NI*, June 19, 1856; Adams to Louisa Adams, Aug. 1, 1850.
3. Adams to Strang, Aug. 1, 1850.
4. Affidavit of Strang, William Townsend, Joseph Ketcham and Finley Page, June 9, 1851, *U.S. v. Strang*, Burton.
5. Adams to Strang, Aug. 14, 1850, in *Adams' New Drama*, Nov. 1850, a broadsheet believed to be the first publication from Strang's press on Beaver Island.
6. Caroline Adams to R. F. Mills, May 7, 1850, *Adams' New Drama*.
7. Ibid.; *NI*, Dec. 12, 1850.
8. *Adams' New Drama*; *Ancient*, p. 26.
9. *Ancient*, pp. 49, 50.
10. Minutes of conferences on Beaver Island, Reorganized Church Archives.
11. *DA*, July 3, 9, 1951.
12. Ibid., June 6, 1851; Covenant book.
13. Minutes of conferences; *DA*, July 8, 1851.
14. *NI*, Dec. 12, 1850, Jan. 1, May 1, 1851; *DA*, July 3, 10, 1851; Abigail Holmes to Strang, Oct. 6, 1850, Beinecke; deposition of Benjamin Austin, *U.S. v. Strang*, Burton.
15. Chauncey Loomis, letter published in *Saints' Herald*, Nov. 10, 1888.
16. *NI*, Dec. 12, 1850; *Ancient*, p. 50.
17. *DA*, July 16, 1851.
18. *NI*, July 24, 1851; *Ancient*, pp. 16–18; Charles M. Harvey, "Fur Traders as Empire Builders," *Atlantic Monthly* 103 (1909): 532.
19. Marion Morse Davis, "Stories of Saint Helena Island," *Michigan History* 10 (1926): 419–23; *Ancient*, p. 23.
20. *Ancient*, pp. 23–25.
21. *NI*, July 24, 1851.
22. *Chronicle* 17 (Summer 1981): 9; *NI*, July 24, 1851; *Michigan Historical Collections* 7 (1886): 202.
23. *NI*, July 24, 1851. The courthouse building still exists on Mackinac Island.
24. *NI*, Dec. 12, 1850; *Michigan Biographies*, 2:159; notes on exami-

nation before O'Malley (apparently in Strang's hand), Oct. 28, 1850, Burton.

25. The first part of this account is based on notes on examination before O'Malley.

26. This part of the narrative is based on an article in *NI*, Dec. 12, 1850.

27. *NI*, May 1, 1851; Eri J. Moore, affidavit, Jan. 2, 1851.

28. Dennis Chidester to Strang, Nov. 12, 1850, Beinecke; *Ancient*, p. 51; election results for Michilimackinac County.

29. *Ancient*, p. 51; *DA*, June 6, 1851; *NI*, May 1, 1851; Eri J. Moore to Governor, Dec. 2, 1850, Executive Office Correspondence.

30. See U.S. census of 1850 for Michilimackinac County.

31. *NI*, Jan. 9, 1851.

32. Strang et al. affidavit, June 9, 1851.

33. Hirshson, *Lion*, pp. 91, 92.

34. *NI*, Jan. 9, 1851.

35. Ibid.

36. Ibid., and Aug. 5, 1852.

37. Ibid., May 1, 1851; *DA*, July 3, 1851; Covenant book; Strang et al. affidavit, June 9, 1851. See also an apparent land deal involving printing office, Aug. 27, 1850, Burton.

38. Moore affidavit, Jan. 2, 1851.

39. *NI*, May 1, 1851.

40. Population figures based on U.S. census of 1850 for Michilimackinac County. There is no breakdown for Beaver Island, but it is clear where the island census starts and ends.

41. Adams to Strang, [Feb.] 18, 1850, Beinecke; Chidester to Strang, Nov. 12, 1850; *NI*, May 1, 1850.

42. Adams to Strang, summer of 1850, Beinecke.

43. Moore affidavit, Jan. 2, 1851; Chidester to Strang, Nov. 12, 1850.

44. Moore affidavit, Jan. 2, 1851; *DA*, July 1, 1851.

45. Moore to Governor, Dec. 2, 1850; *DA*, June 6, 1851.

46. Peter McKinley, affidavit, Dec. 10, 1850, Executive Office Correspondence; Moore affidavit, Jan. 2, 1851; Chidester to Strang, Nov. 12, 1850.

47. *NI*, Jan. 9, 1851.

48. McKinley affidavit, Dec. 10, 1850.

49. Ibid.

50. *NI*, Dec. 12, 1850.

51. McKinley affidavit, Dec. 10, 1850; Moore affidavit, Jan. 2, 1850.

52. *NI*, Jan. 9, 1851; Moore affidavit, Jan. 2, 1851.
53. *NI*, Jan. 9, 1851.
54. Book of the Law, p. 64.
55. Moore affidavit, Jan. 2, 1851.
56. Book of the Law, p. 75.
57. J. W. James to Strang, Jan. 8, 1851, Beinecke.
58. *Ancient*, p. 53; *DA*, July 8, 1851. The date given for the attempted arrest of Moore varies, but the best testimony puts it on Feb. 18.
59. *DA*, July 8, 1851; Strang et al. affidavit, June 9, 1851.
60. This account comes from *DA*, July 8, 1851; depositions of Peaine and Mitchell, *U.S. v. Strang*, Burton.
61. *DA*, July 3, 1851; *NI*, Feb. 6, 1851; Moore to Governor, Mar. 8, 1851, Executive Office Correspondence; Strang et al. affidavit, June 9, 1851; statement of George C. Bates, *U.S. v. Strang*, Burton.
62. *DA*, July 3, 8, 1851; deposition of Mitchell, *U.S. v. Strang*; notes on meetings with Indians, Burton.
63. *Ancient*, p. 53; notes on meetings with Indians; *DA*, June 6, 1851.
64. Strang et al. affidavit, June 9, 1851.
65. *Ancient*, p. 53; *DA*, July 9, 1851.
66. Bates to Crittenden, Mar. 16, 1851, Correspondence of Attorney General, Record Group 60, National Archives.
67. *NI*, Apr. 3, 1851.
68. Ibid.
69. *NI*, May 1, 1851; *Green Bay Advocate*, June 5, 1851; *Ancient*, p. 53.
70. *NI*, May 1, 1851; *Green Bay Advocate*, June 5, 1851.
71. *NI*, May 1, 1951.
72. Strang et al. affidavit, June 9, 1851; *Ancient*, p. 53; *NI*, Feb. 6, 1851.
73. *Ancient*, p. 54; *Green Bay Advocate*, June 5, 1851.
74. *Ancient*, p. 54.
75. Ibid., p. 55.
76. *DA*, July 16, 1851.
77. *Ancient*, p. 55; *DA*, July 1, 9, 1851; letter from Mackinac, Apr. 20, 1851, Burton.
78. *Ancient*, p. 54; *NI*, May 1, 1851.
79. *DA*, June 17, July 16, 1851.
80. Ibid.
81. *NI*, Aug. 5, 1852.
82. *Ancient*, p. 55.

Chapter 9. *The United States v. James J. Strang*

1. Millard Fillmore to John J. Crittenden, Apr. 30, 1851, Crittenden
Papers, Library of Congress, Washington, D.C. Despite what
Strang says in *Ancient*, p. 56, Fillmore did not receive a briefing on
the Mormon situation in Detroit in May; he did not come farther
west than Buffalo that spring. See *DA*, May 1851.
2. *Treaties and Other International Acts of the United States of America*, ed.
Hunter Miller (Washington, D.C., 1931), 2:645, 646; Milo M.
Quaife, "The Iron Ship," *Burton Historical Collection Leaflet* 7 (Nov.
1928): 22; De Vern C. Hulce, "Michigan at Sea," *Michigan History*
55 (1971): 98–100; Herbert R. Spencer, *USS Michigan* (Erie, Pa.,
1966), p. 10.
3. Log of U.S. Steamer *Michigan*, Aug. 12, 13, 1850, May 21, 1851,
Records of Bureau of Naval Personnel, Record Group 24, National
Archives; William A. Graham, secretary of the Navy, to Bullus,
May 9, 1851, Navy.
4. *DA*, May 22, 1851.
5. Log of *Michigan*, May 23, 1851; Bates to Fillmore, June 7, 1851,
Navy; George C. Bates, "The Beaver Island Prophet," *Michigan Historical Collections* 32 (1903): 228–30. This article, first printed in
1877, offers some factual detail in a selectively imaginative history
of Strang's federal trial. The key question: where does the history
end and Bates's desire to tell a good story begin?
6. Bates, "Prophet," pp. 228, 229. The court schedule is in *Acts of the
Legislature*, 1850, p. 232.
7. Bates to Fillmore, June 7, 1851; Bates, "Prophet," p. 229.
8. Log of *Michigan*, May 23, 1851; Bates, "Prophet," pp. 229, 230.
9. Bates to Fillmore, June 7, 1851; Bates, "Prophet," pp. 228–30.
10. Ibid.; *Ancient*, pp. 56, 57.
11. Bates to Fillmore, June 7, 1851; Bates, "Prophet," pp. 230, 231;
log of *Michigan*, May 24, 1851.
12. *NI*, Aug. 14, 1851; *Detroit Free Press*, June 14, 1851; Bates,
"Prophet," p. 231.
13. Bates to Fillmore, June 7, 1851; Bates, "Prophet," p. 231.
14. Strang to Mary Strang and to his parents, May 19, 1851, Beinecke.
15. *Ancient*, p. 57; Bates, "Prophet," p. 231.
16. Log of *Michigan*, May 24, 1851; Bates to Fillmore, June 7, 1851.
17. *NI*, July 24, 1851; *Ancient*, pp. 57, 58.
18. Ibid.

19. Log of *Michigan*, May 24, 1851.
20. *NI*, Oct. 11, 1855. Strang often took the position that the Mormon kingdom was separate from the United States, but that stance did not stop him from holding township and state office.
21. Log of *Michigan*, May 26, 1851; *State of Michigan Gazetteer and Business Directory* (1856–57), p. 35; *Detroit Free Press*, May 27, 1851; *DA*, May 27, 29, 1851.
22. *Detroit Free Press*, May 30, 31, 1851; *DA*, May 28, 1851.
23. Court records, *U.S. v. Strang*, Burton, and in National Archives, Chicago.
24. Court records, *U.S. v. Strang*. The other three defendants were William Townsend, Joseph Ketcham, and Finley Page.
25. *Ancient*, p. 59.
26. *Detroit Free Press*, May 30, 1851.
27. *NI*, July 24, 1851.
28. *NI*, May 1, 1851.
29. Hibbard, *History of Public Land Policies*, p. 458. See also Lucile Kane, "Federal Protection of Public Timber in the Upper Great Lakes," in Carstensen, ed., *Public Lands*, pp. 439–45; D. C. Goddard, acting secretary of the Interior, to W. K. Sebastian, U.S. Senate, Aug. 28, 1850, Correspondence of Secretary of Interior, Record Group 48, National Archives.
30. Court records, *U.S. v. Strang*.
31. *NI*, May 1, July 31, 1851.
32. Ibid., July 31, 1851.
33. Bates, "Prophet," pp. 224, 225.
34. C. D. Fillmore to Millard Fillmore, Nov. 25, 1850, D. Bethune Duffield to Millard Fillmore, Nov. 30, 1850, and J. M. Howard to Millard Fillmore, June 2, 1851, Millard Fillmore Collection, Buffalo and Erie County Historical Society, Buffalo, N.Y.; *Michigan Biographies*, pp. 77, 78; Robert B. Ross, *The Early Bench and Bar of Detroit from 1805 to the End of 1850* (Detroit, 1907), p. 25. Two decades after Strang's trial, Bates was the U.S. attorney for Utah and later a lawyer for the Mormon church there. See *Michigan Historical Collections* 9 (1886): 87.
35. Ross, *Early Bench and Bar of Detroit*, p. 218; Friend Palmer scrapbook, 2:9, Burton; *Michigan Historical Collections* 3 (1881): 38; 22 (1894): 327.
36. *Michigan Historical Collections* 21 (1894): 593; Ross, *Early Bench and Bar of Detroit*, p. 145.

37. *Detroit Free Press*, May 28, 1851.
38. *DA*, June 6, 1851.
39. Ibid.
40. Moses Chase, patriarchal blessing for Warren Post, Nov. 22, 1854, Clarke.
41. *NI*, July 24, 1851.
42. *Ancient*, p. 59.
43. Strang et al. affidavit, June 9, 1851.
44. *DA*, June 6, 1851; *Detroit Free Press*, June 9, 1851.
45. Court records, *U.S. v. Strang*; *Ancient*, p. 59; *DA*, June 13, 1851.
46. Bates telegraphic message to Fillmore, June 11, 1851, Navy.
47. Bates to Fillmore, June 12, 1851, Fillmore Collection, Buffalo and Erie County Historical Society.
48. Peter McKinley affidavit, June 11, 1851, Fillmore Collection, Buffalo and Erie County Historical Society.
49. Fillmore's note on top of Bates's letter, June 12. 1851.
50. Bates to Fillmore, June 7, 1851.
51. *DA*, June 12, 1851.
52. Strang to John S. Barry, June 12, 1851, Executive Office Correspondence.
53. *Detroit Free Press*, June 14, 1851.
54. *DA*, June 16, 1851.
55. Log of *Michigan*, June 17, 1851; Oscar Bullus to William Graham, June 27, 1851, Navy.
56. Log of *Michigan*, June 18, 1851; *DA*, June 21, 1851.
57. *NI*, Jan. 9, 1851.
58. Ibid., Feb. 6, 1851.
59. *DA*, June 21, 1851.
60. *NI*, Aug. 14, 1851.
61. Ibid.; *Detroit Free Press*, June 14, 1851.
62. Ibid.
63. Ibid.
64. *DA*, June 21, 1851.
65. *Detroit Free Press*, June 14, 1851; *NI*, Aug. 14, 1851; *DA*, June 13, 21, July 2, 1851.
66. Williams, *Child of the Sea*, pp. 81, 85, 86.
67. *NI*, Aug. 14, 1851; *Detroit Free Press*, June 14, 1851; *DA*, June 13, 21, 1851.
68. Ibid.; *DA*, July 2, 1851.
69. *DA*, June 13, 1851.
70. Ibid., June 21, 1851.

71. *NI*, Aug. 14, 1851; *Ancient*, p. 61.
72. *DA*, June 12, 13, 21, 1851.
73. *Detroit Free Press*, June 14, 1851; *DA*, July 2, 1851.
74. *DA*, June 13, July 2, 1851.
75. Ibid., June 16, 1851; Williams, *Child of the Sea*, p. 94.
76. *Ancient*, pp. 62, 63; log of *Michigan*, June 18, 1851.
77. Log of *Michigan*, June 18, 1851; Bates, "Prophet," p. 232; *Michigan Historical Collections* 4 (1906): 438.
78. Court records, *U.S. v. Strang*.
79. Depositions of Daniel S. Wheelock, Anderson G. Hopper, and Asa C. B. Field, *U.S. v. Strang*, Burton.
80. Deposition of Wheelock.
81. Depositions of Hopper and others.
82. *Ancient*, pp. 57, 58.
83. Ibid.
84. See depositions of Hopper and Field.
85. Deposition of H. D. MacCulloch, *U.S. v. Strang*, Burton.
86. Deposition of Reuben Field, *U.S. v. Strang*, Burton.
87. Bates, "Prophet," pp. 233, 234.
88. *DA*, June 24, 1851.
89. *State of Michigan Gazetteer*, p. 33; Silas Farmer, *The Story of Detroit* (Detroit, 1926), pp. 456, 457.
90. Court records, *U.S. v. Strang*; *NI*, July 24, 1851. *NI*, July 19, 1855, makes a reference to nine Whigs and three Democrats on the jury.
91. Bates describes Wilkins in the *Michigan Historical Collections* 2 (1880): 179; 22 (1894): 326, 327.
92. *NI*, July 24, 1851, Aug. 24, 1854; court records, *U.S. v. Strang*.
93. Strang et al. affidavit, June 9, 1851.
94. Bates, "Prophet," p. 234.
95. *DA*, June 27, 28, July 3, 1851; *Detroit Free Press*, June 28, 1851.
96. *NI*, Feb. 6, 1851.
97. *DA*, July 1, 3, 1851; deposition of John B. Dorry, *U.S. v. Strang*, Burton.
98. *DA*, July 1, 3, 10, 1851.
99. Deposition of Dorry.
100. Ibid.; *DA*, July 1, 1851.
101. *DA*, July 1, 3, 1851.
102. Depositions of Dorry and Richard O'Donnell, *U.S. v. Strang*, Burton; *DA*, July 3, 1851.
103. Deposition of Peaine, *U.S. v. Strang*, Burton; *DA*, July 3, 1851.

104. Deposition of Jacob Mathes, *U.S. v. Strang*, Burton.
105. Depositions of Mathes and Peaine; *DA*, July 3, 1851.
106. *Detroit Free Press*, June 28, 1851; *DA*, July 3, 1851.
107. *NI*, Jan. 9, 1851.
108. *DA*, June 30, July 3, 1851.
109. The following testimony and cross-examination of George J. Adams comes from his deposition in *U.S. v. Strang*, Burton, and from *DA*, July 3, 9, 1851.
110. Moore to Governor, Mar. 8, 1851, Executive Office Correspondence; *DA*, June 6, July 1, 1851.
111. *DA*, June 6, 1851.
112. Ibid., July 1, 3, 1851.
113. Ibid., July 2, 1851; Strang et al. affidavit, June 9, 1851.
114. *DA*, July 2, 1851.
115. Strang's testimony comes from *DA*, July 2, 1851.
116. Ibid., July 2, 9, 1851.
117. Ibid., July 2, 8, 1851.
118. Ibid., July 9, 1851; *Ancient*, p. 59.
119. Bates, "Prophet," pp. 234, 235.
120. Ibid.; *Detroit Free Press* and DA, July 10, 1851.
121. Ibid.; *NI*, July 24, 1851.
122. *DA*, July 10, 1851.
123. *Detroit Free Press*, July 10, 1851.
124. Court records, *U.S. v. Strang*; *DA*, July 10, 1851.
125. *Ancient*, pp. 64, 65.
126. *NI*, July 24, 1851.

Chapter 10. Gentile Exodus

1. Samuel Graham to Strang, July 8, 27, 1851, Beinecke. In the federal case Graham was charged with trespass on public land, which was not at issue in the trial.
2. Graham to Strang, July 27, 1851.
3. Warren Post, Records of the Quorum of Apostles, 1850–55, Clarke.
4. *NI*, Apr. 13, 1854; *Saints' Herald*, Nov. 10, 1888.
5. Graham to Strang, July 10, 1851, Beinecke.
6. Strang to Graham, Jan. 15, 1853, Burton.
7. M. Strang, *The Diary*, p. 59.
8. Strang to Graham, Jan. 15, 1853.

9. Graham to Strang, July 8, 10, 1851.
10. Graham to Strang, July 8, 1851.
11. Strang to David Strang, Nov. 25, 1852, Clarke.
12. *NI*, March 4, 1852; *Ancient*, p. 64.
13. *NI*, July 24, 1851; *Ancient*, p. 64.
14. Ibid.
15. *NI*, Aug. 14, 1851.
16. *Ancient*, p. 65.
17. Indictment of Strang et al., June 12, 1852, Burton.
18. Eri J. Moore to Governor John S. Barry, Sept. 20, 1851, Executive Office Correspondence.
19. Indictment of Strang et al., June 12, 1852; *Annual Report of the Attorney General of the State of Michigan* (Lansing, 1852), p. 39.
20. Moore to Governor Barry, Sept. 20, 1851.
21. Ibid.
22. *NI*, Sept. 9, 1852.
23. Moore to Governor Barry, Sept. 20, 1851.
24. *Ancient*, p. 65.
25. Williams, *Child of the Sea*, p. 102.
26. Beaver Island land records; *NI*, June 24, 1852.
27. Beaver Island land records; Collar, "Mormon Land Policy," p. 107.
28. Williams, *Child of the Sea*, pp. 87, 88.
29. The story about Betsy McNutt comes from Wingfield W. Watson, in an interview by Quaife, as reported in *The Kingdom of Saint James*, p. 111.
30. *NI*, Mar. 4, 1852.
31. Ibid.
32. Ibid., July 29, Aug. 5, 12, 1852.
33. Ibid., Sept. 9, 1852.
34. Ibid., Nov. 2, 1854.
35. Strang to David Strang, Feb. 10, 1852, Clarke.
36. *NI*, Mar. 4, 1852.
37. Beaver Island land records; Collar, "Mormon Land Policy," p. 105.
38. Ibid.
39. Beaver Island land records; *NI*, June 17, 1852.
40. *NI*, June 8, 1852; Beaver Island land records.
41. *DA*, July 27, 1853. The Mormons themselves, meanwhile, apparently had not paid property taxes for two years. See J. P. King of Mackinac to State Board of Equalization, Aug. 16, 1851, and minutes of Michilimackinac Board of Supervisors, Oct. 15, 1850, Records of Mackinac Island State Park Commission, Lansing, Mich.

42. *NI*, Apr. 22, 1851.
43. *Ancient*, pp. 66, 67.
44. *Laws of Michigan*, 1851, pp. 306–11; *New York Tribune*, July 2, 1853.
45. *Acts of the Legislature*, 1851, pp. 306–11.
46. *New York Tribune*, July 2, 1853.
47. *Ancient*, p. 67.
48. Beaver Island land records; *NI*, Apr. 22, July 22, 1852; *Ancient*, p. 28.
49. *NI*, July 22, 29, Sept. 16, 1852; *Ancient*, p. 28; *New York Tribune*, July 2, 1853.
50. *NI*, July 29, 1852.
51. Ibid., July 22, 1852.
52. *Ancient*, p. 66; *New York Tribune*, July 2, 1853.
53. *New York Tribune*, July 2, 1853.
54. Ibid.
55. *NI*, July 8, 1852; McNutt Diary, p. 4.
56. Book of the Law, p. 59.
57. *NI*, July 8, 1852.
58. As quoted in ibid., July 15, 1852.
59. Ibid.
60. Ibid.
61. *Ancient*, p. 68.
62. Ibid, pp. 68, 69.
63. *NI*, Sept. 2, 1852.
64. Ibid., Aug. 12, 19, 1852.
65. *Ancient*, pp. 67, 68.
66. *NI*, Sept. 9, 16, 1852.
67. Williams, *Child of the Sea*, pp. 87, 142.
68. The story of the departure of the Whitneys comes from ibid., pp. 142–144.

Chapter 11. The King as Legislator

1. *NI*, Oct. 14, 1852; *Ancient*, pp. 69, 70.
2. Ibid.
3. Ibid.; election results for Michilimackinac County; *NI*, Nov. 11, 1852, June 30, 1853.
4. Diary, pp. 30 (22), 73 (40).

5. Ibid.
6. *GH*, Nov. 2, 1848.
7. *NI*, Oct. 14, 1852; election results from Michilimackinac County.
8. *NI*, Nov. 11, 1852; *Ancient*, p. 70.
9. Certificate of election, Nov. 16, 1852, Statements from County Canvassers, Records of Secretary of State, Elections Division, State Archives of Michigan; *NI*, Nov. 11, 1852; *Journal of the House of Representatives of the State of Michigan*, 1853, p. 32; *Ancient*, p. 70.
10. *NI*, Nov. 11, 1852.
11. Strang to David Strang, Nov. 25, 1852.
12. *NI*, Nov. 11, 1852.
13. Strang to David Strang, Nov. 25, 1852; Strang, draft of speech to Michigan House of Representatives, Burton.
14. The following paragraphs are based on Strang's letter to his brother, Nov. 25, 1852.
15. Indictment of Strang, June 12, 1852; Strang's notes giving background of his arrest at the legislature, Burton; *Ancient*, p. 70.
16. Strang's notes on arrest; *NI*, June 24, 1852; *Ancient*, p. 70.
17. Minutes of Michilimackinac Board of Supervisors, Records of Mackinac Island State Park Commission; *Ancient*, p. 71. The jail building still exists on the island.
18. Juliette B. Stucky, *To Lansing with Love* (Lansing, 1960), p. 2; *Michigan Historical Collections* (1880): 133; 6 (1907): 291; 11 (1908): 240–42; 31 (1902): 227; *Michigan History* 38 (1954): 277.
19. Stucky, *To Lansing with Love*, p. 1; *Michigan Historical Collections* 13 (1908): 308; 26 (1896): 643; *Michigan Manual*, 1853.
20. *Journal of House*, pp. 3–11.
21. Ibid., pp. 3–9; *Michigan Manual* (Lansing, Mich.) 1853; *Jackson Citizen*, Feb. 16, 1853.
22. *Journal of House*, p. 11; *Detroit Free Press*, Jan. 5, 1853.
23. *Ancient*, p. 71; *Journal of House*, pp. 11, 12; Strang's notes on arrest; *Detroit Free Press*, Jan. 10, 1853.
24. *Journal of House*, pp. 11–21; *Detroit Free Press*, Jan. 10, 1853; *NI*, May 12, 1853; Strang's notes on arrest.
25. *Journal of House*, pp. 20, 21.
26. Ibid., pp. 17, 18, 23, 25, 40.
27. Ibid., p. 19.
28. Ibid., pp. 32, 33; *Michigan Biographies*, p. 348.
29. *Journal of House*, pp. 33–35; see also *Acts of the Legislature*, 1851, pp. 273, 274.

30. John Farmer, map of Michigan, 1852, State Archives of Michigan.
31. *Journal of House*, p. 52.
32. Journal of Henry Gillman, Burton.
33. The description was from Ludlow P. Hill in Legler, *Moses*, p. 213; *Journal of House*, p. 52.
34. Strang, draft of speech to House of Representatives.
35. *Journal of House*, pp. 52, 53, 64–66.
36. As quoted in *NI*, May 12, 1853; *Ancient*, p. 72.
37. *Journal of House*, pp. 261, 278.
38. *Ancient*, p. 38; *NI*, Apr. 28, 1853; *Journal of House*, pp. 196, 197, 261.
39. *NI*, Apr. 28, 1853.
40. Ibid.; *Journal of House*, p. 261.
41. *Journal of House*, pp. 261, 278; *NI*, Apr. 28, May 5, 1853.
42. *DA*, Feb. 4, 1853; *Journal of House*, pp. 222, 271, 329.
43. *DA*, Feb. 4, 18, 1853; *Detroit Free Press*, Jan. 18, 1853; *NI*, Feb. 2, 1854.
44. *DA*, Feb. 4, 1853; *Michigan Biographies*, p. 273.
45. The debate between Strang and Ely is taken from the *DA*, Feb. 4, 1853.
46. Ibid., Feb. 5, 1853.
47. Ibid., Feb. 10, 24, 25, 1853.
48. Ibid., Feb. 24, 25, 1853; *Journal of House*, p. 353.
49. *Detroit Free Press*, Feb. 15, 1953; *DA*, Feb. 24, 1853; *Journal of House*, p. 399.
50. *DA*, Feb. 23, 1853, quoting the *Ionia Gazette*; *Journal of Senate*, pp. 356, 357.
51. *Journal of House*, pp. 305, 306; *Journal of Senate*, pp. 205, 206.
52. *Jackson Citizen*, Feb. 9, 16, 1853; *Journal of House*, pp. 140, 290–92.
53. *Jackson Citizen*, Feb. 9, 16, 1853.
54. *Michigan History* 61 (1977): 331.
55. *Jackson Citizen*, Feb. 16, 1853.
56. *DA*, Feb. 14, 1853.
57. Ibid., Feb. 24, 1853.
58. *NI*, May 12, 1853.
59. *Battle Creek Journal*, Jan. 28, 1853; Enos Goodrich to Charles E. Stuart, Mar. 7, 1853, Beinecke; Arrington, *Brigham Young*, pp. 226, 227, 246, 251–53.

Chapter 12. Battle of Pine River

1. Minutes of Michilimackinac County Board of Supervisors, Records of Mackinac Island State Park Commission; election results for Michilimackinac County; *NI*, May 12, 1853.
2. *NI*, May 12, 1853.
3. *Ancient*, p. 73; *NI*, June 30, 1853 (includes article from *Detroit Tribune* of May 19, 1853).
4. The story of the attempted arrest is based on accounts in *NI*, June 30, 1853.
5. Ibid.
6. Ibid.
7. Ibid.; "Journal of Anti-Mormon Transactions," May 17, 1853, Records of Mackinac Island State Park Commission.
8. *NI*, June 30, 1853.
9. Strang to *New York Tribune*, July 2, 1853.
10. *NI*, June 30, 1853.
11. Ibid.
12. *New York Tribune*, July 2, 1853.
13. *NI*, June 30, 1853.
14. *DA*, July 27, 1853.
15. *NI*, June 30, 1853.
16. *New York Tribune*, July 2, 1853.
17. *NI*, June 30, 1853.
18. Ibid.; *New York Tribune*, July 2, 1853.
19. Ibid.
20. Ibid.
21. *Ancient*, p. 32.; *New York Tribune*, July 2, 1853.
22. *NI*, June 30, 1853.
23. *Ancient*, p. 88; *NI*, Apr. 28, 1853. The Pine River area is now the City of Charlevoix.
24. Williams, *Child of the Sea*, pp. 144, 145.
25. *NI*, Nov. 11, 1852.
26. *Ancient*, p 89.
27. *NI*, Nov. 11, 1852.
28. Ibid., Apr. 28, 1853.
29. Ibid., Apr. 28, May 12, June 30, 1853.
30. Legler, *Moses*, pp. 209, 211; Williams, *Child of the Sea*. pp. 144, 145; *History of the Grand Traverse Region*, comp. M. L. Leach, first printed in Grand Traverse Herald (1883), reprinted in *Michigan Historical Collections* 32 (1903): 14–175 (quote on p. 107).

31. *Ancient*, p. 89; Williams, *Child of the Sea*, pp. 144.
32. *NI*, Apr. 28, 1853, and *NI* extra of July 14, 1853, printed in Quaife, *Kingdom of Saint James*, pp. 271–75.
33. *NI*, July 14, 1853.
34. William N. MacLeod, "Address to the Inhabitants of Pine River," May 19, 1853, Burton.
35. Ibid.
36. *NI*, Aug. 16, 1855.
37. Williams, *Child of the Sea*, pp. 148, 149; Leach, *History of Grand Traverse*, pp. 107, 108.
38. *NI*, July 14, 1853.
39. Ibid.; *DA*, July 27, 1853; Williams, *Child of the Sea*, p. 150.
40. *DA*, July 27, 1853; Leach, *History of Grand Traverse*, p. 107; Legler, p. 211.
41. *NI*, Oct. 18, 1855.
42. *NI*, July 14, 1853; *DA*, July 27, 1853.
43. Ibid.; Leach, *History of Grand Traverse*, p. 108.
44. *NI*, July 14, 1853.
45. Leach, *History of Grand Traverse*, p. 108; *NI*, July 14, 1853; *DA*, July 27, 1853.
46. *DA*, July 27, 1853.
47. *NI*, July 14, 1853; *DA*, July 18, 1853; *Detroit Free Press*, July 19, 1853.
48. *NI*, July 14, 1853.
49. *DA*, July 18, 1853; *NI*, July 14, 1853; *Bloomington Intelligencer*, July 27, 1853.
50. *Detroit Free Press*, July 17, 1853; Legler, *Moses*, p. 214; *New York Tribune*, July 22, 1853.
51. *New York Tribune*, July 22, 1853; Legler, *Moses*, pp. 214, 215.
52. Ibid.
53. *New York Tribune*, July 22, 1853; *Bloomington Intelligencer*, July 27, 1853.
54. *New York Tribune*, July 22, 1853; Legler, *Moses*, p. 215.
55. Ibid.; *NI*, July 14, 1853.
56. *NI*, June 1, 1854.
57. *NI*, Oct., 18, 1855; *Ancient*, p. 75; Williams, *Child of the Sea*, p. 153; Leach, *History of Grand Traverse*, p. 109.
58. *NI*, Mar. 2, Apr. 13, June 1, 1854.
59. Ibid., Aug. 17, 1854.
60. Collar, "Mormon Land Policy," pp. 112–15.
61. *NI*, Aug. 17, Sept. 28, 1854.

62. Ibid., Apr. 13, June 13, Nov. 2, 1854.
63. Ibid., June 13, Aug. 17, Sept. 28, 1854.
64. *Census and Statistics of the State of Michigan*, 1854 (state made errors in compiling published census; figures used here are from original statements); *NI*, Sept. 28 and Nov. 2, 1854.
65. Statements of census of Peaine and Galilee townships, Burton.
66. *Census of Michigan*, 1854, pp. 386, 412; *NI*, Oct. 11, 1855.
67. *NI*, June 1, Aug. 24, 1854.

Chapter 13. The Drive to Dismember Strang's Empire

1. Report of Board of Canvassers, Nov. 14, 1854, Burton; *NI*, July 5, 1855.
2. Report of Board of Canvassers.
3. Reports of County Canvassers, Nov. 24, 1854, State Archives of Michigan; *NI*, July 5, 1855.
4. Reports of County Canvassers.
5. *DA*, Nov. 22, 1854.
6. *NI*, July 5, Oct. 11, 1855.
7. *NI*, July 5, 1855.
8. Ibid.
9. See statements of census of Peaine, Galilee, and Charlevoix townships and of unorganized territory of Emmet County, Burton.
10. Ibid.
11. *NI*, June 21, 1855; *Ancient*, p. 39.
12. See Michigan Constitution of 1850, Section 1; *NI*, Oct. 11, 1855.
13. *NI*, Oct. 11, 1855; *Census of Michigan*, 1854, p. 377.
14. *NI*, June 14, 1855; Reports of County Canvassers.
15. *NI*, Aug. 24, 1854.
16. See Floyd B. Streeter, *Political Parties in Michigan, 1837–1860* (Lansing, Mich., 1918), pp. 182–203.
17. Myraette (Strang) Losee to David Strang, Jan. 1, 1855, Clarke.
18. *Michigan Manual*, 1855, p. 37; *Michigan Biographies*, p. 425.
19. *Detroit Free Press*, Jan. 5, 17, 1855; *DA*, Jan. 9, 1855; *Michigan History* 61 (1977): 327; *Journal of House*, 1853 and 1855. *Michigan Manual* of 1855 has a seating chart.
20. *Detroit Free Press*, Jan. 7, 17, 1855; *Journal of House*, 1855, p. 10.
21. *Detroit Free Press*, Jan. 10, 1855.
22. *Pontiac Gazette*, Feb. 17, 1855.
23. *Detroit Free Press*, Jan. 10, 1855.
24. *NI*, Feb. 14, 1856.

25. *GH*, Mar. 8, 1849.
26. *Detroit Democrat*, Jan. 26, 1855.
27. *Journal of House*, p. 606. Strang also sought to create townships in Indian territory that would give the Indians both self-government and representation in the legislature. See *DA*, Jan. 12, 1855.
28. *NI*, June 21, 1855.
29. Ibid., June 21, Aug. 24, 1855.
30. *NI*, Aug. 24, 1854.
31. *Journal of House*, pp. 211, 237.
32. *NI*, Dec. 6, 1855, Feb. 14, 1856.
33. *Old Settlers of the Grand Traverse Region*, comp. S. E. Wait and W. S. Anderson (Traverse City, Mich., 1918), p. 46; *NI*, Feb. 14, 1856; Land records, Charlevoix County; *Michigan Biographies*, p. 142; Leach, *History of Grand Traverse*, p. 118.
34. *Lansing State Republican*, Mar. 25, 1856; *The Traverse Region* (Chicago, 1884), p. 175; Leach, *History of Grand Traverse*, p. 109.
35. *NI*, Dec. 6, 1855; Leach, *History of Grand Traverse*, p. 109.
36. *Journal of House*, pp. 225, 296.
37. *NI*, May 31, 1855.
38. *Detroit Democrat*, Feb. 3, 1855.
39. Ibid.; *Journal of House*, p. 296.
40. *Niles Republican*, Feb. 10, 1855.
41. *Jackson American Citizen*, Feb. 7, 1855. Several months later Strang would write that his "last earthly ambition" was appointment to the U.S. Supreme Court. See Strang to Robert McClelland, June 27, 1855, Burton.
42. *Journal of House*, pp. 380, 405, 488; *NI*, June 14, 1855; *Michigan Historical Collections* 1 (1877): 260.
43. *DA*, Feb. 9, 1855.
44. *Journal of Senate*, pp. 325, 390, 391; *NI*, May 31, 1855.
45. Leach, *History of Grand Traverse*, pp. 109, 110; *NI*, May 31, 1855.
46. *NI*, June 14, 1855.
47. Ibid.; *Traverse Region*, p. 176.
48. *NI*, June 14, 1855.
49. Ibid., May 31, June 21, 1855.
50. *NI*, July 19, Aug. 9, 1855.
51. Warren Post, Records of the Quorum of Apostles.
52. *NI*, Aug. 9, 1855.
53. Ibid., July 19, 1855.
54. Ibid.

55. Leach, *History of Grand Traverse*, p. 112.
56. *Lansing State Republican*, June 24, 1856; Leach, *History of Grand Traverse*, p. 113.
57. *NI*, July 19, Dec. 6, 1855.
58. John S. Dixon to J. A. T. Wendell, Sept. 21, 1855, Mackinac Island Collection, 1789–1933, Records of Mackinac Island State Park Commission; *NI*, Dec. 6, 1855; Leach, *History of Grand Traverse*, pp. 111, 112; *Traverse Region*, p. 176.
59. *NI*, Aug. 9, Dec. 6, 1855.
60. Dixon to Wendell, Sept. 21, 1855; Wendell to Dixon, Sept. 24, 1855, Mackinac Island Collection; Leach, *History of Grand Traverse*, pp. 118–20.
61. *NI*, Oct. 18, 1855.
62. Ibid., Nov. 1, 1855; Leach, *History of Grand Traverse*, p. 111.
63. *Traverse Region*, p. 136.
64. Ibid., p. 178; *NI*, Jan., 24, 1856.

Chapter 14. Consecration and Thievery

1. The *Rochester Daily Democrat* as quoted in *NI*, Oct. 11, 1855.
2. *NI*, Oct. 11, 1855.
3. Ibid.
4. Sarah (Strang) Wing to Milo M. Quaife, June 28, 1920, Beinecke; Arrington and Bitton, *Mormon Experience*, p. 190.
5. The "Polygamy" portion of the Book of the Law was printed in *NI*, May 1, 1856.
6. Sarah (Strang) Wing to Quaife, spring of 1920, June 28, 1920, Beinecke; *Strang Family Newsletter*, Apr. 1980, p. 13.
7. Ibid.; Eugenia Phillips (Phoebe's daughter) to Quaife, July 15, 1920, Beinecke. She described her mother as an attractive, witty woman with fair complexion, black hair, and bright blue eyes.
8. E. and C. Strang, "Biographical Sketch," pp. 5, 10; Wingfield W. Watson interview, Dec. 11, 1918.
9. *NI*, June 14, July 19, 1855.
10. E. and C. Strang, "Biographical Sketch," p. 5; minutes of conferences on Beaver Island, pp. 52, 58, 61, 62; Watson interview. Strang's first wife was not on the island after the Detroit trial in 1851, and Hickey's first wife had left before the coronation.
11. Wing to Quaife, spring of 1920.
12. Watson interview.

13. C. Strang, "Why I Am Not a Strangite," p. 460; Clement Strang interview; Clement Strang to Quaife, June 17, 1921, Beinecke. Sarah Strang also had duties outside the home. She was ordained as church teacher and as the general recorder for the baptisms for the dead on Beaver Island; see *NI*, Aug. 9, 1855.
14. *Strang Family Newsletter*, Apr. 1980, p. 12; *Detroit Post and Tribune*, Sept. 19, 1879; Williams, *Child of the Sea*, p. 88.
15. *Michigan Historical Collections* 15 (1909): 285; *NI*, Nov. 1, 1855.
16. *Michigan Historical Collections* 9 (1908): 106–7.
17. Leonard Arrington, "An Economic Interpretation of the 'Word of Wisdom,' " *BYU Studies* 1 (1959): 37–39; Flanders, *Nauvoo*, pp. 244–47; E. and C. Strang, "Biographical Sketch," p. 5.
18. *NI*, Aug. 24, 1854.
19. *NI*, Oct. 18, 1855; E. and C. Strang, "Biographical Sketch," p. 6.
20. Romeo Strang to David Strang, Nov. 18, 1855, Clarke.
21. Ibid.
22. Ibid.
23. *Strang Family Newsletter*, Apr. 1980, p. 12. They were married on May 20, 1855, in a Baptist church near Voree. Strang would be a grandfather for the first time the following spring, when Romeo and Netti had a child on April 3. That offspring of first cousins, a girl, died a month later, however.
24. Romeo Strang to David Strang, Nov. 18, 1855.
25. C. Strang, "Why I Am Not a Strangite," pp. 470–73.
26. Roberts, ed., *History of Church*, 3:180–181; Brodie, *No Man*, pp. 106, 107, 141, 220; Hill, *Joseph Smith*, p. 131. For a look at the Danites and consecration, see Leland H. Gentry, "The Danite Band of 1838," *BYU Studies* 14 (1974): 421–37.
27. Leach, *History of Grand Traverse*, p. 104.
28. *DA*, June 21, 1851.
29. Leach, *History of Grand Traverse*, p. 105.
30. C. Strang, "Why I Am Not a Strangite," p. 463.
31. Thomas Paine, *Age of Reason* (rpt. ed. Baltimore, 1956), p. 6.
32. *NI*, May 31, 1855.
33. Ibid., July 26, 1855.
34. Thomas Bedford interview, *Detroit News*, July 7, 1882.
35. *NI*, July 26, 1855.
36. Ibid., Aug. 23, 1855.
37. Ibid., Nov. 1, 1855.
38. Ibid., Mar. 13, 1856.
39. Ibid., Sept. 20, 1855.

40. Ibid., Oct. 18, 1855.
41. *Lansing State Republican*, Nov. 6, 1855.
42. *NI*, Dec. 6, 1855.
43. Ibid.

Chapter 15. The Conspirators

1. Meteorological Journal, St. James, Beaver Island, Beinecke; *NI*, Mar. 13 and Apr. 3, 1856.
2. Leach, *History of Grand Traverse*, p. 124; *NI*, Apr. 3, 1856.
3. Zenos Wright (son of Phineas Wright), interview by Milo M. Quaife, May 25, 1920, Beinecke; Covenant book; U.S. Census of 1860, Manitou County. For description of Bedford, see clippings of 1882 in Strang Papers, State Library of Michigan.
4. *NI*, Aug. 9, 1855; Leach, *History of Grand Traverse*, p. 123; Thomas Bedford interview, Detroit News, July 7, 1882.
5. Book of the Law, p. 65; *Green Bay Advocate*, Feb. 7, 1905.
6. Hirshson, *Lion*, p. 103.
7. *NI*, Aug. 12, 1852.
8. Ibid., Feb. 14, May 1, 22, 1856.
9. Leach, *History of Grand Traverse*, pp. 122, 123; *Detroit News*, July 7, 1882.
10. Leach, *History of Grand Traverse*, p. 124; *Detroit News*, July 7, 1882. In the *News* article Bedford gave his version of the events that spring; and he was quoted as saying the conversation occurred in late February or early March. Piecing together the date of the whipping from the *Northern Islander* makes it clear the conversation took place on April 1.
11. *Detroit News*, July 7, 1882; Leach, *History of Grand Traverse*, p. 124; *DA*, June 20, 1856.
12. Watson interview.
13. Sarah Wing to Quaife, spring 1920.
14. Leach, *History of Grand Traverse*, p. 124; *Detroit News*, July 7, 1882.
15. *NI*, Apr. 3, 1856.
16. *Detroit News*, July 7, 1882; Leach, *History of Grand Traverse*, p. 124.
17. *NI*, Apr. 3, 1856.
18. *Detroit News*, July 7, 1882.
19. H. P. Brown to Strang, Aug. 29, 1850, Beinecke; *GH*, Mar. 4, 1849; U.S. Census of 1860, Town of Koshkonong, Jefferson County, Wisconsin; Coronation book.
20. *Chicago Tribune*, Oct. 13, 1895; U.S. Census of 1850, Michilimack-

inac County. Wentworth's wife has been called Alvira by a number
of writers. She was Phebe in the 1850 and 1860 censuses and was
called Virginia in the 1870 and 1880 censuses. In the latter three
censuses she was living in Waseca County in Minnesota.

21. Zenos Wright interview; Civil War record of Alexander Wentworth,
National Archives.
22. *NI*, July 14, 1853; "Beaver Island Record," a history of the Strangite church on Beaver Island, p. 37, Clarke. The petition is in
Burton.
23. Wingfield W. Watson to Quaife, May 20, 1920, Beinecke.
24. *NI*, May 22, 1856.
25. Ibid., June 19, 1856.
26. Ibid.
27. Ibid.; Wingfield W. Watson to Quaife, June 19, 1919, Beinecke.
28. *NI*, June 19, 1856.
29. Ibid., *Detroit News*, July 7, 1882; Watson to Quaife, June 19,
1919.
30. Meteorological Journal; *NI*, Apr. 3, May 1, 1856.
31. *NI*, May 1, June 5, 1856.
32. Ibid., June 5, 1856.
33. Ibid., Leach, *History of Grand Traverse*, p. 125; *NI*, May 22, 1856;
letter from James Hutchins in Journal History, Sept. 19, 1870,
Mormon Church Archives.
34. *NI*, May 22, 1856.
35. Ibid., June 19, 1856.
36. Ibid., June 5, 1856.
37. Ibid., June 19, 1856.
38. Ibid., May 22, 1856.
39. The account of this incident is in ibid.
40. Ibid., Mar. 13, May 22, 1856.
41. Ibid., July 19, 1855, May 1, 1856.
42. Ibid., June 5, 19, 1856; Leach, *History of Grand Traverse*, p. 125.
43. See *Lansing Republican*, May 20, 1856, and *Michigan Expositor*, May
31, 1856, for details of school fund apportionment, which did not
include Manitou County.
44. Leach, *History of Grand Traverse*, p. 125; Warren Post, record of assassination, reprinted in the *Journal of History of Reorganized Church*
(Lamoni, Iowa, 1920), 3:74.
45. *NI*, June 5, 1856.
46. The letter of Feb. 8, 1856, is in Clarke.

47. See *NI*, Aug. 23, 1855.
48. Kenneth S. Davis, *Kansas* (New York, 1976), pp. 56, 57, 58.
49. *Lansing State Republican*, May 22, 1856; *Dictionary of American Biography* (New York, 1936), pp. 208–11.
50. Leach, *History of Grand Traverse*, p. 125; Post, record of assassination, p. 74; *Detroit News*, July 7, 1882; *NI*, June 5, 1856.
51. *Detroit News*, July 7, 1882; Log of *Michigan*; *NI*, June 19, 1856.
52. Charles H. McBlair to James C. Dobbin, June 6, 1856, Navy; abstracts of service records, Records of Naval Officers, National Archives; *NI*, June 19, 1856; Edward Callahan, *List of Officers of the U.S. Navy, 1775–1900* (New York, 1901), p. 359; Hulce, "Michigan at Sea," p. 103.
53. McBlair to Charles W. Welsh, Sept. 24, 1856, to Dobbin, June 6, 1856, to Kinsley S. Bingham, June 6, 1856, all in Navy; *Lansing Republican*, June 24, 1856.
54. McBlair to Dobbin, to Bingham, June 6, 1856.
55. Watson interview.
56. McBlair to Bingham, June 6, 1856.
57. Bingham to McBlair, July 1, 1856, Navy; *Lansing State Republican*, June 24, 1856.
58. McBlair to Dobbin, June 6, 1856.
59. *Milwaukee Wisconsin*, June 16, 1856; Log of *Michigan*.
60. *DA*, June 19, 1856.

Chapter 16. Assassination

1. Log of *Michigan*.
2. Charles H. McBlair to Charles W. Welsh, Sept. 24, 1856; Warren Post, record of assassination, p. 74; *NI*, June 20, 1856.
3. Alexander St. Bernard's account of the assassination is printed in the *Detroit Free Press*, June 30, 1889; *NI*, June 20, 1856; for background on St. Bernard, see his letter to William Graham, May 17, 1851, Navy.
4. *NI*, June 5, 1856.
5. E. and C. Strang, "Biographical Sketch," p. 11; *Detroit Free Press*, June 30, 1889, Sept. 20, 1908; St. Bernard to Graham, May 17, 1851.
6. McBlair to Dobbin, June 19, 1856, Navy; *Detroit Free Press*, June 30, 1889; Thomas Bedford interview, *Detroit News*, July 7, 1882; Williams, *Child of the Sea*, p. 96.

7. Warren Post, record of assassination, p. 75; *NI*, June 20, 1856; *DA*, June 20, 1856; Hutchins, letter in Journal History, Sept. 19, 1870; *Detroit News*, July 7, 1882. The reports vary on certain details of the assassination, but there is a consistency in most of the accounts. St. Bernard's version (in *Detroit Free Press*, June 30, 1889) has Strang hanging onto his arm until the shooting stopped and the pistol-whipping began, while other accounts have Strang falling to the ground after the initial shots.

8. *NI*, June 20, 1856; *Detroit News*, July 7, 1882; *Green Bay Advocate*, June 26, 1856.

9. *NI*, June 20, 1856. The dialogue is from Warren Post, record of assassination, p. 75, and Wingfield W. Watson's notes, apparently written within hours of the shooting, Burton.

10. *NI*, June 20, 1856.

11. Bedford's version of the assassination is in the *Detroit News*, July 7, 1882.

12. Ibid.; log of *Michigan*; McBlair to Welsh, Sept. 24, 1856; *NI*, June 20, 1856.

13. Warren Post, record of assassination, p. 75; *NI*, June 20, 1856.

14. McBlair to Dobbin, June 19, 1856; *NI*, June 20, 1856; Watson, notes; abstracts of service records, Records of Naval Officers.

15. *NI*, June 20, 1856; *DA*, June 20, 1856; Warren Post, record of assassination, pp. 75, 76; McBlair to Dobbin, June 19, 1856.

16. Leach, *History of Grand Traverse*, p. 126; McBlair to Welsh, Sept. 24, 1856; *Detroit News*, July 7, 1882.

17. McBlair to George Miller, and Miller to McBlair, June 17, 1856, Navy; Warren Post, record of assassination, pp. 75, 76; McBlair to Welsh, Sept. 24, 1856.

18. Miller to Lewis Cass, June 18, 1856, Navy.

19. McBlair to Welsh, Sept. 24, 1856.

20. *Detroit Free Press*, June 30, 1889.

21. Watson, notes.

22. Ibid.; Warren Post, record of assassination, p. 76.

23. *NI*, June 20, 1856; log of *Michigan*; *Detroit Free Press*, June 20, 1856; McBlair to Dobbin, June 19, 1856; Warren Post, record of assassination, p. 76; Leach, *History of Grand Traverse*, p. 126.

24. Leach, *History of Grand Traverse*, p. 126; log of *Michigan*; *Detroit News*, July 7, 1882.

25. Leach, *History of Grand Traverse*, p. 126; *Detroit News*, July 7, 1882.

26. *Detroit News*, July 7, 1882.

27. Ibid.

28. Ibid.
29. Helen Collar, "Irish Migration," *Journal of Beaver Island History* 1 (1976): 30, 31.
30. Ibid.
31. The *Milwaukee Sentinel* published the news a day earlier.
32. *Detroit Free Press*, June 24, 28, 1856; *NI*, June 20, 1856; Wingfield W. Watson, autobiography, written in 1881, copy in Clarke, p. 19.
33. *Milwaukee Sentinel*, June 28, 1856; Warren Post, record of assassination, p. 76; *DA*, June 3, 1856; *Michigan History* 27 (1943): 79; 60 (1971): 97. Histories about Strang commonly state, in error, that the warship *Michigan*, with the assassins aboard, returned to the scene.
34. *Green Bay Advocate*, June 26, July 3, 1856; *Buffalo Express*, July 2, 1856; *DA*, June 30, 1856.
35. Warren Post, record of assassination, p. 76; *Grand Rapids Eagle*, July 3, 1856; *DA*, June 30, 1856; *Green Bay Advocate*, July 3, 1856.
36. Warren Post, record of assassination, p. 76; *Grand Rapids Eagle*, July 3, 1856.
37. *Grand Rapids Eagle*, July 3, 1856; *Detroit News*, July 7, 1882.
38. *Detroit News*, July 7, 1882.
39. Warren Post, record of assassination, p. 76; *Green Bay Advocate*, July 3, 1856; *Grand Rapids Eagle*, July 3, 1856. Bedford later said that the arrested Mormons were released after questioning in Mackinac.
40. *Green Bay Advocate*, July 3, 1856.
41. *DA*, June 30, 1856.
42. Warren Post, record of assassination, p. 76.
43. Warren Post to Br. Bennett, May 16, 1858, Clarke; Gabriel Strang to John Wake, May 8, 1929, copy in Clarke; Leach, *History of Grand Traverse*, p. 127.
44. Warren Post, record of assassination, p. 77; Leach, *History of Grand Traverse*, pp. 129, 130; Morgan, "Bibliography," p. 75; *NI*, Apr. 3, 1856.
45. *Racine Advocate*, July 2, 1856; *History of Racine and Kenosha Counties*, p. 179.
46. Watson, interview by Quaife, Feb. 3, 1921, Beinecke; *Coldwater Republican*, Aug. 6, 1886; *Delavan Republican*, Jan. 1, 1906. The home that Strang's parents lived in still exists on the site of Voree.
47. Warren Post, record of assassination, p. 77; *Detroit Free Press*, July 2, 1856.
48. *Detroit News*, July 7, 1882; Warren Post, record of assassination,

p. 77; Davis, "Stories of Saint Helena," pp. 423, 428; *Michigan History* 22 (1938): 297.

49. *Niles Republican*, July 19, 1856.

50. *Detroit Free Press*, July 2, 1856; Williams, *Child of the Sea*, p. 175; Davis, "Stories of Saint Helena," pp. 429–31.

51. Warren Post, record of assassination, p. 77; Leach, *History of Grand Traverse*, p. 127; *Detroit News*, July 7, 1882; Zenos Wright interview.

52. Watson's description of the expulsion of the Saints, given in subsequent paragraphs herein, is found in Leach, *History of Grand Traverse*, pp. 128–32.

53. Ibid.; *Green Bay Advocate*, July 17, 1856; *Detroit News*, July 7, 1882; E. and C. Strang, "Biographical Sketch," pp. 13, 14.

54. *NI*, May 22, 1856. Mormons apparently had piled stones on the grave a few days earlier on June 7, the anniversary of Bennett's death.

55. E. and C. Strang, "Biographical Sketch," p. 14; Leach, *History of Grand Traverse*, p. 130.

56. Leach, *History of Grand Traverse*, p. 131.

57. E. and C. Strang, "Biographical Sketch," pp. 13, 14; Clement Strang, interview by Quaife, Feb. 12, 1921.

58. J. S. Comstock to Moses Wisner, early in 1860, to Governor of Michigan, Nov. 23, 1870, both in Executive Office Correspondence.

59. In Leach, *History of Grand Traverse*, pp. 128–32, Watson says that the steamer was the *Buckeye State*'s sister ship, the *Keystone State*, and that it arrived on July 6. It is clear from newspapers, ship schedules, and other sources, however, that the ship was the *Buckeye State* and that it arrived on July 7. See in particular the Mission House register, Records of Mackinac Island State Park Commission, and Warren Post, record of assassination, p. 77.

60. The following incidents involving Watson come from Leach, *History of Grand Traverse*, pp. 131, 132. See also Watson interview, Dec. 11, 1919.

61. Leach, *History of Grand Traverse*, pp. 128, 132; *Niles Republican*, July 19, 1856.

62. Watson, autobiography, p. 20.

63. *Buffalo Express*, July 9, 1856; Leach, *History of Grand Traverse*, p. 128.

64. *Detroit News*, July 7, 1882.

65. Warren Post, record of assassination, p. 77; *Detroit News*, July 7,

1882; *Green Bay Advocate*, May 15, 1856; James C. Mills, *Our Inland Seas* (Chicago, 1910), p. 146.

66. *Detroit Tribune*, July 8, 1856; *DA*, July 8, 1856.
67. *Green Bay Advocate*, July 10, 1856.
68. *DA*, July 11, 1856; *Niles Republican*, July 19, 1856.
69. Sarah Wing to Quaife, June 28, 1920. Strang's son Clement J. suggested that the Mormons, who outnumbered the mob by at least seven to one, were paralyzed because of their "consecration" of Gentile property. If the consciences of the Mormons had been clear, Clement Strang wrote, they would have "given their lives to their holy cause instead of running away like mice from the house-cat." See "Why I Am Not a Strangite," pp. 472, 473.
70. Warren Post, record of assassination, p. 79.
71. Sarah Wing to Quaife, spring 1920.
72. Warren Post, record of assassination, p. 79.
73. Hansen, "Making of King Strang," pp. 212, 213.
74. Stephen Post to Warren Post, Mar. 10, 1856, Reorganized Church Archives.
75. *NI*, May 22, 1856.
76. *Green Bay Advocate*, July 17, 1856.
77. Warren Post, record of assassination, p. 79.
78. E. and C. Strang, "Biographical Sketch," p. 13; Gabriel Strang to John Wake, Apr. 10, 1929, copy in Clarke.
79. Warren Post, record of assassination, p. 79.
80. Ibid.
81. Ibid; Cumming, "Lorenzo Dow Hickey," p. 60.
82. Warren Post, record of assassination, p. 79; *Detroit Free Press*, July 12, 1856.
83. *Milwaukee Daily News*, July 9, 1856; Watson, autobiography, pp. 19, 21.
84. As quoted in the *Niles Republican*, July 19, 1856.
85. Watson, autobiography, p. 20; Watson to Quaife, Apr. 14, 1919, Beinecke.

Epilogue

1. Lewis Cass to James C. Dobbin, June 27, 1856, Navy.
2. Charles H. McBlair to Dobbin, Sept. 10, 1856, and Index of Letters Received, Navy.
3. Charles W. Welsh to McBlair, Sept. 15, 1856, Navy.

4. McBlair to Welsh, Sept. 24, 1856, Navy.
5. Welsh to Cass, Oct. 2, 1856, Navy.
6. J. S. Comstock to Governor of Michigan, late 1859, Executive Office Correspondence; *Journal of House*, 1857, p. 467.
7. Comstock to Governor of Michigan, late 1859.
8. Moses Wisner to Comstock, Jan. 13, 1860, Executive Office Correspondence. The Comstock response is attached to this letter.
9. Reports of County Canvassers, Manitou County, Nov. 4, 1856, State Archives of Michigan; McNutt Diary, p. 4.
10. Williams, *Child of the Sea*, pp. 182, 203, 204; McNutt Diary, p. 4; Collar, "Irish Migration," pp. 46, 47.
11. Williams, *Child of the Sea*, pp. 87, 88, 204, 205, 208; *Detroit News Tribune*, Dec. 7, 1915.
12. McNutt Diary, p. 5; Williams, *Child of the Sea*, p. 189.
13. McNutt Diary, p. 6.
14. U.S. Census of 1860, Beaver Island Township, Manitou County; *Chicago Weekly Democrat*, July 19, 1856; Leach, *History of Grand Traverse*, p. 121; Williams, *Child of the Sea*, pp. 77, 182, 184, 200. The building that housed the Mormon printing office is now a museum on the island.
15. U.S. Census of 1860, Beaver Island Township, Manitou County.
16. U.S. Census of 1860, Janesville Township, Waseca County, Minnesota.
17. Williams, *Child of the Sea*, p. 212.
18. Civil War Record of Alexander Wentworth.
19. Minutes of Michilimackinac Board of Supervisors, Oct. 20, 1856, Records of Mackinac Island State Park Commission.
20. Beaver Island land records, Charlevoix.
21. *Detroit News*, July 7, 1882; U.S. Census of 1880, Chandler Township, Manitou County. See also clippings of 1882, Strang Papers, State Library of Michigan.
22. *Cheboygan Democrat*, July 20, 1882.
23. Clement Strang to Milo M. Quaife, June 29, 1921, Beinecke.
24. Death records of Eaton County, Mich.
25. *Green Bay Advocate*, July 17, 1856.
26. Warren Post, record of assassination, pp. 77, 78.
27. *Strang Family Newsletter*, Apr. 1980, pp. 12, 13; U.S. Census of 1860, Spring Prairie Township, Walworth County; Doyle Fitzpatrick, *The King Strang Story* (Lansing, 1970), pp. 117–32. Fitzpatrick is an authority on the descendants of Strang. Two other children

died before Strang did, Mary in Wisconsin in 1843 and an infant born to Betsy on Beaver Island. Mary had three living children, Elvira four, Betsy three, and Phoebe and Sarah, one each.

28. Sarah Wing to Quaife, June 28, 1920.
29. Interviews of Bruce Flanders, presiding high priest of Strangite church in Burlington, Wis., July 23, 1985, and Nov. 8, 1987.
30. Fitzpatrick, *King Strang*, p. 200. See Gabriel Strang to John Wake, June 23, 1932, copy in Clarke. The grave is adjacent to the Soldiers' Monument.
31. Flanders interviews.
32. Fawn Brodie, in her biography of Joseph Smith, suggested that certain aspects of Smith's behavior could be defined as that of an imposter personality (See *No Man*, pp. 418, 419). A similar case could be made about Strang. Psychiatrist Phyllis Greenacre has written that the imposter personality enjoys the limelight and "putting something over" on his audience. This disorder typically has its roots with an overpossessive mother (which Strang had), which creates an inability to develop a separate indentity and leads to the imposture. It is through the reaction of the audience that the individual seeks to achieve a sense of competence as a man. See Greenacre, "The Imposter," *Psychoanalytic Quarterly* 27 (1958): 359–82.
33. Stephen Post to Warren Post, Dec. 5, 1858, Reorganized Church Archives.

Sources

The most fruitful approach into the life of James J. Strang is through his writing: his diary, correspondence, uncompleted autobiography, and the published work in his newspapers (the *Voree Herald* and its Voree successors, *Zion's Reveille* and *Gospel Herald*, and the Beaver Island paper, the *Northern Islander*) and his books, The Book of the Law of the Lord and *Ancient and Modern Michilimackinac*.

The richest source of letters and other documents relating to Strang is the Beinecke Rare Book and Manuscript Library at Yale University, New Haven, Connecticut. The collection includes hundreds of letters and documents, such as Strang's diary, his uncompleted autobiography, the letter of appointment, the covenant book, the record of the organization of the kingdom, and Milo M. Quaife's notes, including those from interviews. The collection also contains Dale L. Morgan's typewritten notes about a portion of the Strang Papers.

The Burton Historical Collection at the Detroit Public Library is the second most important source of manuscript materials. Included are correspondence, a bound volume that contains most of the original documents from the 1851 federal trial, a draft of Strang's first speech to the Michigan House of Representatives, and the state census records of Beaver Island in 1854.

Another important manuscript collection is in the Clarke Historical Library at Central Michigan University, Mount Pleasant. Other libraries and archives that have manuscript holdings about Strang but not in any one collection are the State Archives of the Michigan History Division, Lansing; the National Archives, Washington, D.C.; the Library and Archives of the Reorganized Church of Jesus Christ of Latter Day Saints in Independence, Missouri; the Library-Archives of the Historical Department of the Church of Jesus Christ of Latter-day Saints in Salt Lake City, Utah; the archives of the State Historical Society of Wisconsin, Madison; and the Mackinac Island State Park Commission in Lansing, Michigan.

For published material about Strang, the required reference is Dale L. Morgan's "A Bibliography of the Church of Jesus Christ of Latter Day Saints (Strangite)," *Western Humanities Review* 5 (1950). This bibliography lists both Strangite and anti-Strangite publications, from broadsides to

books, and where the publications can be found, although the latter list-
ings are incomplete today.

Contemporary newspapers are also a significant source of firsthand
accounts and often provide a balance to the official version of events given
by Strang's publications. The anti-Strangite and newspaper accounts have
to be used with care, but they should not be ignored in fashioning a
credible history.

The following are other books, articles, and contemporary newspapers that I have found especially valuable in writing about Strang and
the Mormons.

BOOKS AND ARTICLES

Adams, Henry. "Charles Francis Adams Visits the Mormons in 1844."
    Proceedings of the Massachusetts Historical Society 68 (1952).
Amann, Peter. "Prophet in Zion: The Saga of George J. Adams." *New
    England Quarterly* 37 (December 1964): 477ff.
Anderson, Richard L. "Reuben Miller, Recorder of Oliver Cowdery's
    Reaffirmations." *BYU Studies* 8 (1968): 277–93.
Arrington, Leonard J. *Brigham Young: American Moses.* New York, 1985;
    Urbana, Ill., 1986.
———. "An Economic Interpretation of the 'Word of Wisdom.'" *BYU
    Studies* 1 (1959): 37–49.
———, and Davis Bitton. *The Mormon Experience.* New York, 1980.
Brodie, Fawn M. *No Man Knows My History.* New York, 1946.
Bush, Lester E., Jr. "Mormonism's Negro Doctrine: An Historical Over-
    view." *Dialogue* 8 (Spring 1973): 11–68.
Collar, Helen. "Mormon Land Policy on Beaver Island." *Michigan History*
    56 (1972): 87–118.
———. "The Pre-Mormon Settlement on Beaver Island, 1837–1852."
    Journal of Beaver Island History 2 (1980): 9–28.
Cross, Whitney R. *The Burned-over District.* New York, 1950.
Cumming, John. "Lorenzo Dow Hickey." *Michigan History* 50 (1966):
    50–75.
Davis, Marion Morse. "Stories of Saint Helena Island." *Michigan History*
    10 (1926): 411–46.
Eberstadt, Charles. "A Letter that Founded a Kingdom." *Autograph Col-
    lectors' Journal* (October 1950).
Ehat, Andrew F. "'It Seems Like Heaven Began on Earth': Joseph Smith
    and the Constitution of the Kingdom of God." *BYU Studies* 20
    (1980): 253–79.

Fitzpatrick, Doyle. *The King Strang Story*. Lansing, Mich., 1970.

Flanders, Robert B. *Nauvoo: Kingdom on the Mississippi*. Urbana, Ill., 1965.

Ford, Thomas. *History of Illinois*. Chicago, 1854.

Foster, Lawrence. *Religion and Sexuality: Three American Communal Experiences of the Nineteenth Century*. New York, 1981; Urbana, Ill., 1984.

Gates, Paul Wallace. "The Role of the Land Speculator in Western Development." In *The Public Lands*, edited by Vernon Carstensen. Madison, Wis., 1968.

Gentry, Leland H. "The Danite Band of 1838." *BYU Studies* 14 (1974): 421–37.

Hansen, Klaus J. "The Making of King Strang." *Michigan History* 46 (1962): 201–19.

———. *Quest for Empire: The Political Kingdom of God and the Council of Fifty in Mormon History*. East Lansing, Mich., 1967.

Hibbard, Benjamin H. *A History of the Public Land Policies*. New York, 1924.

Hill, Donna. *Joseph Smith*. New York, 1977.

Hirshson, Stanley. *The Lion of the Lord*. New York, 1969.

History of the Church of Jesus Christ of Latter-day Saints, edited by B. H. Roberts. Salt Lake City, 1957.

Journal of History of the Church of Jesus Christ of Latter Day Saints. Lamoni, Iowa, 1920.

Journal of the House of Representatives of the State of Michigan. Lansing, 1853, 1855.

Kane, Lucile. "Federal Protection of Public Timber in the Upper Great Lakes." In *The Public Lands*, edited by Vernon Carstensen. Madison, Wis., 1968.

Leach, M. L., comp. *History of the Grand Traverse Region* (1883), reprinted in *Michigan Historical Collections* 32 (1903): 14–175.

Legler, Henry E. *A Moses of the Mormons*. Milwaukee, Wis., 1897. Reprinted in *Michigan Historical Collections* 32 (1903): 180–224.

Lewis, David Rich. " 'For Life, the Resurrection, and the Life Everlasting': James J. Strang and Strangite Mormon Polygamy, 1849–1856." *Wisconsin Magazine of History* 67 (1983): 274–91.

Miller, Reuben. *James J. Strang, Weighed in the Balance of Truth, and Found Wanting*. Burlington, Wis., 1846.

———. *Truth Shall Prevail*. Burlington, Wis., 1847.

Moody, Thurmon Dean. "Nauvoo's Whistling and Whittling Brigade." *BYU Studies* 15 (1975): 480–90.

Morgan, Dale L. "A Bibliography of the Church of Jesus Christ of Latter Day Saints (Strangite)." *Western Humanities Review* 5 (1950): 43–109.

Quaife, Milo M. *The Kingdom of Saint James*. New Haven, Conn., 1930.
Quinn, D. Michael. "The Council of Fifty and Its Members, 1844 to 1945." *BYU Studies* 20 (1980): 163–97.
———. "The Mormon Succession Crisis of 1844." *BYU Studies* 16 (1976): 187–233.
The Record of Norton Jacob, edited by C. Edward and Ruth S. Jacob. Salt Lake City, 1949.
Rich, Russell R. *Ensign to the Nations*. Provo, Utah, 1972.
Strang, Clement J. "Why I Am Not a Strangite." *Michigan History* 26 (1942): 457–79.
Strang, Mark A. *The Diary of James J. Strang*. East Lansing, Mich., 1961.
Strang Family Newsletter, edited by Janet Strang Shott. La Canada, Calif., 1979–82.
Streeter, Floyd B. *Political Parties in Michigan, 1837–1860*. Lansing, Mich., 1918.
Walton, Ivan H. "Developments on the Great Lakes, 1815–1943." *Michigan History* 27 (1943): 72–142.
Williams, Elizabeth Whitney. *A Child of the Sea*. Ann Arbor, Mich., 1905.
Young, Andrew W. *History of Chautauqua County*. Buffalo, 1875.

CONTEMPORARY NEWSPAPERS

Detroit Advertiser, 1851–56
Detroit Free Press, 1851–56
Green Bay Advocate, 1851–56
Jackson (Michigan) *Citizen*, 1852–56
Lansing State Republican, 1855–56
Latter-day Saints' Millennial Star (Liverpool, England), 1842–56
Times and Seasons (Nauvoo, Illinois), 1842–46
Warsaw (Illinois) *Signal*, 1844–46

Index

Adams, Caroline, 112, 118
Adams, George J.: controversial background of, 46, 47; joins Strang, 47; as counselor to Strang, 52, 66, 91, 101, 102, 112, 113, 122; on missions, 53, 65, 66, 111, 112; and polygamy, 79, 80, 82; carries proposal of marriage for Strang, 82; at New York City conference, 83, 85–87; role in establishing kingdom, 91, 105–7; crowns Strang king, 107, 141; named prime minister, 107; breaks with Strang, 112–14; testimony against Strang, 116, 118, 137, 141, 142, 156–60
Adams, Louisa, 111–14, 116–18, 142
Aldrich, Marvin M., 72, 73, 146–48, 258–62
Ancient and Modern Michilimackinac, 289 n
Atkyn, Dr. J.: as Beaver Island photographer, 240, 241; conspirator against Strang, 240–43

Bacon, Samuel P., 105, 219
Baptism for the dead, 77
Baraga, Frederic, 68
Barnes, Caleb P., 7, 32, 56, 57
Barry, Gov. John S., 144, 213
Barton, James, 180, 184–86
Bates, George C.: prosecutes Strang, 128, 133–37, 139, 140, 142, 143, 145, 151–54, 160, 181
Beaver Island: economy of, xi, 73, 74, 114, 115, 208, 209; Mormon settlement of, 67–74, 93, 94; Indians on, 67–70, 73, 96, 97, 125–28, 171–73; described, 68–70, 99, 239, 240; land transactions on, 68, 72, 74, 167, 169, 170, 172, 208; population of, 69–73, 120, 122, 166, 209, 211–13, 239, 245, 269; tabernacle on, 74, 93, 99–101, 103, 106, 167, 248, 259;

elections at, 93, 96, 119, 170, 178–80, 210–13; conflict between Mormons and Gentiles, 93–95, 98, 99, 120–32, 141, 166, 167, 169–77; kingdom established on, 97–99, 105–7; polygamy on, 107–9, 167, 168, 223–26, 240; inheritances on, 109, 110, 208; rival for Mackinac, 114, 115, 196–200, 208, 209; arrests of Mormons on, 129–37, 150, 165; killing of Thomas Bennett on, 142–50; Gentiles driven off, 166, 167, 169–72, 174–77; exodus of Mormons, 256–66
Bedford, Ruth Ann, 233, 235, 236, 271
Bedford, Thomas: whipping of, 233–36; assassin of Strang, 244, 249–53, 267; on Beaver Island after assassination, 254, 255, 262, 268, 270, 271
Belle Isle, 68
Bennett, John Cook: controversial background of, 43–45; joins Strang, 43, 45, 46; and polygamy, 44, 45, 61, 79, 80; as counselor to Strang, 46, 59, 61, 66; and Order of Illuminati, 48–51, 61, 62, 101; trial of, 61; excommunication of, 61, 65; as chicken farmer, 99, 295 n
Bennett, Samuel: wounded by Mormons, 142–50
Bennett, Thomas: conflict with Strang, 124, 127, 128; killed by Mormons, 142–50, 165, 166, 259
Bingham, Gov. Kinsley S., 213–15, 242, 245, 246, 260, 268
Bloomers, 100, 233, 234
Book of Mormon, 34
Book of the Law of the Lord, 97, 127, 141, 224, 256; designates Strang to be king, 97, 98; polygamy provision, 108, 224; other provisions, 124, 125, 159, 173, 234

329

Silver Creek, N.Y., 20, 22, 26, 28
Slavery: the issue of, 120, 213–15
Smith, Aaron, 6–11, 25, 33, 34; breaks
  with Strang, 60–63
Smith, Emma, 42, 43
Smith, Hyrum, 1–4, 6
Smith, James, 258, 260, 261
Smith, Joseph, assassination of, 1–4; vis-
  ited by Strang, 5, 6; described, 5; bap-
  tizes Strang, 6; discussions with Strang,
  6; "appointment" of Strang, 7; selec-
  tion of successor to, 8, 10; translates
  gold plates into Book of Mormon, 33,
  34; relationship with John C. Bennett,
  43–45; and polygamy, 44, 79
Smith, Lucy, 45, 51
Smith, Moses, 9, 10, 25, 40, 42
Smith, Wealthy, 22, 23, 26–28, 58
Smith, William, 8, 45, 46, 51, 65
"Spiritual wife" doctrine. See Polygamy
Steinhelber, Conrad, 254
Stone, E. S., 206, 207
Strang, Abigail (mother), 12, 13, 17, 25,
  31, 57, 89, 214, 256
Strang, Betsy McNutt: marries Strang,
  167, 168; as wife of Strang, 225, 265,
  272. See also McNutt, Betsy
Strang, Clement (father), 12–14, 17, 25,
  31, 57, 214, 227, 256
Strang, Clement (son), 227–29, 271
Strang, David (brother), 12, 22–24, 57,
  181
Strang, Elvira Field: marries Strang, 81–
  83; in East with Strang, 85–91; on island, 100–101, 105, 107, 108, 224,
  225, 227, 234, 260, 272; see also
  Douglass, Charles J., and Field, Elvira
Strang, Harriet (daughter), 214
Strang, James Jesse: phrenologist's report
  on, ix, x; anointed by angel, 4, 7, 9,
  60; described, 4, 35, 36, 53, 109,
  140, 185, 194, 217, 282n; visit to
  Nauvoo, 5, 6; baptized as Mormon and
  ordained as elder, 6; proposes Mormon
  settlement in Wisconsin, 6, 7; receives
  letter of appointment, 7–10, 51,
  53–56, 65; attends conference in Florence, Mich., 8–10; reports vision of

Voree, 10; excommunicated, 10; rival
  for Brigham Young, 11, 36, 37, 57;
  autobiography, 12, 278n; birth of, 12;
  early years, 12, 13; education, 13, 14;
  learning about love, 13–15; diary, 13,
  16, 26; diary code, 13, 16; dreams of
  royalty and empire, 15–17; as debater,
  15, 19, 20, 39; reverses order of first
  two names, 16; studies law, 16, 17, 19,
  20, 26; views on religion, 17–19, 31;
  public speaker, 20; as lawyer, 20, 22,
  26, 32; preoccupation with fame, 20,
  21, 181; involvement in politics, 21,
  31, 178–94, 210–18; land speculator, 21–23, 31, 33, 48, 49, 56, 59;
  relationship with Wealthy Smith, 22,
  23, 26–28, 58; accused of perjury, 23;
  marries Mary Perce, 25, 26, 28–31; on
  passion, 26, 28; named postmaster, 31;
  moves west, 31, 32; children, 31, 32,
  108, 214, 272, 273, 323n; as editor
  and publisher, 31, 41, 42, 59, 71; parallels with Smith, 33–35, 51, 77, 107,
  263, 291n; discovers and translates
  brass plates at Voree, 34, 35; as
  prophet, 37, 50, 51, 61, 62, 80, 106,
  152, 273, 274; publishes Voree Herald,
  37, 38; mission into northern Illinois,
  38–40; sniping at Brigham Young, 41,
  75, 168, 169; names John Cook Bennett and George J. Adams as counselors, 43, 45–47; proclaimed imperial
  primate, 45, 49; homes of, 49, 64, 71,
  102, 167, 269; mission to East (1846),
  51–53, 57; attacks polygamy, 52,
  79–81; on origin of Jesus, 59, 60;
  Pseudo Mormon revolt against at Voree,
  60–63; establishes settlement on
  Beaver Island, 67–74; creates Order of
  Enoch, 76–78; institutes baptism for
  the dead, 77; marries Elvira Field,
  81–83; practices polygamy, 81–83,
  90, 107, 108, 167, 168, 223–25,
  240; mission to East (1849–50), 83–
  91; authorizes priesthood for blacks, 84;
  coronation of, 97, 102, 105–7, 147;
  disciplines George Adams's wife, 112,
  113; undergoes trial on charges of